Political ecologies of the far right

Manchester University Press

Global Studies of the Far Right

Series editors:
Dr Eviane Leidig, Dr William Allchorn, Dr Ariel Alejandro Goldstein

We are living in an unprecedented moment of uncertainty and chaos. The edifice of the old liberal order is starting to crack and a new, illiberal order is appearing on the horizon. The complexity and seriousness of these changes is such that now more than ever scholars are needed to weigh in on – and make sense of – these 'shifting sands'.

This series showcases innovative research from established and early career scholars working on the far right, providing fresh insights on emerging trends and themes within this field of study. It features high-quality single-authored books and edited volumes.

The series is multi-disciplinary, taking in the fields of political science, cultural studies, communication studies, sociology and international relations. More importantly, it aims to be broad in geographical scope, looking at both the Global North and the Global South, as we see new illiberal and authoritarian populist actors increasingly across the globe.

To buy or to find out more about the books currently available in this series, please go to:
https://manchesteruniversitypress.co.uk/series/global-studies-of-the-far-right/

Political ecologies of the far right

Fanning the flames

Edited by Irma Kinga Allen,
Kristoffer Ekberg, Ståle Holgersen
and Andreas Malm

MANCHESTER UNIVERSITY PRESS

Published by Manchester University Press
Oxford Road, Manchester, M13 9PL

www.manchesteruniversitypress.co.uk

British Library Cataloguing-in-Publication Data
A catalogue record for this book is available from the
British Library

ISBN   978 1 5261 6778 1   hardback
ISBN   978 1 5261 6779 8   paperback

First published 2024

Typeset
by New Best-set Typesetters Ltd

Contents

Contents

Figures and tables

Figures

Tables

Contributors

Irma Kinga Allen is an independent Environmental and Energy Humanities scholar. She is the author of *Dirty Coal: Industrial Populism as Purification in Poland's Mining Heartland* (Kungliga tekniska högskolan (Royal Institute of Technology), 2021), a doctoral monograph funded by a Horizon 2020 Marie Curie fellowship that explores the emotional draw of far-right populist politics among a mining community in Upper Silesia, Europe's largest hard-coal region, based on a year's ethnographic fieldwork. She was previously a Zetkin Collective member, collaborating on the book *White Skin, Black Fuel* (Verso, 2021) and co-founding the Political Ecologies of the Far Right conference and network. She currently works as a practitioner on just transition in the UK.

Rod Bantjes is a Professor of Sociology at St Francis Xavier University, Nova Scotia, Canada. He is author of two books and numerous journal articles on social movements and state formation. He is currently applying his research on media archaeology to understanding changing conceptions of space, perception and epistemology.

Sérgio Botton Barcellos is Adjunct Lecturer at the Department of Social Sciences, and Lecturer and Coordinator in the Postgraduate Programme, at the Federal University of Paraíba, Brazil. He holds a doctorate and MA in Social Sciences from the Federal Rural University of Rio de Janeiro in the Postgraduate Programme in Development, Agriculture and Society. Sérgio works with teaching, research and extension projects in the area of Rural and Environmental Sociology with a focus on state, development and public policies; socio-environmental conflicts; rural youth; family and peasant agriculture; sociology of education; and environmental education.

Rodrigo D. E. Campos is a PhD candidate in Politics at the University of York, UK, with a focus on Evangelical base building with police forces in Brazil. He holds an MA in International Relations from the San Tiago Dantas Graduate Programme (São Paulo State University, Campinas State University and Catholic University of São Paulo). His main research interests include religion and violence, security and policing, far-right politics, international political theory, Brazilian politics, and the geopolitics of the Maghreb region. He is also a documentary filmmaker and co-author of the book *No Way to Gaza: A Chronicle of Adventure and Fraud under the Egyptian Blockade* (Middle East Monitor, 2021).

Kristoffer Ekberg is a historian and Associate Senior Lecturer in Human Ecology at Lund University, Sweden. His research focuses on environmental history, and especially business responses and engagement with environmental policy and environmental movements. His most recent publications include the book *Climate Obstruction: How Denial, Delay and Inaction are Heating the Planet*, with Forchtner, Hultman and Jylhä. He is a member of the Centre for Studies of Climate Change Denialism and the Climate Social Science Network.

David Eliot is a PhD student at the University of Ottawa, Canada, and a 2022 Pierre Elliott Trudeau PhD Scholar. He specializes in the study of Artificial Intelligence systems and their effects on society.

Bernhard Forchtner is Associate Professor at the School of Arts, Media and Communication, University of Leicester, UK, and has previously worked as a Marie Curie Fellow at the Institute of Social Sciences at Humboldt University in Berlin, Germany, where he conducted a project on far-right discourses on the environment (Far-RightEco, project number 327595). Recent publications include 'Scepticisms and Beyond? A Comprehensive Portrait of Climate Change Communication by the Far Right in the European Parliament' (*Environmental Politics*, 2022 with B. Lubarda) and the edited volumes *The Far Right and the Environment* (Routledge, 2019) and *Visualising Far-Right Environments* (Manchester University Press, 2023).

Ricardo Gonçalves Severo holds a Doctorate in Social Sciences from the Pontifical Catholic University of Rio Grande do Sul, and an MA in Social Sciences from the Federal University of Pelotas, Brazil. He is Associate Professor of Sociology and Permanent Professor for the Graduate Programme in Education at the Federal University of Rio Grande, Brazil . His main areas of research are sociology of knowledge, sociology of education, political sociology, and sociology of youth.

Ståle Holgersen is a Senior Lecturer in Human Geography at Örebro University, Sweden. He is the author of books including *The Rise (and Fall?) of Post-Industrial Malmö* (Lund University Press, 2014) and *Against the Crisis* (Verso, 2024), and has published articles in journals such as *Antipode, Capital and Class, Human Geography, Planning Theory* and *International Journal of Urban and Regional Research*. He is a member of the Zetkin Collective and the housing-research collective *Fundament*.

Robert B. Horwitz is Professor in the Department of Communication at the University of California, San Diego, USA. The focus of his scholarship is democracy, communication and political reform. He is author of *The Irony of Regulatory Reform: The Deregulation of American Telecommunications* (Oxford University Press, 1989); *Communication and Democratic Reform in South Africa* (Cambridge University Press, 2001); *America's Right: Anti-establishment Conservatism from Goldwater to the Tea Party* (Polity, 2013), and essays on freedom of expression and reflections on contemporary political discourse. Horwitz was Chair of the systemwide University of California Academic Senate, 2021–2022.

Shehnoor Khurram is a PhD candidate in the Department of Political Science at York University in Toronto, Canada. She is also currently a Fulbright Scholar, taking up residency at Georgetown University in Washington D.C., USA. Her fields of interest include international and comparative political economy, development studies, critical security studies, and political ecology. She employs historical sociology and qualitative and archival methodologies in her research. Her doctoral dissertation analyses ISIS' rise to power through the making and unmaking of statehood in Iraq.

Balša Lubarda, PhD, is the Head of Research at the Damar Institute, Montenegro. He was most recently Fulbright Visiting Scholar at the Institute for the Study of Societal Issues, University of California, Berkeley, USA. He is the author of *Far-Right Ecologism: Environmental Politics and the Far Right* (Routledge, 2024), a book based on his doctoral project at Central European University, Austria (2017–2021). Lubarda was founder and head of the Ideology Research Unit at the Far-Right Analysis Network (previously Centre for Analysis of the Radical Right).

Andreas Malm is Associate Professor of Human Ecology at Lund University. His most recent book, together with Wim Carton, is *Overshoot: How the World Surrendered to Climate Breakdown* (London: Verso, 2024).

Amir Massoumian is a PhD student in Anthropology at SOAS University, and a Fellow at the Global Research Network on Parliaments and People, London. His doctoral research focuses on far-right supporters in London. His topics of interest include political exclusion, nostalgia, gender, body politics, and research ethics.

Jacob McLean is a PhD candidate in the Faculty of Environmental and Urban Change at York University, Canada. He studies the political ecology of far-right social movements in Canada. He is also a member of the Zetkin Collective.

Laura Pulido is the Collins Professor in Indigenous, Race, and Ethnic Studies and Geography at the University of Oregon, USA, where she studies

Environmental Justice, White Supremacy, Cultural Memory and Latina/o/x Studies. She is the author of six books, including *Environmentalism and Economic Justice: Two Chicano Struggles in the Southwest* (1996); *Black, Brown, Yellow and Left: Radical Activism in Los Angeles* (2006), and *A People's Guide to Los Angeles* (with Laura Barraclough and Wendy Cheng) (2012). Her current project, *Monumental Denial: U.S. Cultural Memory and White Innocence*, examines how the US represents histories of white supremacy and colonization.

Lisa Santosa is a PhD candidate and Interdisciplinary Center for the Study of Global Change-Mellon Fellow in Human Geography at the University of Minnesota Twin Cities, USA. Her current research project investigates land reform policy in South Africa and its intersection with ethno-nationalism and the historical legacy of settler colonialism. She also incorporates psychoanalytic, critical race, decolonial and feminist methodologies in her research.

Amanda Thomas is a Senior Lecturer in Environmental Studies at Te Herenga Waka Victoria University of Wellington, in Aotearoa New Zealand. She is a Pākehā political geographer interested in whiteness, decolonization and environmental democracy, and has recently published a book, *Stopping Oil: Climate Justice and Hope* (Pluto Press, Melbourne University Press, 2023) with colleagues.

The **Zetkin Collective** is an eco-socialist group of scholars and activists working primarily on the political ecologies of the far right. In addition to **Ståle Holgersen** and **Jacob McLean** (see above), members contributing to the afterword of this volume are: **William Callison**, a Postdoctoral Fellow in the Department of Human Geography at Uppsala University. William's research focuses on the history of neoliberalism, far-right movements and climate denialism. **George Edwards**, PhD candidate at the University of Warwick. George's research considers the role of nationalism in the climate crisis. **Alexandra McFadden**, a researcher and science editor based in Stockholm. Alexandra studies the environmental politics of the far right and conservation ecology and conflicts.

Introduction

Irma Kinga Allen, Kristoffer Ekberg, Ståle Holgersen and Andreas Malm

On 14 May 2022, 18-year-old Payton Gendron drove to a supermarket in Buffalo, upstate New York. His car was loaded with a shotgun, a hunting rifle and a semi-automatic rifle, on which he had scribbled *inter alia* the N-word, 'White Lives Matter', the year '2083' and the name 'Brenton Tarrant'. Inside the supermarket, he found his targets: Black bodies. He gunned them down one after the other – all filmed and livestreamed from the camera mounted on his military-style helmet. When he happened to aim his rifle at a White body behind a counter, he corrected himself, said 'Sorry' and turned elsewhere (Thompson & Balsamo, 2022). He knew what he was there to do. The operation was carefully prepared: Gendron had scouted the area for the densest possible concentration of a Black population. 'All black people are replacers just by existing in White countries', so the mission must be to 'kill as many blacks as possible', he wrote in his 180-page manifesto that he, true to such form, posted online before his action (Gendron, 2022: 5, 57). The most remarkable aspect of this text, beyond its violent racist message, was precisely its utter unoriginality. Gendron had lifted entire sections verbatim from the manifesto penned by his hero Brenton Tarrant before he murdered 51 Muslims in Christchurch, New Zealand, on 15 March 2019. A theme prominent in the plagiarism was ecology.

For Tarrant and his copyist, echoing timeworn racialized Malthusian overpopulation narratives (see for example Erlich, 1968; Hardin, 1974), non-White people are inundating the world with a surfeit of children. If no one stops these brutes, they will replace and potentially extinguish the White race, as well as consume nature to death. In this view, climate breakdown and other aspects of the ecological crisis have the same causal root – too many non-White people. The earth is being overrun by Blacks, Muslims, immigrants and other racial inferiors, who do not know how to appreciate the beauty of nature (see Dyett & Thomas, 2019). As with all other afflictions troubling White people today: Whiteness and nature supposedly share the fate of subjugation at the hands of a racialized, invasive and parasitic enemy.

Ten African Americans were killed in the parking lot and inside the Tops supermarket on that day based on this logic. Like Tarrant, Gendron identified himself as an 'eco-fascist', a self-proclaimed label that was not lost in media reports of the atrocity (Gendron, 2022, for example pp. 10, 164, 168). With this latest act, the heavily armed eco-fascist was becoming a central figure on the stage of contemporary global political violence (see Milman, 2022; Tigue, 2022; for an analysis of Tarrant's ideas, see Malm and Zetkin Collective, 2021: 150–153; and for him and eco-fascism generally, Moore and Roberts, 2022).

Almost exactly ten months earlier, a very different political phenomenon had leapt onto the scene: *American Marxism* by Mark R. Levin. This was not a bloody massacre, but an (innocent?) book. Yet it belonged not to a subculture or extremist fringe, but to the mainstream of the American right – which is to say, these days, pretty far out on the right. When figures were tallied at the end of 2021, no other non-fiction book had sold as many copies in the US (Cadden, 2021). If Gendron had dredged up paragraphs for his composition from the darker corners of the far-right web, Levin, having been a former Reagan government advisor, drew his from the echo-chambers of the vast Republican mediasphere. While Gendron radicalized himself on the controversial, male-dominated online forum 4Chan, Levin was a talk-radio host and star of mainstream Fox News, where he had a show of his own. The thesis of his book is that America is in the process of being occupied and destroyed by Marxists in various guises. Two stand out: Marxists dressed up as critical race theorists – aggressive and dangerous supporters of Black people as against White – and as environmentalists. This was not a new dystopia. The trope of the cultural Marxist conspiracy theory, and its 'long march through the institutions', had become a cornerstone metatheory of the right since the 2010s – a post-Cold War bogeyman with older antisemitic roots too (see Malm & Zetkin Collective, 2021: 300–313 on the genealogy of the cultural Marxist conspiracy theory). Levin, however, gave this theory new life – and a huge audience – ensuring it would add fuel to the fire of today's culture wars and more.

While Gendron did not question the science of climate change, Levin's take on ecology was a more familiar right-wing story. In the chapter '"Climate Change" Fanaticism', he rehashed the most hackneyed themes of climate denialism: there is no trend of warming any more than one of cooling; carbon dioxide is not a pollutant but 'plant food'; the science is fabricated; wind turbines and solar panels spoil landscapes; we cannot live in prosperity without fossil fuels, and they do no harm anyway; if there is any warming at all, it's due to the sun (Levin, 2021: 173; see further examples 139–192, 213–214, 271; on denialism, see McCright & Dunlap, 2011; Lockwood, 2018; Forchtner, 2019; Vowles & Hultman, 2021; Ekberg et al., 2022). As such, he reiterated an anti-environmentalist sentiment that had cemented conservatives of different brands since the 1970s (Boynton, 2015). Now the perpetrators of the climate lie that indirectly wages war against (White) American freedoms should be understood as the same people who condemn Whites in the name of invented grievances (racism) – this time Marxist ideologues. Armed then with the 'twin subjects of race and climate change', for Levin it is this enemy that must be stopped in its tracks before America is a dreamland lost. 'Patriots of America, unite!', he ends his screed (Levin, 2021: 223, 276). In case the subtext wasn't obvious, by that, of course, he means White Americans, the GOP's core fanbase.

For all their contrasts, then, Gendron and Levin share certain troubling features: a conspicuous identification with the extreme political right as against the left; a flag-waving racialized patriotism; a sense of Whiteness being under siege and losing power; an imaginative association between the problem of ecology and enemies of (a White) nation; a fairly keen interest in environmental politics; and, perhaps most significantly, a knack for repetition and unoriginality. With their overlapping analyses – Gendron: non-Whites cause the ecological crisis; Levin: the Marxists who attack Whites cook it up – they place themselves in currents that have been circulating for decades if not centuries, though alarmingly at higher velocity and with greater traction in the past few years. In short, they regurgitate key themes in the political ecologies of the far right, infiltrating into, indeed at times fronting (as in the case of Levin), the mainstream while doing so. In their disparate ways, they fan the flames of White nationalism *and* the ecological crisis itself by totally misplacing its roots, a classic case of disavowal at the crucial hour. For one thing should be clear: to deny this crisis or to blame it on non-Whites are two ways of letting it run its destructive course, with some extra gasoline poured onto the bonfire.

So, what happens when the far right keeps fanning such flames in a rapidly warming world? Not one thing, but many; of this we can be sure. The far right is a distinctly multi-faceted and contradictory force in politics. It is capable of doing one thing and the opposite and creating plenty of havoc in the process. Crucial to watch is particularly how its apparent 'far-ness' may increasingly become a cover for its actual near-ness – its proximity, its growing normalization as it co-opts the centre, and the minds and mythologies of current and no doubt future generations. How will we stay vigilant and alert, recognize and continue to name this phenomenon for what it is? As for global heating itself, it is having, and will continue to have, unforeseeable and potentially numberless impacts on social life, and then it is but one facet of the ecological crisis unfolding around us. How these two variables – the far right and ecology – intersect, indeed feed into and off one another, is the theme of this book. Throwing them into collision with each other, or, rather, recognizing they are inalienably two sides of the same coin, the product of real confluences in the late capitalism of the twenty-first century and its ecological unravelling, is to set the stage for all sorts of flying objects and ricochet effects (Darian-Smith, 2022). What this volume does is to report from the frontline on some of these under-reported encounters, or entanglements in recent times, with an eye towards a future where they horrifically might well become more frequent and explosive. Through 12 chapters and an afterword it highlights the ever-shifting complexities of the political ecologies of the far right in terms of form (from eco-fascism to fossil fascism, and everything in between), geography (spanning four continents), content (from denialism and conspiracy theory, relations to its liberal ideology and masculinity – and much more), and research methodology too (from case studies and ethnographies to visual content analysis and document analysis). This is not simply to document, though that too of course, but to lay bare the inner mechanisms of a dark vein running through our world and how we might continue to do that much-needed ongoing work of recognizing, naming, researching and pushing back against this trend. In doing so we join, and urge, a growing number of scholars turning weary and wary attention to this moment since the mid-2010s.

In particular, this volume is a product of the inaugural Political Ecologies of the Far Right (PEFR) conference that was held at Lund University, Sweden, in November 2019, attracting some 400 scholars and activists, just before the world slid into the pandemic. It was organized by the Human Ecology Division of that university, in collaboration with the Centre for Studies of Climate Change Denial (CEFORCED) at Chalmers University, the research project 'White Skin, Black Fuel' at Uppsala University, the scholar-activist network the Zetkin Collective and the activist group AG Hedvig. The scientific rationale for the conference was the observation that the growing intersection of far-right and anti-environmentalist politics around the world – which had seemingly burst forth out of nowhere in the era of Trump – had been massively understudied (see also Lockwood, 2018). In their review of the field, Lubarda and Forchtner (2022) note that indeed early scholarship in this vein was highly focused on the history of environmental thought within the Nazi party in Germany, and maintained a distinct interest in Europe alone (and often Western Europe at that). Since the late 2010s, or the second half of Trump's reign, perhaps unsurprisingly, in a case of academia catching up with the world, broader studies focused on the contemporary moment have since proliferated. The increased interest in the intersection of far-right actors and the environment was shown especially by the exploration of climate denial and far-right thought (see Forchtner, 2019). From Cara Daggett's work on American petro-masculinity (2018), Irma Kinga Allen's research on Polish coal-based industrial populism (2021), and especially with the publication of *White Skin, Black Fuel* by Andreas Malm and the Zetkin Collective in 2021, the dangers of 'fossil fascism', or the high-risk conflation of fossil fuels and far-right thought and activity, became more prominent within a now burgeoning field of research.

Yet, as the PEFR conference itself attempted to highlight, broader ecological issues beyond climate and energy were largely conspicuous by their absence. Likewise, geographically the focus still often remained on the Global North. This volume, while keeping an eye solidly on the irrefutable centrality of climate politics, thus also places reports on a wider range of environmental topics (veganism, land degradation, biodiversity loss) from the capitalist core next to ones from those regions where the political ecologies of the far right have so far received less attention. In doing so, it joins calls for a transnational, postcolonial understanding of the far-right phenomenon (Masood & Nisar, 2020; Zhang, 2020; Pinheiro-Machado & Vargas-Maia, 2023), here with an explicit ecological focus. Featuring some of the outstanding contributions from the PEFR conference, forming just a subset of much larger material that cannot be reproduced outside of an event of that kind, it marks the entrance of far-right ecologies, or varying shades of eco-fascism, as a now global force calling for serious and urgent scholarly attention on the political ecological world stage. With chapters on Brazil, New Zealand, Canada, Nigeria and South Africa, this volume seeks to throw a diverse set of lights on how the far right operates within and through the ecological crisis – which is nothing if not global. Through this, it highlights how planetary ecology is indeed increasingly the irrefutable stage set, rather than mere backdrop, for the spreading wildfire that is the contemporary far-right presence.

The expansion in scale, of course, raises questions on the universality of a concept such as 'the far right'. What do we mean by the term? Especially as the signified object is, as already argued, anything but clear-cut and monolithic. In the following pages, it will be represented by parties, astroturfs, armed outfits, individuals and even robots, which adds to the almost bewildering multifariousness of 'the' far right. If there is any final impression we wish to leave the reader with, it is of the complexity and contradictoriness of the subject at hand, rather than its uniformity, however monotonous it might appear in its nastiness. Thus, rather than getting bogged down in potentially interminable discussions of where the category of the far right begins and ends in definitive terms, a debate which has, so far, unhelpfully led to the orientalist exclusion of Global South actors due to a Western-centric reading of the term (see Masood & Nisar, 2020), we have allowed it to be used in somewhat differing senses – but generally as an umbrella term. A term encompassing a kind of right-wing politics that elevates specific values such as authoritarianism, ethno-nationalism, traditional norms, homogeneity, anti-intellectualism and physical violence, usually overlapping with misogyny and the acceptance and aggressive promotion of racialized, gendered (status quo) hierarchies, belying a steadfast resistance to any ideals of human equality. These values, crucially to this volume, tend to be couched in, justified by and mobilized through ideas of nature and the environment. In these ideas lie the assortment of matches it uses to set an overheated world ablaze.

Not all of them at once, however, must feature to be recognized as being part of the far-right family – not even, we argue, the concept of the nation, whose restoration is typically considered a central tenet of especially fascist thought. This volume, in the interests of retaining vigilance of its future iterations, in fact highlights how far-right forces can also fire imaginations and actions on both smaller and bigger political scales. Boko Haram, for instance, is certainly not animated by nationalist commitment to Nigeria or any other worldly nation-state; it primarily propagates a religious ideology, but it shares other recognizable features of the far-right family – notably extreme authoritarianism, misogyny, intolerance and fetishization of violence.

Challenging also the misperception that the far right operates at some extreme opposite and distant end to everyday realities, represented only by the likes of Gendron and his ilk, we also wish to illuminate how some aspects of far-right thought and practice find banal resonance among a wider population (see also Allen, 2021), filtering also into, and shaping, the mainstream, as with Levin's example.

In that sense, the 'far' right is always very near – often as near as family, the familiar, the metaphor of family resemblance is also symbolically apt – and might, as ecological events continue to unfold in iteration with other crises, attract surprise followers through providing novel answers through spectacle, a sense of seductive belonging (via exclusion), and through overt action and reaction, as shown in various contributions to this book. By remaining open to the novel forms and places through which the far right might appear, the book aims to take the ethos and practices of those we disagree with seriously in an effort to understand the political Other at face value, as a highly malleable and insidious force to be reckoned with. Through the various chapters we hope to convey not only an exposure of a politics we must fight but also to understand and explain what makes this politics attractive for some, and how is that achieved? As such, we are perhaps most interested in not what the far right *is* as such, but what it *does* – sow hatred, anger, exclusion, Othering, suspicion, violence mixed with ecological havoc, too. Only with an attentiveness to this series of swirling features and how they continue to morph and merge can we keep track of the developments with that vigilance which they deserve.

This book focuses on the far right's *ecology* – or indeed ecolog*ies*. While similar terminological debates as with the 'far right' could be had about the concept of 'political ecology' and its definition, its immediate amenability to the intentionally plural form highlights the direction in which we travel. We seek to pay close attention to how material environments, environmental issues and ideas are expressed and mobilized in multiple guises for political ends, through, for example, propaganda, conspiracy, history, technology, movements and lived experience. As such, Lubarda's notion of 'far-right ecologisms', rather than, again, eco-fascism as a singular set of ideas, is closer to the mark in how we approach this terrain (Lubarda, 2020). Since much research on far-right politics and the environment so far has been focused on the realm of ideas alone, by emphasizing political ecology we also want to stress material aspects of both how the far right are ultimately (anti)ecological in their politics, and how environments are necessarily both a precondition and an outcome of them. Ecology, as we hope the reader will have begun to glean, should not be seen as a factor extraneous to the far right, something that smashes into it from the outside or vice versa. Rather, the far right is – much as any other force in politics – always already ecological, just as it has irreducible gender and class dimensions. Indeed, because the far right has been present in Western politics since the French Revolution – its very positionality defined by extreme hostility to its universalist ideals – it must be contextualized as having had a key historical hand in the creation, and perpetuation, of the present climate crisis (though of course it is not itself responsible alone, that would let far too many mainstream actors off the hook).

Most crucially, the far right has typically been the most fanatical friend of fossil-fuelled technologies. The Italian and German fascists gave the development of automobiles and airplanes critical momentum. Long before their years in power, steamboats and railroads had spanned the globe through routes and tracks laid down in the belief that White people were superior human beings; long after, non-fascist elements of the far right have continued to champion oil, gas, coal and their derivatives with reference to one or other cherished notion of supremacy (for this history, see Malm & Zetkin Collective 2021; for a history of coloniality and climate change, see Ghosh, 2021). In the present volume, to take but one example, Robert B. Horwitz shows how, in the key case of the US, the Republican right has mixed an increasingly far-out religious ideology with the promotion of petroleum into what he calls 'fossil fuel authoritarianism'.

Based on this genealogical relation, much of far-right posturing at the present conjuncture should thus be viewed as *anti*-ecological or, perhaps better, anti-environmentalist, in the sense that it, as we saw earlier, opposes measures for addressing the crisis (proposed by those pesky Marxist green fanatics), while retaining its own peculiar form of ecological relation. A primary way this attitude is manifested is, as with Levin, in the denial of the existence of anthropogenic climate change. The far right has long engaged in the most blatant denial of climate science – and, we should add, ditto suffering – and this is probably also the most researched aspect of its political ecologies (see e.g. McCright & Dunlap, 2003; Anshelm & Hultman, 2014; Forchtner & Kølvraa, 2015; Forchtner, 2019; Hess & Renner, 2019; Vowles & Hultman, 2021). But the topic is, unfortunately, anything but exhausted. As Bernhard Forchtner illustrates in his chapter, insights into the emotional appeal of far-right climate denial can be gained by looking at the imagery deployed. In the age of the social media spectacle, the visual image is among the most effective instruments for spreading denial. As the case of Levin's national bestseller suggests, these ideas have a remarkable capacity for self-replication and hold sway over significant segments of voters in a key country such as the US – but for how long?

Overt climate denial, observers have long predicted, must soon go out of business. With more knowledge and first-hand experience, with ever more wildfires and droughts, with *even more* researchers saying the same thing about the climate crisis, it would seem unthinkable that the far right can stay impervious to the realities of a world aflame. But several chapters in this volume demonstrate how the anti-climate politics of the far right rather has nine lives and more to go. In her contribution, Laura Pulido studies how far-right segments of the Oregon public responded to the devastating wildfires of 2020: by denying any link to the climate crisis and instead blaming supposed arsonists from Black Lives Matter and Antifa (on such narratives of innocence see also Norgaard, 2012 and Loftin, 2023). David Eliot and Rod Bantjes point to a fresh technological tool that could give climate denial a new lease of life: sophisticated and apparently convincing texts produced by means of Artificial Intelligence, the prospect of which the latest ChatGPT phenomenon only speeds up. Armed with AI writer bots, far-right agents might penetrate various barriers against untruths and sow deeper seeds of doubt about the severity and nature of climate disasters. Popular climate denial is far from a thing of the past: as Rodrigo D. E. Campos, Sérgio B. Barcelos and Ricardo G. Severo detail in their chapter, it continues, as of this writing, to rule Brazil; while in Canada, as Jacob McLean makes clear in his, it has channelled oppositional forces that call for even more aggressive extraction of coal, oil and gas. Such populist tendencies have for several years been an expression in climate and environmental policy (see e.g. Allen, 2021; Bosworth, 2021; McCarthy, 2019; Ofstehage et al., 2022). We are unlikely to have heard the last word from this brand of the far right, with its various inflections of denying the realities of the climate crisis.

This is so because denial is constantly evolving in close relation to more 'mainstream' approaches, indeed feeds off them, highlighting their complicity. As several contributors suggest, the politics of the centre is not always antithetical to denial: much of it rather proceeds on the assumption that global heating can be continuously ignored in deed (if not necessarily in word). Ståle Holgersen examines how the important case of Norway – the largest oil and gas producer in Europe – has generated a symbiosis between 'delayers' and 'deniers'. While the former fall back on a 'fossil ideology' contending that Norwegian oil is uniquely good for humanity, the latter deny any existence of a problem altogether. But they are united in almost identical petroleum policies, nourish and give legitimacy to each other, and as long as the centrist 'fossil ideology' remains dominant, various spin-offs of denial are to be expected. Again – the 'far' is more near than anticipated (see also Ekberg & Pressfeldt, 2022). On the other side of the Atlantic, meanwhile, the spectre of Trumpism has refused to go away after the presidential election of 2020 and hovers over many of the pages in this book.

And yet the far right is Janus faced: alongside climate denial and fossil fuel boosterism sits an opposite profile – one threaded through the manifesto of Gendron, self-proclaimed foot-soldier of eco-fascism. This is the tradition – again, as old as the far right itself – of valorizing nature, the local landscape, the soil and forests and mountains of the nation, the natural order. Aliens and subversives must not trespass against that order, the far right has always averred. Its fascination with nature as source of purity and good has been alive since at least the nineteenth century. Several studies have examined how the classical fascists – the Nazis, above all – had an interest in animal welfare, national parks, and hunting and wildlife practices (e.g. Armiero & Graf von Hardenberg, 2013; Uekötter, 2006; Biehl & Staudenmeier, 2011; Brüggemeier, et al. 2005). Today, this tradition often translates into nostalgic and romantic notions of the simpler, more authentic rural life, at a remove from the global and urban hustle and bustle of the IPCC or the UNFCCC; the far right has yet to make international climate politics an object for anything else than repudiation and derision. And (much like the Nazis), even the far right that portrays itself as the truest guardian of agrarian traditions often slips into advocacy of unrestricted extractivism and entrepreneurial freedom. In its most fervent form it appears, as we have caught a dreaded glimpse of, as eco-fascism, sadly not something to be brushed aside as irrelevant, a yesteryear bogeyman. But how does the far right and the environment intersect and manifest today?

Amanda Thomas here investigates one of the most highly publicized acts of eco-fascist violence in recent years, the Christchurch massacre – inspiration for Gendron – and more precisely its afterlife in the ideas of the ultra-nationalist outfit, Action Zealandia. Here, too, the far right has umbilical cords to its innocent-looking surroundings. Thomas raises some uncomfortable questions about the links between the ideology of the eco-fascist fringe and the culture of purportedly benevolent, enlightened Whiteness in New Zealand. A similar connection between Whiteness implanted through settler-colonial aggression and a concern to protect and preserve the fruits of the land (for some) is found in South Africa, the case studied by Lisa Santosa (see also McFadden, 2023). Back in the erstwhile metropolis, White men can ruminate on how best to purify themselves and their environment from polluting elements. In his close ethnography of a group of 'traditionalists' in London, Amir Massoumian pinpoints how vegan diets and environmental concerns can be mobilized by individuals on the very farthest right of the spectrum: here the pure and clean body is a line of defence against Jewish emasculation and despoliation. Such notions of defending a supposedly threatened masculinity either by turning towards eco-fascist 'restoration' or through the rejection of climate science and climate action have been identified as a key feature of far-right environmental thought (see e.g. Daggett, 2018, 2021; Allen, 2021; Benegal & Holman, 2021; Darwish, 2021; MacGregor & Paterson, 2021; Loftin, 2023). The far right is certainly able to put its own spin on the latest aspects of ecological crisis, for purposes that are anything but new.

In her original take on the nexus, Shehnoor Khurram lays bare how the drying out of Lake Chad and other climate-induced miseries in northern Nigeria have fuelled the Boko Haram insurgency, and how it should be understood as a form of far-right terror – not an innately Islamic, African or otherwise distantly barbaric terrorism, but a manifestation of trends in the totality of 'the Capitalocene'. On a conceptual level Khurram's chapter puts the notion of the far right as a Western phenomenon into question and distorts the ideas of far and near, inside and outside. How will groups like Boko Haram make use of coming rounds of climate suffering in the Global South and elsewhere? Khurram's chapter makes for disturbing reading and insists on tracking the political ecologies of the far right beyond the *locus classicus* of European politics.

Global heating is only one of many vectors of misery which feed this phenomenon: the present decade has also given us COVID-19, a zoonotic disease with roots in deforestation, wildlife trading and other facets of the biodiversity crisis. How has the far right responded to and deployed it? Largely by denying the existence of the pandemic and resisting measures for containing it, while accusing elites of conspiracy. In his chapter, Balsa Lubarda looks at the differences and significant overlaps between far-right interventions in the climate and those in the corona crisis (see also Forchtner & Özvatan, 2022). The 'Freedom Convoy' occupying central Ottawa in early 2022 (Murphy, 2022) marked a continuation of the 'United We Roll' campaign analysed by McLean; as in Eastern Europe, the Canadian far right that had recently denied climate now protested corona measures with vehemence. Given the likelihood of new zoonotic diseases – not to mention the many other unknown unknowns of the ecological crisis: from the effects of pharmaceutical pollution of rivers to those of insect collapse – this is another conjunction with a future ahead of it. More far-right responses will spring up as certainly as more crises will erupt. Ideas about ecology on the far right have a remarkably long lifetime and stubborn persistence. This makes them amenable to replication and further elaboration, in theory or practice.

This is not to say that ecological crises deterministically lead to far-right politics, but that the far right, as this volume highlights, is increasingly demonstrating itself to be an actor well versed in using ecological crises to its benefit. Indeed, with a wide palette of compelling historical myths and modernized narratives to draw on in this vein, the far right might be best prepared to take advantage of the opportunities they present to capture political ground over and above other forces coldly cashing in on disaster but forgetting to draw the crowds. That all ecological crises can, and no doubt will, come with racist explanation in tow therefore needs to be taken deadly seriously (Holgersen, 2022). The far right will continue to march, or perhaps rather drive its jeeps and trucks, through Ouagadougou as much as through Ottawa. And certainly, its ideas, its tracts and manifestos, know no borders, circulating within the underbelly of the virtual world without stoppage. If we are not vigilant, far-right mobilizations will be there to offer their ideological politics dressed as clear-eyed explanation. And in informational and imaginary vacuums, charged with fear and insecurity, such politics can and will take hold. Any artificial restriction of our purview, therefore, to these now global zones, would risk leaving out the most affected areas and people, where forces of the far right might find highly fertile ground – among the dispossessed, disturbed and disorientated, including in ecological terms.

How can we pre-empt and fight back against this insidious infestation of these scenes? One obligation, surely, is to maintain a glaring spotlight on their machinations through rigorous research and analysis. In addition to encouraging the expansion of the study of the political ecology of the far right geographically, therefore, the volume also seeks to showcase the wide range of methodologies that might be used to do so: ranging from quantitative to qualitative methods, engaging with interviews, ethnographic field observations, images, emerging technologies, analysis of policy documents and other written texts, as well as scrutinizing social media. Through this, the present volume is intended to stimulate further research on the political ecologies of a far right in perpetual motion, offering a number of innovative entry points for tracking developments on the ground.

It is also the hope of the editors, that – just as with the PEFR conference, whose secondary rationale was the recognition that knowledge exchange between sectors of academia (students and scholars of the far right and of ecology) and of social movements (for climate justice, against racism and fascism) were few and far between – this volume will find wide readership among those with boots on the ground confronting this politics head on. Scholars and activists have spoken far too little to one another, just as pro-environmentalist, anti-racist and anti-far-right movements have. With the second Political Ecologies of the Far Right conference in 2024, held this time at the University of Uppsala, and in offering the final afterword in this volume to the scholar-activist Zetkin Collective, we hope to contribute to greater collaboration and cross-fertilization in the building of a united front against this assault on a liveable world for all. No one with an interest in combatting climate or ecological catastrophe and fighting injustices between people – in particular those relating to race and ethnic origin – can afford to ignore the political ecologies of the far right. They will tragically leave their mark on the years ahead, fanning fast-spreading flames.

Acknowledgements

Andreas Malm would like to thank Formas 2018–01702; Ståle Holgersen would like to thank Formas 2018–01702 and Vetenskapsrådet 2020–04164; Kristoffer Ekberg would like to thank the Swedish Energy Agency 2018–002424, 46178–1 and Formas 2022–01844.

References

Allen, I. K. (2021). Dirty Coal: Industrial Populism as Purification in Poland's Mining Heartland. Doctoral thesis, KTH Royal Institute of Technology.

Anshelm, J., & Hultman, M. (2014). *Discourses of Global Climate Change: Apocalyptic Framing and Political Antagonisms*. Abingdon: Routledge.

Armiero, M., & Graf von Hardenberg, W. (2013). Green Rhetoric in Blackshirts: Italian Fascism and the Environment. *Environment and History*, 19(3): 283–311. doi:10.3197/096734013X13690716950064.

Benegal, S., & Holman, M. R. (2021). Understanding the Importance of Sexism in Shaping Climate Denial and Policy Opposition. *Climatic Change*, 167(3): 1–19.

Biehl, J., & Staudenmaier, P. (2011). *Ecofascism Revisited: Lessons from the German Experience*. Porsgrunn: New Compass Press.

Bosworth, K. (2021). 'They're treating us like Indians!' Political Ecologies of Property and Race in North American Pipeline Populism. *Antipode*, 53(3): 665–685.

Boynton, Alex (2015). Confronting the Environmental Crisis? Anti-environmentalism and the Transformation of Conservative Thought in the 1970s. Doctoral thesis, University of Kansas.

Brüggemeier, F.-J., Cioc, M., & Zeller, T. (2005). *How Green were the Nazis? Nature, Environment, and Nation in the Third Reich*. Ohio: Ohio University Press.

Cadden, M. (2021). USA Today's bestselling book of 2021 is.... *USA Today*, 30 December.

Daggett, C. (2018). Petro-masculinity: Fossil Fuels and Authoritarian Desire. *Millennium*, 47(1): 25–44.

Daggett, C. (2021). Energy and Domination: Contesting the Fossil Myth of Fuel Expansion. *Environmental Politics*, 30(4): 644–662.

Darian-Smith, E. (2022). Deadly Global Alliance: Antidemocracy and Anti-environmentalism. *Third World Quarterly*, 44(2): 1–16.

Darwish, M. (2021). Nature, Masculinities, Care, and the Far-Right. In P. M. Pulé & M. Hultman (eds), *Men, Masculinities, and Earth: Contending with the (m) Anthropocene*, Cham: Springer International Publishing, pp. 183–206.

Dyett, J., & Thomas, C. (2019). Overpopulation Discourse: Patriarchy, Racism, and the Specter of Ecofascism. *Perspectives on Global Development and Technology*, 18(1–2): 205–224.

Ehrlich, P. R. (1968). *The Population Bomb*. New York: Ballantine.

Ekberg, K., & Pressfeldt, V. (2022). A Road to Denial: Climate Change and Neo-liberal Thought in Sweden, 1988–2000. *Contemporary European History*, 31(4): 627–644.

Ekberg, K., Forchtner, B., Hultman, M., & Jylhä, K. M. (2022). *Climate Obstruction: How Denial, Delay and Inaction Are Heating the Planet*. London: Routledge.

Forchtner, B. (2019). *The Far Right and the Environment: Politics, Discourse and Communication*. Abingdon: Routledge.

Forchtner, B., & Kølvraa, C. (2015). The Nature of Nationalism: Populist Radical Right Parties on Countryside and Climate. *Nature and Culture*, 10(2): 199–224.

Forchtner, B., & Özvatan, Ö. (2022). De/legitimising Europe through the Performance of Crises: The Far-Right Alternative for Germany on 'Climate Hysteria' and 'Corona Hysteria'. *Journal of Language and Politics*, 21(2): 208–232.

Gendron, P. (2022). You Wait for a Signal While Your People Wait for You. Manifesto.

Ghosh, A. (2021). *The Nutmeg's Curse: Parables for a Planet in Crisis*. Chicago: University of Chicago Press.

Hardin, Garrett (1974). Lifeboat Ethics: The Case Against Helping the Poor. *Psychology Today*, 8: 800–812.

Hess, D. J., & Renner, M. (2019). Conservative Political Parties and Energy Transitions in Europe: Opposition to Climate Mitigation Policies. *Renewable and Sustainable Energy Reviews*, 104: 419–428.

Holgersen, S. (2022). *Krisernas Tid: Ekologi och Ekonomi under Kapitalismen*. Göteborg: Daidalos.

Levin, M. (2021). *American Marxism*. New York: Threshold Editions.

Lockwood, M. (2018). Right-Wing Populism and the Climate Change Agenda: Exploring the Linkages. *Environmental Politics*, 27(4): 712–732. doi.org/10.1080/09644016.2018.1458411.

Loftin, Mac (2023). 'The Crime of Innocence': Baldwin, Bataille, and the Political Theology of Far-Right Climate Politics. *Political Theology*, 24(6): 1–17.

Lubarda, B. (2020). Beyond Ecofascism? Far-Right Ecologism (Fre) as a Framework for Future Inquiries. *Environmental Values*, 29(6) 713–732. doi.org/10.3197/096327120X15752810323922.

Lubarda, B., & Forchtner, B. (2022). The Far Right and the Environment: Past–Present–Future. In V. A. Bruno (ed.), *Populism and Far-Right: Trends in Europe*. Milan: EDUCatt.

MacGregor, S., & Paterson, M. (2021). Island Kings: Imperial Masculinity and Climate Fragilities. In P. M. Pulé & M. Hultman (eds), *Men, Masculinities, and Earth: Contending with the (m)Anthropocene*, Cham: Springer International Publishing, pp. 153–168.

Malm, A., & Zetkin Collective (2021). *White Skin, Black Fuel: On the Danger of Fossil Fascism*. London and New York: Verso Books.

Masood, A., & Nisar, M. A. (2020). Speaking Out: A Postcolonial Critique of the Academic Discourse on Far-Right Populism. *Organization*, 27(1): 162–173.

McCarthy, J. (2019). Authoritarianism, Populism, and the Environment: Comparative Experiences, Insights, and Perspectives. *Annals of the American Association of Geographers*, 109(2): 301–313.

McCright, A. M., & Dunlap, R. E. (2003). Defeating Kyoto: The Conservative Movement's Impact on US Climate Change Policy. *Social Problems*, 50(3): 348–373.

McCright, A. M., & Dunlap, R. E. (2011). The Politicization of Climate Change and Polarization in the American Public's Views of Global Warming, 2001–2010. *Sociological Quarterly*, 52(2): 155–194.

McFadden, A. (2023). Wardens of Civilisation: The Political Ecology of Australian Far-Right Civilisationism. *Antipode*, 55(2): 548–573.

Milman, O. (2022). Buffalo suspect may be latest mass shooter motivated by 'eco-fascism'. *The Guardian*, 17 May, www.theguardian.com/us-news/2022/may/17/buffalo-shooting-suspect-eco-fascism?fbclid=IwAR2pWsgcGFMVv79moyXXk8d2wul8_U0L94x2sS_KaximaQP73kCFr_BUt2w (accessed 24 November 2023).

Moore, S., & Roberts, A. (2022). *The Rise of Ecofascism: Climate Change and the Far Right*. New Jersey: John Wiley & Sons.

Murphy, J. (2022). Freedom Convoy: Why Canadian truckers are protesting in Ottawa. *BBC News*, 29 January, www.bbc.com/news/world-us-canada-60164561 (accessed 8 March 2022).

Norgaard, K. M. (2012). Climate Denial and the Construction of Innocence: Reproducing Transnational Environmental Privilege in the Face of Climate Change. *Race, Gender & Class*, 19(1/2): 80–103.

Ofstehage, A., Wolford, W., & Borras, S. M. (2022). Contemporary Populism and the Environment. *Annual Review of Environment and Resources*, 47(1): 671–696.

Pinheiro-Machado, R., & Vargas-Maia, T. (2023). Why We Need a New Framework to Study the Far Right in the Global South. *Global Dialogue*, 13(1): 16–18.

Thompson, C., & Balsamo, M. (2022). Buffalo shooter targeted Black neighborhood, officials say. *AP News*, 16 May.

Tigue, C. (2022). How mass shootings, climate change and eco-fascism got tied together. *InsideClimateNews.org*, 27 May, https://insideclimatenews.org/news/27052022/how-mass-shootings-ecofascism-and-climate-change-got-tied-together/ (accessed 24 November 2023).

Uekötter, F. (2006). *The Green and the Brown: A History of Conservation in Nazi Germany*. Cambridge: Cambridge University Press.

Vowles, K., & Hultman, M. (2021). Scare-Quoting Climate: The Rapid Rise of Climate Denial in the Swedish Far-Right Media Ecosystem. *Nordic Journal of Media Studies*, 3(1): 79–95.

Zhang, Chenchen (2020). Right-Wing Populism with Chinese Characteristics? Identity, Otherness and Global Imaginaries in Debating World Politics Online. *European Journal of International Relations*, 26(1): 88–115.

1

Purity, place and Pākehā nature imaginaries in Aotearoa New Zealand[1]

Amanda Thomas

This chapter starts with a description of the massacre of Muslims in Ōtautahi Christchurch.

On 15 March 2019, a white man pulled up to Al Noor mosque in Ōtautahi Christchurch and began shooting people attending Friday afternoon prayers. There were 190 people gathered there on a fine autumnal day. Livestreaming, he sprayed bullets into the gathered worshippers. After five deadly minutes, he drove 6 kilometres to the Linwood Islamic Centre. There he killed more worshippers among the hundred gathered, before fleeing with the intention of travelling to a third mosque (Brown, 2020). He was stopped soon after by police. Ultimately, he killed 51 people and wounded many more. The worshippers he killed were from a range of backgrounds – some born in Aotearoa New Zealand, some were immigrants or former refugees. They included a three-year-old, a father and son who were worshipping together, students, doctors, restaurant owners (Royal Commission of Inquiry, 2020).[2]

Almost instantly, messages of solidarity from horrified people flooded all forms of media, and decorated mosques and people's front gates (see Arkilic, 2021; Aslam 2019). One image of two women holding each other, drawn by artist Ruby Jones, was accompanied by the message 'this is your home and you should have been safe here'. Other messages repeated Prime Minister Jacinda Ardern's statements that 'they [Muslims] are us [New Zealanders]', and 'this is not us'. These sentiments were well intended, as people grappled with the horror of what happened and sought to comfort the Muslim community, and, it must be said, our(white)selves.

However, Muslim and Māori activists and community leaders soon contested portrayals of the massacre as exceptional and at odds with the *true* nature of Aotearoa New Zealand. Nishhza Thiruselvam (2019) describes the attack as both shocking and unsurprising; the Muslim community had repeatedly warned state agencies of the threats they face (Rahman, 2019). The Al Noor mosque had been targeted by fascists since September 11, and concerns had grown in the five years preceding the massacre. More broadly, Tina Ngata (2019) and Moana Jackson (2019) draw a direct line from the colonization of Aotearoa to the massacre, pointing to the central logic of white supremacy. As Sahar Ghumkhor (2019) wrote in the days after:

> This oscillation of 'they' (the barbarian) and 'us' (the fully civilised human) reveals the precarious nature of a Muslim's life and its place in the nation. Colonial governance has historically relied on exactly the same distinction of human/non-human, us/them in order to legitimise its mission to 'civilise' and provide a rationale for the violent strategies it uses to manage native populations.

The widespread statement, therefore, that 'this was not us', 'profoundly invalidates the complex reality and history of Aotearoa/New Zealand, as experienced by those of us living beyond the rose-tinted lens of white liberal sensibilities' (Thiruselvam, 2019: 62).

One aspect of the connection between the massacre and colonial governance is the underpinning ideas about nature. The shooter's motivations draw on familiar far-right tropes; nostalgia for some imagined pre-immigration past (obviously nonsensical in a [post]colonial place), extreme racism and Islamophobia. In his 74-page manifesto, a document that is banned in Aotearoa New Zealand, the shooter criticizes '[r]ampant urbanization and industrialization, ever expanding cities and shrinking forests, a complete removal of man from nature' and proclaims that 'Green nationalism is the only true nationalism.' He labels himself 'an Ethno-nationalist Eco-fascist', describing his views as 'Ethnic autonomy for all peoples with a focus on the preservation of nature, and the natural order'. Ross and Bevensee (2020: 4) identify the 'cognitive dissonance' of anti-imperial and green narratives like those included in the manifesto of the Christchurch shooter. But rather than exploring this dissonance, or trying to make sense of his actions and ideas, I argue that just as white supremacy is connected to everyday racism, the shooter's eco-fascism and mainstream white New Zealand ideas about nature are connected on a spectrum of white utopianism. This spectrum runs the gamut of the extreme, overt violence of eco-fascism through to the buried violence of white ideas about wilderness and pure nature in Aotearoa New Zealand (Sargent, 2001). Pākehā, or white, nationalism emphasizes the importance of place and natures while actively ignoring how that place attachment was formed (Bell, 2006). This chapter will explore this central thread through the emergence of a new white supremacy group, Action Zealandia (AZ), in the wake of the massacre. This group espouses ideas of white identity under threat, alongside deep ecology and pride in colonization. Through this example, I argue that to understand and confront eco-fascism, the points of continuity and divergence with banal whiteness and colonialism in Aotearoa New Zealand need to be revealed.

In the next section, I explore 'Pākehāness' – white New Zealand identity – and how it relates to nature. I then describe the emergence of Action Zealandia and its eco-fascism. This is connected to a third section about the state: through decisions about who is a 'terrorist' and who needs surveillance, the state has promoted white utopias by attempting to suppress decolonization movements that would see land returned to Māori, and continue to 'other' Muslims from white utopias.

In exploring these themes, I am mindful of critiques of white studies, that I risk further centring whiteness when it already dominates much research and scholarship. And I am aware of my own position as a white person, and that my work relies heavily on the ideas of Indigenous folks, people of colour and Muslim communities. However, careful and critical examination of whiteness is necessary to highlight and excavate embedded colonialism and challenge the idea that Pākehā bear no culpability for the broader ecosystem that fed the shooter's murderous desires. In addition, Indigenous folks and communities of colour are tired of having to speak back to and educate Pākehā (see for instance Mire, 2019). Instead, they ask us to work on ourselves. So this chapter is an attempt to do some of that work by criticizing the way Pākehā have constructed nature here – places cleansed of Indigenous people and sovereignty and thereby rendered pure – and the multiple violences this construction has necessitated and permitted.

Pākehā identity and pure nature

The intention of colonizers coming to Aotearoa New Zealand from England was clear – to transplant English society, and build a better version of it (Cupples et al., 2007). The aspirations for a good life, and the sense that it is possible to build that, led Sargent (2001: 14) to argue that Aotearoa 'New Zealand appears to have developed a stronger utopian tradition than any other country'. Better-than-England narratives dominated in Ōtautahi Christchurch for 150 years as the city built and fed an English identity through carefully curating nature and space. Spaces used by Māori as meeting and trading areas, marked by particular indigenous flora, were turned into monuments for British royalty (McCrone, 2013). The city's Botanic Gardens were designed to reflect Englishness and order, and were positioned as the opposite to uncivilized, unruly native flora (Glynn, 2009). Like other colonized places, space has been portrayed in binaried terms; wildernesses and true nature are imagined to be elsewhere, outside the city borders (Howitt, 2001). The kind of wild nature that would inspire awe was at the doors of the city for colonizers to venture out and be re-created in (Sargent, 2001), but always with the safety of the domesticated city to retreat to.

Whiteness studies in (post)colonial societies has interrogated the power and privileges afforded through whiteness and the way white societal structures are positioned as 'normal'. There is a growing, cross-disciplinary body of work that explores whiteness in Aotearoa New Zealand. In this work, 'Pākehāness' is unpacked and examined. Pākehā is a word from the Māori language that has come to signify non-Māori of European descent. It is at times a controversial term; some white people mistakenly understand it to be an insult, or insist that 'we are all kiwis'. For those who do identify as Pākehā, including me, this identification is often claimed to demarcate our difference from Europeans and other white people; we may not have strong attachments to Europe and see our identity is quite separate from that distant continent. Pākehā, as an identity, locates us in this place, in relationship with Māori and with this land (see Jones, 2020).

It can, however, be a problematic way of identifying. Gray et al. (2013) argue that in naming ourselves as Pākehā, we avoid naming ourselves as white, and in this way race and structural racism are pushed out of identity definition. Their research explored what whiteness meant for people who identified as 'Pākehā'. For Gray et al.'s (2013) participants, rejecting the label of white was an intentional way to distinguish themselves from skinheads.

Yet whiteness is fundamental to colonization and colonialism. Drawing on the work of Yogarajah (2018), Thiruselvam (2019) writes that Pākehā have a rose-tinted version of self that reflects an 'angel complex' where white New Zealand ignores the institutional nature of racism because we are not as bad as, not as racist as, Australia, the birthplace of the mosque shooter. In claiming, for example, that this was 'not us', people implicitly and sometimes explicitly centre the fact that the killer was Australian and came to live in Aotearoa New Zealand with the intention of committing a massacre (see Royal Commission of Inquiry, 2020).

Gray et al. (2013: 99) argue that when people self-label as Pākehā to distinguish ourselves from skinheads and fascists, we:

> risk diverting attention from the relationship that exists between all white people in this country. While not attempting to deny the differences that exist between white people, highlighting the 'hegemonic whiteness' that transcends these distinctions (Hughey, 2010; Lewis, 2004), emphasises the group cohesion created by whiteness; in particular, the benefits shared by living in a society founded on the basis of white supremacy.

Lawn (2015: 263; drawing on Bell, 2014) argues that this attempt to wriggle out of a white identity is common across (post)colonial states. Settler imaginaries share 'a set of common discursive manoeuvres – fantasies of unity, myths of origin, entrenched narratives of innocence, the appropriation of authenticity – by which settler cultures have sought to secure a distinct identity from the imperial centre and legitimate their habitation on indigenous territories'.

Similar discursive manoeuvres, that locate problematic whiteness as 'elsewhere' and outside of mainstream Pākehāness were explored in research by Audrey Kobayashi (2009) when she visited Ōtautahi Christchurch. She describes a 2004 rally that was organized in response to racist violence, and specifically anti-Asian racism, in the city. There were three particular discourses evident in reaction to the rally: discourses of denial (that racism is contained with the far right, not everyday people), of affront (it is insulting to claim that there is racism) and discourses of whiteness that Othered non-white people. These discourses were echoed after the 2019 massacre; racialized people were simultaneously Othered – 'they' – and enfolded into the discourse of denial – racism is from elsewhere, specifically the far right, and Australia.

As well as these discursive manoeuvres that place racism 'elsewhere' and fail to acknowledge the white supremacy that pervades contemporary Aotearoa New Zealand, Avril Bell (2006) argues that Pākehā 'belonging' is focused on attachment to place, attachment that is claimed by an active forgetting of how we came to be here – through the violence of colonialism and the persistent denial of Māori sovereignty. This is evident, for example, in the ways that Pākehā 'claim authenticity' (Lawn, 2015).

Within te ao Māori (the Māori world), a pepeha is a way of emplacing yourself when making introductions. For Māori it often involves tracing the waka (vessel) that ancestors arrived on, tribal affiliations, and mountains and waterways that people are genealogically connected to. The function of the pepeha is to locate yourself in relation to others and the landscape. The politics of Pākehā doing pepeha are complicated but it is common for Pākehā to not know where our ancestors are from, and be proud of this ignorance. Instead, Pākehā will often dodge this aspect and talk about the places we grew up, or the mountains and rivers we love. This is a 'collective wilful amnesia' (Jones, 2020: 203) that erases colonialism and seeks to place Pākehā alongside Māori as belonging to this place, and only this place, and therefore as Indigenous. In doing so, non-white/Pākehā migrants are Othered over and over again, persistently rendered as outsiders to a bicultural utopia (Nasr, 2020).

Nature, and particularly, wild and pure nature, is portrayed as the unproblematic, apolitical canvas upon which a bicultural national identity is created (Bond et al., 2015; Ginn, 2008). The links between nature and wilderness and national identity abound, from appeals to 'tidy kiwis' to clean up litter, through to tourism marketing campaigns that promote Aotearoa New Zealand as '100% pure'. The long-running 100 per cent pure campaign is typically accompanied by imagery from national parks of a landscape devoid of humans, with clean rivers and the promise of wilderness. Around 30 per cent of Aotearoa New Zealand's land area is in national parks with strict rules and norms about who enters, how and what they are allowed to do there. But, like all colonized places, wild and pure landscapes are places violently cleansed of Indigenous folks.

Coombes and Hill (2005) chart some of the mechanisms by which Māori were alienated from their land, for national parks to be formed later. For instance, through the infamous Kemp purchase in 1848, the Crown paid Ngāi Tahu, an iwi (tribe) with attachment to and responsibility for much of the South Island including Ōtautahi Christchurch, two thousand pounds for most of the island (and a third of the entire country). Ngāi Tahu were effectively coerced into the purchase arrangement, and promises made to them to create reserves were never fulfilled (Waitangi Tribunal, 1991). Prominent national parks were created from the land taken through the Kemp purchase; these parks, characterized by soaring, snow-capped mountains and alpine lakes, often feature as examples of 100 per cent purity. In other parts of the country – such as Taranaki and Te Urewera – land was confiscated from Māori, sometimes as punishment for disloyalty to the Crown, and later became part of the conservation estate (Coombes and Hill, 2005). The rules established to regulate these spaces criminalized many activities that underpinned Māori livelihoods, like hunting birds (Coombes, 2020).

As iwi continue to work their way through 'settlement' processes, whereby the Crown makes *some* atonement for breaches of the foundational Te Tiriti o Waitangi / Treaty of Waitangi, returning these wild places to Māori is off the table. In 2009, the Prime Minister at the time ruled out returning one national park to the Tūhoe iwi because 'he felt that, however the Crown got to own Te Urewera [National Park] was irrelevant, it was now public land and all New Zealanders owned it, and loved it and admired it. Even more so perhaps than Tūhoe people' (Kruger, 2017). According to this narrative, non-Māori love and admiration for the national park, and public ownership administered by the (post)colonial state, both erase and justify colonial violence; non-Tūhoe may love it more and therefore be more deserving and better caretakers of the land. Tūhoe have been subjected to wave after wave of Crown-sanctioned violence that has created and maintained a wilderness, and attempted to alienate people from land and to violently suppress movements for tino rangatiratanga (supreme chieftainship, its values and practices) (Aikman, 2017; Coombes, 2020; Kruger, 2017). While there have been significant gains in drawing Māori knowledges and values alongside Eurocentric ideas of environmental management, the kind of decolonization that sees land and sovereignty returned seems like a long way off.

Pākehā identity, through our wilful amnesia, draws heavily on connection to place rather than claims of culture or history (Bell, 2006). We are stubbornly resistant to attempts to get us to acknowledge how we came to be here (Elkington et al., 2020). The effects of this are evident through the way space is ordered and represented. Nature is, for the most part, out there, in national parks that are portrayed as 100 per cent pure, ahistorical and apolitical wild places.

Action Zealandia

Discourses of purity can also be found in the more overtly racist and violent narratives of eco-fascist groups. Just three months after the mosque massacres, a new group, Action Zealandia, emerged out of the remains of the Dominion Movement, an alt-right group. By 2021, AZ was the largest white supremacist group in Aotearoa New Zealand. The number of active members is relatively small – one report puts the number at 30 – but this number is not insignificant in a national population of 5 million (Weir, 2021a, 2021b). There are no known links between the Christchurch shooter and domestic white supremacist groups prior to the massacre (Royal Commission of Inquiry, 2020),[3] but AZ members have praised his violence (Weir, 2021a). The group, therefore, is a useful case study for examining the particularities of fascism, and especially eco-fascism, in the context of post-massacre Aotearoa New Zealand and understanding the ongoing threat of racist and xenophobic violence.

Action Zealandia is explicitly for fit and able-bodied, white, heterosexual men, who 'are the foundation of strong communities and successful families'.[4] The group's website lists their 'ideals' as self-improvement, New Zealand European identity, community building, nationalism and sustainability. Under each ideal is an explanation, and these broadly reflect an anti-capitalist, anti-globalization version of white nationalism. Since July 2019, AZ has published articles on its website, and monthly activity reports that include anonymized photos of group members stickering university campuses and the offices of Members of Parliament, banner drops in support of 'Boers' and boycotts of China, and members boxing, going on tramps in the bush[5] and up mountains, and cleaning up rubbish.

The group writes about 'demographic integrity' and criticizes abortion as a threat to a 'healthier and stronger' nation, a concern rooted in white fears of 'replacement' by people of colour. It is a 'duty', according to the group, to remain a majority in 'our homelands'. The idea of Aotearoa New Zealand as a homeland is developed in a different way from Pākehā described earlier, who learn a pepeha but refuse to identify links with Europe as a way of trying to claim a version of indigeneity. In contrast, the claim to Aotearoa New Zealand being a white homeland is made by rehashing racist tropes of Māori – as undeveloped, savage, destructive – and in need of civilization. Through colonization and white labour, Europeans built this country, they state. Like other fascist groups, they create myths that romanticize and falsify white history – for instance by claiming that Māori gave sovereignty to Britain – while also essentializing racism through claims that it is natural for people with shared ethnic identities to want to be together. Multiple posts on their website trace the origins and praise the actions of white colonizers.

Guest comments on its website congratulate the group for not targeting Muslim communities, and publicly a spokesperson has described the 15 March massacre as having mostly negative effects on white nationalists. However, investigation by the White Rose Society (2020) has shown the group building international connections with neo-Nazi groups and threatening Muslim communities in Aotearoa New Zealand. For example, in conversations on Telegram with the Nordic Resistance Movement, some AZ members have praised the mosque shootings (Clark, 2020b). Further, in the lead-up to the one-year commemorations of the massacre, an AZ member was arrested after threatening Al Noor mosque, and other members plotted a terror cell and discussed buying weapons on the black market (White Rose Society, 2020). So, while the membership of AZ is not large its white supremacy is violent and does target Muslims. As Clark (2023: 51) writes, the 'men of Action Zealandia are not driven to a violent ideology by marginalisation, but by entitlement, and a disdain – if not outright hatred – for genuinely marginalised groups'.

Eco-fascist groups can be identified by their belief that the world is overpopulated and white men have been unfairly attacked (Ross and Bevensee, 2020), particularly by Jewish and non-white people. According to AZ, most environmental damage comes from Africa, India, China and South America, places that are, they claim, the source of overpopulation. In typically neo-Malthusian language, they contend that 'in nature there is no equality. ... If we are not striving to overcome, we are not European.' Environmental degradation is one of the threats to be overcome because '[w]e care about our people and their future, so of course preserving the environment for future generations is a primary concern. Not conserving the habitat and ecosystems for other life forms is tantamount to the downfall of our own people.' The notion that white New Zealanders and nature are fundamentally intertwined is repeated elsewhere; one commenter draws parallels with nineteenth-century Germany and its protection of forests from industrialization, therefore protecting Germany itself.

Their trips into the bush or climbing mountains are written about as antidotes to, and escape from, modern urban life, as overcoming adversity and conquering nature while building camaraderie. In this sense, they echo the mosque shooter's fears of urban degeneracy. One regional AZ group, for example, described their day trip into a national park: 'Exposed to snow, rain, clouds, and extremely strong winds, they marched onwards through the tussock towards their objective.' Activity reports about bush walks are often accompanied by photos of members – with their faces blurred – gathered at mountain summits or on rocky outcrops holding a New Zealand flag or AZ symbol. In other activity reports, AZ members report cleaning up others' degeneracy by picking up litter from beaches. 'As always,' they write, 'thank your local nationalists from preventing rubbish causing damage to the environment.'

The way these activities are described reflects pioneering, frontier narratives about the colonization of Aotearoa New Zealand. Tropes about early colonizers relate to the figure of the 'man alone', forging his way through sheer hard work, not constrained by the class dynamics of Britain. The man alone tamed the land, and remade the entire economy of the country. As is obvious, this narrative is deeply gendered; men are at the centre of work to remake wild land (Cupples et al., 2007). The hyper-masculine (white) rural figure continues to shape national identity, although its dominance is waning. AZ's militaristic masculinity – boxing on the beach, marching through the tussocks – reflects the toxic masculinity of fascism (el-Ojeili, 2018).

Gilbert and Elley (2020, see also Cunningham et al., 2022; Ford, 2020) trace the history of white supremacist groups in Aotearoa New Zealand, and the way that in the decade leading up to the massacre in Ōtautahi Christchurch, little attention was paid to these groups by the public. There is still very limited public discussion about groups like Action Zealandia, and the discussion that does happen is the result of a few journalists and anti-fascist groups, like Paparoa and Tāmaki Anti-Fascist Action.

The state

In March 2019, state security agencies had no strategies relating to the far right and threats to Muslim communities (Clark, 2020a). This is despite a long thread of the far right targeting Māori, Muslims and people of colour. Neo-Nazi groups have been active for more than 50 years, attacking synagogues in the 1960s, fire bombing a marae (meeting house) at the bottom of the South Island in the 1980s, organizing street patrols targeting Pasifika youth in Christchurch in the 2000s, and dumping pigs' heads at the Al Noor mosque in the 2010s (Ford, 2020).

In the face of white supremacy and Islamophobia, the Islamic Women's Council of New Zealand (2019) 'made intense efforts to engage with the New Zealand government in the five years before the Christchurch mosque killings, seeking protection and support for an increasingly vulnerable and exposed Muslim community'. State security agencies were so focused on supposed threats *from* the Muslim community that white supremacists and the alt-right were almost entirely absent from their briefings to the Prime Minister. Despite apologies after the massacre by security agencies, police and state agencies have continued their lacklustre response to threats from the far right against Muslim and Jewish communities (see, for instance, Daalder, 2020). In the weeks before the two-year anniversary of the massacre, a new threat was made against the two mosques where the massacre took place. The anonymous anti-fascist group Paparoa tipped the police off about the threat, and has criticized the domestic spy agency's inadequate response (Scotcher, 2020).

In addition to surveilling Muslims, state agencies have directed their attention to Māori sovereignty activists. Māori never ceded sovereignty, a fact that is profoundly troubling to Pākehā claims to being of this land, and to the settler colonial state's legitimacy. Any discussion of nature and the environment in Aotearoa New Zealand directly relates to questions of sovereignty – who decides what counts as nature and the relationships that can exist with that nature.

In 2007, the state raided the homes of Māori sovereignty, anarchist and environmental justice activists across the country. In a post-9/11 world, there seemed to be pressure to directly identify and confront a terrorist threat. The raids particularly targeted Tūhoe in Te Urewera, where police erected illegal road blocks, stopped a school bus full of children and terrorized families. The raids were framed as 'anti-terror' operations, a label that has been hard to shift, despite the fact that no one was prosecuted for terrorism. Of the 18 people who were arrested, only four were successfully prosecuted for firearms offences. Aikman (2017: 69) argues that the raids on Tūhoe were 'not exceptional, but routine functions of the settler colonial state' and their efforts to secure sovereignty. Tūhoe have been subjected to punitive actions by the Crown, including the confiscation of much of their land, since the mid-1800s. Much of this land was turned into a national park, the same park that the Prime Minister ruled out returning because New Zealanders love it just as much as (if not more than) Tūhoe. In other examples, attempts to assert tino rangatiratanga (supreme chieftainship, its values and practices) have been met with an overwhelming police presence, or the involvement of the military. For example, when one of Tūhoe's neighbouring iwi (tribes), Te Whānau-ā-Apanui, attempted to stop seismic surveying in their ocean territory, the navy assisted the police to arrest an iwi leader.

The New Zealand state plays a pivotal role in underpinning white utopias. This role is most apparent in this case study in relation to the framing of 'threat' and ideas about who the threat was against (Bargh, 2012). The colonial state has always understood the central threats to territorial sovereignty to be from claims of tino rangatiratanga – and all its possible implications for the wilderness constructed through colonization (Coombes, 2020) – and from incursions by non-white and non-Christian 'Others' across borders. As Aikman (2017: 59) argues, 'state sovereignty is articulated through on-going acts of violent legitimation', in this instance the violence enacted through state security agencies' choices about who to surveil and target, and who to ignore.

Continuity and divergence in white ideas about nature

Colonialism, banal whiteness and eco-fascism exist in relation to each other; exploring the points of convergence and divergence is an important part of anti-fascist and decolonial political projects. As Hala Nasr (2020) argues, terrorism rooted in white supremacy is intimately connected to everyday racism. From the beginning of the colonial project in Aotearoa, particular nature discourses have had material impacts on the land and Indigenous people. The pure and wild spaces that are preserved through the large tracts of land locked into national parks are fundamental to national identity. This national identity is not an exclusively Pākehā identity; people from a range of backgrounds value and seek to preserve these spaces. What distinguishes the relationship between wilderness and Pākehā is that it is fundamental to Pākehā nationalism to forget and erase how Pākehā came to be here, and the violence that was used to dispossess Māori of these same places. Through this ignorance, Pākehā are able to maintain our own sense of innocence and claim that racist violence is not us. Banal Pākehāness often seeks to locate us as also Indigenous, and this is partly done by disavowing our ancestral ties to Europe (Elkington et al., 2020). In this way, we make similar claims to this being our 'homeland' to the eco-fascist group, Action Zealandia. That group, however, does not deny connections to Europe. Instead, it amplifies European pioneering myths and attempts to build white pride in connections to colonial Europe, and Britain in particular.

Across the eco-fascism of the shooter and Action Zealandia, and the refusal of the state and Pākehā to grapple with the violence through which wilderness areas were created, there is a positioning of Eurocentric ideas, if not white people, as the rightful caretakers of nature. Banal Pākehāness, the state and AZ share a presumption that preservationist conservation is the best, perhaps the only way, of maintaining nature. For the state, there have been shifts towards co-management with Māori, and recognition of the personhood of nature. However, the refusal to repatriate national parks reflects the supremacy of white ideas about wilderness (Coombes, 2020), and a prioritizing of the connection to and 'love' for these places that 'all' New Zealanders feel. When Māori sovereignty activists have sought the kind of decolonization that sees land returned, they have often been surveilled or subject to police or occasionally military action. AZ are more overtly racist in the way they try to position white people as the natural caretakers of the environment. Māori needed civilizing through colonization, they argue, and migrants and non-white foreigners represent a constant threat to the environment and sustainability. Similarly, for the Christchurch shooter, 'invaders' threaten the integrity of place. Across this spectrum of white ideas, there is also a shared construction of true, wild nature as out there, beyond the city. This was apparent from the earliest colonizers of Ōtautahi Christchurch who understood the city as a place for domesticated nature, reflected in the English gardens.

Sargent (2001) argues that one of the key features of Pākehā identity that emerged from utopian traditions was conformity – there is a reasonably narrow spectrum of what is acceptable in Aotearoa New Zealand culture. The radical fringes are typically small and not well tolerated, but some researchers demonstrate there has been a recent rise of the far right and worry about what that means in the context of climate change (Campion and Phillips, 2023). The extreme rhetoric of Action Zealandia has, for the most part, not taken hold. And while I am placing mainstream Pākehā ideas about nature on a spectrum of white utopia with eco-fascism, it is important to distinguish liberal white identity from fascism (el-Ojeili, 2018).

Most Pākehā were and (largely) still are horrified by the mosque killings, although white fragility has also limited the extent of self-analysis that should have followed, including a reckoning with similar acts of violence committed by the colonial state in the 1800s (see McConnell, 2020). When Pākehā insisted 'this is not us', we denied that white violence characterized the earliest encounters with Aotearoa, and has continued through the dispossession of Māori land and the Othering of non-white migrants. The idea that 'this is not us' was able to take hold because of our 'collective wilful amnesia' (Jones, 2020: 203) of our own migrant histories, and the myth of a bicultural utopia built through wild and pure nature. As Moana Jackson (2019) writes:

> In many ways, today's white supremacists are the most recent and most extreme colonisers. The Christchurch terrorist was therefore not some 'lone wolf' psychopath. He may have acted alone, but he drew upon the shared ideas and history that still lurk in the shadows of every country that has been colonised.

They – the barbarian white supremacists – are us – emerging from Pākehā, white society. Without an honest accounting of whiteness in its full spectrum, the actions of the (post)colonial state, and the impact of white utopic ambitions, there will always be the risk of eco-fascist myths taking hold.

Notes

1 Aotearoa is the Māori-language name for what is known in English as New Zealand. The convention of writing 'Aotearoa New Zealand' acknowledges that Māori never ceded sovereignty, and that settler colonialism persists.
2 An independent inquiry was commissioned by the New Zealand Government 10 days after the shootings. The commission conducting the inquiry was strongly criticized by the Muslim community for excluding them, and a relatively closed process that precluded them from making meaningful contributions to both the terms of reference and the inquiry itself – see Danzeisen (2020).
3 The shooter was, however, active in Australian, and other, far-right online groups (McGowan, 2020).
4 In this section, I haven't included direct links for the quotes included to avoid driving traffic to AZ's website. I have struggled with whether or not to name the group concerned; some activists advocate not naming them so as to limit their reach. This approach is also reflected in an almost blanket refusal within Aotearoa New Zealand to use the name of the mosque shooter in order to deny him the notoriety he craved. However, I named AZ in this chapter because one consequence of *not* naming is a widespread ignorance of groups like this, and therefore a lack of discussion and understanding of the (very real) threat they present.
5 In Aotearoa New Zealand, forests are often referred to as 'the bush'.

References

Aikman, P. J. W. E. (2017). Trouble on the Frontier: *Hunt for the Wilderpeople,* Sovereignty and State Violence. *SITES: New Series,* 14(1): 56–79.

Arkilic, A. (2021). The Christchurch Shooting and the 2020 New Zealand Election. In S. Levine (ed.), *Politics in a Pandemic: Jacinda Ardern and New Zealand's 2020 election.* Wellington: Victoria University Press, pp. 225–239.

Aslam, R. (2019). Christchurch Mosque Shooting: Reflections and Confessions. *Ethical Space: The International Journal of Communication Ethics,* 16(4): 48–56.

Bargh, M. (2012). Community Organizing: Māori Movement-Building. In A. Choudry, J. Hanley and E. Shragge (eds), *Organize! Building from the Local for Global Justice.* Oakland, CA.: PM Press, pp. 123–131.

Bell, A. (2006). Bifurcation or Entanglement? Settler Identity and Biculturalism in Aotearoa New Zealand. *Continuum,* 20(2): 253–268.

Bell, A. (2014). *Relating Indigenous and Settler Identities: Beyond Domination.* Houndmills: Palgrave Macmillan.

Bond, S., Diprose, G. and McGregor, A. (2015). 2Precious2Mine: Post-Politics, Colonial Imaginary, or Hopeful Political Moment? *Antipode*, 47(5): 1161–1183.

Brown, T. (2020). Christchurch mosque attack victims address gunman: 'we did not deserve your actions'. *RNZ*, 24 August, www.rnz.co.nz/news/national/424297/christchurch-mosque-attack-victims-address-gunman-we-did-not-deserve-your-actions (accessed 13 November 2023).

Campion, K. and Phillips, J. (2023). The Exclusivist Claims of Pacific Ecofascists: Visual Environmental Communication by Far-right Groups in Australia and New Zealand. In B. Forchtner (ed.), *Visualising Far Right Environments: Communication and the Politics of Nature*. Manchester: Manchester University Press, pp. 43–62.

Clark, B. C. (2020a). Encounters with the far right part 1. *Webworm with David Farrier*, www.webworm.co/p/alt-right-pt1 (accessed 13 November 2023).

Clark, B. C. (2020b). Encounters with the far right part 2. *Webworm with David Farrier*, www.webworm.co/p/alt-right-pt2?fbclid=IwAR1_qVy23m_rq7XI0hAKZGI8ueEk_z-wjO2w0mHWpFMdAHT1gyHQd6K7o0E (accessed 13 November 2023).

Clark, B. C. (2023). *Fear: New Zealand's Hostile Underworld of Extremists*. Auckland: Harper Collins.

Coombes, B. (2020). Nature's Rights As Indigenous Rights? Mis/recognition through Personhood for Te Urewera. *Espace Populations Sociétés*, 1–2. doi.org/10.4000/eps.9857.

Coombes, B. and Hill, S. (2005). 'Nā whenua, nā Tūhoe, ko D.o.C te partner' – Prospects for Comanagement of Te Urewera National Park. *Society and Natural Resources*, 18, 135–152.

Cunningham, M., La Rooij, M. and Spoonley, P. (eds) (2022). *Histories of Hate: The Radical Right in Aotearoa New Zealand*. Dunedin: Otago University Press.

Cupples, J., Guyatt, V. and Pearce, J. (2007). 'Put a jacket on you wuss': Cultural Identities, Home Heating, and Air Pollution in Christchurch New Zealand. *Environment and Planning A*, 39: 2883–2898.

Daalder, M. (2020). Online, nobody knows you're a terrorist: extremists targeted me. *Stuff.co.nz*, 21 December, www.stuff.co.nz/opinion/300189381/online-nobody-knows-youre-a-terrorist-extremists-targeted-me (accessed 13 November 2023).

Danzeisen, A. (2020). Justice has not been served in Royal Commission report into terrorist attack on Christchurch mosques. *NZHerald*, 8 December, www.nzherald.co.nz/nz/aliya-danzeisen-justice-has-not-been-served-in-royal-commission-report-into-terrorist-attack-on-christchurch-mosques/ESVK2TJLQQ7ULZOFQTY3KN2QHY/ (accessed 13 November 2023).

Elkington, B., Kiddle, R., Jackson, M., Mercier, O. R., Ross, M., Smeaton, J. and Thomas, A. (2020). *Imagining Decolonisation*. Wellington: BWB.

El-Ojeili, C. (2018). Keywords: Post-fascism. *Counterfutures*, 6: 100–118.

Ford, K. (2020). Mapping the New Zealand Far Right. *Peace Review: A Journal of Social Justice*, 32(4): 504–511.

Ghumkhor, S. (2019). The hypocrisy of New Zealand's 'this is not us' claim. *Al Jazeera*, 20 March, www.aljazeera.com/indepth/opinion/hypocrisy-zealand-claim-190319104526942.html (accessed 13 November 2023).

Gilbert, J. and Elley, B. (2020). Shaved Heads and Sonnenrads: Comparing White Supremacist Skinheads and the Alt-Right in New Zealand. *Kōtuitui: New Zealand Journal of Social Sciences, Online*, 15(2): 280–294.

Ginn, F. (2008). Extension, Subversion, Containment: Eco-nationalism and (Post) colonial Nature in Aotearoa New Zealand. *Transactions of the British Institute of Geographers*, 33(3): 335–353.

Glynn, K. (2009). Contested Land and Mediascapes: The Visuality of the Postcolonial City. *New Zealand Geographer*, 65: 6–22.

Gray, C., Jaber, N. and Anglem, J. (2013). Pakeha Identity and Whiteness: What Does It Mean To Be White? *SITES*, 10(2): 82–106.

Howitt, R. (2001). Frontiers, Borderings, Edges: Liminal Challenges to the Hegemony of Exclusion. *Australian Geographical Studies*, 39(2): 233–245.

Islamic Women's Council of New Zealand (2019). Submissions of the Islamic Women's Council of New Zealand to the Royal Commission of Inquiry into the attack on Christchurch mosques on 15 March 2019. *iwc.nz*, 29 August, https://islamicwomenscouncilnz.co.nz/submissions-iwcnz/ (accessed 17 November 2023).

Jackson, M. (2019). The connection between white supremacy and colonisation. *E-Tangata*, 24 March, https://e-tangata.co.nz/comment-and-analysis/the-connection-between-white-supremacy/ (accessed 13 November 2023).

Jones, A. (2020). *This Pākehā Life: An Unsettled Memoir*. Wellington: BWB.

Kobayashi, A. (2009). 'Here we go again': Christchurch's Antiracism Rally as a Discursive Crisis. *New Zealand Geographer*, 65: 59–72.

Kruger, T. (2017). We are not who we should be as Tūhoe people. *E-Tangata*, 18 November, https://e-tangata.co.nz/identity/tamati-kruger-we-are-not-who-we-should-be-as-tuhoe-people/ (accessed 13 November 2023).

Lawn, J. (2015). Review: Relating Indigenous and Settler Identities: Beyond Domination. *New Zealand Sociology*, 30(1): 263–270.

McConnell, G. (2020). I spent a year watching the alt-right after the devastating Christchurch terror attacks. *Stuff.co.nz*, 12 March, www.stuff.co.nz/national/christchurch-shooting/120161318/i-spent-a-year-watching-the-altright-after-the-devastating-christchurch-terror-attacks (accessed 13 November 2023).

McCrone, J. (2013). Ngāi Tahu's reach shapes new city. *Stuff.co.nz*, 19 January, www.stuff.co.nz/the-press/news/8198076/Ngai-Tahus-reach-shapes-a-new-city (accessed 13 November 2023).

McGowan, M (2020). Christchurch shooter was active with Australian far right groups online but escaped police attention. *The Guardian*, 8 December, www.theguardian.com/world/2020/dec/08/christchurch-shooter-was-active-with-australian-far-right-groups-online-but-escaped-police-attention (accessed 13 November 2023).

Mire, G. (2019). Christchurch terror attacks: Kiwis need to 'stop living in denial' and acknowledge racism exists in Aotearoa. *1 News Now*, 18 March, www.tvnz.co.nz/one-news/new-zealand/christchurch-terror-attacks-kiwis-need-stop-living-in-denial-and-acknowledge-racism-exists-aotearoa?variant=tb_v_2 (accessed 13 November 2023).

Nasr, H. (2020). Memorial through action. *Economic and Social Research Aotearoa*, 20 March, https://esra.nz/memorial-through-action/ (accessed 13 November 2023).

Ngata, T. (2019). What does a safe, just Aotearoa look like? *The Non-Plastic Māori*, 19 March, https://thenonplasticmaori.wordpress.com/2019/03/19/what-does-a-just-safe-aotearoa-look-like/ (accessed 13 November 2023).

Rahman, A. (2019). We warned you. We begged. We pleaded. And now we demand accountability. *The Spinoff*, 17 March https://thespinoff.co.nz/society/17–03–2019/we-warned-you-we-begged-we-pleaded-and-now-we-demand-accountability/?fbclid=IwAR0lS7wxM_5_237ttEKMUpNSGvBuKoDh86VKvs6gspoYCGd9rE5EIoLec84 (accessed 13 November 2023).

Ross, A. R., and Bevensee, E. (2020). Confronting the rise of eco-fascism means grappling with complex systems. *CARR Research Insight 2020.3*. London: Centre for Analysis of the Radical Right.

Royal Commission of Inquiry (2020). *Ko tō tātou kāinga tēnei*. Report: Royal Commission of Inquiry into the Terrorist Attack on Christchurch Masjidain on 15 March 2019. https://christchurchattack.royalcommission.nz/ (accessed 13 November 2023).

Sargent, L. T. (2001). Utopianism and the Creation of New Zealand National Identity. *Utopian Studies*, 12(1): 1–18.

Scotcher, K. (2020). Person who alerted police to mosque threat had met man arrested. *RNZ*, 9 March, www.rnz.co.nz/news/political/437940/person-who-alerted-police-to-mosque-threat-had-met-man-arrested (accessed 17 November 2023).

Thiruselvam, N. (2019). Care Ethics and Narratives of the 'Grateful Refugee' and 'Model Minority': A Postcolonial Feminist Observation of New Zealand in the Wake of the Christchurch Terror Attacks. *Women's Studies Journal*, 33(1/2): 62–70.

Waitangi Tribunal (1991). *The Ngāi Tahu Land Report. Waitangi Tribunal, Department of Justice*, https://forms.justice.govt.nz/search/Documents/WT/wt_DOC_68476209/Wai27.pdf (accessed 17 November 2023).

Weir, E. (2021a). Fascism 2.0: lessons from six months in New Zealand's largest white supremacist group. *Critic Te Arohi*, 9 August, www.critic.co.nz/features/article/9610/fascism-20-lessons-from-six-months-in-new-zealands (accessed 13 November 2023).

Weir, E. (2021b). Investigation sheds light on Aotearoa's largest neo-Nazi group. *Critic Te Arohi*, 9 August, www.critic.co.nz/news/article/9609/investigation-sheds-light-on-aotearoas-largest-neo (accessed 13 November 2023).

White Rose Society (2020). Max Newsome ('Matt') and Action Zealandia, *White Rose Society*, 10 March, https://thewhiterosesociety.writeas.com/max-newsome-matt-and-action-zealandia (accessed 13 November 2023).

Yogarajah, M. (2018). (Lack of) citizenship and Canada's angel complex. *Public Policy & Governance Review*, 20 March, https://ppgreview.ca/2018/03/20/lack-of-citizenship-and-canadas-angel-complex/ (accessed 17 November 2023).

2

Boko Haram in the Capitalocene: assemblages of climate change and militant Islamism in Nigeria

Shehnoor Khurram

The world is in the throes of an existential calamity brought on by climate change. While the physical impacts of global warming are frightening, so too are the social and political aspects of adaptation, which can take reactionary and repressive forms. In his infamous 2002 'Letter to America', Osama bin Laden criticized the US for its contribution to climate change (Bodetti, 2019). He wrote, 'You have destroyed nature with your industrial waste and gases more than any other nation in history. Despite this, you refuse to sign the Kyoto agreement so that you can secure the profit of your greedy companies and industries' (*The Guardian*, 2002). In 2017, the Afghan Taliban critiqued the US intervention in Afghanistan for the environmental destruction that it wrought, stating, 'The US invasion destroyed many sectors of Afghanistan, including the environment, in a very bad way and for the long term. The Islamic Emirate of Afghanistan has the perfect plan for environmental protection through planting trees' (Bodetti, 2017). In Somalia in 2018, Al-Shabaab banned plastic bags because they pose 'a serious threat to the well-being of humans and animals alike' (Dahir, 2018). It is no longer possible to avoid interacting with the discourses and materiality of our current ecological crisis. Unfolding globally, it is devastating ecosystems, killing human and non-human life, decimating livelihoods, destroying infrastructure, stressing national political economies, and more (Eklöw & Krampe, 2019: 4). From politicians to far-right groups to ordinary citizens, everyone is reacting to these changes. Violent insurgent groups are also joining the conversation in unprecedented and peculiar ways. While the protection of nature is a part of the rhetoric of some militant Islamist movements, other groups take advantage of the consequences of climate change. Most notably, in Nigeria, Boko Haram has used the dwindling Lake Chad as a weapon of war.

Violent militant Islamist movements have emerged as major political contenders across the world. In tandem, ecological crises are intensifying in their urgency. Both are transforming and redefining the security landscape, creating significant implications for global peace and security. But how, when and why do they intersect? This chapter addresses this question through a case study of Boko Haram in Lake Chad, an epicentre of climate catastrophe. The conflict has reached such troubling magnitudes that the World Food Programme declared it a Level 3 emergency, stating 'The Sahel is a tragic masterclass in how violence and extreme weather feed into each other' (WFP, 2020). I conceptualize the nexus of climate change and militant Islamist violence as consisting of an array of interacting geopolitical, socio-economic, ecological and discursive components. Specifically, the Capitalocene, colonialism, neoliberalism and the social hierarchies of class/race/gender/ethnicity/religious co-determine the climate change–militant Islamism matrix in nonlinear, nondeterministic and complex ways (Chalecki, 2001). Dominant media, policy and academic discourses contribute to this assemblage by offering analyses that suffer from a racist and Islamophobic schema that renders the crisis ahistorical and depoliticized. This chapter critically reviews this literature and offers a re-reading of the crisis that considers the social, political, economic and ecological elements of the crisis. I argue this nexus is a political puzzle that must be understood as the historically specific expression of the contradictions of the Capitalocene.

I highlight two major mechanisms of the effect of climate on militant Islamism: first, climate change exacerbates violent conflicts surrounding natural resources. Water scarcity has allowed Boko Haram to weaponize the access and use of Lake Chad to carry out its religio-political agenda. Secondly, climate change is intensifying precarity, making affected populations more vulnerable to recruitment by militant Islamist groups because they offer alternative livelihoods that coincide with their political and socio-economic grievances. This cumulatively provides a fertile ground for insurgent groups to increase their membership and access to valuable resources, making it more viable for them to achieve their objectives. The argument develops in four parts: the first section examines whether Boko Haram can be classified as a far-right movement; the second part sketches the contours of the Lake Chad conflict; the third portion assesses the existing literature; and the fourth section analyses Boko Haram's weaponization of Lake Chad in its struggle to establish an Islamic caliphate in Nigeria. I conclude by outlining an agenda for further research.

Boko Haram – terrorism or far-right populism?

Boko Haram is a militant Islamist movement that emerged in Nigeria's Muslim-majority North. Boko Haram turned into a violent anti-state insurgent movement in 2009 with the explicit aim of toppling the secular state and implementing a Salafist Islamic caliphate (Ekhomu, 2019). A majority of the scholarly and mdia analyses have examined the group through the terrorism/War on Terror lens that focuses on Boko Haram's anti-state and anti-Western motivations, explaining its existence through the prism of the 'mad Muslim terrorist' (Patel, 2014: 202). These discourses are grounded in an orientalist binary between the civilizational and racial superiority of the West versus the inferiority of the barbarous East, in which the

> wild, untameable Muslim is solely defined by his passion rather than his politics, and [his] mindset is so evil and so irrational that people of the civilized white West cannot understand it ... the psychologizing discourses of the Muslim mind turn political actions into their emotions, their instability (of character), and their 'passion,' which is constructed as apolitical and a sign of their anti-modernity (as opposed to the rational, civilized, and modern white Westerner). (Patel, 2014: 204)

Such discourses decontextualize these groups from their complex political, economic and social contexts, consequently obscuring decades of Western colonial and imperial intervention that engender varying degrees of violent and non-violent resistance. Given that the 'mad Muslim terrorist' cannot be rational, it becomes possible to reject engaging with their actions, like suicide bombing, in a political manner as acts of resistance (Patel, 2014). This resistance is perceived to be a threat to the white political economic order, and thus it can only be cured by the civility of the West through either indefinite incarceration and torture or total elimination, ultimately giving imperialist nations moral superiority and legitimizing imperial policies (Edwards, 1989: 655; Patel, 2014: 212).

In stark contrast, discourses on the far right in the Global North take seriously the ideological, political and economic underpinnings of far-right populism and violence. These narratives portray white people as rational, complex and imperfect beings whose actions can be understood in relation to the broader social landscape in which they emerge – a privilege denied to the 'mad Muslim terrorist' from the Global South. Interestingly, organizations from the Global South are often overlooked within conventional far-right discourses, which are premised on the Eurocentric, orientalist and racist assumption that the 'normal' Global North is undergoing certain 'abnormal' changes that create far-right populism, while the possibility of such changes in the Global South is not addressed because within the 'always-assumed-to-be-uncivilized, the undeveloped [Global South], the question of "abnormality" is always foreclosed' (Masood and Nisar, 2020: 163). It is thus no coincidence that terrorism studies overwhelmingly focus on movements from the Global South, whereas far-right discourses exclusively examine the Global North. Calling one form of reactionary violence, militant Islamism, terrorism but not considering another form, right-wing extremist violence, as terrorism is an inherently political position, which reveals prejudicial assumptions held about the nature of terrorism and terrorists (van Elk, 2016: 153). Classifying the Boko Haram crisis as one of terrorism rather than the far right implies that the 'far right' is an aberration in the Global North deserving of its own analytical category, but it constitutes 'regular politics' in the Global South. Such frameworks inevitably lead to neoliberal technocratic and militarized solutions that do not combat the root causes, and, in many cases, worsen the violence.

There is budding literature that points to how the far right and militant Islamism are two sides of the same coin, phenomena with shared driving forces – the Capitalocene (Jarvis, 2022; Buckingham & Alali, 2020; Bakali, 2019). The Global Network on Extremism and Technology (Wegener, 2020), a major research institution dedicated to the study of far-right violence, points to the connections between the far-right and militant Islamist movements: dissatisfaction with the socio-economic consequences of neoliberalism; monolithic nationalist identity; xenophobia and anti-immigrant sentiment; a claim to speak for ordinary citizens whose interests are no longer well represented by traditional politics; patriarchal domination; anti-democratic/ anti-state tendencies; distrust of mainstream and government media, and a need to establish their own media networks to disseminate their ideology; and religious antagonism and a call for a return to 'tradition' (Gusterson, 2017: 210; Masood & Nisar, 2020: 167). In a project of experimentation, I analyse Boko Haram through the lens of the far right, as a movement rooted in an alienated and oppressed populace and a religious ideology that is capable of articulating its grievances. The Capitalocene assemblage, explored in section four, demonstrates how similar structural processes that are stoking far-right violence across the Western world are the same ones shaping militant Islamist violence in Africa and beyond.

The anatomy of the Lake Chad crisis

In 2019, the Intergovernmental Panel on Climate Change (IPCC) cautioned that land, which provides the 'food, feed, fibre, fuel, and freshwater' that humanity needs to survive, is under threat from rising global temperatures that are causing unprecedentedly high rates of water scarcity. This is acutely felt in Africa, where the temperature is increasing 1.5 times faster than the global average, causing a sharp decrease in available freshwater (Nett & Rüttinger, 2016: 24). Populations that live in drylands, like in the African Sahel, are exposed to extreme risks like water stress, drought and desertification, and habitat degradation (Carbon Brief, 2019). Nigeria is one of the most climate-vulnerable countries in the world (Fasona & Omojola, 2005: 5). The IPCC has found that it is losing an estimated 35,000 square kilometres of agricultural lands to desertification, coupled with drastic reductions in rainfall (Werz & Conley, 2012: 21). This is troubling because agriculture comprises approximately 22 per cent of its gross domestic product and 35 per cent of employment (World Bank, 2021; FAO, 2020). Environmental degradation threatens the livelihoods of around 40 million people, who now face unemployment and poverty (Ojoye, 2016).

Lake Chad is at the centre of this ecological crisis. A transboundary zone that borders four countries – Nigeria, Cameroon, Chad and Niger – it was once Africa's second-largest wetland and fourth-largest lake, and it was the sixth-largest lake in the entire world, with a surface area of about 25,000 square kilometres (Gao et al., 2011). It lies in an endorheic basin on the southern margin of the Sahara Desert, making it a primary source of freshwater for drinking, sanitation, fishing and irrigation for the production of staple commodities such as cotton, rice and maize (Owonikoko & Momodu, 2020: 1305). The lake fluctuates seasonally because it is shallow and flat, only reaching a depth of 7 metres, making it sensitive to desertification and precipitation variability (Rizzo, 2015: 13). Coe and Foley (2001) and Gao et al. (2011) report that since the early 1960s, rainfall over the basin has decreased significantly at the same time that irrigation has increased dramatically, negatively impacting the lake's biomass recovery rates. As a result, the lake has shrunk by roughly 90 per cent over 35 years, reaching its lowest point in 2004 at 532 square kilometres (Rizzo, 2015: 14). In 2003, the United Nations (UN) classified the lake as one of the ten most water-impoverished regions in the world (UNEP, 2018). Hydrological and biophysical changes arising from climate change have contributed to the degradation of pasturelands, reduction in the livestock population, 60 per cent decline in fish stocks, loss of vegetation, and depletion of grazing land (Nett & Rüttinger, 2016; Gao et al., 2011).

The drastic reductions in water supply, quality and accessibility have critical social, economic and political consequences (Okpara et al., 2017). The social effects of climate change depend on the adaptive capacity of economic, cultural and political systems (Buhaug et al., 2015: 2). Lake Chad operates in a degree of lawlessness because the Nigerian state lacks the human, technical and administrative control to manage water scarcity (Okpara et al., 2017: 311). In the absence of social safety nets, climate change has generated continuous cycles of mass migration, poverty, food insecurity, unemployment and more (Owonikoko & Momodu, 2020: 1302). In this chaos, contestations over the control of water emerge, as insurgent groups, who are vying for state power, use the shrinking sources of water as a 'political tool, a material source of power, a weapon during wars and a means of violence' to advance their interests (Daoudy, 2020: 1349). In parallel to the deteriorating ecological conditions, a crisis of insurgency is also erupting in Lake Chad – perpetrated by Boko Haram (Nett & Rüttinger, 2016).

In 2015, Boko Haram expanded into the Lake Chad region, gaining control over the dwindling water source and establishing itself as the premier political authority (Maza et al., 2020: 8). The lawlessness of the basin has provided the group with a safe haven to protect itself from attacks by the Nigerian military (Comolli, 2017). Designated as the world's deadliest terrorist group in 2015 by the Global Terrorism Index, Boko Haram has taken the lives of over 31,000 people since 2011 in the Lake Chad region through abductions, suicide bombings, assassinations and beheadings (Global Terrorism Index, 2015; Watts, 2004: 2). Boko Haram's control over the basin has allowed it to operate more freely in the region. It is estimated that the group has destroyed approximately 75 per cent of the water infrastructure in the Northeast in an attempt to control the surrounding population (Ekhomu, 2019: 141). For example, it has been known to poison valuable water sources, like wells and streams, used by the military during their counter-terrorism missions near and around the basin as a means to deter them from further encroaching into the lake (Nett & Rüttinger, 2016: 15). This has made the water dangerous for humans and livestock by proxy, leading to the rise of waterborne illnesses, like typhoid (Hugh, 2019: 11).

Further, Boko Haram and its affiliate, Islamic State in West Africa use control of the lake and its economic activity, like cross-border trade routes, to finance their activities (Bressler, 2020: 20). Before Boko Haram gained control, the fish and red pepper trade was a major source of exports for the Nigerian economy, generating approximately ₦19 billion per year and providing almost 300,000 people with employment (Oxfam, 2017: 3). But climate change has depleted fish stocks, creating a large reserve of unemployed fishers. The few who have continued to fish have faced new levies and taxes since Boko Haram took over (Salkida, 2020). HumAngle, a local news agency, reports that fishers have to pay around ₦15,000 every two weeks for fishing rights (Salkida, 2020). Those who are unable to pay face dire consequences: in 2014, Boko Haram killed 48 fishers by drowning them in the lake (BBC, 2014); in 2017, Boko Haram killed 'at least 31 fishers' (AFP, 2017); in 2020, Boko Haram killed 'at least 50 fishers' (BBC, 2020). In response to these brutal acts, the Nigerian state banned the production and trade of fish and red pepper (Mahmood & Ani, 2018). The Borno Fish Producers' Association has reported a ₦500 million loss in business per year because of Boko Haram's changes to the production, collection of taxes and control over access to the lake (Okoye, 2021). Climate change and Boko Haram's violence are pushing people into extreme marginality, which is ground for recruiting new fighters (Nett & Rüttinger, 2016: 48; Salkida, 2020). Control over the lake allows the group to carry out its religio-political agenda while also creating an informal cash-based illicit and criminal economy network for financial power (Igwe, 2021; Salkida, 2020).

These volatile conditions allow Boko Haram to recruit more easily as the escalation in its violence corresponds to the increase in its membership (Vivekananda and Born, 2018; MacEachern, 2018; Watts, 2017; David et al., 2015). For insurgent movements, steady and continuous recruitment is a matter of survival as the membership size determines access to resources and human capital to carry out their goals (Maza et al., 2020: 2). Boko Haram's chief recruitment tactic includes financial incentives and manipulating anti-state sentiment using religious vernacular as a tool for radicalization. Through field research, David et al. (2015: 72) and Scott MacEachern (2018: 163) have found that the group's foot-soldiers primarily consist of people from the poorest communities. Aghedo and Osumah (2012: 861) note from their field research that the upsurge in Boko Haram's membership since 2009 'largely relates to the depth of feeling about socioeconomic injustice, marginalization, and human insecurity'.[1] Indeed, many researchers have found that many individuals join Boko Haram primarily for monetary benefits. Suicide bombers are reportedly paid large sums of money to carry out attacks amounting to ₦10 million. For example, Mohammed Manga carried out a suicide-bombing attack on the Nigerian police headquarters in Ajuba, and he was paid ₦4 million, which he willed to his family (Onapajo & Uzodike, 2012: 27, 29). Boko Haram has also been reported to offer an income of approximately ₦3000 per month (Maza et al., 2020: 6). The UN Counter-Terrorism Committee found that it 'pays between $30 and $312 per mission for women weapons carriers' (UNCTED, 2019: 18). There is a clear correlation between recruitment and monetary gains. David et al. (2015: 90) write that it 'offer[s] not just material well-being but also promises a greater after-life, indeed stands the chance of being very attractive to the destitute youths and children who are not sure where their next meal will come from, let alone any future life prospect'.

The increase in membership and the escalation in violence has led to the displacement of over 2.5 million people across the North (Watts, 2004: 2). Boko Haram's increasing presence in neighbouring countries, like Cameroon, has prevented people from seeking asylum out of Nigeria, causing millions of Internally Displaced Peoples to be trapped in towns controlled by Boko Haram where murder, sexual assault, hunger and destruction of the environment are fixtures of daily life (Osuoka & Haruna, 2019: 7). With mobility severely limited, there is an increased strain placed on already fragile natural resources, like freshwater. *Caritas Canada* found that 'the admixture of a blighted ecology with the presence of Boko Haram insurgents' has broken the region's social fabric, demolishing relations among families and between generations (Osuoka & Haruna, 2019: 7). Boko Haram exploits the conditions of precarity by offering financial incentives and alternative livelihood options, acting as the first responders to climate change in the absence of the state (Nett & Rüttinger, 2016: 3). This reveals important implications for ecological futures if militant far-right movements continue to amass power. Similar situations can unfold globally if/when a weakened state cannot handle extreme climate crises and emboldened far-right movements use that void to exploit the environment in their (counter)hegemonic struggle.

Two general patterns can be discerned. First, Boko Haram weaponizes scarce water in an attempt to fill the void left by the state, consequently establishing itself as the premier political authority and strengthening its informal illicit and criminal economy network (Skah & Lyammouri, 2020: 22). A vicious cycle emerges in which climate change exacerbates insecurity that militant Islamist movements exploit to their advantage, which creates further instability and destruction of the environment (Nett & Rüttinger, 2016: 17). Secondly, the deteriorating climate conditions have a detrimental impact on the agricultural sector, which in turn devastates traditional livelihoods, producing tremendous poverty that becomes fertile ground for recruitment (Nett & Rüttinger, 2016: 46). It is in this context that Lake Chad has now become the convergence point of a complex crisis of climate change *and* militant Islamist violence (Owonikoko & Momodu, 2020: 1308). In 2017, the UN Security Council declared it one of the world's worst humanitarian crises in the last decade, stating that 'climate change was shaping the peace and security landscape' in Lake Chad (Skah & Lyammouri, 2020: 19). What has the existing research said about the causes of these dual calamities? What solutions does it offer? The following section critically assesses the extant literature.

Critically interrogating the existing literature

Since the early 2000s, the academic and policy community has sought to understand the climate change–militant Islamist matrix. The general consensus is that climate change is 'a threat multiplier' that does not itself cause conflict but interacts with existing vulnerabilities to produce militant Islamist violence (Ahmed, 2011: 348). The differences in the literature stem from which existing threats authors privilege over others (European Union Institute for Security Studies, Raineri, 2020: 3). Some argue that ethno-religious cleavages and state dysfunction drive the climate change–militant Islamist nexus

(Rapoport, 2004). Thomas Homer-Dixon offers a conservative perspective of ecological scarcity, population pressure and 'grievances articulated by groups organized around clear social cleavages, such as ethnicity or religion' that foster intrastate conflict over access to valuable resources (Homer-Dixon & Blitt, 1998). He argues that Boko Haram can be attributed to 'a limited state presence and poor governance, underdevelopment and unemployment, environmental pressures enhanced by the receding waters of Lake Chad and desertification, and a deep history of Islamic conservatism' (Homer-Dixon & Blitt, 1998: 18). Werz and Conley (2012: 16) add that climate change aggravates the existing dangerous combination of seasonal migration, rapid population growth, a weak state, and ethnic frictions between the Christian Yoruba and the Muslim Hausa-Fulani, fuelling 'terrorism'. Rudincová (2017: 112) locates Boko Haram in the global 'Islamic revivalist movement' that is inspired by 'deeply traditional Islamism based on the rejection of all Western and anti-Islamic influences'. Though she argues that religion itself is not a source of conflict, when climate change interacts with the revivalist movement, terrorism is a likely outcome, especially if the state is too weak to effectively manage sectarian and religious clashes (Rudincová, 2017). Price and Elu assert that West Africa is especially susceptible to 'climate-induced Islamist terror' because it has a long history of 'Fulani and Hausa affinities for Islamic theocracy' (2016: 1; 2017). Schleussner et al. (2016: 9216) add that 'ethnicity appears to play a prominent and almost ubiquitous role' in the conflict. Smith (2007: 270) argues that the issues in Nigeria are rooted in 'sectarian clashes and religious differences' that turn violent with the intensification of climate change. King and Burnell (2017: 67) state that 'war is dramatically higher in countries with inter-ethnic social tensions. These divisions play a greater role than poverty, income inequality.' Cumulatively, the authors argue in favour of strengthening the state through good governance mechanisms as a means of managing sectarian and ethno-religious contestations.

The second body of literature examines political and economic issues, like livelihood insecurity, unemployment and poverty, and corrupt governance. Kohler et al. (2019: 19) argue that the co-optation of scarce resources by militant Islamist groups 'impact[s] the vulnerable in society where there are populations affected by climatic events, especially those living in drought-stressed regions'. They advocate strategies that aim to reduce the risks of conflict through international cooperation and governance mechanisms (Kohler et al., 2019). Eklöw and Krampe (2019) highlight state failure and corrupt political elites as elements that make up the climate change–militant Islamist matrix. Podesta and Ogden (2008: 118) emphasize factors such as wealth inequality and state failure, finding that the clash between these factors and climate change leads to an increase in militant Islamist violence.

They argue that this poses grave national security and foreign policy challenges to the US. They advocate for greater intervention by the international community, particularly the US, who must play a central role as a first responder by investing in strategies like offshoring 'sea basing' platforms that do not require host countries' consent (Podesta & Ogden, 2008: 133). De Coning and Krampe (2020: 18) add that climate change erodes the capacity of states to mitigate militant Islamism, so they emphasize greater Western intervention to empower and strengthen the national state, promote good governance and employ greater police-military intervention.

Despite the differences between the two literatures, the authors all offer a risk-oriented approach in which climate change acts as a 'threat multiplier' that leads to conflict when it interacts with other elements, like ethno-religious tensions and demographic pressures. Another similarity is that they place blame on the Nigerian state, which is portrayed as having a tendency towards corruption, authoritarianism and clientelism – making it unfit to handle crises of this nature (Rizzo, 2015). The solution proposed by authors at both ends of the spectrum is straightforward: Nigeria must strengthen its state by investing in enhancing good governance programmes, social welfare policies, development and law enforcement (Werz & Conley, 2012: 21). Others also advocate for greater intervention from the international community and global cooperation on climate change mitigation and sustainable growth policies (Podesta & Ogden, 2008; Nett & Rüttinger, 2016).

While this research appears to be logically sound, it is limited in its explanatory value. Two main problems emerge. First, narrow emphasis is placed on mechanistic connections deduced from abstract variables and rational choice thinking. The various factors are theorized as existing in a vacuum, unrelated to each other, and divorced from the broader global political economy – the Capitalocene. The authors present diverse independent variables, like weak governance, climate change and ethno-religious tensions, as wholly distinct recipe ingredients, which, when mixed together, inevitably lead to conflict. Such narratives erase the interdependence of these elements, disembedding them from the 'broader set of historically bounded and politically contingent social relations that underpin them' (Gonzales-Vicente, 2020: 104). This leads to ahistorical and apolitical explanations that overlook the systemic causes and interrelations of ecological crises and religion-based violence (Ahmed, 2011: 340). The second issue is that it offers technical, neoliberal policies that address the *symptoms* of the crisis rather than its root causes. These solutions comprise greater state intervention, securitization of climate change and increased militarization, all of which carry the potential of deepening the conditions of abjection that create violence in the first place.

These dominant perspectives miss how climate change and militant Islamist violence are manifestations of deeper systemic crises rooted in exploitative capitalist social relations. In contrast, a political economy approach sees Capitalocene as a *totality*, and examines its various parts (ex. weak governance) in relation to the whole system (ex. crisis of political economy brought about by the neoliberal stage of Capitalocene). Socio-ecological crises are produced in the context of historically specific political and socio-economic systems, and whether or not they lead to armed conflict depends on existing relations of power at local, national and transnational scales, and on how those relations are configured by structures of imperialism, colonialism and capitalism. Given that the above-mentioned literatures do not acknowledge and interrogate the systems at play, they conceal the underlying causes of the crisis and disembed climate change and militant Islamist violence from each other, thus rendering them politically nonactionable (Ribot et al., 2020: 61). Doing so sanitizes the impacts of the destructive tendencies of the Capitalocene in generating both climate change *and* militancy, thereby tacitly legitimizing an exploitative system as a natural and undisputable given that cannot be subject to debate or reform. Further, treating the various elements as independent variables leads to the reification of abstract notions of the primacy of the state (Ahmed, 2011: 349, 343).

The argument that weak governance leads to a tragedy of the commons where climate change-induced scarcity generates violent contestation over valuable resources does not recognize that the state exists in a complicated web of global capitalist relations that, in part, dictates how it can respond to climate crises. Such narratives, and their corresponding solutions of good governance, are, in effect, offering a moral critique of the state by pathologizing the Nigerian state as anti-democratic and authoritarian (Wengraf, 2018: 17). These racist undertones imply that the state is innately prone to corruption and mismanagement, unable to self-govern and requiring supervision from the international community, who must step in to save the citizens who are trapped in primordial violence (Wengraf, 2018: 17). This is a complete dismissal of the devastating impacts of Western colonial and imperial interventions that have eroded the state structure over time[2] (Ahmed, 2011: 345). It also does not account for neoliberalism, which has hollowed out the state and undermined its capacity to protect citizens and environments against the harsh vicissitudes of capitalism (Beckman, 1991: 70). Nor do they take seriously the Global North's historic colonial accountability for climate change, which has caused severe ecological crises across the Global South (Gonzalez, 2015). It simply regurgitates the hackneyed and clichéd mantras that those suffering from poverty need economic development that their supposedly felonious governments are denying them. Moreover, by focusing on 'terrorism' discourses and obscuring the geopolitical context of the crisis, the above-mentioned literatures im/explicitly portray militant Islamist movements as irrationally evil apparitions that come into existence sporadically and unexplainably and turn into messianic demagogues who manipulate deteriorating conditions for their own benefit. This rhetoric draws on essentialist assumptions that do not make distinctions between Islam as a faith and militant Islamism as a political ideology emerging out of particular social relations. Militant Islamism is depicted as a static and unchanging ideology that has existed uninterrupted in Nigerian history. This casts Nigerian peoples as 'variously villains, victims, or pawns', in which the Muslim-majority North is discussed as though it is predisposed to violence (Ribot et al., 2020: 48). Such discourses divert attention away from class struggle towards flawed analyses of ethno-religious tensions. Although some studies adopt class-derived rhetoric (e.g. poverty), basic analyses of class struggle are missing, and class is treated as epiphenomenal to weak governance.

This leads to the *securitization* of the crisis, which is a 'redundant conceptualization of global systemic crises [like climate change] purely as potential "threat-multipliers" of traditional security issues' like militant Islamist violence (Ahmed, 2011: 351). The conjecture is that regions that carry geopolitical interest for capitalist states, that also happen to be Muslim majority and resource rich (e.g. Nigeria contains Africa's largest oil revenues), will also be sites of armed conflict that require militarizing measures, like the War on Terror (Ahmed, 2011: 351). This causes the problematization of entire religious and ethnic groups that are 'Othered' as belligerent and threatening, which consequently justifies violence against them to prevent any challenges to capital accumulation (Ahmed, 2011: 354). Rather than meaningfully addressing the contradictions of the Capitalocene that generate socio-ecological crises, culpability is displaced onto rebellious social groups. Instead of advocating for systemic solutions like anti-fracking policies in Nigeria and emissions reductions for Western countries, it adopts militaristic counter-terrorism solutions, which fuel vast profit-accumulating systems. Strengthening the repressive apparatuses of the state thus becomes a necessary solution to the crisis, but in reality serves to protect the transnational and national capitalist classes' interests in the Nigerian oil industry (Wengraf, 2018: 17).

A cursory look into the War on Terror in Nigeria affirms this reality. Crises, like Lake Chad, are used to justify and expand the US military footprint in West Africa through the US African Command (AFRICOM) (Feldstein, 2018). From 2016 to 2020, the US Department of State provided USD$7.1 million for training, equipment and advisory support to the Nigerian military for its operations against Boko Haram (United States Department of State, 2022; Barraza, 2021). US Brigadier General Thomas Tickner has stated, 'We recognize the growing significance our work in Africa has on achieving our national security goals. Having a permanent presence on the continent allows us to better leverage our capabilities to support AFRICOM's and the State Department's desired objectives' (Barraza, 2021). US interests are couched in 'security' language, but in actuality it serves to protect Western exploitation of Nigerian oil – both the strategic interests in oil and the physical infrastructure of oil extraction. Further, militarized security responses have only worsened the situation in Nigeria as 'there has long been anecdotal evidence that the Nigerian security agencies may have killed as many Nigerians as Boko Haram in certain time periods' (Campbell, 2014: 13).

Exposing the taken-for-granted logics and problematic conceptions of security and militant Islamism that are so often unquestioningly repeated in ecological discourses is necessary because they have material implications on the way those committed to ecological justice mobilize politically, economically, socially and ecologically, and they have consequences for how ecological imperialism and neoliberal extractivism adapt to preserve their interests (Baldwin and Erickson, 2020: 5). In the following section, I offer a materialist examination of the climate change–militant Islamist matrix in Lake Chad.

A climate change–militant Islamism nexus assemblage

The existing research is unable to explain the Lake Chad disaster as a historical *totality*. To grasp the root causes of the conflict, it is necessary to situate the dynamics of Lake Chad within the historical and contemporary socio-ecological and political-economic power structures that influence its rise and transformation. Instead of presenting temporal narratives of progression towards development or regression into barbarity, which feature prominently within neoliberal discourses, we need to view the various elements of the whole as 'forever shifting, crumpling, and multiplying, disappearing and reappearing' (Puar, 2005: 130).

This is important in explaining why in this particular moment, the Boko Haram crisis has unfolded the way it has and why similar situations either do or do not materialize elsewhere. By linking the economic to the political to the social to the ecological, we can understand the Lake Chad crisis as stemming from the contradictions of Capitalocene, where militant Islamist violence is not simply a side effect of worsening ecoclimatic events, but rather is a symptom of the wider social dislocation caused by capitalist subjugation. This phenomenon is mirrored in far-right populist literature that locates the rise of the far right in the West as a response to the devastating socio-economic impacts of neoliberalism, which suggests continuity in the crisis and effects of the Capitalocene globally. These transnational links further affirm that the Boko Haram case does not need to be analysed as separate from the far-right literature. This directly attacks the orientalist and Islamophobic roots of terrorism literature that casts Boko Haram as distinct because of its religious foundations.

The socio-ecological crisis unfolding in Nigeria is intimately connected to capital's exploitation of its two most valuable sources: humans and the earth. Where the depletion of Lake Chad is an ecological consequence of infinite economic growth on a finite planet, the militant Islamism of Boko Haram is a social consequence of class struggle and of the exploitation of humans in a capitalist system. Both crises emerge from and are embedded in the Capitalocene, so they cannot be discussed as separate from one another or divorced from the capitalist political economy, which '[annihilates] the human and natural substance of society' (Polanyi, 1944: 3). The next part will trace some important elements of the *whole* that converge to give birth to the conflict.

Capitalocene

'Humans transformed environments from the very beginning,' but capitalism radically altered these dynamics by ushering in a new era of social relations in which nature was deployed for large-scale commodity production and exchange and profit maximization (Moore, 2017: 610). Termed the 'Capitalocene', it is composed of ecological regimes dictated by the laws of motion of ever-expanding capital accumulation (Foster et al., 2010: 71).

Capitalocene is a way of organizing relations between nature, humans and work for accumulation that relies on 'cheapened' nature, which renders food, labour, energy and raw materials accessible for appropriation. This necessitates waves of global expansion through imperialism, which has demanded the construction of global webs of racialized and gendered domination (Moore, 2017: 607, 609). The West's development has been dependent on the underdevelopment of the Global South through unequal ecological exchange facilitated by violent colonialism (Adelman, 2019: 38). Today, the transnational capitalist class has a carbon footprint that is estimated to be 175 times more than the world's poorest 10 per cent (Malm, 2016: 248). Science has confirmed that since 1989, just 100 multinational corporations headquartered in the West, like fossil fuel producer Shell, are responsible for 71 per cent of industrial greenhouse gas emissions (Griffin, 2017: 10). These emissions are directly linked to the intensification of desertification and droughts in the Global South, which are causing water scarcity in drylands like the Sahel (Griffin, 2017: 10). The ecological impacts of colonialism, fossil fuel use, and exploitation of cheap natures are outsourced to the Global South, while their benefits are reaped by the Global North (Diffenbaug & Burke, 2019: 9808). So, despite being responsible for a significantly smaller share of greenhouse gas emissions, the Global South faces more extreme impacts of climate hazards, while possessing far fewer material adaptation resources.

As Gonzalez (2015: 422) outlines, the North–South ecological divide occurs along four injustices. First, it is distributive injustice because the Capitalocene emerged in the Global North, but it has produced the harshest impact in the Global South. Secondly, it is procedural injustice because the Global North dominates multilateral governance organizations, giving them an upper hand during environmental treaty negotiations that allows them to protect their interests and ignore the needs of the Global South. Thirdly, it is corrective injustice because the Global North owes the Global South a significant ecological debt, which it refuses to acknowledge. Lastly, it is social injustice as the Capitalocene continues to facilitate ecological imperialism (Gonzalez, 2015: 422).

Colonialism

The Capitalocene enveloped Nigeria during Britain's colonization in the nineteenth century. The imperial expansion focused on expropriating raw materials and importing British goods to the newly constructed Nigerian market. The region was fragmented into three zones, Southern, Northern and Western, with each region specializing in an agricultural export commodity (Uwazurike & Mbabuike, 2004: 203). These regions also comprised distinct ethno-religious groups: Hausa-Fulani Muslims in the North, the Yoruba in the West and the Ibo Christians in the South (Watts, 2017: 60).

British rule aimed at consolidating differences of class, ethnicity, religion and region to prevent unification (Uwazurike & Mbabuike, 2004: 203). This was coupled with the combined and uneven development of capitalism across Nigeria (Wengraf, 2018: 24). Lagos, in the South, was established as the crown colony, and efforts were made to construct a railroad network and other infrastructure to facilitate trade. The North did not receive the same kind of investment, so it was plagued by low levels of development; these 'colonial differences produced postcolonial disparities', leading to a stark schism between the regions today (Thurston, 2017: 25).

At independence in 1960, Nigeria inherited a political and economic machine that was predicated on a regime of violence in which an alliance of the domestic bourgeois class and foreign capital ensured that the country continued to operate as a 'citadel of neocolonial domination' (Beckman, 1982: 39). Post-colonial Nigeria became an export-enclave economy dependent on the exportation of goods from the agricultural sector (Beckman, 1982). Given its relatively strong position, the South gained dominance, while the North has lagged behind and struggled to use political power to generate economic development, leading to higher rates of unemployment, illiteracy and poverty (David et al., 2015: 10). This period was marked by developmentalist state approaches that sought to protect labour and natural resources to a degree (David et al., 2015). However, the advent of neoliberalism in the 1970s signalled a new global regime of ecological imperialism, ending the developmental state approach, and entrenching the Washington Consensus (Moore, 2018: 10).

Neoliberalism

Since the 1940s, oil has become a structural requirement for capital accumulation. Post-independence, Nigeria's southern Delta, which contains the world's tenth-largest oil reserves, became a geopolitical hotspot for petroleum extraction (Gonzalez, 2015: 411). In the 1970s, a heavily indebted Nigeria transformed from an agriculture-dominated economy towards a petroleum economy, in which multinational conglomerates, like Shell, worked with the state to employ exploitative practices to keep costs low (Watts, 2004: 59). This exacerbated uneven development because the South was established as a centre of accumulation, so its economic and political development was prioritized to create a favourable environment for foreign investment, while the agriculture-dominated North was left behind (Wengraf, 2018: 27).

These processes were facilitated by neoliberalism, which subordinated labour and environments to finance imperialism through the complex debt schemes of the structural adjustment programmes enforced by the International Monetary Fund (IMF) (Wengraf, 2018: 27). In 1986, General Babangida implemented a series of stringent economic and political reforms in exchange for debt repayment assistance from the IMF, which included trade liberalization, elimination of labour and environmental regulations, privatization of public goods and state-owned industries, austerity, gutting public sector wages and jobs, and the intensification of export production to service foreign debt (Watts, 2004: 61). The state retreated from social welfare provisioning and invested in carceral apparatuses to protect the continual flow of oil from rising social unrest (Wengraf, 2018: 35). These structural changes have largely only benefited foreign capital and the domestic bourgeois class. They have adversely affected democratic rule, created crises of legitimacy for successive governments, caused irreparable harm to the environment, reduced the state's institutional capacity, intensified socio-economic inequalities and generated a 'survivalist culture and a politics of ethnic mobilization' (Udoh, 2020: 202; Watts, 2004: 61).

Today, oil accounts for over 80 per cent of Nigeria's GDP (World Bank, 2018). Shell produces 43 per cent of Nigerian oil through gas flaring;[3] in 2002, the World Bank noted that 'flaring in Nigeria had contributed more greenhouse gases to the Earth's atmosphere than all other sources in sub-Saharan Africa combined' (Stockman et al., 2009: 11). Despite facing substantial legal scrutiny over human rights abuses, pollution and oil spills, Shell refuses to change its practices, and the state refuses to hold it accountable (Amnesty International, 2020). A great rift has emerged in which the state gains unprecedentedly high revenues from oil sales, which are partially reinvested in southern infrastructure, while rates of unemployment, precarity and poverty increase at alarmingly high speeds, especially in the North, where 'Muslim populations stood in a more attenuated relation to oil wealth' (Gonzalez, 2015: 411; Watts, 2017: 32). The poverty rate in the North is approximately 75 per cent, in stark contrast to the South, where the poverty rate is estimated to be 27 per cent (Faluyi et al., 2019: 2). In 2008, former Governor of the Central Bank of Nigeria, Chukwuma Soludo, observed that astronomical levels of poverty in the country had become a 'northern phenomenon' (David et al., 2015: 87). This precarity, alienation and exclusion are produced and reproduced, pushing disenfranchised people towards the margins to the most dangerous zones of climate change, forcing them to rely on shrinking resource bases without any alternatives (Malm & Esmailian, 2013: 487).

Crisis of social reproduction

The neoliberal state has been plagued with the declining capacity to deliver public goods, including basic survival needs like healthcare, affordable housing, food security, clean water and more, especially in regions suffering from water scarcity, like Lake Chad (Maza et al., 2020: 99). As a result, 44 per cent of children under five suffer from chronic malnutrition, which is roughly 14.5 million children who are at risk of dying or not developing into healthy adults (World Bank, 2018: 53). Underrepresented and neglected by the national government, citizens feel estranged from political processes because they are unable to influence the political economy that shapes their lives (Ribot et al., 2020: 60). The breakdown of the social safety net has prevented people from relying on the state or their traditional social networks. Neoliberal policies displace the cost, risk and burdens of economic insecurity from the state onto the individual, who must now search for alternative sources of protection. This leads to hyper-individualism in which each individual is responsible and accountable for their own well-being, and success and failures are perceived as personal failings, rather than structural oppression (Cooper, 2017: 13).

With the elimination of the protective cover of democratic safeguards and faced with indefinite social dislocations, people turn to other forms of associations to construct social solidarities and express a collective will (Cooper, 2017: 89). In the North, this crisis of social reproduction is politicized in distinct ethnic and religious ways. Northern Nigerians 'facing a lifetime of indefinite precarity are doing what they can to transform their situations. They are motivated often to their deaths, not by here-and-now hardships, but by deeply human concerns for their own and their families' future' (Ribot et al., 2020: 48). As the Capitalocene disrupts livelihoods, erodes social cohesion and displaces entire social groups from their ancestral lands, the resulting disenfranchisement, marginalization and social disconnection turn people towards Boko Haram.

Conclusion

The climate change–militant Islamist nexus emerges in these tensions, struggles and contradictions. Boko Haram is speaking to the ongoing crisis of planetary life and how societies react and adapt to climate change, especially in reactionary ways. Lake Chad has emerged as a site of violent contestation as a result of the assemblages of Capitalocene. The rise in insurgency cannot be reduced to essentialist narratives of ideology or 'global Islamic revivalist movements'. In this instance, it is clear that Islamic militancy of poor young Nigerian men is an expression of violent political protests that are comparable to other forms of regressive opposition to the Capitalocene, like violent far-right movements in Europe. By ignoring these histories and systems, and displacing blame onto other factors, as the mainstream literature has done exceptionally well, it provides the Global North and its adjacent non-governmental organizations and international financial institutions with narratives that depoliticize the conflict and downplay their responsibilities while at the same time creating an avenue for further imperialist intervention through the War on Terror.

This chapter is a modest effort to ground the links between climate change and escalation of militant Islamist violence in a concrete case study and provide the momentum for more detailed discussions on various climate change–militant Islamist relations from critical perspectives. In doing so, I aim to contribute to the political ecologies of the far-right literature and to the broader body of scholarship on the social responses to the Capitalocene. Moving forward, there is a pressing need to examine how gender relations, connections to transnational militant Islamist movements like ISIS, and cross-border recruitment influence the climate change–militant Islamist nexus.

Notes

1 Similar grievances are fuelling far-right upswells across Europe and North America. Gusterson (2017: 211) writes, 'even as the white working class is engulfed by a claustrophobic sense of being trapped in decaying local communities, a vibrantly

fluid transnational and cosmopolitan urban lifeworld has evolved, buoyed by the expanding economies of international finance, information technology, biomedicine, and social media.'
2 This does not account for the capitalist state as a system of power itself that constitutes and sustains environmentally destructive capital accumulation.
3 Gas flaring is the combustion of gases generated during the oil and gas extraction process. Gas flaring dramatically increases the number of greenhouse gases emitted in comparison to other forms of extraction.

References

Adelman, S. (2019). Justice, Development and Sustainability in the Anthropocene. In P. Cullet & S. Koonan (eds), *Research Handbook on Law, Environment and the Global South*. Cheltenham: Edward Elgar Publishing, pp. 14–31.
AFP (2017). Boko Haram kill 31 fishermen in Nigeria. *Arab News*, 7 August.
Aghedo, I., & Osumah, O. (2012). The Boko Haram Uprising: How Should Nigeria Respond? *Third World Quarterly*, 33(5): 853–869.
Ahmed, N. M. (2011). The International Relations of Crisis and the Crisis of International Relations: From the Securitisation of Scarcity to the Militarisation of Society. *Global Change, Peace & Security*, 23(3): 335–355.
Amnesty International (2020). 2020 could be Shell year of reckoning. *Amnesty International*, 10 February 2020, www.amnesty.org/en/latest/news/2020/02/nigeria-2020-could-be-shell-year-of-reckoning/ (accessed 24 April 2023).
Bakali, N. (2019). Challenging Terrorism as a Form of 'Otherness': Exploring the Parallels between Far-Right and Muslim Religious Extremism. *Islamophobia Studies Journal*, 5(1): 99–115.
Baldwin, A., & Erickson, B. (2020). Introduction: Whiteness, coloniality, and the Anthropocene. *Environment and Planning D: Society and Space*, 38(1), 3–11. doi.org/10.1177/0263775820904485.
Barraza, A. (2021). USACE establishes permanent presence in Africa to support key missions. *US Army*, 2 March, www.army.mil/article/243825/usace_establishes_permanent_presence_in_africa_to_support_key_missions (accessed 20 November 2023).
BBC (2014). 'Boko Haram' kills 48 Nigerian fishermen near Chad. *BBC News*, 23 November, www.bbc.com/news/world-africa-30167886 (accessed 20 November 2023).
BBC (2020). Lake Chad attack: 'dozens of fishermen' killed near Cameroon border. *BBC News*, 3 January, www.bbc.com/news/world-africa-50987123 (accessed 20 November 2023).
Beckman, B. (1982). Whose State? State and Capitalist Development in Nigeria. *Review of African Political Economy*, 9(23): 37–51.
Beckman, B. (1991). Empowerment or Repression? The World Bank and the Politics of African Adjustment. *Africa Development/Afrique et Développement*, 16(1): 45–72.

Bodetti, A. (2017). The Taliban want to go green. *Vox News*, 19 April, www.vice.com/en/article/8qpqmb/the-taliban-want-to-go-green (accessed 24 April 2023).

Bodetti, A. (2019). 'Greening the desert': what drives militants' environmentalism? *The New Arab*, 5 March, www.newarab.com/analysis/greening-desert-what-drives-militants-environmentalism (accessed 20 November 2023).

Bressler, T. (2020). Drought and Extremism: How Climate Change Impacts the Power of Boko Haram in Northeastern Nigeria. Bachelor Thesis, Lund University.

Buckingham, L., & Alali, N. (2020). Extreme Parallels: A Corpus-Driven Analysis of ISIS and Far-Right Discourse. *Kōtuitui: New Zealand Journal of Social Sciences Online*, 15(2): 310–331.

Buhaug, H., Benjaminsen, T. A., Sjaastad, E., & Theisen, O. M. (2015). Climate Variability, Food Production Shocks, and Violent Conflict in Sub-Saharan Africa. *Environmental Research Letters*, 10(12). doi.org/10.1088/1748-9326/10/12/125015.

Campbell, J. (2014). *US Policy to Counter Nigeria's Boko Haram*. Council Special Report no. 70, November, Council on Foreign Relations.

Carbon Brief (2019). In-depth Q&A: the IPCC'S special report on climate change and land. *Carbon Brief*, 8 August, www.carbonbrief.org/in-depth-qa-the-ipccs-special-report-on-climate-change-and-land/ (accessed 20 November 2023).

Chalecki, E. (2001). *A New Vigilance: Identifying and Reducing the Risks of Environmental Terrorism*. Report, Pacific Institute for Studies in Development, Environment, and Security.

Coe, M. T., & Foley, J. A. (2001). Human and Natural Impacts on the Water Resources of the Lake Chad Basin. *Journal of Geophysical Research: Atmospheres*, 106(D4): 3349–3356.

Comolli, V. (2017). The Evolution and Impact of Boko Haram in the Lake Chad Basin. *Humanitarian Practice Network*, 70(2): 7–10.

Cooper, M. (2017). *Family Values: Between Neoliberalism and the New Social Conservatism*. New York: Zone Books.

Dahir, A. (2018). One of the WORLD'S deadliest terrorist groups wants to ban plastic bags. *Quartz News*, 12 July, www.carbonbrief.org/in-depth-qa-the-ipccs-special-report-on-climate-change-and-land/ (accessed 20 November 2023).

Daoudy, M. (2020). Water Weaponization in the Syrian Conflict: Strategies of Domination and Cooperation. *International Affairs*, 96(5): 1347–1366.

David, O. J., Asuelime, L. E., & Onapajo, H. (2015). *Boko Haram: The Socioeconomic Drivers*. Switzerland: Springer International Publishing.

De Coning, C., & Krampe, F. (2020). Multilateral cooperation in the area of climate-related security and development risks in Africa. NUPI Report no 4/2020, Norwegian Institute of International Affairs.

Diffenbaugh, N. S., & Burke, M. (2019). Global Warming has Increased Global Economic Inequality. *Proceedings of the National Academy of Sciences*, 116(20): 9808–9813.

Edwards, D. B. (1989). Mad Mullahs and Englishmen: Discourse in the Colonial Encounter. *Comparative Studies in Society and History*, 31(4): 649–670.

Ekhomu, O. (2019). *Boko Haram: Security Considerations and the Rise of an Insurgency*. New York: CRC Press. doi.org/10.4324/9780203710838.

Eklöw, K., & Krampe, F. (2019). *Climate-Related Security Risks and Peacebuilding in Somalia*. Stockholm: Stockholm International Peace Research Institute (SIPRI).

European Union Institute for Security Studies, Raineri, L. (2020). Sahel climate conflicts? When (fighting) climate change fuels terrorism. *Publications Office of the European Union*, https://data.europa.eu/doi/10.2815/790429 (accessed 20 November 2023).

Faluyi, O. T., Khan, S., Akinola, A. O. (2019). Nigeria and the Resource Question: Theoretical Understanding. In *Boko Haram's Terrorism and the Nigerian State: Federalism, Politics and Policies*. Cham: Springer, pp. 45–56.

Fasona, M. J., & Omojola, A. S. (2005). Climate Change, Human Security and Communal Clashes in Nigeria. Paper presented at the International Workshop on Human Security and Climate Change, Asker, Norway. 21–23 June. doi:10.13140/2.1.2218.5928.

Feldstein, S. (2018). Do terrorist trends in Africa justify the U.S. military's expansion? *Carnegie Endowment for International Peace*, 9 February, https://carnegieendowment.org/2018/02/09/do-terrorist-trends-in-africa-justify-u.s.-military-s-expansion-pub-75476 (accessed 28 November 2023).

Food and Agriculture Organization of the United Nations (FAO) (2020). FAO in Nigeria: Nigeria at a glance. *FAO*, www.fao.org/nigeria/fao-in-nigeria/nigeria-at-a-glance/en/ accessed 28 November 2013).

Foster, J. B., Clark, B., & York, R. (2010). *The Ecological Rift: Capitalism's War on the Earth*. New York: NYU Press.

Gao, H., Bohn, T. J., Podest, E., McDonald, K. C., & Lettenmaier, D. P. (2011). On the Causes of the Shrinking of Lake Chad. *Environmental Research Letters*, 6(3): 034021.

Global Terrorism Index (2015). Measuring and understanding the impact of terrorism – privacy international. *Institute for Economics and Peace*, https://privacyinternational.org/sites/default/files/2018-02/Global%20Terrorism%20Index%202015,%20Institute%20for%20Economics%20&%20Peace.pdf (accessed 28 November 2023).

Gonzalez, C. G. (2015). Bridging the North–South Divide: International Environmental Law in the Anthropocene. *Pace Environmental Law Review*, 32: 407.

Gonzalez-Vicente, R. (2020). The Liberal Peace Fallacy: Violent Neoliberalism and the Temporal and Spatial Traps of State-Based Approaches to Peace. *Territory, Politics, Governance*, 8(1): 100–116.

Griffin, P. (2017). The Carbon Majors Database. CDP Carbon Majors Report 2017.https://cdn.cdp.net/cdp-production/cms/reports/documents/000/002/327/original/Carbon-Majors-Report-2017.pdf (accessed 20 November 2023).

Guardian, The (2002). Full text: Bin Laden's 'Letter to America'. Appeared 24 November, link removed 15 November 2023.

Gusterson, H. (2017). From Brexit to Trump: Anthropology and the Rise of Nationalist Populism. *American Ethnologist*, 44(2): 209–214.

Homer-Dixon, T., & Blitt, J. (eds) (1998). *Ecoviolence: Links among Environment, Population and Security*. Lanham: Rowman & Littlefield.

Hugh, B. (2019). Unemployment, Terrorism, and Water Scarcity Compounded in WANAME Region by Climate Change. Student research report, Center for Anticipatory Intelligence. www.usu.edu/cai/files/studentpaper-hugh.pdf (accessed 20 November 2023).

Igwe, U. (2021). We must understand terrorist financing to defeat Boko Haram and Nigeria's insurgents. *Africa at LSE*, 12 August, https://blogs.lse.ac.uk/africaatlse/2021/08/03/terrorist-financing-economy-defeat-boko-haram-nigeria-insurgents/#:~:text=It%20is%20believed%20that%20many,insurgents%20out%20of%20their%20way (accessed 4 December 2022).

IPCC (2019). Special report: climate change and land. *IPCC*, www.ipcc.ch/srccl/ (accessed 28 November 2023).

Jarvis, L. (2022). Critical Terrorism Studies and the Far-Right: Beyond Problems and Solutions? *Critical Studies on Terrorism*, 15(1): 13–37.

King, M. D., & Burnell, J. (2017). The Weaponization of Water in a Changing Climate. In C. Werrell & F. Femia (eds), *Epicenters of Climate and Security: The New Geostrategic Landscape of the Anthropocene*, Centre for Climate & Security, pp. 67–73.

Kohler, C., Dos Santos, C. D., & Bursztyn, M. (2019). Understanding Environmental Terrorism in Times of Climate Change: Implications for Asylum Seekers in Germany. *Research in Globalization*, 1: 100006.

MacEachern, S. (2018). *Searching for Boko Haram: A History of Violence in Central Africa*. Oxford: Oxford University Press.

Mahmood, S. & Ani, N. C. (2018). Factional dynamics within Boko Haram. *Africa Centre for Strategic Studies*, 6 July, https://africacenter.org/security-article/factional-dynamics-within-boko-haram/ (accessed 28 November 2023).

Malm, A. (2016). Who Lit this Fire? Approaching the History of the Fossil Economy. *Critical Historical Studies*, 3(2): 215–248.

Malm, A., & Esmailian, S. (2013). Ways In and Out of Vulnerability to Climate Change: Abandoning the Mubarak Project in the Northern Nile Delta, Egypt. *Antipode*, 45(2): 474–492.

Masood, A., & Nisar, M. A. (2020). Speaking Out: A Postcolonial Critique of the Academic Discourse on Far-Right Populism. *Organization*, 27(1): 162–173.

Maza, K. D., Koldas, U., & Aksit, S. (2020). Challenges of Countering Terrorist Recruitment in the Lake Chad Region: The Case of Boko Haram. *Religions*, 11(2): 139–165.

Moore, J. W. (2017). The Capitalocene, Part I: On the Nature and Origins of our Ecological Crisis. *Journal of Peasant Studies*, 44(3): 594–630.

Moore, J. W. (2018). The Capitalocene Part II: Accumulation by Appropriation and the Centrality of Unpaid Work/Energy. *Journal of Peasant Studies*, 45(2): 237–279.

Nett, K., & Rüttinger, L. (2016). Insurgency, terrorism and organised crime in a warming climate: analysing the links between climate change and non-state armed groups. *Climate Diplomacy and Adelphi*, October, https://climate-diplomacy.org/sites/default/files/2020-10/CD%20Report_Insurgency_170724_web.pdf (accessed 20 November 2023).

Ojoye, T. (2016). Receding Lake Chad leaves 40 million jobless, says minister. *PUNCH Newspaper*, 1 November, https://punchng.com/receding-lake-chad-leaves-40-million-jobless-says-minister/ (accessed 4 December 2023).

Okoye, F. (2021). Nigeria: We lose N500m weekly to Boko Haram – Borno fish producers. *Fisheries Committee for the West Central Gulf of Guinea*, 6 March, https://fcwc-fish.org/other-news/nigeria-we-lose-n500m-weekly-to-boko-haram-borno-fish-producers (accessed 28 November 2023).

Okpara, U. T., Stringer, L. C., & Dougill, A. J. (2017). Using a Novel Climate–Water Conflict Vulnerability Index to Capture Double Exposures in Lake Chad. *Regional Environmental Change*, 17(2): 351–366.

Onapajo, H., & Uzodike, U. O. (2012). Boko Haram Terrorism in Nigeria: Man, the State, and the International System. *African Security Review*, 21(3): 24–39.

Osuoka, I., & Haruna, A. (2019). Boiling Over: Global Warming, Hunger and Violence in the Lake Chad Basin. *Development and Peace – Caritas Canada/ Social Action, Social Development Integrated Center*. https://devp.org/wp-content/uploads/2023/09/Boiling_over_report_2019_EN.pdf (accessed 20 November 2023).

Owonikoko, S. B., & Momodu, J. A. (2020). Environmental Degradation, Livelihood, and the Stability of Chad Basin Region. *Small Wars & Insurgencies*, 31(6): 1295–1322.

Oxfam (Begum, S. & van Lookeren Campagne, A.) (2017). Red Gold and Fishing in the Lake Chad Basin: Restoring Destroyed Livelihoods and Protecting People in Niger's Diffa Region. *Oxfam, Briefing Note*.

Patel, S. (2014). Racing Madness: The Terrorizing Madness of the Post-9/11 Terrorist Body. In L. Ben-Moshe, C. Chapman, & A. C. Carey (eds), *Disability Incarcerated: Imprisonment and Disability in the United States and Canada*. New York: Palgrave Macmillan, pp. 201–215.

Podesta, J., & Ogden, P. (2008). The Security Implications of Climate Change. *Washington Quarterly*, 31(1): 115–138.

Polanyi, K. (1944). *The Great Transformation: Economic and Political Origins of Our Time*. New York: Rinehart.

Price, G. N., & Elu, J. U. (2016). Global warming and cross-state Islamist terrorism in Nigeria. Department of Economics, Morehouse College, Atlanta GA, 30314.

Price, G. N., & Elu, J. U. (2017). Climate Change and Cross-State Islamist Terrorism in Nigeria. *Peace Economics, Peace Science and Public Policy*, 23(3). doi.org/10.1515/peps-2016-0047.

Puar, J. K. (2005). Queer Times, Queer Assemblages. *Social Text*, 84–85: 121–139.

Rapoport, D. C. (2004). The Four Waves of Modern Terrorism. In A. K. Cronin & J. M. Ludes (eds), *Attacking Terrorism: Elements of a Grand Strategy*. Washington, D. C.: Georgetown University Press pp. 46–73.

Ribot, J., Faye, P., & Turner, M. D. (2020). Climate of Anxiety in the Sahel: Emigration in Xenophobic Times. *Public Culture*, 32(1): 45–75.

Rizzo, J. (2015). A shrinking lake and a rising insurgency: migratory responses to environmental degradation and violence in the Lake Chad basin. http://labos.ulg.ac.be/hugo/wp-content/uploads/sites/38/2017/11/The-State-of-Environmental-Migration-2015-13-29.pdf (accessed 20 November 2023).

Rudincová, K. (2017). Desiccation of Lake Chad as a Cause of Security Instability in the Sahel Region. *GeoScape*, 11(2): 112–120.

Salkida, A. (2020). How Boko Haram sustain operations through international trade in smoked fish. *Premier Times*, 26 April, https://www.premiumtimesng.com/news/headlines/389916-how-boko-haram-sustain-operations-through-international-trade-in-smoked-fish.html?tztc=1 (accessed 20 November 2023).

Schleussner, C. F., Donges, J. F., Donner, R. V., & Schellnhuber, H. J. (2016). Armed-Conflict Risks Enhanced by Climate-Related Disasters in Ethnically Fractionalized Countries. *Proceedings of the National Academy of Sciences*, 113(33): 9216–9221.

Skah, M., & Lyammouri, R. (2020). The climate change–security nexus: case study of the Lake Chad Basin. RP-20/08. *Policy Center for the New South*, 26 June, www.policycenter.ma/publications/climate-change-security-nexus-case-study-lake-chad-basin (accessed 20 November 2023).

Smith, P. J. (2007). Climate Change, Weak States and the 'War on Terrorism' in South and Southeast Asia. *Contemporary Southeast Asia*, 264–285.

Stockman, L., Rowell, A., & Kretzmann, S. (2009). Shell's Big Dirty Secret. Insight into the world's most carbon intensive oil company and the legacy of CEO Jeroen van der Veer. *Friends of the Earth*, June, www.foeeurope.org/sites/default/files/publications/foe_shells_big_dirty_secret_0609.pdf (accessed 20 November 2023).

Thurston, A. (2017). *Boko Haram: The History of an African Jihadist Movement*. Princeton: Princeton University Press.

Udoh, I. (2020). Oil Production, Environmental Pressures and Other Sources of Violent Conflict in Nigeria. *Review of African Political Economy*, 47(164): 199–219.

UNCTED (United Nations Counter-Terrorism Committee Executive Directorate) (2019). Nigeria training module on gender dimensions of criminal justice responses to terrorism. *United Nations Office on Drugs and Crime*, www.unodc.org/pdf/terrorism/Web_stories/UNODC_Nigeria_Gender_Training_Module.pdf (accessed 6 December 2023).

United Nations Environment Programme (2018). The tale of a disappearing lake. *UNEP*, 28 February, www.unep.org/news-and-stories/story/tale-disappearing-lake (accessed 28 November 2023).

United States Department of State (2022). U.S. security cooperation with Nigeria. *U.S. Department of State*, 14 April, www.state.gov/u-s-security-cooperation-with-nigeria/ (accessed 4 December 2023).

Uwazurike, P., & Mbabuike, M. (2004). Nigeria's Perennial Problem of Nationhood, Democracy and Development on the Wages of Social Negative Capital. *Dialectical Anthropology*, 28: 203–231.

Van Elk, N. (2016). What's In a Name? Asymmetries in the Evaluation of Religiously Motivated Terrorism and Right-Wing Motivated Violence in the Context of the 'Refugee Crisis'. *Journal for Deradicalization*, (8): 153–177.

Vivekananda, J., & Born, C. (2018). Lake Chad region: climate-related security risk assessment. *Expert Working Group on climate-related security risks. Adelphi*, July, https://adelphi.de/system/files/mediathek/bilder/Lake%20Chad%20Region%20-%20Climate%20related%20security%20risk%20assessment.pdf (accessed 20 November 2023).

Watts, M. (2004). Resource Curse? Governmentality, Oil and Power in the Niger Delta, Nigeria. *Geopolitics*, 9(1): 50–80.

Watts, M. J. (2017). Frontiers: Authority, Precarity and Insurgency at the Edge of the State. 32, https://doi.org/10.4000/espacepolitique.4336.

Wegener, F. (2020). Striking similarities between Islamist terrorism and violent right-wing extremism. *Global Network on Extremism and Technology*, 18 September, https://gnet-research.org/2020/09/18/striking-similarities-between-islamist-terrorism-and-violent-right-wing-extremism/ (accessed 20 November 2023).

Wengraf, L. (2018). *Extracting Profit: Imperialism, Neoliberalism and the New Scramble for Africa*. Chicago: Haymarket Books.

Werz, M., & Conley, L. (2012). Climate change migration and conflict in Northwest Africa: rising dangers and policy options across the Arc of tension. *Center for American Progress*, www.americanprogress.org/wp-content/uploads/sites/2/2022/06/climate_migration_nwafrica.pdf (accessed 20 November 2023).

WFP (2020). Central Sahel emergency. *World Food Programme*, www.wfp.org/support-us/stories/central-sahel-the-humanitarian-emergency-the-world-is-ignoring#:~:text=The%20Sahel%20is%20a%20tragic,job%20opportunities%20and%20social%20services (accessed 4 December 2023).

World Bank (2018) International Development Association's Project Appraisal Document on a proposed credit in the amount of SDR 156.5 million and a proposed grant in the amount of US$7 million from the Global Financing Facilitating to the Federal Republic of Nigeria for an Accelerating Nutrition Results in Nigeria Project. *World Bank*, https://documents1.worldbank.org/curated/en/910491530329489994/pdf/NIGERIA-NUTRITION-PAD-05252018.pdf (accessed 28 November 2023).

World Bank (2021). Employment in agriculture (% of total employment) (modeled ILO estimate) – Nigeria. *World Bank Open Data*, https://data.worldbank.org/indicator/SL.AGR.EMPL.ZS?locations=NG (accessed 28 November 2023).

3

Wildfire rumours and denial in the Trump era

Laura Pulido

In September 2020 the US West coast was on fire. Though wildfires frequent this region, they were unprecedented in their breadth, heat and destruction (Oregon Department of Forestry, 2020). The fires were not unexpected. Scientists have warned for decades that the western US would experience heightened wildfires with global warming. Numerous factors contributed to the explosive fires, including drought, higher temperatures and a history of fire suppression (Lindsey, 2020; Sickinger, 2020; see also Oregon Forest Resources Institute, n. d.).[1]

While the fires were predictable, less anticipated was the response from rural and rural-identified communities. Just southeast of Portland, rumours circulated that Antifa and Black Lives Matters (BLM) activists were deliberately setting fires and terrorizing rural residents with violence and looting. Such rumours spread rapidly and created havoc for first responders trying to evacuate imperilled communities. Building on the rumours, some locals set up illegal checkpoints, threatened journalists and 'outsiders', and refused to evacuate in order to protect their communities from the imagined invaders (Kristof, 2020).

These events illuminate the complexities of cross-cutting denial in a polarized political landscape. I argue that the rumours reflect the fusion of two forms of denial: climate denial and racial denial. Though scientists explained the fires, many rural residents embraced a false narrative linked to larger anxieties and anger, including socialist take-overs, unpatriotic anti-racists, domestic terrorists and threats to the white nation. In this chapter I explore how white nationalism informs multiple anxieties on the right, including climate change. While the right is animated by many currents, it has been fuelled by racism and white nationalism for decades (Lowndes, 2008). Moreover, at this moment the white nation is facing grave challenges, which have triggered profound rage and anxiety (Anderson, 2016; O'Connor, 2021).

The white nation is an imagined political community in which whites and whiteness are the central subjects (Thobani, 2007). Currently, the white nation fears it is being decentred and white innocence is being called into question. White innocence is the belief that whites are not responsible for the US's history of racial violence and dehumanization, including settler colonization, slavery and racial discrimination (Inwood, 2018). This obviously requires denying the structural nature of US racism and the privileged status of whiteness. Though white supremacy and its denial have varied over the centuries, overt racism resurfaced with the election of Barack Obama (2008) and Donald Trump's 2015 presidential campaign. Obama's election, as a Black president, incensed the white nation and Trump's campaign rode that racist fury. Trump's infamous declaration that Mexicans were rapists shattered any pretence of the US as a 'post-racial' society. The overt racism of Trumpism, coupled with the police killing of George Floyd in May 2020, led many to see US racism as structural for the first time.

Global condemnation of Floyd's murder and widespread support of BLM brought the US close to a racial reckoning, which the right has resisted. Though antagonistic towards BLM for numerous reasons, the right fiercely opposed the movement's claim of systemic racism. To admit structural racism rather than individual racists would undermine the 'goodness' of white settlers (Hixson, 2013: 21) and question how whiteness became privileged. This has triggered a crisis for the white nation as its moral authority and very existence rest on denying structural white supremacy.

Thus, in this moment, two crises – climate change and white nationalism – converged. This convergence is not accidental but the product of threats centuries in the making. Given that they profoundly undermine both physical and social environments, they engender intense emotions, including resentment, victimization, uncertainty, rage and denial. Physical threats to homes, communities, landscapes and livelihoods are coupled with challenges to white power and its attendant values of personal freedom and resistance to 'state tyranny'. Though rage is the most visible response (Anderson, 2016; Inwood, 2019), it can mask multiple emotions and anxieties, as noted above. Because intense, collective emotions in highly politicized contexts can inspire action and societal change, they are called 'political emotions' (Olson, 2016; Antadze, 2020). The wildfire rumours are the result of political emotions triggered by an array of material and ideological threats at multiple scales.

In this chapter I first discuss the concept of denial and then outline the Oregon wildfires. I then examine the structural elements of the rumours, why this happened in Oregon and the larger political landscape. Finally, I consider how the rumours constitute entwined forms of climate and racial denial.

Denial

Stanley Cohen defines denial as 'assertions that something did not happen, did not exist, is not true or is not known' (2001: 3). Denial ensues when the truth is too disturbing or threatening to be accepted. People may repress, disavow, lie or reinterpret the truth. Climate change has triggered multiple forms of denial (van Rensburg, 2015), with Norgaard (2019) arguing for a spectrum in which apathy is one extreme and disinformation another. In the US, where climate change is deeply politicized (MacInnis and Krosnick, 2020), denial is more complex. Norgaard (2011: 181) argues that the US fossil fuel industry's campaign of 'organized denial' (Klein, 2015: ch. 1; Leonard, 2019; Mayer, 2016: ch. 8; O'Connor, 2017; Oreskes and Conway, 2010) created doubt, which led millions to embrace literal and implicatory denial as well as apathy. This is especially true for conservatives (McCright and Dunlap, 2011). This doubt, coupled with the Republican Party's power, for decades effectively blocked any meaningful effort to address climate change (Drennen and Hardin, 2021).

In contrast to apathy, doubt and disinformation, the denial articulated by rural Oregonians is more complex and warrants close investigation. Given the suddenness of the fires, the denial was certainly not premeditated. People actually *believed* they were being targeted by outsiders – despite the fact that the entire West coast was in flames. Indeed, many were willing to risk their well-being to protect their communities from BLM and Antifa.

This denial, while not entirely conscious, hardly emerged out of thin air. Rather, it illustrates the link between socio-cultural factors and climate attitudes, including values like freedom, individualism (Leiserowitz, 2006) and far-right ideologies (Forchtner, 2018a, 2018b). Traditionally, scholars believed that better information would result in people accepting the truth, but recent research argues for treating denial and conspiracies as part of the larger social formation. This includes studying the worldviews and contexts which produce denial (Fischer, 2019) and conceptualizing conspiracy theories and disinformation as forms of cultural failure (Guilhot, 2021).

I examine how one element of the social formation intersects with climate denial – white nationalism. Though rural-identified communities face economic decline and state abandonment, most white, rural Oregonians, like much of rural America, have become increasingly invested in white nationalism. Rural areas have historically been more conservative than cities, but they have energized the right, as various tendencies congealed into Trumpism (Lowndes, 2018; Marantz, 2019; O'Connor, 2021; Read, 2020b; Selsky, 2021). Trumpism exceeds the man and exists as a powerful political force that dominates the political landscape of the right. While the economic devastation wrought by neoliberalism is often seen as the source of US rural populism and authoritarianism, this overlooks the importance of white nationalism (Roman-Alcalá et al., 2021), which can contribute to unanticipated outcomes. For example, rural areas often vote against their economic interests because they are anti-state (HoSang and Lowndes, 2019). Residents feel the state has betrayed them as it prioritizes urban elites and racial Others (Hochschild, 2016). Trump tapped into this anger, and drawing on deep reservoirs of white nationalism, repeated the Republican Party's Southern Strategy, which foregrounded racial resentment (Inwood, 2019; Lowndes, 2008). The recognition that Trumpism offers enabled rural voters to express their emotions, which was important in a time of change and precarity (Hochschild, 2016).

The contemporary right is characterized by disinformation, rumours and conspiracy theories (Marantz, 2019). Such narratives serve multiple functions, including offering paths for politicization, providing explanations in overwhelming times, relieving collective tension (Karuka, 2019: 5) and creating rigid binaries. According to Daggett, the right employs melodramatic narratives, which are a 'highly dramatic and emotive form that constructs polar opposites of good and evil' (2020: 2). Such narratives, which may not be based on facts, collectively create meta-narratives in which diverse dramas, events and processes can be understood. Hochschild (2016) calls such meta-narratives 'the deep story', reminding us how smaller narratives build on and are connected to each other. The right's deep story centres on loathing the government, racial resentment, a loss of respect and anger at those advancing, seemingly at their expense. Thus, there are similarities in the beliefs that COVID is a hoax, Trump won the 2020 election and anti-racists started wildfires – they all fit into a deep story.

The Oregon wildfires

Early September 2020 was hot and sunny in Oregon. Because of tremendous heat and high pressure east of the Cascade Mountains (Figure 3.1), an unusual hot, dry wind blew into western Oregon creating an 'east wind' event. While such winds are common in California, they are rare in western Oregon. The hot winds, dry lightning and parched forest quickly caught fire and burned a vast area.

Many on the right, including then-President Trump, argued that insufficient logging caused the fires, what Gavin (2020) calls the 'fuels narrative'. Evidence suggests, however, that much of the burned land was privately owned and had been previously clear-cut (see also Bendix, 2020). Because private forests often operate as tree plantations, they are characterized by clear cutting

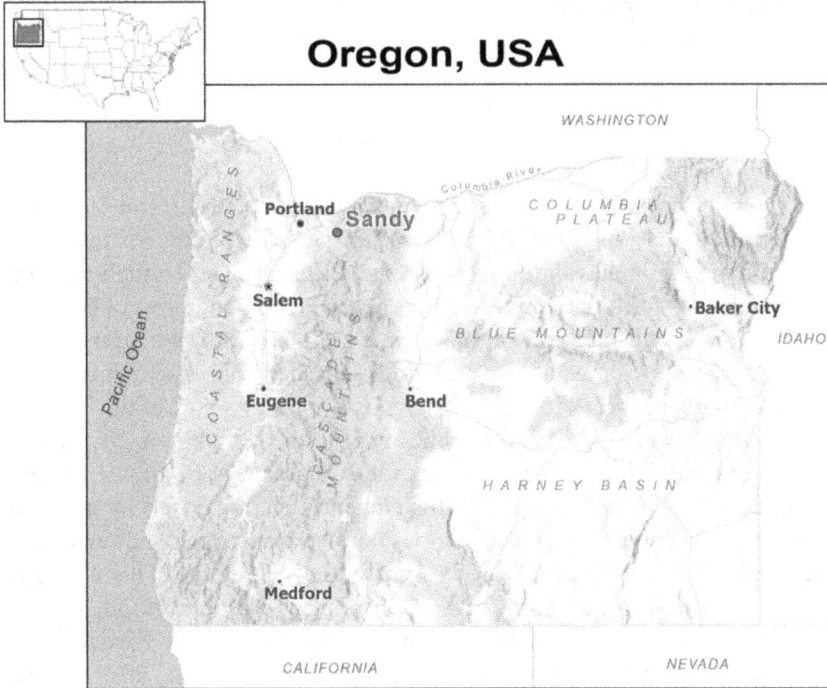

3.1 Map of Oregon, USA. Created by Sophia Ford

and young saplings, both of which enabled fires to spread at rates that precluded effective firefighting. Gavin found that in the Holiday Fire west of Eugene, one of the many fires that burned in Oregon in September 2020, the timber giant, Weyerhaeuser, is the largest landowner. In this fire, over 70 per cent of the burned areas employed clear-cut rotation forestry (Gavin, 2020). In contrast, public lands, which have been managed through clear cutting, prescribed burns and regular thinning, were characterized by second-growth forests and were better able to withstand the fires.

As the fires spread, evacuation warnings were issued, and community evacuation plans implemented. Entire communities, including Talent and Phoenix, were burned. Others, such as Blue River, were partially destroyed. Hundreds lost their homes and belongings. The McKenzie River, which draws thousands every summer, was significantly damaged. The air in Oregon and Washington registered as the most polluted on the planet, and for almost two weeks residents were confined indoors. By 3 October 2020, Oregon had sustained over two thousand fires encompassing over a million acres; 40,000 people were displaced; thousands of structures destroyed; and 9 people were dead (Powell, 2020; Templeton, 2020). The fires, which were partially caused by global warming (Buis, 2021), were a traumatic event for all Oregonians.

The wildfire rumours

The rumours first appeared on social media on 9 September and continued for approximately one week. Data was drawn from Sandy, a small town approximately 30 miles southeast of Portland (Figure 3.1). Though rumours existed throughout rural Oregon, they were most intense southeast of Portland, at the rural–urban interface. Sandy has a population of just over 12,000 and is 75 per cent white. Latinas/os/x and Asians are the primary communities of colour, with smaller Native and Black populations. As part of the Portland metro, Sandy has experienced significant growth, including a 20 per cent population increase over the past decade. Originally part of the Oregon Trail, it became a timber town and is currently characterized by a service economy. While much of rural Oregon is impoverished, Sandy has an above-average household income of $73,443 (US Census, 2019). This is due to Portland's expanding economy and its proximity to Mount Hood, a major recreational area. It is precisely because of its closeness to Portland that Sandy defines itself 'in opposition to Portland values' (Yau, 2021). Thus, Sandy is a rural-identified community rather than a rural one, reflecting its location at the rural/urban nexus.

A university research assistant who was from Sandy joined various social media groups to access local data. Data was drawn from YouTube, Parler, Twitter and Facebook – the latter accounting for approximately 70 per cent of all postings. We counted approximately a hundred original postings, some of which were shared hundreds of times, as well as dozens of comments. Comments provided the richest data, totalling over a thousand. Original postings included photographs, videos, screen shots of text messages, and news stories which people responded to. The original postings typically offered 'evidence' of arson and other illegal activity. But because of poor quality, it was usually unclear what was happening. Alternatively, there were clear images of neutral objects, like a parked car, but accompanied by a nefarious narrative. Given heightened anxiety and an extant deep story, such images fuelled more rumours. The most common postings were second-hand accounts of threatening events, such as the following: 'I found out yesterday that my brother-in-law's friend caught someone putting a mattress in his field and pouring gasoline on it. Then our neighbours tells us her friend caught someone trying to light some taped-together m100s … in her driveway.' [2] Note how the actors are several steps removed from the person reporting.

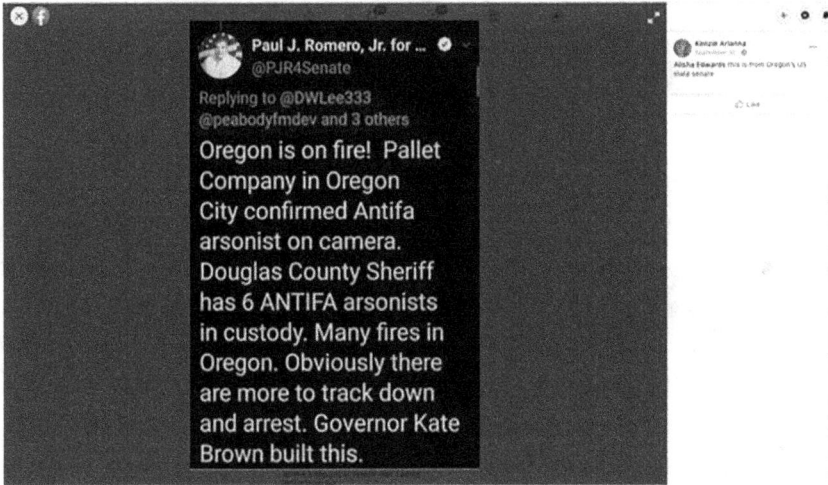

3.2 Post by Oregon political candidate Paul Romero Jr., distributed via Facebook

Most postings were from private individuals, but a sheriff, police association, conservative pundits and a political candidate also spread rumours (see Figure 3.2). Law enforcement investigated the claims, found them meritless (Palma, 2020) and sought to curb them (see Figure 3.3). Consequently, social media platforms stopped posting the rumours and removed some. Though they ceased to exist digitally, the extent of their influence is unknown. Measurable impacts include first responders answering rumour-based calls rather than protecting communities. Clackamas County, where Sandy is located, reported a 405 per cent increase in calls (Clackamas County Sheriff's Office, 2020). Moreover, because some refused to evacuate, firefighters' lives were further jeopardized.

While some impacts can be measured, the rumours themselves cannot. Besides reflecting the social formation, they reproduced a melodramatic discourse grounded in anger, resentment, fear and victimization. A close reading of the data revealed a narrative structure composed of four elements: 1) Arson is not climate change; 2) Antifa/BLM are the arsonists/terrorists; 3) There is a cover-up conspiracy; and 4) Those who don't believe this are the real denialists.

Act 1 – Arson is not climate change

The rumours were anchored by denying the fires' connection to global warming. Instead, those posting insisted that the fires were due to arson. Any suggestion that they were *not* caused by arson was angrily refuted.

FBI Portland ✓
@FBIPortland

000

Reports that extremists are setting wildfires in Oregon are untrue. Help us stop the spread of misinformation by only sharing information from trusted, official sources.

> " FBI Portland and local law enforcement agencies have been receiving reports that extremists are responsible for setting wildfires in Oregon. With our state and local partners, the FBI has investigated several such reports and found them to be <u>untrue</u>.
>
> *1 of 2*
>
> SPECIAL AGENT IN CHARGE LOREN CANNON
> Federal Bureau of Investigation
>
> FBI PORTLAND DIVISION

11:20 AM · Sep 11, 2020 · Hootsuite Inc.

12.3K Retweets   **2.7K** Quote Tweets   **16.8K** Likes

3.3 Tweet by FBI Portland on misinformation, 11 September 2020

Actually, most fires are due to direct human action, such as smouldering campfires, but that is not arson. Denying the role of climate change was embedded in larger narratives and conspiracies:

Q sent me.[3] Let's call this what it really is. This is Domestic Terrorism by paid mercenaries of the Democrat party. This is not about 'climate fires.' This is ARSON.

Yes, these idiots have been running around setting fires and the mainstream media tries to attribute it to climate change, but we all know the truth ... its extremist groups antifa/blm. Nobody is fooled by those world-class retards.

The wildfires were no accident. Antifa Leftists are starting fires to BURN THE COUNTRY DOWN.

Believe what you want but these fires aren't just popping up out of nowhere by chance[.] Yes, some started from power lines being down etc but this many fires at once happening this broadly is too strange.

These quotes contain features common to all the postings, including references to 'Q', condemnation of the Democratic Party and allusions to larger attacks. People saw themselves as victims of the Democratic Party and Antifa/BLM, which in turn, draws on white grievance, a political emotion central to the right.

Three components of climate denial can be identified. First, there is the physical experience of wildfires, whose unprecedented nature facilitates false explanations. Secondly, the arson narrative built on decades of climate denial by the right (McCright and Dunlap, 2011). Thus, denying climate change was a familiar practice. And lastly, there was a readily available alternative explanation, or deep story (Hochschild, 2016), which aligned with contemporary national events: anti-racists seeking to destroy the country.

Act 2 – Antifa/BLM are responsible

Assuming the fires were caused by arson, the question is, who are the arsonists? The answer: Antifa and BLM. It is important to understand the relationship between these two formations. BLM is a multiracial mass movement led by Black people which foregrounds anti-racism. Antifa is a largely white, anarchist formation that seeks to support BLM. Antifa has a larger agenda than anti-Black racism, as it is also anti-capitalist and rejects non-violence, unlike BLM (Read, 2020c). Though Antifa is far smaller than BLM, it figures prominently in the right's imaginary: it is concrete evidence of violent leftists. Consequently, many quickly extrapolated arson to shooting, looting and threatening rural white communities: 'Any truth to the rumor that these [fires] have been set? ... They're reporting that "antifa" is starting fires to block exits, last report is that shots are being fired at evacuees.' Such exaggerated violence suggests an existential crisis stemming from wildfires *and* challenges to whiteness.

The Democratic Party was considered a secondary culprit as it purportedly enabled Antifa/BLM. 'As Antifa/BLM set fire to the Pacific Northwest, Joe Biden labeled President Trump a "climate arsonist." Really? What warped alternate reality are Democrats living in?' The idea of climate arson is significant as it attributes climate change to individual actors rather than larger anthropogenic forces. Moreover, it overlooks decades of 'climate defiance' (Daggett, 2020) on the part of the Republican Party, in which it has refused to act to address climate change.

The reality is there *was* a pre-existing connection between Antifa/BLM and fire. During the racial justice protests of 2020, Antifa set fires in Portland, which BLM largely opposed (Read, 2020c). Although wildfires and protest fires are distinct, the summer protests predisposed many on the right to connect Antifa/BLM with fire. Despite over 93 per cent of BLM protests being peaceful (Armed Conflict Location and Event Data Project, 2020), media coverage highlighted looting and fires, which exacerbated the wildfire rumours. While biased coverage was important, such narratives also suggest latent, underlying anxieties.

> Who has been rioting? Who has been protesting? Who has been starting fires? ... Isn't [it] Antifa and BLM who have been saying 'we are going to burn it all down.'

> Antifa has been setting fires nightly in Oregon and Washington for the past 100 days. Time to implement the death penalty for arson.

> antifa is not a group ... but they sure as hell light off a lot of fires ... It's not hard to connect the dots.

What evidence existed for such claims? One man was arrested for arson in the neighbouring state of Washington. Because he had been arrested at a 2014 BLM protest, he was portrayed as a member of Antifa, which was sufficient proof to many of criminality. Despite the paucity of evidence, claims of arrests abounded: 'People are getting caught left and right for Arson. (I mean in the dozens).' But, in fact, no known members of BLM/Antifa were arrested (Palma, 2020), which inspired the next part of the narrative arc.

Act 3 – It's a conspiracy

As mentioned earlier, law enforcement and the mainstream media quickly refuted rumours and admonished people to stop spreading them (Figure 3.3). Sandy residents saw such pleas as efforts to protect arsonists from blame, which in turn indicated a larger conspiracy. As claims of arson were rejected by authorities, disinformation morphed into a conspiracy in which the Oregon government, including Governor Kate Brown, the Democrats and the mainstream media, were scheming to obscure the truth. Some demanded that the Governor be tried for treason for her refusal to pursue Antifa/BLM while Oregon was under COVID restrictions. The logic was as follows:

> Sad that these people have no idea WHAT's really going on, AND WANT TO WAIT AFTER PEOPLE DIE AND THEIR HOMES ARE BURNED TO THE GROUND ... WAITING TO DO SOMETHING ... OH AND LET'S KEEP LAW ABIDING PEOPLE LOCKED DOWN WHILE YOU ALLOW OTHERS TO BURN, LOOT, AND MURDER IN PRIVATE ... LIKE ANTIFA

WILL OBEY CURFEW … LIKE ANTIFA WILL OBEY LAWS … HAVE THEY YET?

This is an example of how multiple crises and their attendant anxieties and anger were merged into conspiracy theories.

The flip side of the conspiracy was false victimization: 'The system protects antifa and BLM terrorists. Imagine the narrative if even one Trump supporter or white supremacist was caught setting fires. We are on our own. hashtag – whitelivesmatter.' The phrase, 'we are on our own' hints at the sense of betrayal on the part of the state towards white victims. The belief that a Trump supporter would automatically be prosecuted is untrue, as most domestic terrorism is by white supremacists, who have rarely been pursued (Department of Homeland Security, 2020; Benner et al., 2021). Because such claims are demonstrably false, they emanate from larger grievances, as they reflect the deep story.

Because the right generally supports law enforcement, its rejection of arson claims was difficult to accept. Although law enforcement found no basis to support the rumours, one officer did implicate Antifa. A Clackamas County Sheriff Deputy publicly stated, 'Antifa mother fuckers are causing hell.' He was put on administrative leave and a statement refuting the comment was issued. These actions were seen as evidence of a conspiracy: the officer was punished for speaking the truth.

In contrast, dismissing the mainstream media was easy. The mainstream media has been discredited by the right due to its liberal bias, as epitomized by Trump's phrase, 'fake news'. Not only did most posts reject the mainstream media, but dissension was not tolerated. For example, the few who supported law enforcement's findings encountered pushback:

> Of course the left wing media outlets don't want people thinking it's antifa! This … page … will probably post next: 'Antifa was busy all night checking on rural communities, leaving gasoline for returning property owners in case they need it … Later in the week they plan to hand out gifts to Portland and surrounding areas. This page is losing its purpose quickly, need to change the name to 'Sandy liberal bias information.'

Ironically, BLM *did* aid fire evacuees in Portland (Davis-Cohen, 2020), but this was never acknowledged. When the Portland-based *Oregonian* announced that the arson rumours were false, someone responded, 'I don't believe *The Oregonian* for one second.'

Act 4 – Disbelief

The final arc of the story is disbelief that not everyone shared this narrative. Commentators were incredulous that some could not see what was so obvious. Such supposed blindness precluded an effective public response, which presumably was to arrest Antifa/BLM members. 'People's blindness is what is dangerous to this community. Wake up folks[,] bad people are doing bad things.' Or, 'We know who set the fires, there's enough video and pictures all over social media to show the proof! It's the same people that have been setting fires downtown! Why is that so hard to figure out?'

In short, people chose to believe the fires were due to arson rather than climate change, they blamed anti-racist activists, fabricated conspiracies, positioned themselves as victims and condemned those who disagreed. Clearly, residents felt besieged and enraged. The question becomes, why did they feel so vulnerable and threatened by imagined terrorists? How is this connected to white supremacy? And, why is this happening in Oregon?

Political polarization and the Oregon right

Oregon, with a relatively small population (4,270,000), is considered a liberal, quirky state. Known for its environmentalism and pioneering drug-legalization, it has a long history of protest, hippies and whiteness. Besides a white population, Oregon and the Pacific Northwest loom large in the white imaginary, as seen in efforts to create a white homeland (Wright, 2020). One reason whiteness is so prominent is because the region was the last part of the continental US settled by Anglo-Americans. As part of US westward expansion, Lewis and Clark's 'Corps of Discovery' did not arrive in Oregon until 1805 and it did not achieve statehood until 1859. Subsequent to Anglo-American arrival, many Native people died from disease and survivors were forcibly relocated to reservations on the coast and eastern Oregon (Barber, 2019; Lewis and Connolly, 2019). Through treaties, massacres, wars and laws, including the Oregon Land Donation Act (Coleman, 2019), Native people were stripped of their land, homes and way of life. White racial violence was central to it all.

White supremacy enabled Indigenous removal which made land available for white settlement. Settlers decided to join the US as a free state to avoid any Black people (Thoennes and Landau, 2019). Besides outlawing Black residents, settlers also restricted Asian communities. To justify and sanitize this history, settlers created a pioneer narrative which erased racial violence (Carpenter, 2020), cultivated white innocence and celebrated Manifest Destiny (Horsman, 1981).

In recent decades Oregon has become increasingly diverse. Latinas/os/x are now 12 per cent of the population, Asians 6 per cent, and Native and

Black populations each constitute 3 per cent. While many Latinas/os/x and Native peoples are rural and live throughout the state (Sandoval and Rodine, 2020), Portland is the most diverse and liberal city in Oregon. Home to 2.5 million, the Portland area is surrounded by expansive forests and agricultural areas, which are far more conservative (Hibbard et al., 2011). Though right-wing politicians represent the vast eastern portion of Oregon, liberals represent the population centres of Portland, Salem and Eugene. Consequently, Portland has emerged as a flash point for clashing racial and political ideologies, leading some to call it a 'proxy in the culture wars' (Pereira, 2021). Sandy is deeply implicated in this geography, as it is a 'shatterbelt' where rural and urban meet. While Sandy has the economic benefits of Portland (US Census, 2019; Mechling, 2020), it embraces a rural politics.

Rural Oregon is a kaleidoscope of political ideologies and formations, including those advocating for decreased regulation (especially extractive industries), gun rights, white nationalism, religious freedom, Christianity, anti-vaxxers and accelerationists, who promote civil war. They are united, however, in their opposition to the state and urban elites, advocating for limited regulation and local control. HoSang and Lowndes (2019) note that rather than directing their ire against, say, the timber industry for abandoning the area (Schick et al., 2020), residents blame environmental regulations and the state. Anti-statism was evident in the 2016 occupation of a Wildlife Refuge in eastern Oregon. Led by the Bundy family and its followers, it ended in a shoot-out with federal authorities (Inwood and Bonds, 2017, but see Walker, 2018). Others, hoping to escape liberal governance, seek to create a state where rural, conservative, white, Christian values prevail (Wright, 2020).

Environmental governance reflects Oregon's rural/urban tensions, as seen in conflicts over logging, climate change and endangered species. Besides opposing state regulation, rural areas note that they are disproportionately harmed by such policies. Given their minority status, Republicans employ various strategies to assert themselves. For example, rather than voting on a climate change bill in 2018, they fled the state, thereby preventing a quorum (Leber and Breland, 2020).

Extractive industries have been instrumental in helping to organize Oregon's right. A growing political force, Timber Unity, for example, purportedly advocates for farmers, logging communities and truckers. As such, it harkens back to the Sagebrush Rebellion of the 1980s. With financial support from logging interests and even Donald Trump, it helped organize the legislative walkouts and protests against climate legislation (Leber and Breland, 2020). Protests included tractors and trucks circling the capital, a powerful symbol of the white, male, rural subject, which gained ascendency in the Trump era (Carian and Sobotka, 2018).

Racism on the right is complex. As a political movement comprising up to one-third of the US, it embodies various forms of racism. The racial violence of the 2017 'Unite the Right' rally in Charlottesville appalled many, prompting the right to adopt softer language and include Black, Indigenous and people of colour in their organizations (Lowndes, 2021; Ross, 2020; HoSang and Lowndes, 2019). Enrique Tarrio, for instance, an Afro-Cuban, became a leader of the Proud Boys. Increasingly, the racial rhetoric has shifted from abstract white supremacy to protecting the white nation and Western values (Marantz, 2017).

These events build on decades of growing white grievance (Inwood, 2019), economic precarity, anti-statism and increased violence. The white nation feels threatened by the 'browning of the nation' (Jardin, 2019), the election of a Black president (Williamson et al., 2011) and multiculturalism (Bartels, 2020). Such tendencies have been exacerbated by the US's War on Terror which emphasized US vulnerability to terrorism (Ackerman, 2021). The Oathkeepers, a militia group, illustrate how multiple threats combine to form an amorphous conspiracy theory (Jamin, 2018):

> We face an open, now obvious insurrection against our Constitution being waged by the American Marxist left; by the Democratic Party which the radical left has captured; by their many Deep State allies; their Muslim Brotherhood led Jihadist allies; their foreign allies such as Communist China; and globalist elites such as George Soros. All of these enemies, both foreign and domestic, are now engaged in an assault on our Republic, intent on its destruction. (Oathkeepers, 2020)

The murder of George Floyd was a precipitous event that intensified an already polarized political culture. Millions saw the murder as outrageous and began re-evaluating the nature of US racism. As a racial critique developed, Confederate and colonial statues were toppled. Although the protests occurred throughout the US, they were most pronounced in urban centres, reinforcing the urban/rural divide. This clash was palpable in Portland, which saw protests for over a hundred consecutive nights, including street fights between the right and anti-racist activists (Read, 2020a).

This is the immediate backdrop to the wildfire rumours. While they are informed by multiple issues, white rage is central. In keeping with the contemporary right, the rumours drew on coded organizing frames that were not overtly racist but were saturated with racial meaning and reproduced white supremacy (Lowndes, 2021). These frames deny structural racism and annunciate who belongs and who does not. Below I briefly review three frames: communism, 'patriots', and 'law and order.'

Organizing frames

Communism

Communism provides an overarching frame for the right's contemporary discourse. For the right, communism and socialism are existential dangers that must be resisted, with force if necessary. Despite the demise of the Soviet Union, the communist threat persists in the idea that cultural Marxism seeks to destroy Western culture (Jamin, 2018), in China's ascendancy and the 'state-overreach' associated with the pandemic. The right places BLM/Antifa in this camp because anti-racists are categorized as socialist threats intent on destroying the US. BLM is not a communist front, but there are individuals who identify as socialist, while Antifa stands for anti-fascist. Regardless, one repeatedly hears that BLM is Marxist and socialist, and therefore must be resisted.

There is a long history of connecting anti-racism and communism in the US. Communism and socialism were routinely used to delegitimize Black and Mexican-American anti-racist and labour activists (Bernstein, 2011; Kelley, 1990). Prior to the twenty-first century, charges of communism implied foreign interference, which was intolerable during the Cold War. Consequently, such charges discredited anti-racist activism. This had several implications. First, it implied that people of colour were incapable of building effective organizations and movements. Instead, it was assumed that the Soviets were behind US anti-racist campaigns (Bernstein, 2011). Secondly, dismissing anti-racism as a communist plot implies that people of colour were satisfied with their racial status. Supposedly they had no need or desire to seek change. This, in itself, is a remarkable form of denial. Today, the right sees BLM and its allies as 'unAmerican' and it is incumbent upon 'true patriots' to defend the US.

Antifa occupies a special place in the right's imagination. A loosely organized group of activists, Antifa has committed to challenging the right and fascism with physical violence if necessary. Its goal, it says, is to defend protestors. Nonetheless, it has been inflated by the right into a massive, organized armed force committed to Marxism. In reality, it is far smaller and less organized than groups like Patriot Prayer and Boogaloo Bois, which were on the offensive throughout Trump's ascent. The two are simply not comparable, but Antifa is mentioned more often than BLM by those spreading rumours (see Benner et al., 2021). Antifa is an ideal strawman. For one, it is mostly white, thus condemning Antifa avoids charges of racism. Secondly, as the only segment of the racial justice movement willing to engage in violence and that embraces an anti-fascist and leftist identity, it is the manifestation of a supposed global Marxist take-over.

Patriot

The term 'patriot' has gained increasing traction across the right and was strategically used by then-President Trump to characterize his supporters. One wildfire post by a vigilante read: 'I've been doing this every night. Stopping at all these checkpoints and meeting more and more Patriots! It's awesome!' 'Patriot' is a powerful ideological term which serves to legitimate and make respectful the right's racial terror, whether it is attacking the US capitol in January 2021 (Venkataramanan, 2021), shooting BLM protestors (Korecki and Cadelago, 2020) or creating armed checkpoints. The right discredits those who disagree with them as being 'unpatriotic'. Such persons have no legitimacy or standing in the body politic, including the millions of BLM supporters, who are seen as intent on destroying the US.

'Patriot' is a strategic and sufficiently robust term that includes diverse peoples. Indeed, the Three Percenters' (2020) webpage stated, 'patriotism is color blind'. People of colour can be patriots but anti-racist activists cannot. For people of colour to be patriots, they must accept the continued privileging of the white nation, which a minority has always been willing to do (HoSang and Lowndes, 2019). Patriots not only oppose efforts to create racial justice, but they also demonize such activists, labelling them 'UnAmerican'.

Law and order

The phrase 'law and order' builds on a long history of connecting cities, crime and people of colour. Although Portland was the site of nightly protests in support of BLM, including looting and fires, it is the right that has rammed cars into activists, shot people, used pepper spray on protestors and attacked the US capitol (Department of Homeland Security, 2020; Deveraux, 2021). Right-wing activists claimed they were needed because mayors were not controlling the protests, therefore it was up to patriots. One counter-protestor explained, 'We're just sick and tired of the lawlessness for 100-plus days in Portland. There has to be some accountability' (Biggs in Read, 2020a).

The law and order frame is deeply contradictory. First, as previously noted, anti-racist activists are not a serious threat. According to the Department of Homeland Security, 'white supremacist extremists will remain the most persistent and lethal threat in the Homeland through 2021' (2020: 27). Secondly, law enforcement's negation of the rumours around the wildfires caused confusion and eroded confidence in the only segment of the state that the right trusted. One Facebook user posted, 'I'm so confused … So are we with law enforcement or no? When we hear "defund the police," we are with them. When the sheriff tells us Antifa isn't setting the fires, they are government and not to be believed' (in Abcarian, 2020). This confusion stems from the deep connection between law enforcement and white supremacy. Whites exhibit the highest levels of support for law enforcement because of its historic role in protecting whiteness, including property, bodies and space (The Opportunity Agenda, n. d.). This support has led to the 'Back the Blue' movement in which mostly white people defend the police against BLM's claims. According to its website, 'with radical leftist protestors constantly vilifying our local heroes, it is our job to stand up and defend their honor' (Back the Blue, 2021). Because BLM's claims of systematic police brutality conflict with law enforcement's 'honor', counter-protestors actively oppose racial justice, as it undermines claims to white innocence.

Conclusion

Denial is woven throughout the wildfire rumours. Denying the racial violence and white supremacy upon which the US was built has been essential to building a viable nation, as the truth does not offer a 'useable past' (Hixson, 2013). Acknowledging the truth occurs episodically and is highly contentious, as the white nation is invested in denying it. BLM and its allies' insistence that Black lives actually matter, implies that they have not previously mattered. It requires accepting that the US has historically over-valued and privileged white lives at the expense of Black lives (Taylor, 2016), which undermines white innocence. In turn, this threatens the central narrative of the US as a land of equality, freedom and a meritocracy. This racial crisis, which has been postponed for centuries, coupled with unprecedented wildfires, produced political emotions resulting in the rumours.

The right and rural-identifying communities are not alone in denying climate change. While most Americans accept climate change, we remain apathetic and unwilling to change (Norgaard, 2011; Antadze, 2018). But the right's denial is not just inertia. Instead, it creates fabrications that draw on deep anxieties which require intense energy and imagination. The right's denial is not the path of least resistance, but is more akin to 'climate defiance' (Daggett, 2020).

Climate change poses serious threats to the right, including government intervention, globalism and elite dominance (Forchtner, 2018b; Klein, 2015). For much of the right, refusal to accept climate change is not about the science, but fear of the policy implications (van Rensburg, 2015) and challenges to its worldview (Klein, 2015). While the policy changes may be objectionable, they also undermine cherished values, including limited government. Thus, denying climate change for rural-identified Oregonians is part of a larger worldview encompassing one's identity, community, beliefs and lifestyle. While climate denial has existed for decades and racial denial for centuries, in this particular moment they merged. As the climate crisis worsens, we can expect to see similar fusions along various lines of power and difference.

Notes

1 US policy suppressed fire on public lands for over a century, creating highly combustible forests.
2 All quotes are reprinted as in the original unless otherwise stated. M100s are firecrackers.
3 'Q' is short for Q-Anon, a conspiracy in which Donald Trump is saving the world from paedophiles and cannibalistic Democrats and global elites (Healy, 2020).

References

Abcarian, R. (2020). The rumor mill in Oregon has got the wildfires figured out – it's all Antifa's fault. *Los Angeles Times*, 16 September.

Ackerman, S. (2021). *The Reign of Terror*. New York: Penguin Books.

Anderson, C. (2016). *White Rage: The Unspoken Truth of Our Nation's Divide*. New York: Bloomsbury.

Antadze, N. (2018). The Politics of Apathy: Trumping the Ethical Imperative of Climate Change. *Ethics, Policy & Environment*, 21(1): 45–47.

Antadze, N. (2020). The Emotional Regime of Apathy, Trump, and Climate Injustice. In Barney Warf (ed.), *Political Landscapes of Donald Trump*. New York: Routledge, pp. 311–321.

Armed Conflict Location and Event Data Project (2020). Demonstrations & political violence in America, new data for Summer 2020. https://acleddata.com/ (accessed 3 March 2021).

Back the Blue (2021). www.actforamerica.org/activism/back-the-blue (accessed 4 March 2021).

Barber, K. (2019). We Were at Our Journey's End. *Oregon Historical Quarterly*, 120(4): 382–413.

Bartels, L. (2020). Ethnic Antagonism Erodes Republicans' Commitment to Democracy. *PNAS*, 117(37): 22752–22759.

Bendix, J. (2020). Western wildfires – there is no 'silver bullet,' but there are things to be done. *The Hill*, 7 October, https://thehill.com/opinion/energy-environment/519970-western-wildfires-there-is-no-silver-bullet-but-there-are-things/ (accessed 12 October 2020).

Benner, K., Goldman, A., and Kanno-Youngs, Z. (2021). Search for threats on left as far-right peril brewed. *New York Times*, 31 January.

Bernstein, Shana (2011). *Bridges of Reform: Interracial Civil Rights Activism in Twentieth Century Los Angeles*. New York: Oxford University Press.

Buis, Alan (2021). The climate connections of a record fire year in the West. *NASA Global Climate Change*, 22 February, https://climate.nasa.gov/blog/3066/the-climate-connections-of-a-record-fire-year-in-the-us-west/ (accessed 23 October 2023).

Carian, E., and Sobotka, T. C. (2018). Playing the Trump Card: Masculinity Threat and the 2016 Presidential Election. *Socius: Sociological Research for a Dynamic World*, 4 (January–December). doi.org/10.1177/2378023117740699.

Carpenter, M. (2020). Pioneer Problems: 'Wanton Murder,' Indian War Veterans, and Oregon's Violent History. *Oregon Historical Quarterly*, 121(2): 156–185.

Clackamas County Sheriff's Office (2020). News release: Tales from Clackamas wildfire patrols. *Facebook* post, 12 September, www.facebook.com/clackcosheriff/posts/3319587008127163 (accessed 18 February 2021).

Cohen, S. (2001). *States of Denial*. Cambridge: Polity Press.

Coleman, K. (2019). 'We'll All Start Even': White Egalitarianism and the Oregon Donation Land Claim Act. *Oregon Historical Quarterly*, 120(4): 414–437.

Daggett, C. (2020). The Melodrama of Climate Change Denial. *Green European Journal*, 11 March, www.greeneuropeanjournal.eu/the-melodrama-of-climate-change-denial/ (accessed 23 October 2023).

Davis-Cohen, S. (2020). Mutual aid response during fires shows Black Lives Matter is building community. *Truthout*, 18 September, https://truthout.org/articles/mutual-aid-response-during-fires-shows-black-lives-matter-is-building-community/ (accessed 4 March 2021).

Department of Homeland Security, US (2020). Homeland threat assessment. October 2020, www.dhs.gov/publication/2020-homeland-threat-assessment (accessed 24 February 2021).

Devereaux, R. (2021). Capitol attack was culmination of generations of far-right extremism. *The Intercept*, https://theintercept.com/2021/01/23/capitol-riot-far-right-extremism/ (accessed 3 March 2021).

Drennen, A., and Hardin, S. (2021). Climate deniers in the 117th Congress, *Center for American Progress*, 20 March, www.americanprogress.org/article/climate-deniers-117th-congress/ (accessed 24 November 2023).

Fischer, F. (2019). Knowledge Politics and Post-truth in Climate Denial: On the Social Construction of Alternative Facts. *Critical Policy Studies*, 13(2): 133–152.

Forchtner, B. (2018a). Climate change, Holocaust denial and the 'lies of our time'. *Centre for Analysis of the Radical Right*, 19 December, www.radicalrightanalysis.com/2018/12/19/ (accessed 21 February 2021).

Forchtner, B. (2018b). 'The people, the climate and "globalism"'. *Centre for Analysis of the Radical Right*, 25 July, www.radicalrightanalysis.com/2018/07/25/the-people-the-climate-and-globalism-the-radical-right-on-climate-change/ (accessed 21 February 2021).

Gavin, D. (2020). In Oregon's 2020 fires, highly managed forests burned the most. Firefighters United for Safety, Ethics & Ecology, *Spotfire! Blog*, 25 September, https://fusee.org/fusee-blog (accessed 12 October 2020).

Guilhot, N. (2021). Bad information. *Boston Review*, 23 August, https://bostonreview.net/politics/nicolas-guilhot-bad-information (accessed 1 October 2021).

Healy, M. (2020). What is driving bogus pedophilia claims? *Los Angeles Times*, 20 October.

Hibbard, M., Seltzer, E., Weber, B., and Emshoff, B. (2011). *Toward One Oregon*. Corvallis: Oregon State University Press.

Hixson, W. (2013). *American Settler Colonialism: A History*. London: Palgrave Macmillan.

Hochschild, A. (2016). *Strangers in Their Own Land*. New York: The New Press.

Horsman, R. (1981). *Race and Manifest Destiny*. Cambridge: Harvard University Press.

HoSang, D., and Lowndes, J. (2019). *Producers, Parasites, Patriots: Race and the New Right Wing Politics of Precarity*. Minneapolis: University of Minnesota Press.

Inwood, J. (2018). 'It is the innocence which constitutes the crime': Political Geographies of White Supremacy, the Construction of White Innocence, and the Flint Water Crisis. *Geography Compass*, 12(3): 1–11.

Inwood, J. (2019). White Supremacy, White Counter-revolutionary Politics, and the Rise of Donald Trump. *EPC: Politics and Space*, 37(4): 579–596.

Inwood, J., and Bonds, A. (2017). Property and Whiteness: The Oregon Standoff and the Contradictions of the Settler State. *Space and Polity*, 21(3): 253–268.

Jamin, J. (2018). Cultural Marxism: A Survey. *Religious Compass*, 12(1–2): 1–12.

Jardin, A. (2019). *White Identity Politics*. Cambridge: Cambridge University Press.

Karuka, M. (2019). *Empire's Tracks*. Berkeley: University of California Press.

Kelley, R. (1990). *Hammer and Hoe*. Chapel Hill: University of North Carolina Press.

Klein, N. (2015). *This Changes Everything*. New York: Simon & Schuster.

Korecki, N., and Cadelago, C. (2020). With a Hand from Trump, the Right Makes Rittenhouse a Cause Celebre. *Politico*, 1 September, .www.politico.com/news/2020/09/01/trump-rittenhouse-kenosha-support-407106 (accessed 18 February 2021).

Kristof, N. (2020). Flames that won't die out so easily. *New York Times*, 20 September.

Leber, R., and Breland, A. (2020). The Oregon GOP's favorite anti-environment group is awash in racism and violent threats, *Mother Jones*, 6 March.

Leiserowitz, A. (2006). Climate Change Risk Perception and Policy Preferences. *Climatic Change*, 77: 45–72.

Leonard, C. (2019). *Kochland: The Secret History of Koch Industries and Corporate Power in America*. New York: Simon & Schuster.

Lewis, D., and Connolly, T. (2019). White American Violence on Tribal Peoples on the Oregon Coast. *Oregon Historical Quarterly*, 120(4): 368–381.

Lindsey, R. (2020). Drought emerges across the Pacific Northwest in Spring 2020. National Oceanic and Atmospheric Agency, 26 May, www.climate.gov/news-features/event-tracker/drought-emerges-across-pacific-northwest-spring-2020 (accessed 29 September 2020).

Lowndes, J. (2008). *From the New Deal to the New Right*. New Haven: Yale University Press.

Lowndes, J. (2018). The GOP had an uneasy relationship to the far right. Until Trump. *Washington Post*, 16 September.

Lowndes, J. (2021). How the far right weaponized America's democratic roots. *New Republic*, 10 August, https://newrepublic.com/article/163210/far-right-proud-boys-tea-party-myth (accessed 30 September 2021).

MacInnis, B., and Krosnick, J. (2020). *Climate Insights 2020: Surveying American Public Opinion on Climate Change and the Environment*. Report: Partisan Divide. *Resources for the Future*, https://media.rff.org/documents/Climate_Insights_2020_Partisan_Divide.pdf (accessed 25 November 2023).

Marantz, A. (2017). The alt-right branding war has torn the movement in two. *New Yorker*, 6 July.

Marantz, A. (2019). *Antisocial: Online Extremists, Techno-utopians, and the Hijacking of the American Conversation*. New York: Viking.

Mayer, J. (2016). *Dark Money: The Hidden History of the Billionaires Behind the Rise of the Right*. New York: Anchor Books.

McCright, A., and Dunlap, R. (2011). Cool Dudes: The Denial of Climate Change Among Conservative White Males in the United States. *Global Environmental Change*, 21(4): 1163–1172.

Mechling, A. (2020). A portrait of poverty in Oregon. *Oregon Center for Public Policy*, 7 August, www.ocpp.org/2020/08/07/poverty-oregon/ (accessed 24 October 2023).

Norgaard, K. (2011). *Living in Denial: Climate Change, Emotions, and Everyday Life*. Cambridge: MIT Press.

Norgaard, K. (2019). Making Sense of a Spectrum of Climate Denial. *Critical Policy Studies*, 13(4): 437–441.

Oathkeepers (2020). Oathkeeper's critical message to patriots on election day – and after. 3 November, https://oathkeepers.org/2020/11/oath-keepers-critical-message-to-patriots-on-election-day-and-after/ (accessed 9 November 2020).

O'Connor, B. (2017). How fossil fuel money made climate change denial the word of God. *Splinter*, 8 August, https://splinternews.com (accessed 17 February 2021).

O'Connor, B. (2021). *Blood Red Lines: How Nativism Fuels the Right*. Chicago: Haymarket Books.

Olson, E. (2016). Geography and Ethics II: Emotions and Morality. *Progress in Human Geography*, 40(6): 830–838.

Oregon Department of Forestry (2020). ODF fire history 1911–2020, www.oregon.gov/odf/Documents/fire/odf-century-fire-history-chart.pdf (accessed 3 March 2021).

Oregon Forest Resources Institute (n. d.). State of fire: fire in Oregon forests, https://oregonforests.org/node/186 (accessed 3 March 2021).

Oreskes, N., and Conway, E. (2010). *Merchants of Doubt*. New York: Bloomsbury Publishing.

Palma, B. (2020). Is Antifa setting wildfires in Oregon? *Snopes*, 10 September, updated 17 September, www.snopes.com/fact-check/antifa-starting-fires-oregon/ (accessed 24 October 2023).

Pereira, I. (2021). Why liberal Portland has become a focal point for the far right. *abcNEWS*, 5 September, https://abcnews.go.com/US/liberal-portland-focal-point/story?id=79731161 (accessed 9 September 2021).

Powell, M. (2020). Fire crews continue to make progress on wildfire containment in Oregon. *Oregon Public Radio*, 3 October.

Read, R. (2020a). Proud Boys organizer to Trump: 'We're ready!!'. *Los Angeles Times*, 1 October.

Read, R. (2020b). Far right members join Oregon Trump caravan. *Los Angeles Times*, 8 September.

Read, R. (2020c). Portland anarchists spark backlash. *Los Angeles Times*, 16 November.

Roman-Alcalá, A., Graddy-Lovelace, G., and Edelman, M. (2021). Authoritarian Populism and Emancipatory Politics in the Rural United States. *Journal of Rural Studies*, 82: 500–504.

Ross, A. (2020). Interview with author. 22 October.

Sandoval, G., and Rodine, S. (2020). Ranchitos: Immigrant Integration via Latino Sustainable Agriculture, *Latino Studies*, 18: 151–173

Schick, T., Davis, R., and Younes, L. (2020). Big money bought the forests, small logging communities pay the price. *ProPublica*, 11 June, https://features.propublica.org/oregon-timber/severance-tax-cut-wall-street-private-logging-companies/ (accessed 24 November 2023).

Selsky, A. (2021). Far-right lawmaker takes over Oregon GOP in larger US shift. *Associated Press*, 22 February, https://apnews.com/article/donald-trump-elections-oregon-coronavirus-pandemic-presidential-elections-ede993ae236ab4af15247ff33fa23b39 (accessed 3 March 2021).

Sickinger, T. (2020). Oregon historic wildfires: unusual but not unprecedented. *The Oregonian*, 12 September, www.oregonlive.com/news/2020/09/oregons-historic-wildfires-the-unprecedented-was-predictable.html (accessed 3 March 2021).

Taylor, K.-Y. (2016). *From #BlackLivesMatter to Black Liberation*. Chicago: Haymarket Books.

Templeton, A. (2020). 2 people remain missing in Oregon's devastating fires. *Oregon Public Broadcasting*, 24 September.

The Opportunity Agenda (n. d.). Racial divide in attitudes towards the police … www.opportunityagenda.org/explore/resources-publications/new-sensibility/part-iv (accessed 24 February 2021).

Thobani, S. (2007). *Exalted Subjects: Studies in the Making of Race in Canada*. Toronto: University of Toronto Press.

Thoennes, P., and Landau, J. (2019). Constitutionalizing Racism: George H. William's Appeal for a White Utopia. *Oregon Historical Quarterly*, 120(4): 468–487.

Three Percenters – Original (2020). Who is the Three Percenters? www.thethreepercenters.org (accessed 9 November 2020).

US Census (2019). Quick facts, Sandy. emberwww.census.gov/quickfacts/fact/table/sandycityoregon/PST120219#PST120219 (accessed 9 September 2021).

Van Rensburg, W. (2015). Climate Change Scepticism: A Conceptual Re-evaluation. *Sage Open*, April–June, 1–13.

Venkataramanan, M. (2021). Gosar calls Jan. 6 Capitol attackers 'peaceful patriots'. *Arizona Republic*, 12 May, www.azcentral.com/story/news/politics/arizona/2021/05/12/rep-paul-gosar-calls-jan-6-us-capitol-attackers-peaceful-patriots/5063404001/ (accessed 1 October 2021).

Walker, P. (2018). *Sagebrush Collaboration*. Corvallis: Oregon State University Press.

Williamson, V., Skocpol, T., and Coggin, J. (2011). The Tea Party and the Remaking of Republican Conservativism. *Perspectives on Politics*, 9(1): 25–43.

Wright, R. (2020). Liberty State: Territorializing Whiteness in the Northwest. Paper presented at the Annual Meetings of the Association of American Geographers, April.

Yau, J. (2021). Small-town Sandy hosts a public stand-off over LGBTQ rights. *Willamette Weekly*, 21 March, www.wweek.com/news/2021/03/21/small-town-sandy-hosts-a-public-standoff-over-lgbtq-rights-and-the-proud-boys-resurface/ (accessed 9 September 2021).

4

United they roll? How Canadian fossil capital subsidizes the far right

Jacob McLean

It was a frigid day. The convoy, which consisted of about a hundred trucks ranging from small pickups to large commercial transports, had departed five days earlier from Red Deer, Alberta. After 3500 km of trucking, they had arrived in the nation's capital and pulled up in front of the snow-covered Parliament Hill.

In the driver's seat of a semi-truck, a white man wearing a reflective yellow vest got on his walkie-talkie and gave the order. The entire convoy erupted in a deafening cacophony of honking horns, drowning out all conversation and thought. The horns seemed to scream, 'Today, you political elites, with all your chattering, will be silent. Today, you will listen to us.'

I snapped photos and took short videos as I headed towards the crowd.

A makeshift sign propped up in the flatbed of a pickup read, 'Trudeau! Your job: protect our borders like you protect your own home and family. Do your job! No carbon tax. Canada absorbs more CO_2 than it produces!!! No migration pact. No illegals. No United Nations. Canada Strong!'

'Support Canadian agriculture – carbon taxing destroys Canadian economy – put the grain in the train and oil in the pipe', read another. It also featured a little cartoon mascot: a smiling steak in a cowboy hat encouraging the viewer to 'eat beef', connecting the dots between high-carbon energy infrastructure and high-carbon lifestyles.

Yellow vests and variations of the slogan 'I love Canadian oil and gas' were pervasive.

I arrived at the front of the convoy. Emblazoned onto the hood of the lead truck was the convoy's official logo. The logo featured a Canadian maple leaf, inside of which a young soldier stood at attention, saluting the skies where two military helicopters flew. To the left of the helicopters, two oil derricks protruded over the horizon, towering into the blue sky. Black silhouettes of people, representing the movement, fringed the bottom, superimposed by the words, 'United We Roll for Canada'.

Yellow Vests Canada and the United We Roll convoy

The *gilets jaunes* (yellow vest) movement erupted in France in November 2018 as a protest against President Emmanuel Macron's plan to increase fuel taxes. The fluorescent yellow high-visibility vest was chosen as the symbol of the movement, since French motorists are required by law to travel with one at all times (Cigainero, 2018). Initially, there was ambiguity as to the political orientation of the protests, as hundreds of thousands of people from across the political spectrum poured into the streets, without affiliation to a political party or trade union. Kipfer (2019: 212) writes that 'while their original demand (to repeal the gas tax hike) resonated with the populist and far Right, their demands evolved because of a dynamic of collective mobilization that kept putting the vests in touch with movements rooted in other subaltern social spaces'. As a result of this intermingling with progressive actors, after Macron reversed course and repealed the gas tax rise on 5 December 2018, their demands broadened in a decidedly left-wing direction, and came to include calls to raise the minimum wage and retirement benefits, and to reintroduce a wealth tax that Macron had cut (Chrisafis, 2018). While it would be possible to misconstrue the *gilet jaunes'* opposition to the gas tax as anti-ecological, Bejar-Garcia (2020) encourages us to view it as a protest against 'unfair climate policies that targeted the lower-class while leaving the upper-class largely unaffected'. Instead, the *gilets jaunes* favoured policies that simultaneously tackle climate change and economic inequality (Kipfer, 2019; Mehling, 2018).

Yellow vest protests quickly spread around the world, though they had very little in common with the original or with one another except for the symbolism of the vest (Lucardi & Brancati, 2019). In Canada, the symbol was quickly claimed by the right. Active from December 2018 and now dormant, Yellow Vests Canada (YVC) demanded looser environmental regulations on the oil and gas industry and stricter immigration policies. The movement attracted members of far-right hate groups like the Proud Boys and the Soldiers of Odin, and the activity of YVC Facebook groups drew controversy for their racist and violent discourse (Mosleh, 2018). At the height of the movement, Evan Balgord, the Executive Director of the Canadian Anti-Hate Network, believed that YVC had the 'greatest potential for radicalization leading to violence' in the country (Mussett, 2019).

This chapter focuses on the 'crescendo' of the movement: the United We Roll convoy, which drew national media attention when YVC activists drove transport trucks from Red Deer, Alberta to protest outside the Canadian parliament in Ottawa, Ontario. The chapter is divided into four main sections. In the first section, I contextualize Canada, and the province of Alberta in particular, as a place where fossil capital plays a hegemonic role in the political economy.[1] In the second section, I advance an argument about the origins of the YVC movement, contending it was a 'subsidized public' with two main tributaries: 'extractive populist' groups funded by fossil capital, and far-right anti-immigrant groups emboldened by the 'Trump effect' (Gunster et al., 2021; Malm & the Zetkin Collective, 2021; Perry et al., 2019).[2] In the third section, I show how fossil capital began to lose control of the very movement it subsidized: YVC represented the fruition of fossil capital's extractive populist strategy of mobilizing a base of pro-oil and gas activists, but, as the base asserted its agency over the direction of the movement, pushing it further right, fossil capital lost control over demands and messaging, posing significant public relations risks. In the fourth section, I propose dividing fossil capital into class fractions based on size, and argue that doing so is useful for analysing fossil capital's relationship to the far right. I reflect on why 'big fossil capital' distanced itself from YVC, while segments of 'small fossil capital' funded and participated in the convoy. I conclude with brief notes on how the alliance between fossil capital and the far right has morphed in the years since United We Roll.

Fossil capitalism in Canada

The landlocked western province of Alberta is Canada's largest producer of natural gas, conventional oil and coal, and, most famously, is home to the third-largest proven oil reserves in the world in the form of bituminous sands, also known as oil or tar sands (Natural Resources Canada, 2016). Given the importance of oil to the province, Alberta is sometimes referred to as a 'first world petro-state' or 'petroculture', terms that attune us to the ways in which the economic dominance of oil in Alberta has ripple effects at the levels of politics, culture and ideology (Adkin, 2016b: 3; Wilson et al., 2017).

A key aspect of fossil capital's hegemony over Alberta is the premise that fossil fuel extraction is in the best interests of Albertans and Canadians in general, a concept captured by the phrase 'the Alberta Advantage'. According to Adkin (2016a: 78), the term, which was coined by conservative Premier Ralph Klein (1992–2006), is essentially a euphemism for neoliberal governance that stresses low taxes, limited government and a business-friendly regulatory environment, especially with regards to the oil and gas industry. The Alberta Advantage, a boisterous celebration of a neoliberal political culture premised on extractivism, lends credence to the widespread belief that Alberta is the 'heartland of Canadian conservatism' (Stewart & Sayers, 2013: 250).[3]

The political project of conservative Prime Minister Stephen Harper (2006–2015), who came out of the Alberta-based right-wing populist Reform

Party, has been characterized as the '"Albertization" of Canada' (Shrivastava & Stefanick, 2015: 19). Writing in the collection *Petrocultures: Oil, Politics, Culture*, Darin Barney conceptualizes the Harper era as an effort to graft oil extraction onto Canadian identity writ large, remaking the country into a 'pipeline nation' (2017: 88). While there is certainly a large segment of the Canadian population who embraced this material and ideological project, it also encountered intense opposition, especially from Indigenous peoples and environmentalists.[4]

This opposition helped foment an anti-Harper voting bloc, which coalesced around the Liberal Party of Canada, led by Justin Trudeau, who became Prime Minister in 2015 (Gibillini, 2015). While Trudeau has been superior to Stephen Harper on the climate file, his approach is characterized by what has been called a 'grand bargain', referring to Trudeau's insistence that Canada can simultaneously reduce its emissions and continue to develop the Alberta oil sands (Ballingall, 2021). Trudeau's approach to the climate crisis has therefore been characterized as 'the new denialism', meaning a form of climate denialism that does not deny the existence of anthropogenic climate change, but denies the policy implications of adequately mitigating it (Daub et al., 2021; Klein & Daub, 2016). In 2021, Trudeau's 'new denialism' resulted in Canada acquiring the dubious distinction of being the only G7 economy whose emissions have risen since signing the Paris Agreement, with the oil sands being largely to blame (Austen & Flavelle, 2021). And yet, despite his explicit support for the oil and gas industry, including the nationalization of the Trans Mountain oil sands pipeline, Trudeau's modest (and inadequate) climate policies have been met with fury from Canada's right wing.

Extractive populism and the Trump effect: subsidizing the Yellow Vests

For Gunster et al. (2021: 198), extractive populism is 'an emerging effort to position extractivism as under attack from elites, as an economic and political project that demands popular mobilization to defend, and as a democratic expression of the public will to fight for an industry that serves the common good'. Gunster et al. trace the origins of extractive populism to the Canadian Association of Petroleum Producers, the largest oil and gas industry association in Canada, which, in 2014, created a campaign called 'Canada's Energy Citizens' (CEC). Wood (2018) shows how CEC marked a conscious shift by the Canadian fossil fuel industry, which historically had relied primarily on lobbying to secure political influence, towards 'grassroots' mobilization.[5] The idea was to counter the environmental left by adopting its tactics and tools: petitions, letters to politicians and protests. Canada Action (CA), founded in 2010 as a small company making pro-oil and gas t-shirts, has grown into the most prolific extractive populist group in terms of the number of protests and events it has organized. Despite claiming to be 'grassroots', CA is backed by fossil capital, which donates to it, bulk orders its 'I Love Canadian Oil and Gas' merchandise, and encourages its employees to attend CA rallies (Linnitt, 2020; Markusoff, 2018).

Following Wood (2018) and Gunster et al.'s (2021) interpretation of CEC, I conceive of these extractive populist groups not as 'astroturf' (i.e., fake grassroots) but as a 'subsidized public', a term coined by Walker (2014) in his study of the political influence of public consultants and PR firms in the US. For Walker, the term 'subsidized public' refers to a phenomenon wherein 'corporations, trade associations, wealthy advocacy organizations, and campaign groups utilize the services of public affairs consultants to lower the costs of participation for targeted activist groups' (2014: 10). While the term 'astroturf' may be politically useful for drawing attention to the CEC and CA's corporate origins, it implies that participants in such groups are 'dupes, or hired guns', and ignores the extent to which such campaigns are willingly picked up by citizens (Wood, 2018: 78). Rather than view participants in such campaigns as victims of 'corporate ventrilo-quism', as Schneider et al. (2016: 5) term it, the concept of 'subsidized public' ascribes political agency to both the corporate backers of subsidized campaigns and the participants themselves, thereby encouraging researchers to explore participant motivations alongside those of corporations.

Throughout 2018, these extractive populist campaigns were holding increasingly well-attended rallies, especially in Alberta, where they counter-protested and outnumbered anti-pipeline protesters on a number of occasions and were picking up significant mainstream media attention (CBC News, 2018a, 2018c; Rieger, 2018). Towards the end of the year, when the *gilets jaunes* movement erupted in France, the extractive populist movement in Canada was reaching new heights in terms of on-the-ground organizing capacity and mobilization. In Alberta, truck convoys became a common form of protest in November and December, with attendance ranging from a few hundred vehicles to over a thousand at one particularly large event where Andrew Scheer, then-leader of the Conservative Party of Canada (CPC), spoke (CBC News, 2018b; Issawi, 2018, 2019). The main Yellow Vests Canada Facebook page was launched in early December, and soon many protesters were wearing yellow vests to attend these extractive populist protests, often organized by Canada Action, in addition to organizing their own weekly yellow vest protests every Saturday (Doherty, 2018; King, 2018).

In addition to these extractive populist groups, the other main tributary to the Yellow Vests Canada movement was a network of far-right anti-immigrant groups, emboldened by what Perry et al. (2019: 144) call 'the Trump effect', which refers to the increase in violent hate crimes and hate group activity in Canada following the election of Donald Trump in 2016. Indeed, according to Evan Balgord, Executive Director of the Canadian Anti-Hate Network, YVC 'is unique in that it is bringing together the anti-Muslim, alt-right neo-Nazi and ultra-conservative elements that make up the far-right movement but don't always play nicely together or overlap' (qtd in Metcalf, 2018). However, the Trump effect in Canada also refers to the rightward shift of mainstream electoral politics, especially with regards to the CPC, who seemed to view Trumpism with envy, and wished to emulate it (Perry et al., 2019: 158–159). In September 2018, the People's Party of Canada (PPC) splintered off of the CPC to form Canada's first far-right populist national political party, led by Maxime Bernier, who resigned from the CPC in 2017 after narrowly losing the leadership race to Andrew Scheer. In this context, with the electoral success of Trumpism and additional right-flank pressure being applied by the PPC, the CPC drifted further rightward, as exemplified by their opposition to the non-binding UN Migration Pact in late 2018, which they erroneously argued would infringe on Canada's sovereignty, thus playing into far-right conspiracies of a 'one-world government' and bringing such ideas to the mainstream (Coyne, 2018).

From Yellow Vests to United We Roll

In the discussion section of CA's Facebook event page for a 17 December 2018 rally, one participant commented, 'I'll be there. Are we doing the yellow vests thing?' CA responded, 'No yellow vests please. That's not what we are promoting!' One participant's response is instructive: 'ouch! The very people wearing the yellow vests are who truly support the pipelines.' CA did not want to be associated with the yellow vests, but the public they had subsidized into action insisted on heading in that direction. Against CA's wishes, yellow vests became a regular appearance at CA-organized protests (Antoneshyn, 2018).

CA spearheaded the original plan for a pro-oil and gas convoy to Ottawa, initially calling it the Resource Coalition Convoy (Brooks, 2019). When YVC made plans to support the convoy with their own contingent, CA would once again try to distance themselves. When asked about his move-ment's connections to YVC, Cody Battershill, the founder and lead spokes-person for CA, responded, 'There's been many things said by people wearing yellow vests that I think are horrible. There's no room for racism .... We gotta stay focused on staying positive, respectful, and non-partisan' (Ener-gyNow, 2019). Despite this, Canada Action intended to proceed with the convoy, knowing full well it would inevitably be joined by the yellow vests, as so many of their rallies had that winter (Jaremko, 2019).

Thus, Canada Action appears to have entered into a phase of trying to discipline and coordinate the messaging of the YVC convoy so as to avoid embarrassment for associating with them. In another interview, Battershill, referring to the YVC convoy, said, 'They've assured us that they're very much focused on energy and resources and pipelines, and I've just expressed to them that … for me personally I just look at the yellow vests as being a French thing from France. And I think we should stay focused on Canadian symbols' (Rieger, 2019). Battershill here belies his refusal to work with YVC, suggesting that he had been in dialogue with YVC activists to collaborate on messaging and symbolism. As we shall see, despite receiving assurances of YVC's willingness to stay on a united message with Canada Action, Battershill would be let down by his decidedly unpolished allies.

Battershill was not alone in making efforts to control the messaging of the twin convoys. He was joined by a chorus of elites, including journalists and politicians of all stripes, who aimed to discursively separate the 'good' elements of the movement from the 'bad' by encouraging the groups to focus their demands on energy and avoid the issues of immigration, the UN, 'globalism' and son on. Even Alberta New Democratic Party (NDP) leader, then-Premier Rachel Notley, participated in this discursive project of disciplining the movement. When asked by a reporter, 'What concerns do you have about the growing militancy of the yellow vest movement in Alberta?', Notley responded:

> Well, I'm not necessarily sure that it's growing, one way or the other as people become more and more aware of what some of the underpinnings of that movement are. You know, some of the folks that are working on putting together the convoy, the Canada Action group, I think that they're working very hard to provide a forum for working people. … We need to be reasonable and stick to the issues and not let these kinds of protests be taken over by people with more extreme views. (Hames, 2019)

That even Notley would come out in support of Canada Action's convoy displays the extent to which fossil capital has captured Albertan politicians. Notley tried to distinguish the 'good' convoy from the 'bad', refusing to concede the degree to which the two overlap. In doing so, Notley lends legitimacy to an industry-funded organization, name dropping and applauding the efforts of Canada Action (falsely claiming the group provides a forum driven by working people, rather than fossil capital) while failing to understand their role in fomenting the extractive populist movement that would soon sweep her from power.

Unlike the industry-funded convoy, whose message could be highly disciplined since it came from a hierarchical top-down structure using professionally made protest signs and messaging, YVC was a leaderless movement with activists who were often explicitly bigoted, conspiratorial and violent in their messaging. A typical CA sign, for example, might say, 'Bill C-69 is All Risk & No Reward', whereas a typical YVC sign might say, 'Trudeau for Treason' and depict a man hanging from a noose. While CA and elites like Notley clearly tried to discipline YVC's messaging, the latter proved impossible to control. Thus, on 14 January Canada Action cancelled the Resource Coalition convoy, leaving the YVC convoy to go it alone. Many activists who had signed up for the Canada Action convoy promptly switched to the YVC convoy after the former was cancelled, further demonstrating the fluidity and cross-pollination between the movements (Keller, 2019).

The YVC convoy itself, however, would quickly experience further divisions, as the key organizer, Glen Carritt, owner of an oilfield fire and safety company, split off to start yet another convoy to Ottawa. Carritt expressed a desire to make the rally accessible to all individuals, not just yellow vests, so left the YVC convoy and founded the United We Roll convoy. Carritt's project would end up attracting more support, and eventually the YVC convoy was cancelled altogether, and folded into United We Roll. Though the name change certainly suggests an attempt to distance the convoy from the yellow vests, on 9 February Carritt made it clear that, 'We still stand behind the "yellow vests," but whether you want to wear the yellow vest or not, we welcome all respectful, hard-working Canadians' (Keller, 2019). Despite yellow vesters still clearly being a welcome component of the movement, conservative politicians lined up in support of United We Roll and both the leaders of the CPC and PPC went on to give speeches at the final rally in Ottawa.

Cillia & McCurdy (2020: 673–675) observe that the mainstream media provided similar social cover for the convoy. While right-wing outlets like Post Media explicitly praised the convoy, liberal mainstream media followed a pattern that echoed efforts to separate the good parts of the movement from the bad, providing some critical coverage of the convoy's associations with the xenophobic and far-right YVC movement, while providing generally uncritical coverage of the movement's association with industry, and thereby upholding the hegemonic interests of fossil capital. The Canadian Anti-Hate Network, on the other hand, argues that the mainstream media's coverage of the convoy ignored the hundreds of examples of overt racism and death threats directed at Muslim Canadians on YVC social media, and thereby whitewashed the convoy as driven by 'legitimate economic concerns' and not hate (Canadian Anti-Hate Network, 2019). However, this latter critique overlooks the extent to which climate denialism and its twin, fossil fuel boosterism, are far from being expressions of legitimate economic concerns, but have instead become central to the political project of the contemporary far right, as recent scholarly research has begun to uncover (Forchtner et al., 2018; Hultman et al., 2019; Malm & the Zetkin Collective, 2021). By trying to separate out the movement's racism from its fossil fuel boosterism, politicians and mainstream media dangerously legitimized the climate denialist aspects of the movement. Inversely, in its attempt to discredit the movement, the Canadian Anti-Hate Network strategically downplayed its fossil fuel boosterism, and claimed the movement was mainly an anti-immigrant one. The downside to this strategy, though, is that it does not challenge the legitimacy of fossil fuel boosterism and climate denialism, and overlooks the extent to which they have become key planks of the far right's political worldview, and themselves constitute a type of fascistic politics.

On the role of small fossil capital

Fossil capital needs ideologies of racialized and gendered hierarchies to complement its drive for accumulation, and so the far right is, in some ways, a logical political home for it. Preston (2017), for example, describes the tar sands as 'racial extractivism', drawing attention to the ways in which tar sands extraction is predicated on the white supremacist and settler colonial dispossession of Indigenous peoples. Similarly, Daggett (2018) uses the term 'petro-masculinity' to highlight the ways in which misogyny, whiteness and fossil capitalist extractivism are materially and ideologically linked. As she puts it, 'privileged subjectivities are oil-soaked'; the combustion of fossil fuels has historically been primarily to the benefit of white men, and they are relatively well insulated from the immediate effects of climate change, so it only makes sense that they form the core demographic of climate denialism (Daggett, 2018: 27; Krange et al., 2019; McCright & Dunlap, 2011).

Despite fossil capital's need for these aspects of far-right ideology, there are political and reputational risks associated with openly allying with the far right, and these risks must be managed. Despite a decade of the Harper government shifting the country right, Canada maintains a commitment to and popular support for multiculturalism, which Ambrose and Mudde (2015) credit with preventing the rise of a Canadian far-right political party. While the creation of the PPC has ended Canada's exceptionalism in that regard, the party remains relatively marginal, having failed, despite a rise in its vote total, to win a single seat in the September 2021 election. Meanwhile, public polling continues to suggest the majority of Canadians support immigration (Neuman, 2021). In the context of popular support for multiculturalism, fossil capital risks being perceived as bigoted or even 'un-Canadian' by openly allying itself with the far right. This appears to have been part of the calculation made by Canada Action in navigating its relationship with the very public it subsidized. However, fossil capital is not a monolith, and, while Canada Action eventually chose to distance itself from the convoy, other segments of fossil capital got closer.

While fossil capital is a class fraction of capital (see note 1), fossil capital can itself be divided into further class fractions, and these categories have analytical importance for the study of the far right in Canada. Statistics Canada defines the size of a business based on how many employees it has: small (1 to 99 employees), medium (100 to 499 employees) and large (500 or more employees) (Government of Canada, n. d.). I propose that these demarcations could form the basis of an attempt to distinguish between small, medium and big fossil capital, and argue that these distinctions, particularly between big and small, are a useful heuristic for understanding fossil capital's relationship to the far right.

Most critical discussion of the industry's role in fuelling climate change (and climate denialism) focuses attention on big fossil capital. There are good reasons for this, and attention to the ownership of the Alberta tar sands demonstrates why. In 2017, the 'Big Five' companies of Canadian oil and gas collectively owned 79.4 per cent of Canada's bitumen production capacity (Hussey et al., 2021: 38).[6] Such production capacity means this 'oligopolistic core' of companies controls obscene levels of wealth (in 2017, their gross profit was greater than the province of Alberta's revenue for that year), which allows them to make investment decisions that shape the entire industry, 'effectively exerting control over the myriad of small and medium-sized service firms that depend on their activities' (Hussey et al., 2021: 40–41). Thus, from a climate perspective, big Canadian fossil capital deserves to be the focus of attention and admonition: the assets that big fossil capital controls could make or break Canada's climate change mitigation efforts, and, as we have seen, through its reach into civil society with extractive populist groups like Canada Action and the Canadian Association of Petroleum Producers, big fossil capital plays a key role in fomenting climate denialism and delay. Less attention, however, has been paid to the role of small fossil capital.

Upon reviewing the many photographs I had taken on the day of the United We Roll convoy rally in Ottawa, I started to take note of the company names printed on the convoy trucks: the Big Four were nowhere to be seen. Instead, the convoy was dominated by small and medium-sized businesses.[7] In order to pull off a protest convoy of industrial vehicles, one first requires access to these vehicles, access that regular workers do not have. In at least one case that I know of, a driver was actually being paid by their boss to participate in the convoy.[8] Other drivers would either have received their boss's permission to take a company truck (an explicit sign of endorsement of the event) or were themselves small business owners. Indeed, one of the lead organizers of the convoy, Glen Carritt, owns an oilfield fire and safety company – OP Fire & Rescue – and drove the convoy's lead truck. In addition to drawing its participants from the ranks of small business, the convoy was directly funded by small companies, including many oil and gas service companies, who gave large amounts in their own name to the convoy's GoFundMe page.[9] The participation of small businesses in the convoy raises important questions for scholars of climate change and the far right concerning the role of the petite bourgeoisie in funding denial and supporting fascistic politics.

Scholars of fascism and the far right note the importance of the petite bourgeoisie as the class base for far-right political movements, including classical fascism and contemporary right-wing populism in the US and Canada (Davidson, 2015; Perry et al., 2019: 147). The list of businesses which participated in or donated to the convoy shows that the petite bourgeoisie of fossil capital did, indeed, form a key base of support for the far-right United We Roll convoy. Small fossil capital was seemingly more comfortable than big fossil capital with being publicly connected to the movement. As I have suggested, this is partially because big fossil capital has more to lose in terms of its reputation. It may also be because, as a registered non-profit, CA's activities need to be non-partisan; thus, YVC's constant demonization of and death threats towards Trudeau may have posed potential legal risks.

Is it possible, however, that small fossil capital (and perhaps privileged segments of what Malm & the Zetkin Collective (2021) call the 'fossilized proletariat') are more reactionary than big fossil capital? This is a puzzle for future research to solve, so I will only offer some brief speculation. For big fossil capitalists, ensconced in their glass office towers and removed from the spatial and temporal rhythms of extraction, the only goal is abstract surplus-value. Small fossil capitalists, on the other hand, who often own *and operate* their businesses, are on-the-ground: driving trucks, laying pipe, getting their hands dirty, enmeshed in and committed to the materiality of fossil capitalism as a way of life and as an identity. While much attention is paid to big fossil capital's role in fuelling climate denialism, big fossil capitalists are, by definition, few in number, and cannot by themselves muster the street forces required for something so ominous as 'fossil fascism' (Malm & the Zetkin Collective, 2021). Those studying the political ecology of the far right would do well to turn their attention towards the class fractions likely to make up the shock troops of fossil fascism. Small fossil capitalists, unable to accept the loss of livelihood and fearing for their class status, all too eagerly swallow climate denialist conspiracies. After one conspiratorial pill is taken, it becomes easier to take more.

Beyond United We Roll

Since YVC plateaued with the United We Roll convoy, the movement has largely abandoned the yellow vest as a symbol but has moved on to other campaigns and demands. When the CPC failed to unseat Justin Trudeau in the October 2019 election, anger in Alberta boiled over, fuelling Wexit (a pun on Brexit), a movement whose key demand is that western provinces separate and form a new country. The Wexit movement, whose slogan was 'Make Alberta Great Again', attracted many former YVC activists (including Wexit's founder, Peter Downing) and would fuel the creation of a number of new western separatist political parties, most notably the Wildrose Independence Party of Alberta, which at one point rose to 20 per cent in provincial polling (Fournier, 2021).

The United We Roll brand continued past the initial convoy. In February 2020, when the Indigenous-led anti-fossil fuel movement #ShutDownCanada was spreading across the country in solidarity with the Wet'suwet'en struggle against the Coastal GasLink pipeline, Canada Action spent $21,000 on Facebook ads denouncing the protest blockades, second only to Coastal GasLink itself (Rocha et al., 2020). Once again proving willing to be the street forces for big fossil capital, United We Roll planned to travel to and intimidate a rail blockade established by Indigenous and climate activists west of Edmonton. By the time they arrived on the afternoon of 19 February, other counter-protesters had already dismantled the blockade, forcing the Indigenous and climate activists to leave. United We Roll did a 'victory lap' around the vicinity and posed for a picture on the now-cleared rail line with Canada Action-inspired signs reading, 'I Love Canadian Energy' (Ramsay, 2020).

During the pandemic, many former yellow vesters became part of the anti-lockdown, anti-mask and anti-vaccine 'Freedom movement', which culminated in the Freedom Convoy in February 2022, labelled by the Canadian Anti-Hate Network as 'United We Roll 2.0' (Anderson, 2021; Canadian Anti-Hate Network, 2022). Extractive populist groups like Canada Action, on the other hand, held off on organizing protests and rallies during the pandemic. Even now, with almost all restrictions lifted, there are few signs that the pro-oil and gas street movement is close to returning to its 2018–2019 peak. There are some signs, however, that the Freedom movement is morphing into a movement against climate policies, such as a February 2023 protest in Alberta against 15-minute cities (Green, 2023). The innocuous urban planning concept, which aims to have all life's necessities and amenities within a 15-minute walk, has, like the carbon tax, the migration compact and public health restrictions before it, come to be seen by the far right through the lens of the globalist conspiracy theory – that is, as yet another manifestation of a tyrannical, socialist plot to restrict individual freedoms. At the time of writing, though, the Freedom movement in Alberta is largely focused on electoral politics; having successfully ousted Jason Kenney as Premier, they are working to ensure the UCP's new far-right leader, Danielle Smith, defeats the NDP in the May 2023 election (Magusiak, 2023). Regardless of whether she receives a mandate from Albertans, Smith's premiership and the social forces behind her rise will be a fruitful case for further studies of fossil capitalism and the Canadian far right.

Notes

1 Malm & the Zetkin Collective (2021) distinguish between fossil capital and primitive fossil capital. They follow Malm's earlier work, where he uses the term 'fossil capital' to refer to all capital that relies on fossil fuel combustion in order to accumulate surplus-value (Malm, 2016: 279–326). Malm & the Zetkin Collective (2021: 16) build on and refine this term by distinguishing primitive fossil capital as the class fraction of fossil capital that locates, extracts, refines and transports fossil fuels to market. For the purposes of this chapter, I use the term 'fossil capital' to refer to primitive fossil capital. In this formulation, then, fossil capital is a class fraction of capital in general, and capital in general remains reliant on fossil fuel combustion for accumulation.
2 I define the terms 'subsidized public', 'extractive populist' and 'Trump effect' below.
3 Alberta was governed by conservative parties for an uninterrupted 80 years: the Alberta Social Credit Party (from 1935–1971) and the Progressive Conservative Association of Alberta (from 1971–2015). In the 2015 election, the right-wing vote was split between Progressive Conservatives and the further-right Wildrose Party, which the social democratic Alberta New Democratic Party exploited on its path to victory. In 2017, however, the Progressive Conservatives and Wildrose would merge, forming the United Conservative Party, which swept the New Democrats from power in 2019.
4 For more on Indigenous-led social movement opposition to the tar sands, see the excellent collection, *A Line in the Tar Sands: Struggles for Environmental Justice* (Black et al., 2014).
5 While I agree with Gunster et al. and Wood about the significance of CEC's grassroots turn, neither mention the Ethical Oil Institute, which was operational from 2011 to 2014 and which, I think, should be viewed as a predecessor, even a pioneer, of extractive populist discourse, though it did not adopt the on-the-ground organizational tactics of later groups like CEC and Canada Action. For more on

the Ethical Oil Institute and its ties to CPC staffers and far-right ideologue Ezra Levant (founder of Rebel News), see CBC News (2014).

6 With Cenovus purchasing Husky, the 'Big Five' are now the 'Big Four': Suncor, Canadian Natural Resources Limited, Imperial Oil and Cenovus.

7 Small fossil capitalists included: DD2, Jerry Mainil Ltd, Johner Oilfield Construction, MasTec Canada, OP Fire & Rescue, Pongo Holdings Ltd, Schell Equipment and Tankers Transfer Services. Other small capitalists included: Hamilton Haulage and Landscaping, Kel-Can Mechanical Ltd, National Motor Coach Systems Ltd, Stu's Trucking, Summit Motors Ltd and The Tree Whisperer. Note: this list is not comprehensive, but rather pulled from photographs the author took of the convoy's Ottawa rally.

8 This was told to me by a journalist who covered the convoy, and who interviewed numerous participants.

9 List of companies among top donors to United We Roll, retrieved from GoFundMe, which shows the top donations to any campaign: Alberta Auto and Truck Repair Inc., Black Gold Fishing Services, CD Oilwell Servicing Ltd, Collicutt Energy, Connate Water Solutions Inc., DAZ Management Inc., DHH Dynamic Heavy Haul Ltd, Drewberry Hotel Yellow Vests Lloyminster, Ensign Energy (the only big fossil capitalist company to donate in its own name), PipeSak Incorporated, Starco Ag. Ltd and Subterra HDD.

References

Adkin, L. (2016a). Alberta's Neoliberal Environment. In Laurie E. Adkin (ed.), *First World Petro-politics: The Political Ecology and Governance of Alberta*. Toronto: University of Toronto Press, pp. 78–113.

Adkin, L. (ed.) (2016b). *First World Petro-politics: The Political Ecology and Governance of Alberta*. Toronto: University of Toronto Press.

Ambrose, E., & Mudde, C. (2015). Canadian Multiculturalism and the Absence of the Far Right. *Nationalism and Ethnic Politics*, 21(2): 213–236.

Anderson, D. (2021). COVID denialism and the Alberta context. *CBC News*, 16 January, www.cbc.ca/news/canada/calgary/covid-denialism-conspiracy-masks-alberta-1.5874969 (accessed 1 November 2023).

Antoneshyn, A. (2018). Hundreds of oil supporters rally in central Alta. *CTV Edmonton*, 29 December, https://edmonton.ctvnews.ca/hundreds-of-oil-supporters-rally-in-central-alta-1.4234874 (accessed 1 November 2023).

Austen, I., & Flavelle, C. (2021). Trudeau was a global climate hero. Now Canada risks falling behind. *New York Times*, 21 April, www.nytimes.com/2021/04/21/world/canada/trudeau-climate-oil-sands.html (accessed 1 November 2023).

Ballingall, A. (2021). Justin Trudeau said Canadians could have it all on energy and the environment. It isn't working. *Thestar.Com*, 21 January, www.thestar.com/politics/federal/2021/01/21/justin-trudeau-said-canadians-could-have-it-all-on-energy-and-the-environment-it-isnt-working.html (accessed 1 November 2023).

Barney, D. (2017). Who We Are and What We Do: Canada as a Pipeline Nation. In S. Wilson, A. Carlson & I. Szeman (eds), *Petrocultures: Oil, Politics, Culture*. Montreal: McGill-Queen's University Press, pp. 78–119.

Bejar-Garcia, C. (2020). France's Yellow Vest Movement and the global debate on climate change. *Harvard International Review*, 28 April, https://hir.harvard.edu/frances-yellow-vest-movement-and-the-global-debate-on-climate-change/ (accessed 1 November 2023).

Black, T., D'Arcy, S., & Weis, T. (eds) (2014). *A Line in the Tar Sands: Struggles for Environmental Justice*. Toronto: PM Press.

Brooks, S. (2019). Resource Coalition Convoy heading to Ottawa in February. *Energeticcity.ca – Local News from Northeast B.C.*, 4 January, https://energeticcity.ca/2019/01/04/resource-coalition-convoy-heading-to-ottawa-in-february/ (accessed 1 November 2023).

Canadian Anti-Hate Network (2019). Factcheck: CBC misrepresents Yellow Vests Canada Movement, makes no mention of death threats. *Canadian Anti-Hate Network*, 14 February, www.antihate.ca/factcheck_cbc_misrepresents_yellow_vests_canada_movement_makes_no_mention_of_death_threats (accessed 1 November 2023).

Canadian Anti-Hate Network (2022). The 'Freedom Convoy' is nothing but a vehicle for the far right. *Canadian Anti-Hate Network*, 27 January, www.antihate.ca/the_freedom_convoy_is_nothing_but_a_vehicle_for_the_far_right (accessed 1 November 2023).

CBC News (2014). Greenpeace calls for Elections Canada probe of ethical oil. *CBC News*, 8 April, www.cbc.ca/news/politics/greenpeace-calls-for-elections-canada-probe-of-ethical-oil-1.2602284 (accessed 1 November 2023).

CBC News (2018a). Alberta is in 'crisis' over low energy prices, Trudeau acknowledges, as thousands protest in Calgary. *CBC News*, 22 November, www.cbc.ca/news/canada/calgary/justin-trudeau-calgary-financial-downturn-frustration-1.4916309 (accessed 1 November 2023).

CBC News (2018b). 'We will not stop': truck convoy, rally in Nisku show support for oil and gas industry. *CBC News*, 23 December, www.cbc.ca/news/canada/edmonton/town-hall-andrew-scheer-nisku-convoy-truckers-pipeline-oil-and-gas-1.4952283 (accessed 1 November 2023).

CBC News (2018c). Albertans rally against 'problematic' Bill C-69. *CBC News*, 12 October, www.cbc.ca/news/canada/calgary/alberta-bill-c69-rally-1.4859917 (accessed 1 November 2023).

Chrisafis, A. (2018). Who are the gilets jaunes and what do they want? *The Guardian*, 7 December, www.theguardian.com/world/2018/dec/03/who-are-the-gilets-jaunes-and-what-do-they-want (accessed 1 November 2023).

Cigainero, J. (2018). Who are France's Yellow vest protesters, and what do they want? *NPR*, 3 December, www.npr.org/2018/12/03/672862353/who-are-frances-yellow-vest-protesters-and-what-do-they-want (accessed 1 November 2023).

Cillia, B. D., & McCurdy, P. (2020). No Surrender. No Challenge. No Protest Paradigm: A Content Analysis of the Canadian News Media Coverage of the 'Yellow Vest Movement' and the 'United We Roll Convoy.' *Canadian Review of Sociology/Revue Canadienne de Sociologie*, 57(4): 656–680. doi.org/10.1111/cars.12304.

Coyne, A. (2018). Andrew Scheer steers hard to right on UN migrants pact. *National Post*, 5 December, https://nationalpost.com/news/canada/andrew-coyne-andrew-scheer-steers-hard-to-right-on-un-migrants-pact (accessed 1 November 2023).

Daggett, C. (2018). Petro-masculinity: Fossil Fuels and Authoritarian Desire. *Millennium*, 47(1): 25–44.

Daub, S., Blue, G., Yunker, Z., & Rajewicz, L. (2021). Episodes in the New Climate Denialism. In W. K. Carroll (ed.), *Regime of Obstruction: How Corporate Power Blocks Energy Democracy*. Edmonton: Athabasca University Press, pp. 225–248.

Davidson, N. (2015). The Far-Right and 'the Needs of Capital'. In R. Saull, A. Anievas, N. Davidson & A. Fabry (eds), *The Longue Durée of the Far-Right: An International Historical Sociology*. Abingdon: Routledge, pp. 129–152.

Doherty, B. (2018). Hundreds protest at Calgary pro-oil rally as Nenshi insists 'this isn't about entitled Albertans'. *Thestar.Com*, 17 December, www.thestar.com/calgary/2018/12/17/calgary-pro-oil-rally-to-kick-off-at-city-hall-at-noon.html (accessed 1 November 2023).

EnergyNow (2019). Cody Battershill – discussing the upcoming Official the Resource Coalition Convoy to Ottawa!, *EnergyNow*, 7 January, www.youtube.com/watch?v=BmTwe4N1xP4 (accessed 1 November 2023).

Forchtner, B., Kroneder, A., & Wetzel, D. (2018). Being Skeptical? Exploring Far-Right Climate-Change Communication in Germany. *Environmental Communication*, 12(5): 589–604.

Fournier, P. J. (2021). The splintering of the right in Alberta: 338Canada. *Macleans. Ca*, 16 June www.macleans.ca/politics/338canada-the-splintering-of-the-right-in-alberta/ (accessed 1 November 2023).

Gibillini, N. (2015). 'Harper awoke a sleeping giant': First Nations break election records. *CTVNews*, 20 October, www.ctvnews.ca/politics/election/harper-awoke-a-sleeping-giant-first-nations-break-election-records-1.2619227 (accessed 1 November 2023).

Government of Canada (n. d.). Key small business statistics – November 2019 – SME research and statistics. *Innovation, Science and Economic Development Canada*, www.ic.gc.ca/eic/site/061.nsf/eng/h_03114.html#1.1 (accessed 16 August 2021).

Green, A. C. (2023). Yegunited protests 15 minute cities in Edmonton. *Alberta Report*, 10 February, www.westernstandard.news/alberta/yegunited-protests-15-minute-cities-in-edmonton/article_60c96d48-a97d-11ed-ab80-6fe8798210db.html (accessed 1 November 2023).

Gunster, S., Neubauer, R., Bermingham, J., & Massie, A. (2021). 'Our Oil': Extractive Populism in Canadian Social Media. In W. K. Carroll (ed.), *Regime of Obstruction: How Corporate Power Blocks Energy Democracy*. Edmonton: Athabasca University Press, pp. 197–224.

Hames, E. (2019). Don't dismiss them as 'crackpots': who are Canada's yellow vest protesters? *CBC News*, 11 January, www.cbc.ca/news/canada/edmonton/yellow-vests-canada-alberta-1.4974721 (accessed 1 November 2023).

Hultman, M., Björk, A., & Viinikka, T. (2019). Far-Right and Climate Change Denial: Denouncing Environmental Challenges via Anti-establishment Rhetoric, Marketing of Doubts, Industrial/Breadwinner Masculinities Enactments and

Ethno-nationalism. In B. Forchtner (ed.), *The Far Right and the Environment: Politics, Discourse and Communication*. London: Routledge, pp. 121–135.

Hussey, I., Pineault, É., Jackson, E., & Cake, S. (2021). Boom, Bust and Consolidation: Corporate Restructuring in the Alberta Oil Sands. In W. K. Carroll (ed.), *Regime of Obstruction: How Corporate Power Blocks Energy Democracy*. Edmonton: Athabasca University Press, pp. 35–59.

Issawi, H. (2018). Massive pro-pipeline rally and truck convoy in Nisku snarl traffic on QEII Highway. *Thestar.Com*, 19 December, www.thestar.com/edmonton/2018/12/19/massive-pro-pipeline-rally-and-truck-convoy-in-nisku-causes-massive-delays-on-qeii-highway.html (accessed 1 November 2023).

Issawi, H. (2019). Pro-oil convoy sets course for Ottawa to protest carbon pricing, among other things. *Thestar.Com*, 14 February, www.thestar.com/news/canada/2019/02/14/one-convoy-to-pool-them-all-pro-oil-caravan-sets-course-for-ottawa.html (accessed 1 November 2023).

Jaremko, D. (2019). Online confusion about convoys to Ottawa reveals different organizer priorities. *JWN Energy*, 5 January, www.dailyoilbulletin.com/article/2019/1/7/online-confusion-about-convoys-to-ottawa-reveals-d/ (accessed 1 November 2023).

Keller, J. (2019). Canadian 'yellow vests' join in anti-government convoy: protestors inspired by the French cause have faced scrutiny in Alberta and other parts of the country. *The Globe and Mail*, 9 February, A.16.

King, M. (2018). Calgary yellow vest protesters target economy, immigration at rally – Calgary. *Globalnews.ca*, 15 December, https://globalnews.ca/news/4766936/calgary-yellow-vest-rally/ (accessed 1 November 2023).

Kipfer, S. (2019). What Colour is Your Vest? Reflections on the Yellow Vest Movement in France. *Studies in Political Economy*, 100(3): 209–231.

Klein, S., & Daub, S. (2016). The new climate denialism: time for an intervention. *Policy Note*, 22 September, www.policynote.ca/the-new-climate-denialism-time-for-an-intervention/ (accessed 1 November 2023).

Krange, O., Kaltenborn, B. P., & Hultman, M. (2019). Cool Dudes in Norway: Climate Change Denial among Conservative Norwegian Men. *Environmental Sociology*, 5(1): 1–11. doi.org/10.1080/23251042.2018.1488516.

Linnitt, C. (2020). 'Grassroots' oil and gas advocacy group Canada Action received $100,000 from ARC Resources. *The Narwhal*, 24 June, https://thenarwhal.ca/canada-action-received-100-thousand-from-arc-resources/ (accessed 1 November 2023).

Lucardi, A., & Brancati, D. (2019). Yellow vest protests erupt in Iraq, Bulgaria and beyond – but don't expect a 'yellow wave'. *The Conversation*, 5 February, http://theconversation.com/yellow-vest-protests-erupt-in-iraq-bulgaria-and-beyond-but-dont-expect-a-yellow-wave-110692 (accessed 1 November 2023).

Magusiak, S. (2023). Here are the right-wing political action groups organizing to help Danielle Smith win Alberta's next election. *PressProgress*, 19 January, https://pressprogress.ca/here-are-the-right-wing-political-action-groups-organizing-to-help-danielle-smith-win-albertas-next-election/ (accessed 1 November 2023).

Malm, A. (2016). *Fossil Capital: The Rise of Steam Power and the Roots of Global Warming*. London: Verso Books.

Malm, A., & the Zetkin Collective (2021). *White Skin, Black Fuel: On the Danger of Fossil Fascism*. London: Verso Books.

Markusoff, J. (2018). Alberta's handful of anti-pipeline protesters wage a lonely war. *Macleans.Ca*, 26 May, www.macleans.ca/news/canada/albertas-handful-of-anti-pipeline-protestors-wage-a-lonely-war/ (accessed 1 November 2023).

McCright, A. M., & Dunlap, R. E. (2011). Cool Dudes: The Denial of Climate Change among Conservative White Males in the United States. *Global Environmental Change*, 21(4): 1163–1172. doi.org/10.1016/j.gloenvcha.2011.06.003.

Mehling, M. (2018). Emmanuel Macron's carbon tax sparked gilets jaunes protests, but popular climate policy is possible. *The Conversation*, 10 December, http://theconversation.com/emmanuel-macrons-carbon-tax-sparked-gilets-jaunes-protests-but-popular-climate-policy-is-possible-108437 (accessed 1 November 2023).

Metcalf, K. (2018). Yellow Vests Canada: the far right go high visibility. *Ricochet*, 17 December, https://ricochet.media/en/2461 (accessed 1 November 2023).

Mosleh, O. (2018). Two detained after clash between yellow vests and counter protesters outside Alberta Legislature. *Thestar.Com*, 5 December, www.thestar.com/edmonton/2018/12/15/yellow-vests-clash-with-counter-protestors-at-alberta-legislature-and-churchill-square.html (accessed 1 November 2023).

Mussett, B. (2019). What it's like monitoring Canada's Yellow Vest Movement every day. *VICE*, 8 May, www.vice.com/en_ca/article/9kxkwp/what-its-like-monitoring-canadas-yellow-vest-movement-every-day (accessed 1 November 2023).

Natural Resources Canada (2016). Oil resources. *Natural Resources Canada*, 11 February, www.nrcan.gc.ca/energy/energy-sources-distribution/crude-oil/oil-resources/18085 (accessed 1 November 2023).

Neuman, K. (2021). Canadian public opinion about immigration and refugees – Fall 2021 (Focus Canada). *Environics Institute for Survey Research*, www.environicsinstitute.org/projects/project-details/canadian-public-opinion-about-immigration-and-refugees---fall-2021 (accessed 1 November 2023).

Perry, B., Scrivens, R., & Mirrlees, T. (2019). Epilogue: The Trump Effect on Right-Wing Extremism in Canada. In B. Perry & R. Scrivens. *Right-Wing Extremism in Canada*. Cham: Springer, pp. 143–172.

Preston, J. (2017). Racial Extractivism and White Settler Colonialism: An Examination of the Canadian Tar Sands Mega-projects. *Cultural Studies*, 31(2–3): 353–375.

Ramsay, C. (2020). Counter-protesters tear down CN rail blockade in west Edmonton. *Global News*, 19 February, https://globalnews.ca/news/6568202/wetsuweten-rail-blockade-edmonton-acheson-industrial-area/ (accessed 1 November 2023).

Rieger, S. (2018). Anti- and pro-pipeline rallies face off as Enbridge shareholders meet in Calgary. *CBC News*, 10 May, www.cbc.ca/news/canada/calgary/line-3-protest-calgary-1.4656242 (accessed 1 November 2023).

Rieger, S. (2019). Duel of the convoys as yellow vests and Canada Action both set sights on Ottawa. *CBC News*, 8 January, www.cbc.ca/news/canada/calgary/alberta-pipeline-convoys-1.4969238 (accessed 1 November 2023).

Rocha, R., Yates, J., & Bellemare, A. (2020). Groups linked to oil companies funded Facebook ads denouncing the rail blockades. *CBC News*, 4 March, www.cbc.ca/news/canada/coastal-gas-link-rail-blockades-facebook-1.5484039 (accessed 1 November 2023).

Schneider, J., Schwarze, S., Bsumek, P. K., & Peeples, J. (2016). *Under Pressure: Coal Industry Rhetoric and Neoliberalism*. London: Palgrave Macmillan.

Shrivastava, M., & Stefanick, L. (2015). Introduction: Framing the Debate on Democracy and Governance in an Oil-Exporting Economy. In M. Shrivastava & L. Stefanick (eds), *Alberta Oil and the Decline of Democracy in Canada*. Edmonton: Athabasca University Press, pp. 3–28.

Stewart, D. K., & Sayers, A. M. (2013). Albertans' Conservative Beliefs. In J. Farney & D. Rayside (eds), *Conservatism in Canada*. Toronto: University of Toronto Press, pp. 249–267.

Walker, E. T. (2014). *Grassroots for Hire: Public Affairs Consultants in American Democracy*. Cambridge: Cambridge University Press.

Wilson, S., Szeman, I., & Carlson, A. (2017). On Petrocultures: Or, Why We Need to Understand Oil to Understand Everything Else. In S. Wilson, A. Carlson & I. Szeman (eds), *Petrocultures: Oil, Politics, Culture*. Montreal: McGill-Queen's Press, pp. 3–19.

Wood, T. (2018). Energy's Citizens: The Making of a Canadian Petro-public. *Canadian Journal of Communication*, 43(1): 75–92.

5

Thunberg, not iceberg: visual melodrama in German far-right climate change communication

Bernhard Forchtner

Icebergs and icescapes have long been iconic in climate imagery (O'Neill, 2020) – imagery which has recently been complemented by representations of the climate activist Greta Thunberg. Such imagery is of particular relevance in our increasingly mediatized world in which the persuasive nature of visuals is often taken for granted. Indeed, this persuasiveness is pointedly summarized by Joffe (2008: 86), who argues that a visual 'is emotive, absorbed in an unmediated fashion, vivid and memorable, and "proves" the authenticity of the event depicted'. It is due to these characteristics that scholars in the fields of environmental/climate change communication have increasingly analysed the uses of imagery (for reviews, see Hansen, 2018; O'Neill & Smith, 2014).

Yet, while substantial research on environmental/climate change-related imagery exists, and while there has long been research on visual analysis of far-right communication (for recent examples, see Doerr, 2021; Hokka & Nelimarkka, 2020; Freistein & Gadinger, 2020), the emerging field of study on environmental/climate change communication by the contemporary far right (Mudde, 2019) is only now beginning to take a 'visual turn' (see Forchtner, 2023). Such analysis is, however, crucial as visuals play a leading role in propagating, maintaining and bolstering far-right ideologies (their problem definitions, interpretations and solutions) in society at large, including anti-progressive environmentalist attitudes and worldviews. Indeed, images not only convey knowledge and articulate (far-right) subjectivities, but construct 'appropriate' emotions too as Joffe, in the above quote, makes clear. And, as we shall see, images of Greta Thunberg, rather than icebergs, appear to play a crucial role.

Against this background, this chapter proposes a pathway forward into analysis of environmental imagery to deepen our understanding of how visuals operate in furthering far-right agendas at this crucial moment in time. More specifically, the chapter does so by providing a case study of the German far right. This case promises relevant insights in light of Germany's lively contemporary far right, particularly the recent emergence of Alternative für Deutschland (AfD), and a long history of (research on) imagining and politicizing the link between nation and nature in far-right frames. This stretches from the nineteenth century to the early twentieth century, and furthermore includes National Socialism (with its complex, contradictory history regarding environmental aspects), and renewed efforts to 'make ecology right again' during the second half of the twentieth century as well as the early twenty-first century (see Biehl & Staudenmaier, 1995; Geden, 1996; Olsen, 1999; Forchtner & Özvatan, 2019). In analysing the German far right, this chapter furthermore proposes a mixed-methods architecture which can serve as a starting point for further analyses of visual environmental communication by the far right. Drawing on wider visual environmental communication research, this is achieved by taking three complementary perspectives (from quantitative content and frame analysis to qualitative semiotic analysis), and asking the following research questions: 'Which themes dominate far-right visual climate change communication?', 'What frames are utilized in the investigated communication?' and 'How are knowledge and subjectivities constructed via these images?'

Responding to these questions, this chapter, first, introduces proposed methods of data collection and data analysis. Secondly, it analyses the corpus of images from three perspectives, considering themes, frames and semiotic details. This analysis illustrates that, for example, the German far right is considerably invested in Othering Thunberg and what she represents, clearly trumping concern over icebergs. Here, I draw on the concept of melodrama, which I will elucidate later, to understand far-right meaning making, thus adding to existing scholarship by discussing how melodramatic Othering is *visually* constructed. The chapter closes with a summary of findings.

Methodology

This analysis of visual climate change communication draws on images taken from five key print media across the German far-right spectrum over a period of 18 months, from July 2018 to December 2019. These sources are instrumental in the ideological reproduction of significant parts of the far right in Germany and include: the least extreme, weekly *Junge Freiheit* (Young Freedom), of which, because of the high number of articles published, I only consider texts from the front page and its focus, background, forum, and nature and technology pages. *Junge Freiheit* is accompanied by the monthly *Compact* and the monthly *Zuerst!* (First!) – all three support the AfD (in varying ways). Also included are the monthly party newspaper of the extreme-right National Democratic Party of Germany (since 2023: The

Homeland), *Deutsche Stimme* (German Voice) and the ecological quarterly *Umwelt & Aktiv* (Environment & Active; ideologically and personally, the magazine was connected to the National Democratic Party of Germany and closed at the end of 2019). Given the explorative nature of this case study, this corpus will be analysed as one instead of considering these sources separately, though it is worth noting that subsequent studies should address potential differences between rather radical and rather extreme actors (as well as between, for example, party and non-party actors).

More specifically, this corpus comprised regular articles, short columns and advertisements for previous issues (while excluding book reviews and letters to the editors) which featured 'climate' (e.g. *Klimawandel* [climate change] and *Klimaerwärmung* [climate warming]) and/or 'CO_2' in the title, the lead paragraph or as superimposed writing in the title image. Consequently, terms such as 'energy transition', 'diesel', 'ecology' and 'Thunberg' alone were not considered sufficient. This kept the corpus concerned with the general phenomenon, thus avoiding a biased set of data as, for example 'Thunberg' would have introduced a particular focus. The period investigated is realizable in the context of one chapter, enables analysis of climate change communication prior to the outbreak of COVID-19, and includes key events, such as the rise of Thunberg/the Fridays for Future movement and the European Parliament elections in May 2019. Thereafter, I isolated all images (photographs, scientific figures, cartoons, infographics and artistic representations) from these texts, only excluding images of journalists next to their regular column/editorial. This resulted in a corpus of 97 texts, of which 69 contained at least one image – 166 images in total.[1] *Compact* features 51 images across 19 articles, *Junge Freiheit* 50 images across 39 articles, *Zuerst!* 32 images across 15 articles, *Deutsche Stimme* 19 images across 13 articles, and *Umwelt & Aktiv* 14 images across 11 articles.

Drawing on and combining procedures utilized in the wider literature on visual environmental communication (Culloty et al., 2019; Rebich-Hespanha et al., 2015; Wozniak et al., 2015; DiFrancesco & Young, 2011), I subsequently analysed the material from three complementary perspectives, combining quantitative and qualitative approaches. First, I conducted a *descriptive content analysis*: what actors (individual and collective ones), policies and technologies, elements of nature as well as graphs and figures are present in the analysed images (one image can contain more than one theme, see DiFrancesco & Young, 2011). While the approach to coding was inductive, emerging themes proved largely in line with findings on non-far-right images by others (e.g., DiFrancesco & Young, 2011; Rebich-Hespanha et al., 2015; Metag et al., 2016). Simultaneously, I coded the positive or negative valorization of images (with only two of them coded 'unclear') by considering the status of the depicted within the entire text.

Secondly, I carried out an *interpretative frame analysis*, utilizing, again, the method of quantitative content analysis. Within the analysis of visual communication of environmental issues and, especially, climate change, there is a rich literature on frame analysis, though the concept of frame is not always transparently utilized or demarcated from other concepts (for an overview, see Schäfer & O'Neill, 2017). I therefore draw on Entman's (1993: 52) definition: 'to frame is to select some aspects of a perceived reality and make them more salient in a communicating text, in such a way as to promote a particular problem definition, causal interpretation, moral evaluation, and/or treatment recommendation'. I identified such frames inductively, though they ended up being largely in line with observations present in the existing literature on far-right climate change communication (e.g., Forchtner, 2019). In coding image frames, I coded only an image's dominant frame. While images might convey more than one frame, this was a pragmatic decision in light of the interpretative nature of the analysis. I considered only the image, any superimposed written text and the image's caption text when deciding the frame (for other cases of such coding, see Culloty et al., 2019; O'Neill, 2013) as, in the context of this study, I wanted to avoid reproducing meaning conveyed through the written mode. Instead, I focused on the semiotic contribution made by an image (which is not to deny that an image's meaning might ultimately depend on its written context too).

Thirdly, I provide a *qualitative analysis* of two images to understand their persuasiveness, how, through semiotic choices, they construct subjectivities. The selection of these two images is informed by the results of step two: that is, I analysed images conveying the two most frequent frames. This analysis draws on categories proposed by Kress and van Leeuwen (2006) and their claim that images construct different kinds of imaginary social relationships between their producer and their receiver; the viewer and the represented subject; and the represented subjects themselves. That is, images play their part in constructing viewers' subjectivity as, first, images 'demand' or 'offer': the former happens through, for instance, direct eye contact between represented subject and viewer ('demanding' something from the viewer) while the latter positions the viewer as an 'invisible onlooker', turning the depicted into an object of one's gaze (Kress & van Leeuwen (2006: 119). Secondly, frame size affects social 'closeness', ranging from close enough to touch ('personal distance') to close enough for interaction ('social distance') and further away ('public distance'). Thirdly, angle can convey hierarchy: a low angle tends to indicate the superiority of the represented subject in relation to the onlooker, while a high angle does the opposite. In addition, a frontal angle, in relation to the represented subject, invites full involvement, while a more sideways angle, or even shots from behind, does so less. These rules have to be understood as social conventions; thus, they are not universally valid but open to adaptation and reinterpretation within particular contexts. Further semiotic choices include size, tone and focus to give or deny salience, and colour. The latter denotes persons, events and objects, and affects relationships through, for example, association. For example, the colour green is commonly linked to environmental activism in Western cultures while a colour's intense saturation can indicate intense emotion. These categories represent only a limited part of a possible methodological toolkit, though they are particularly valuable in the following analysis due to their focus on imagined relationships and the subjects which arise from them.

Thunberg, not iceberg

Starting this analysis of visual climate change communication by the far right, it is worth noting that existing research has regularly identified *people* as the main element in mainstream news media reporting on climate change (Culloty et al., 2019; O'Neill, 2013; DiFrancesco & Young, 2011). Is that any different from far-right imagery? Who and what populates the latter? Taking the first steps towards understanding this communication, a *descriptive content analysis* reveals that the theme of 'Actors' dominates, with 96 out of 121 being *people* (Table 5.1). The latter are thus by far the most significant theme in the entire corpus, something in line with the aforementioned research. However, this raises two questions: who is depicted and how?

The most numerous category of *people* is 'environmentalist'; and although far-right publications have often celebrated 'their' predecessors in the field of environmental protection, this is hardly happening in the context of this corpus, probably due to the focus on climate change towards which significant parts of the far right, in a variety of ways, have been sceptical (e.g. Moore & Roberts, 2022; Malm & the Zetkin Collective, 2021; Forchtner, 2019; for book-length analyses with a focus on Germany, see Quent et al., 2022; Sommer et al., 2022). Indeed, only one out of the 47 images containing environmentalists is valorized positively. Eighteen images feature the Swedish climate activist Thunberg, making her the single most often pictured person. Her centrality in this corpus is in line with findings on social media posts by the AfD (Boren & Kahya, 2019) and results reported in an analysis of Swedish far-right media (Vowles & Hultman, 2021).

The second most numerous kind of *people* depicted after Thunberg are politicians (only three out of 14 are valorized positively), mostly German ones such as Chancellor Angela Merkel. Scientists come third, though they are worth mentioning as five out of 10 are valorized positively, thus indicating

Table 5.1 Themes

Theme	Occurrences (number of texts containing at least one relevant image)	Occurrences (in total)
Actor	52	121
People	46	96
Environmentalist	27	47
Politician	10	14
Scientist	8	10
Ordinary person/worker	6	6
Unspecific mass	4	6
Other*	10	13
Non-people actor	18	25
Collective environmentalists (e.g., represented by symbols of Extinction Rebellion and the Green Party)	8	10
Media/press	7	10
Other*	5	5
Policy and technology	24	51
Green policy and technology	16	32
Wind turbine	12	14
Green policy	5	10
Alternative transport	5	6
Other*	2	2
Fossil fuel-related policy and technology	14	19
Fossil fuel technology	9	10
Transportation	7	9
Nature	19	28
Natural environment and landscape	9	13
The planet (including disaster)	6	6
Animal	3	4
*Other**	5	5
Graph and figure	6	6
Other*	5	5

*Includes themes which occurred three or fewer times in both types of occasion.

once again (Forchtner et al., 2018) that the far right has not abandoned scientific, or rather scientific sounding, claims making, but that the struggle against an allegedly oppressive hegemony is also fought in the field of science. Further persons include ordinary people and workers (6; see Figure

5.2, discussed below) and unspecific masses, primarily related to the topic of overpopulation (6). In the theme of *non-people actors* depicted, media, in particular the press, stand out. This element largely comprises cover pages by 'mainstream' news media which feature alleged scare stories of looming climate disaster (10). Fear communication has long been part of climate change communication, though its efficacy has been questioned (e.g. O'Neill & Nicholson-Cole, 2009). Yet, the far right has not only ridiculed the matter, but has also long attacked 'the lying press', a well-known trope since Trump at the latest, even though its use in Germany dates back much further (Koliska & Assmann, 2019).

Following Actor, the theme of Policy and Technology is divided into *green* and *fossil fuel-related* ones, the former being present significantly more often (32 and 19 times respectively). However, this does not point to a celebration of a 'green agenda'; rather, these images are always valorized negatively. Here, wind turbines stand out as targets; they constitute 14 of these 32 elements. Indeed, turning to Nature, a third key theme, depictions of the natural environment and landscapes dominate, elements which often appear in relation to (allegedly disastrous) wind turbines. As discussed below, this concerns a typical criticism present in far-right opposition to climate change policies. Furthermore, and connected to the above comment on fear communication, while disaster-imagery exists, these visuals are used to ridicule climate action and to illustrate climate activists' irrationalism (see below). Moreover, while we have already seen that Thunberg is 'on display', there are almost no polar bears, no melting ice(bergs), that is, what has otherwise counted as iconic in the context of representing climate change elsewhere (Born, 2019; Chapman et al., 2016; though O'Neill, 2020: 18 reports that the polar bear has become a 'tired and hackneyed icon'). Thus, for the far right, communicating climate change is very much about Thunberg rather than (melting) icebergs, constructing a particular 'problem' which, subsequently, calls for (far-right) subjects and their solutions. Of course, this is not surprising given the agenda driving the investigated corpus: one which hardly supports climate action. For example, a polar bear might cause audiences to worry about the impact of climate change (e.g. Metag et al., 2016), though those within the far right might, in line with the written text, perceive the animal as living proof of societal hysteria.

Finally, the least common theme concerns graphs and figures which act as anchors of objectivity; or, more precisely, as simulations of 'hard facts' via which various types of climate change scepticisms are supported. Indeed, of the six graphs and figures, three support evidence scepticism, with others problematizing policy responses.

In a second analytical step, I approach the visual data from the perspective of an *interpretative frame analysis* (Table 5.2). Drawing on Entman's

Table 5.2 Frames

Frames	Occurrences [number of texts containing at least one relevant image]	Occurrences [in total]
Irrationalism	29	46
Unclear	17	28
Economic harm	8	19
Politicized/instrumental activism	12	15
Endangered freedom	7	8
Hypocrisies	6	8
Environmentally harmful climate policies	6	8
Prudence/reasonableness	5	7
Natural cause	5	6
Wind turbines as a blight	4	5
Overpopulation	3	4
Other*	9	12

*Includes frames which occurred three or fewer times in both types of occasion.

aforementioned definition of frame, frames act as 'interpretative *storylines* that set a specific train of thought in motion' (Nisbet & Newman, 2015: 325, italic added), 'storylines' which define a problem and propose ways forward. By far the most widely used frame was 'Irrationalism'. That is, nearly 30 per cent of the analysed images fell into this category, identifying hysteria and (religious) delusion as the problem 'caused' by, for example, the negatively evaluated political and cultural elite, who are separated from the far right's own insights and standards of rationality and sanity. This frame is well known from research on climate change communication by the far right (Forchtner, 2019) and, concerning religious metaphors in particular, has also featured in conservative climate change communication (Atanasova & Koteyko, 2017). Othering facilitated by this frame draws heavily on depictions of Thunberg (15 of 46 images which facilitate this frame feature her). This frame (and the less often mobilized one which states 'our' sanity: 'Prudence/reasonableness') is particularly connected to melodrama (discussed below in more detail) which gives rise to subjects being 'whole' and 'pure', and in no need to engage with their continuously pathologized villains/opponents ('madness' and 'sect' are commonly used words, see Figure 5.1, discussed below).

This is also visible in the frame 'Economic harm' (where individual and national economic pain is viewed negatively, caused by the politics of, for instance, a detached, globalist elite and can only be halted through supporting the right, that is, Right forces), though this frame is less widespread than 'Irrationalism'. While this contrasts with findings in other research (e.g. Forchtner & Lubarda, 2022), this is likely due to the significance of, first, Thunberg during the investigated period: she was clearly perceived as a threat, symbolizing climate-friendly societal transformation which threatens traditional masculine biographies and lifestyles (Vowles & Hultman, 2021; Hultman et al., 2019; Daggett, 2018). Secondly, the visual depiction of a person, and thus their Othering, is arguably more easily achieved than that of a process, economic or otherwise (the analysis of Figure 5.2, concerning this frame, in fact points to the rhetorical force generated by the inclusion of an individual).

Taking stock, the two main frames account for more than a third of all images and are examples of process ('Irrationalism') and response ('Economic harm') scepticism (see van Rensburg, 2015, who separates scepticism towards the status and existence of climate change from process and response scepticism towards scientific/public knowledge generation processes and policy supposed to tackle climate change respectively; for an adoption of this typology in research on the far right in the European Parliament, see Forchtner & Lubarda, 2022). Indeed, as I coded the basic stance taken by entire texts, 'only' 17 out of 97 contained evidence scepticism. No doubt, this is considerable, but it indicates that not even the far right is primarily engaged in what Mann (2021) calls the 'old climate war', that is, fighting the physical evidence of climate change.

What is furthermore notable in the context of this chapter is the way in which frames were identified (considering the image itself, superimposed written text and the caption, but excluding the title of the article and the wider text), resulting in a significant number of images which could not be coded (28 images). This does not mean that these images carried no frame. Rather, it illustrates that by not considering the wider written text as an 'anchor' (see Barthes, 1977 [1964: 37–41]), images are often too polysemic to be 'correctly' understood, that is, in line with the written mode. This is not specific to this analysis (see DiFrancesco & Young, 2011; Hansen and Machin, 2013) – and it should not lead to forgo visual analysis or only to conduct visual analysis hand in hand with full analysis of the written mode. The latter might not only go beyond what is possible in many projects, but would also run the danger of reproducing the primacy of the written mode instead of stressing what images are capable of doing. Indeed, I decided not to include the wider written text when coding frames precisely because I was interested in understanding what images alone do – and how they do it.

Let me finally comment on three intriguing, though numerically less significant 'environmentalist' frames: first, eight images frame responses to climate change as 'Environmentally harmful'. This concerns, for example, the effect wind turbines have on birdlife. Indeed, while wind turbines are common symbols of changing times as O'Neill (2020) shows in her longitudinal analysis of news media in the US and the UK, pointing to the effect on birdlife has been a common means of deflection by the far right as well as other opponents of climate action, even though this argument has been put into perspective (e.g. Mann, 2021: 128). Secondly, aesthetic landscape concerns drive the negative framing of wind turbines (5). Such concerns have a long history in far-right communication about the environment and, thus, Forchtner and Kølvraa (2015) highlight the aesthetic as one of the three dimensions through which the far right makes sense of the national environment – from celebrating the beauties of 'our land' to the aforementioned concerns over its blight. And indeed, Hansen (2019: 46) stresses that visuals depicting the environment draw from historically and culturally resonant ideas of nature, for example romantic views, something likely to be of relevance concerning far-right imagery of, for example, the countryside and forests. Lastly, four images speak to the frame 'Overpopulation'. The latter has, again and again, been shown to feature in far-right communication about the environment (see already Olsen, 1999), but its significance in contemporary climate change communication by the far right has been questioned (e.g. Forchtner & Lubarda, 2022). This study is no exception, though it is notable that all cases of this classic theme (which points to the 'fate' of race, be it understood biologically or culturally) feature in the ideologically most extreme publications of the corpus, *Deutsche Stimme* and *Umwelt & Aktiv*.

Looking back and considering the depictions of themes and frames, the far right's visual climate change communication, most clearly in the case of images of the political opponent, facilitates visual melodrama. Knowledge and subjectivity emerging from melodrama revolve around clear-cut boundaries and denial of complexity, and, thus, the polarization of 'good' and 'evil'.[2] Subjects arising from melodramatic narrativization are particularly characterized by untroubled wholeness and certainty, rather than ambiguity and doubt as in, for example, tragic or ironic stories. Indeed, studies have argued that melodrama is 'the principal mode for uncovering, demonstrating, and making operative the essential moral universe in a post-sacred era by polarising good and evil, calling for the expulsion of the latter' (Brooks, 1976: 15). Hence, melodrama facilitates a '"*space of innocence*"' (Williams, 2001: 28) with Wagner-Pacifici (1986: 283) similarly noting that melodrama facilitates 'intermittent identification and alienation as the audience is pulled in … to sing the praises of the "hero" but is not encouraged to contemplate or participate in a confrontation of the complexities of the moment'. Analyses of melodrama relevant in the context of this chapter have been put forward by, for example, Falasca-Zamponi (1997) on how Mussolini performed melodrama, stressing what other nations did wrong in order to hold down Italy and, turning to contemporary climate change, Daggett (2020) who lucidly speaks of far-right melodrama in the US.

Relatedly, Lubarda's (2020) conceptualization 'far-right ecologism' includes 'Manichaeism' as a core ideological element while scholars of the populist far right have emphasized the Manichaean as a crucial part of populism and its division of the world into 'good' and 'bad' (e.g. Mudde, 2007: 63). However, I view the construction and nature of such sharp divides, including the antagonism between 'pure people' and 'corrupt elite', as better understood when explicitly located at the foundational level of narrative (as it is through this form that knowledge and identity are constituted). Be that as it may, the desire for moral clarity is neither limited to populism nor the far right: as I have outlined, melodrama provides certainty and untroubled wholeness on the side of the subject, separating 'good' from 'evil'. As such, it has also, at times, characterized left-wing articulations, something which Anker (2014) considers in her analysis of left theory. Without doubt, melodrama has also featured prominently in environmental campaigns against, for example, nuclear energy and multinational oil and gas companies – but while melodrama's denial of complexity and polarizing force aids mobilization, the feeling of certainty resulting from melodrama does not facilitate reflexive subjectivities, as can be seen in the corpus investigated here.[3]

Returning (and connecting this) to images, the latter play a key role in the construction of identity – in the case of images analysed in this chapter: single, static ones. While they cannot act as a sequence of events, they can evoke narratives (depending on the background knowledge of readers) and/ or illustrate the written mode. Thus, following Ranta (2010: 1), I argue that images can represent 'components of action sequences familiar to the beholders, sometimes only by rendering a specific, arrested moment which can activate a wider, mentally imagined event schema'. They do so, as we have heard, with vividness, emotiveness and immediacy, and thus tie together networks of associations and affects (Carah, 2014: 138). As such, they are loci of boundary making, of identity making, and recent research has highlighted the significance of digital circulation of images to reproduce emotions and identities (e.g. Hokka & Nelimarkka, 2020; Proitz, 2018). Yet, images in print media too articulate shared worlds, and emotions facilitated in sources analysed in this chapter include despising the transgressing Other and self-righteousness. The centrality of sharp demarcation and vilification of the Other facilitated via visual melodrama is visible in the

5.1 'Climate madness' (*Compact* magazine, November 2019)

overall negative valorization of the images of, for example, politicians and alternative energy sources: 135 of them are valorized negatively while only 29 are positively valorized (two are unclear).

Finally, I complete this analysis of melodramatic depictions of themes and frames via a *qualitative analysis* of two images which illustrate the two most dominant frames ('Irrationalism' and 'Economic harm'). Figure 5.1 is a cover of *Compact* (November 2019), featuring Thunberg next to the writing 'Climate madness. Revolt of the end time sects'.[4] The first part of the title, 'Climate madness', is highlighted through the use of colour, with red conventionally signifying importance/danger. This image was coded as 'Irrationalism' (frame), 'Environmentalist' (theme) and 'negative' (valorization), and clearly furthers a melodramatic reading. The image itself is based on a widely circulated shoot taken during Thunberg's attack on world leaders in Davos in 2019, using a filter to make the photograph look like an oil painting/achieve a particular style.[5]

Compact cut the frame, for instance the magazine did not include Thunberg's right hand with her pointing finger, opting for a close-up through which viewers are put in personal (touching) distance. While this is potentially a way to construct social closeness, here it enables a closer look at 'the object's' supposedly 'deranged' character. Indeed, due to the facial expression, personal distance does not create intimacy, but strengthens the viewer's impression of her being aggressive and hateful. The use of a filter accentuates this and acts to 'de-real' her. As other shots of Thunberg exist from this event (with a similar facial expression), the camera angle too deserves attention: here, Thunberg does not look into the viewer's eyes; instead, the viewer is positioned as an 'invisible onlooker' as she looks off frame, away from the viewer. Indeed, van Leeuwen explains the effect of depicting a person from the side as 'symbolic objectivation'. Hence, people represented like Thunberg are represented 'as objects for our scrutiny, rather than as subjects addressing the viewer with their gaze and symbolically engaging with the viewer in this way' (van Leeuwen, 2000: 333, 339).

This depiction, exemplifying Thunberg's 'madness', is embedded in a broader discourse infantilizing her (and the Fridays for Future movement), one through which her widespread representation as a pure steward of earth is scorned by those allegedly in-the-know. Instead of taking this activism and her emotional response seriously, viewing her outrage as a serious judgement (on emotions as 'a potential avenue to "the reasonable view"'/reason, see Hochschild, 2012: 30 and Habermas, 1998:4f, respectively), the unsettling power of her agenda and performance is rendered as impractical and naïve by those defending the status quo. While such infantilization is a banal manifestation of ageism, it is, simultaneously, compounded by historical, handed down perceptions of women as irrational and, more specifically, hysterical (Scull, 2011). Indeed, infantilization sits at the beginning of a spectrum of misogyny, ranging from infantilization of, to violence against, women (Manne, 2019: 68). Vowles and Hultman (2021) too find Thunberg being represented as emotional and irrational, noting that such efforts resemble the treatment of Rachel Carson in the United States in the 1960s whose *Silent Spring* famously warned against the indiscriminatory use of pesticides.

In the context of this chapter's focus on Thunberg, Manne's (2018: 106–113) observation that women who are not happy to provide, but who demand, are experienced as a threat to what Hultman et al. (2019: 128) refer to as climate denialists' 'life project', one linked to patriarchy, fossil capitalism and 'petro-masculinity' (Daggett, 2018), rings true. Following this line of thought, and although this is not to establish a direct line between the militant Free Corps of the early twentieth century and the far right of the early twenty-first century, the perception of women as a threat furthermore points to Theweleit's (2018: 91) analysis of male fantasies in which good women are pure, such as mothers, while others appear as, for example, hysterically aggressive.[6] Even more so, Theweleit (2018: 100) speaks of some men 'assigning a penis to a certain type of woman … and fear[ing] their own castration from this penis. These men see "communism" as a direct attack on their genitals.' This fear was connected to women supposedly carrying weapons under their skirts. While such fear is not relevant today, we can replace 'communism' with 'left' or 'liberal', while the weapon is Thunberg's words, an interpretation supported by the fact that her open mouth is prominently placed at the very centre of the image.[7]

Figure 5.2 is also taken from *Compact*, though this time the image carries the frame 'Economic harm' and appears at the beginning of an article, filling the upper half of the page, right above the headline ('The big rip off'). A symbol for lack of money (empty pockets) is present at the centre of the image and further supported by the peculiar way the man's hands (especially his thumbs) are presented: turned slightly outwards (i.e. towards the viewer) as if saying 'there is *really* nothing left' and 'there is *really* nothing I can do'. The lead paragraph continues this theme, claiming that 'the CO2-tax is coming!' and that energy will become more expensive for the 'average Joe' as the 'state scoffs the citizens in order to be able to spend more money

5.2 'The big rip off' (*Compact* magazine, July 2019: 23)

on so-called refugees' (the caption text similarly speaks of 'Pockets empty. Treasury full' and the government's desire to take more money from its citizens). Yet, while this text clearly supports the way this image will be read, the image is able to speak for itself.

The image not only signifies lack of money, but also communicates loss of control which, arguably, often gives rise to feelings such as frustration, despair and anger. Given the frame size, viewers are encouraged to feel close to the man and his plight. The second feature instantly noticeable is the lack of a face. This differs sharply from Figure 5.1, especially as viewers might reasonably assume that this person is facing the viewer. And yet, this can be read as, first, lack of voice (there is no mouth; he is decapitated, voiceless, a helpless gesture being the only way to communicate), which feeds into the populist playbook of pure, ordinary people being constantly silenced by 'the corrupt elite'. Secondly, this enables this person to become a true 'average Joe', representing all those to whom populists claim to give voice due to the de-individualized nature of the person. Thus, the voice of ordinary 'citizens' is transferred to the (populist far-right) magazine which becomes the mouthpiece of this 'average Joe' able to save 'us' from the doings of an antagonistic elite.

The fact that this is indeed an 'average Joe', possibly a blue-collar worker, is furthermore supported by the man's clothes: jeans and a shirt, both nice but neither trousers nor a white office shirt (with the rolled-up sleeves further indicating the man's 'hands-on' occupation). This interpretation is supported by the background: a former industrial site, now in ruins; presumably the reason for the man's empty pockets. Among others, the scenery includes a smokestack which commonly symbolizes industrial pollution, though this symbol, much like that of the polar bear, has been subverted by climate sceptics (O'Neill, 2020) and, in this image, recalls lost prosperity (and voice). The rather flat, dull, low-saturated green superimposed on this scenery signifies, first, distance and a broody mood – making the thriving industry a thing not directly accessible, a thing of the past to be looked at nostalgically. Secondly, it is a semiotic resource demarcating good from evil, that is, 'us' from those unreasonable greens who are responsible for this decline (given that today 'green' also signifies environmentalism). Indeed, it is important to note that what this image achieves, through combining a rotten industrial site and an individual, is to signify that economic harm is done to both the livelihoods of individual workers and to the (economic) potency of the nation as it points to the often-raised threat of 'deindustrialization'.

Finally, the composition of man and ruin also connotes a particular kind of masculinity and, as such, a link between 'being manly' and employment, industrial labour to be precise, which is indeed heavily connoted with a traditional understanding of masculine identity (on industrial/breadwinner masculinity see Vowles & Hultman, 2021; Hultman et al., 2019 and on 'petro-masculinity', see Daggett, 2018).

Conclusion

In this chapter, I have argued for the systematic, multi-perspective analysis of images when studying far-right environmental communication, taking climate change communication by the German far right as a case study. Looking back, what can be learned from this analysis, both empirically and with regards to the methodological procedure?

First, and responding to the study's research questions, images analysed in this case study stress themes and frames similar to those highlighted in existing work on written communication about climate change by the far right, both inside and outside of Germany. This includes attacks on people and policies and technologies – first and foremost, Thunberg and wind turbines – which the far right perceives as the real threat (instead of, for example, melting icebergs). These images frame Others as deluded, hysteric, mad or even part of a pseudo-religious cult as well as being responsible for economic harm done to the nation and its individual members. Furthermore, the dominance of these frames points to the significance of process and response scepticism which, again, confirms existing research on the written mode in far-right climate change communication. The analysis of visuals also confirms existing work on the written mode in that ideas of traditional masculinity and misogyny play a role in these representations and feed into the construction of the looking subject. Importantly, I argue that subjects emerging from these representations are melodramatic ones, 'pure' and 'innocent', which know no subtlety while guaranteeing moral clarity and righteousness. However, the fact that visual analysis appears to confirm existing findings regarding the written mode does not render it redundant. Studying other cases might (a) provide different results as the visual and the written mode might pull in different directions (see DiFrancesco & Young, 2011). Arguably more important is (b) the fact that the visual mode is emotive, vivid and memorable, as mentioned at the beginning of this chapter; in short, that it is particularly persuasive in constituting knowledge and subjects. This is especially relevant as images might be the only thing which people actually consider when browsing a newspaper/magazine (or their social media accounts). Thus, understanding images provides more comprehensive insights into far-right communication. Finally, and going beyond the far right, the analysis has illustrated similarities and differences between mainstream news sources and far-right media, for example regarding the centrality of persons in images and the use of iconic symbols respectively.

Secondly, in analysing the German case, I proposed a mixed-method approach for further studies on visual communication by the far right. This approach brought together three complementary perspectives: first, a descriptive, quantitative content analysis illustrated the elements present in the investigated images. Secondly, an interpretative, quantitative frame analysis pointed to dominant (and not so dominant) ways in which these visuals are used, while, thirdly, a qualitative analysis of two images showed how detailed and systematic semiotic analysis adds to a comprehensive understanding of data. This mix adds to existing proposals regarding combinations by, for instance, Rebich-Hespanha et al. (2015), DiFrancesco and Young (2011) and Wozniak et al. (2015), and offers a foundation for further, method-related considerations. For example, while O'Neill and others have done much to illuminate the perception of climate change visuals among the wider public, this mix of methods highlights the need for the field to also consider the reception of such imagery among far-right publics. Here, too, the 'visual turn' in the analysis of far-right environmental communication promises key insights on the workings and effects of political ecologies of the far right.

Acknowledgement

I am grateful to Anders Hansen, Balša Lubarda and Özgür Özvatan, as well as the editors Irma Allen, Kristoffer Ekberg and Ståle Holgersen, for helpful comments on earlier versions of this chapter. All mistakes remain my own.

Notes

1 Texts which did not contain images largely belonged to *Junge Freiheit*.
2 Genres are social conventions which render individual narratives predictable, such as, first and foremost, romance, comedy, tragedy and irony (Frye, 1957; White, 1973; see Forchtner, 2016 for a review). Melodrama is one such genre, one which Jameson (2002: 102) described as 'a degraded form of romance' (this is plausible, given that Frye, 1957: 195 characterizes romance as a genre of narrative in which 'subtlety and complexity are not much favored'). Of course, the significance of melodrama in the analysed corpus does not mean that all texts are melodramatic as some are present in, for example, a low mimetic mode (see Smith, 2012).

3 Indeed, due to high levels of certainty and lack of reflexivity, melodrama facilitates blocking opportunities for collective learning processes to take place (Forchtner, 2016). For a less critical view on environmental melodrama, see Kinsella et al. (2008).

4 Other key issues are also introduced on the cover, but other than 'Eco-dictatorship. A green pioneer warns', they are not relevant in the context of this chapter.

5 See www.nnn.de/deutschland-welt/panorama/Greta-Thunberg-Von-jetzt-an-nur-noch-Death-Metal-id25797697.html (accessed 15 February 2021).

6 The Free Corps referred to here were paramilitary groups which emerged in the wake of Germany's defeat in World War I and largely comprised veterans. Mostly national-conservative/far right, they fought both internal (left-wing) revolts, such as the January uprising in Berlin in 1919, which included the murder of Rosa Luxemburg and Karl Liebknecht by Free Corps, and at the German Reich's eastern border.

7 In fact, the communist scare is not that far off in the eyes of some on the far right who perceive climate change policies, and even environmental policies more generally, as a ploy to further a communist/socialist agenda. For more on the Cultural Marxism conspiracy theory in general and with regards to the climate in particular, see Malm and the Zetkin Collective (2021: 300–313).

References

Anker, E. (2014). *Orgies of Feeling: Melodrama and the Politics of Freedom*. Durham: Duke University Press.

Atanasova, D., & Koteyko, N. (2017). Metaphors in Guardian Online and Mail Online Opinion-Page Content on Climate Change: War, Religion, and Politics. *Environmental Communication*, 11(4): 452–469.

Barthes, R. (1977 [1964]). *Image, Music, Text*. London: Fontana.

Biehl, J., & Staudenmeier, P. (1995). *Ecofascism: Lessons from the German Experience*. Oakland: AK Press.

Boren, Z., & Kahya, D. (2019). German far right targets Greta Thunberg in anti-climate push. *Unearthed*, 14 May, https://unearthed.greenpeace.org/2019/05/14/germany-climate-denial-populist-eike-afd/ (accessed 11 February 2020).

Born, D. (2019). Bearing Witness? Polar Bears as Icons for Climate Change Communication in *National Geographic*. *Environmental Communication*, 13(5): 649–663.

Brooks, P. (1976). *The Melodramatic Imagination: Balzac, Henry James, Melodrama, and the Mode of Excess*. New Haven and London: Yale University Press.

Carah, N. (2014). Curators of Databases: Circulating Images, Managing Attention and Making Value on Social Media. *Media International Australia*, 150(1): 137–142.

Chapman, D., Corner, A., Webster, R., & Markowitz, E. (2016). Climate Visuals: A Mixed Methods Investigation of Public Perceptions of Climate Images in Three Countries. *Global Environmental Change*, 41: 172–182.

Culloty, E., Murphy, P., Brereton, P., Suiter, J., Smeaton A., & Zhang, D. (2019). Researching Visual Representations of Climate Change. *Environmental Communication*, 13(2): 179–191.

Daggett, C. (2018). Petro-masculinity: Fossil Fuels and Authoritarian Desire. *Millennium*, 47(1): 25–44.

Daggett, C. (2020). The Melodrama of Climate Change Denial. *Green European Journal*, 19: 122–128.

DiFrancesco, D., & Young, N. (2011). Seeing Climate Change: The Visual Construction of Global Warming in Canadian National Print Media. *Cultural Geographies*, 18(4): 517–536.

Doerr, N. (2021). The Visual Politics of the Alternative for Germany (AfD): Anti-Islam, Ethno-nationalism, and Gendered Images. *Social Sciences*, 10(1). doi.org/10.3390/socsci10010020.

Entman, R. (1993). Framing: Towards Clarification of a Fractured Paradigm. *Journal of Communication*, 43(4): 51–58.

Falasca-Zamponi, S. (1997). *Fascist Spectacle: The Aesthetics of Power in Mussolini's Italy*. Berkeley: University of California Press.

Forchtner, B. (2016). *Lessons from the Past? Memory, Narrativity and Subjectivity*. London: Palgrave Macmillan.

Forchtner, B. (2019). Climate Change and the Far Right. *WIREs Climate Change*, 10(5), August. doi.org/10.1002/wcc.604.

Forchtner, B. (ed.) (2023). *Visualising Far-Right Environments: Communication and the Politics of Nature*. Manchester: Manchester University Press.

Forchtner, B., & Kølvraa, C. (2015). The Nature of Nationalism: Populist Radical Right Parties on Countryside and Climate. *Nature+Culture*, 10(2): 199–224.

Forchtner, B., & Lubarda, B. (2022). Scepticisms and Beyond? A Comprehensive Portrait of Climate Change Communication by the Far Right in the European Parliament. *Environmental Politics*, 32(1). doi.org/10.1080/09644016.2022.2048556.

Forchtner, B., & Özvatan, Ö. (2019). Beyond the German Forest: Environmental Communication by the German Far Right. In B. Forchtner (ed.), *The Far Right and the Environment*. London and New York: Routledge, pp. 216–236.

Forchtner, B., Kroneder, A., & Wetzel, D. (2018). Being Skeptical? Exploring Far-Right Climate-Change Communication in Germany. *Environmental Communication*, 12(5): 589–604.

Freistein, K., & Gadinger, F. (2020). Populist Stories of Honest Men and Proud Mothers: A Visual Narrative Analysis. *Review of International Studies*, 46(2): 217–236.

Frye, N. (1957). *Anatomy of Criticism: Four Essays*. Princeton: Princeton University Press.

Geden, O. (1996). *Rechte Ökologie: Umweltschutz zwischen Emanzipation und Faschismus*. Berlin: Elefanten Press.

Habermas, J. (1998). A Genealogical Analysis of the Cognitive Content of Morality. In *The Inclusion of the Other: Studies in Political Theory*. Cambridge: Polity, pp. 3–48.

Hansen, A. (2018). Using Visual Images for Showing Environmental Problems. In A. Fill & H. Penz (eds), *The Routledge Handbook of Ecolinguistics*. New York and London: Routledge, pp. 179–195.

Hansen, A. (2019). Environmental Communication Research: Origins, Development and New Directions. In B. Forchtner (ed.), *The Far Right and the Environment*. London and New York: Routledge, pp. 38–55.

Hansen, A., & Machin, D. (2013). Researching Visual Environmental Communication. *Environmental Communication*, 7(2): 151–168.

Hokka, J., & Nelimarkka, M. (2020). Affective Economy of National-Populist Images: Investigating National and Transnational Online Networks through Visual Big Data. *New Media & Society*, 22(5): 770–792.

Hochschild, A. (2012). *The Managed Heart*. Berkeley: University of California Press.

Hultman, M., Björk, A., & Viinikka, T. (2019). Far-right and Climate Change Denial: Denouncing Environmental Challenges via Anti-establishment Rhetoric, Marketing of Doubts, Industrial/Breadwinner Masculinities Enactments and Ethno-nationalism. In B. Forchtner (ed.), *The Far Right and the Environment*. London and New York: Routledge, pp. 121–135.

Jameson, F. (2002). *The Political Unconscious: Narrative as a Socially Symbolic Act*. London and New York: Routledge.

Joffe, H. (2008). The Power of Visual Material: Persuasion, Emotion and Identification. *Diogenes*, 217: 84–93.

Kinsella, W. J., Bsumek, P. K., Walker, G. B., Kinsella, W. J., Check, T., Peterson, T. R., & Schwarze, S. (2008). Narratives, Rhetorical Genres, and Environmental Conflict: Responses to Schwarze's 'Environmental Melodrama'. *Environmental Communication*, 2(1): 78–109.

Koliska, M., & Assmann, K. (2019). Lügenpresse: The Lying Press and German Journalists' Responses to a Stigma. *Journalism*, 22(11). doi.org/10.1177/1464884919894088.

Kress, G., & van Leeuwen, T. (2006). *Reading Images: The Grammar of Visual Design*. London: Routledge.

Lubarda, B. (2020). Beyond Eco-fascism? Far Right Ecologism (FRE) as a Framework for Future Inquiries. *Environmental Values*, 29(6): 713–732.

Malm, A., & the Zetkin Collective (2021). *White Skin, Black Fuel*. London: Verso.

Mann, M. (2021). *The New Climate War: The Fight to Take Back Our Planet*. London: Scribe.

Manne, K. (2019). *Down Girl: The Logic of Misogyny*. London: Penguin.

Metag, J., Schäfer, M., Füchslin, T., Barsuhn, T., & von Königslöw, K. (2016). Perceptions of Climate Change Imagery: Evoked Salience and Self-efficacy in Germany, Switzerland, and Austria. *Science Communication*, 38(2): 197–227.

Moore, S., & Roberts, A. (2022). *The Rise of Ecofascism: Climate Change and the Far Right*. Cambridge: Polity.

Mudde, C. (2007). *Populist Radical Right Parties in Europe*. Cambridge: Cambridge University Press.

Mudde, C. (2019). *The Far Right Today*. Cambridge: Polity.

Nisbet, M., & Newman, T. (2015). Framing, the Media, and Environmental Communication. In A. Hansen & R. Cox (eds), *The Routledge Handbook of Environment and Communication*. Oxon and New York: Routledge, pp. 325–338.

Olsen, J. (1999). *Nature and Nationalism*. New York: St. Martin's Press.

O'Neill, S. (2013). Image Matters: Climate Change Imagery in US, UK and Australian Newspapers, *Geoforum*, 49: 10–19.

O'Neill, S. (2020). More Than Meets the Eye: A Longitudinal Analysis of Climate Change Imagery in the Print Media. *Climatic Change*, 163: 9–26.

O'Neill, S., & Nicholson-Cole, S. (2009). 'Fear won't do it': Promoting Positive Engagement with Climate Change through Visual and Iconic Representations. *Science Communication*, 30(3): 355–379.

O'Neill, S., & Smith, N. (2014). Climate Change and Visual Imagery. *WIREs Climate Change*, 5: 73–87.

Proitz, L. (2018). Visual Social Media and Affectivity: The Impact of the Image of Alan Kurdi and Young People's Response to the Refugee Crisis in Oslo and Sheffield. *Information, Communication and Society*, 21(4): 548–563.

Quent, M., Richter, C., & Salheiser, A. (2022). *Klimarassismus: Der Kampf der Rechten gegen die ökologische Wende. Wie Rechtsaußenparteien den Klimawandel für sich nutzen*. Munich: Piper.

Ranta, M. (2010). Narrativity and Historicism in National Socialist Art. *kunsttexte. de*, 3: 1–14.

Rebich-Hespanha, S., Rice, R., Montello, D., Retzloff, S., Tien, S., & Hespanha, J. (2015). Image Themes and Frames in US Print News Stories about Climate Change. *Environmental Communication*, 9(4): 491–519.

Schäfer, M., & O'Neill, S. (2017). Frame Analysis in Climate Change Communication: Approaches for Assessing Journalists' Minds, Online Communication and Media Portrayals. In M. Nisbet, S. Ho, E. Markowitz, S. O'Neill, M. Schäfer, & J. Thaker (eds), *Oxford Encyclopedia of Climate Change Communication*. Oxford University Press. doi.org/10.1093/acrefore/9780190228620.013.48.

Scull, A. (2011). *Hysteria: The Disturbing History*. Oxford: Oxford University Press.

Smith, P. (2012). Narrating Global Warming. In J. C. Alexander, R. N. Jacobs & P. Smith (eds), *The Oxford Handbook of Cultural Sociology*. Oxford: Oxford University Press, pp. 745–760.

Sommer, B., Schad, M., Kadelke, P., Humpert, F., & Möstl, C. (2022). *Rechtspopulismus vs. Klimaschutz? Positionen, Einstellungen, Erklärungsansätze*. Munich: oekom.

Theweleit, K. (2018). *Männerphantasien*. Berlin: Matthes & Seitz.

Van Leeuwen, T. (2000). Visual Racism. In M. Reisigl & R. Wodak (eds), *The Semiotics of Racism: Approaches in Critical Discourse Analysis*. Vienna: Passagen. 333–350.

Van Rensburg, W. (2015). Climate Change Skepticism: A Conceptual Re-evaluation. *SAGE Open*, 5(2): 1–13.

Vowles, K., & Hultman, M. (2021). Greta Thunberg as hysterical PR-puppet? When climate science was turned into an enemy by Swedish far-right media. The Green Room-seminar at Linköping University, 20 May.

Wagner-Pacifici, R. (1986). *The Moro Morality Play: Terrorism as Social Drama.* Chicago: University of Chicago Press.

White, H. (1973). *Metahistory: The Historical Imagination in Nineteenth-Century Europe.* Baltimore: Johns Hopkins University Press.

Williams, L. (2001). *Playing the Race Card: Melodramas of Black and White from Uncle Tom to O. J. Simpson.* Princeton: Princeton University Press.

Wozniak, A., Lück, J., & Wessler, H. (2015). Frames, Stories, and Images: The Advantages of a Multimodal Approach in Comparative Media Content Research on Climate Change. *Environmental Communication,* 9(4): 469–490.

6

Delayers and deniers: centrist fossil ideology meets the far right in Norway

Ståle Holgersen

The US politician Alexandria Ocasio-Cortez tweeted on 25 February 2019 that 'Climate delayers aren't much better than climate deniers. With either one if they get their way, we're toast' (Cantor, 2019). Groups that constantly argue postponing the needed action and groups that deny climate science altogether certainly come from two distinct ideological, political and social traditions. But they can co-exist, and even arguably strengthen each other. This is indeed the case in Norway.

The dominant view on oil and gas production in Norway – which I will call the Norwegian fossil ideology – is that Norway can *both* produce more oil and gas *and* contribute to saving the planet. This is a Norwegian version of capitalist climate governance. Its proponents acknowledge that climate change is primarily caused by humans, support international negotiations and are deeply worried by every new report from the International Panel on Climate Change (IPCC). The Norwegian fossil ideology is more than anything about *delaying* into a distant future the one thing Norway needs to do: stop extracting oil and gas.

By contrast, the Norwegian far-right Progress Party (Fremskrittspartiet) comes from a classical *denialist* position.[1] However, to be accepted by the Conservative Party as a governing coalition partner it adjusted its position, officially accepting the Norwegian fossil ideology of delay. When in government, between 2013 and 2020, denialism nonetheless remained a strong tendency within the party itself.

Accepting or denying that climate change is primarily caused by human activity are in most respects two very different positions. But in the real life of capitalism and its form of climate governance, such a distinction can become quite blurry. Despite significant differences, the two positions co-existed within the same government and even within the Progress Party. This was only possible due to some important similarities between the positions – and key words here are business friendliness and nationalism – but most important: the two positions are in Norway grounded on more or less the exact same policy for oil and gas extraction. The Progress Party could both enter and leave the government with hardly any changes in Norway's oil and gas policy. Denial and the Norwegian fossil ideology can even provide mutual legitimacy: the climate ideology appears as the 'sensible' big brother of denialism, and denialism can flourish where the national fossil ideology for decades has obscured any reasonable climate debate.

The chapter proceeds in five sections. The first describes the Norwegian fossil ideology as a convenient position for climate delayers and the next three discuss developments within the Progress Party: how it originated in climate denialism (#2), how this altered to allow it to join government (#3) and yet how denialism never died (#4). In the fifth and final section we analyse relations between denying and delaying, between climate denialism and the Norwegian fossil ideology, and identify how the different positions can nourish, legitimize and even strengthen each other.

The Norwegian fossil ideology

Contemporary Norwegian fossil ideology was born in the early 1990s.[2] During the 1970s and 1980s the official petroleum policy was to extract in a 'moderate tempo'. The main concern was economic, to avoid the Dutch disease – that is, that an increase in a specific sector could damage the overall economy – and an overheated economy, but even arguments about environmental concerns (about oil spills and birds and fish) were present. This changed from the early 1990s: now the aim became to extract as much as possible, and then invest the money in financial markets and government bonds. Concerns about the Dutch disease were considered 'solved' through establishing the Oil Fund (currently named the Government Pension Fund of Norway) in 1990.[3] It is worth noting that Jens Stoltenberg – the then Minister of Industry and Energy, later Prime Minster for the Labour Party in 2000–2001 and 2005–2013 – even indicated that future problems related to climate could undermine the value of Norwegian petroleum wealth. (On the history of Norway's climate policy, see for example Ryggvik, 2010, 2013; Ryggvik & Kristoffersen, 2015; Sæther, 2019.)

The core of the Norwegian fossil ideology is that *Norwegian* oil and gas is not a problem. This ideology is produced through a series of opportunistic arguments, which are highly flexible and vary over time. There is no space here for a thorough discussion of the content but, based on a critical analysis of public arguments from oil companies, politicians and experts, we can identify eight important arguments.

First, Norwegian governments have been active promoters of the dream of a worldwide market for CO_2 quotas – arguably the mainstay of the resource-economic capitalist climate ideology (see for example Martiniussen, 2013). Secondly, Norwegian oil and gas is supposedly the 'cleanest' in the world (e.g. Ryggvik, 2013).[4] Thirdly, Norwegian gas will replace coal in Europe (e.g. Sæther, 2019). The fourth argument is based on technology optimism: through 'CO2-cleansing' and 'negative-emission technologies' Norway can solve its own emissions problem (e.g. Anker, 2018). Fifthly, sponsoring poorer countries to do something: for instance, Norway became the largest contributor to the 'Reducing emissions from deforestation and forest degradation' (REDD) mechanism (e.g. Trædal, 2018: 128). Sixthly, that Norwegian energy will globally 'pull millions of people out of poverty' (quote from a 'fact-book' published by the Oil and Energy Department in 2011 (see Sæther, 2019: 83, 85–91). Seventhly, any critique of Norwegian oil and gas production is disrespectful to workers within these sectors (for examples, see Trædal, 2018: 254). And finally: Norway is only *producing* the oil and gas, if the world really wants fewer emissions, they should reduce their *consumption* (see for example Holmgren, 2019).

Malm and the Zetkin Collective argue that capitalist climate governance can be described as 1) postponing any showdown with fossil capital into the distant future; 2) imposing no serious limits on accumulation; and 3) opening up novel opportunities for the generation of profit; or, in short: 'a form of climate governance that harnesses the energies of capital' (2021: 29). The Norwegian fossil ideology is a particular expression of this. Through the said arguments, discussions are steered in certain directions, away from larger pictures of global warming and into technicalities: to which *degree* is Norwegian oil and gas replacing coal; to which *degree* will Norwegian production be replaced by other countries; to which *degree* is carbon capture and storage possible or not; how is carbon trading affecting people there and there and there; exactly how energy efficient are production processes in Norway compared with any other country; exactly how *cost efficient* is it to cut emissions on the supply or the demand side? Not infrequently discussions end on a level with so many technicalities that only a handful of experts are able to really contribute (see also Ihlen, 2009: 57; Ryggvik, 2013: 74; Fæhn, et al. 2017). One core aspect is 'business friendliness', but we can also mention pure greenwashing, technological optimism and, not least, the role of nationalism. The idea that other countries *and* Norway need to cut emissions is seldom on the table. It is taken for granted that if 'we' reduce emissions someone – not as stupid as us, most likely an evil dictator – will take the money 'we' could have made. In 2019 Johan Sverdrup, a field meant to keep pumping crude oil at least until the year 2070, opened. If Norwegian fossil ideology is so suitable for legitimizing extracting oil and gas decades into the future, is there any need for climate denialists?

The Progress Party: from deniers to delayers on its way to power

The Progress Party has a long history of climate denialism.[5] Founded in 1973 by Anders Lange as an anti-tax party, it has always lived in the tension between economic liberalism and conservative nationalism. Immigration rose to the top of the party's agenda in the 1980s, not least in the 1987 election, where the party nearly doubled its share of the vote from 6.3 per cent to 12.3 per cent. The immense focus on immigration continued into the new millennium and always under the leadership of Carl I. Hagen, the doyen of the party and leader for 28 years, between 1978 and 2006. Some polls in 2002 showed the Progress Party as the largest party in the country, and in the 2003 regional elections it became the single largest party in the counties of Vestfold and Rogaland (the latter also being the centre of oil administration in Norway). Opinion polls around 2006–2008 often showed support of over 30 per cent (Vg.no, 2008), and this remained over 25 per cent for much of the following years. The logical next step was therefore to move from being a 'rebellion' and 'populist' party into a proper governing party. It helped in this respect that Hagen was replaced by Siv Jensen as leader in 2006. But to be accepted as coalition partner in any government, the party also needed a new environmental policy.

When Norway wanted to be an international role model for sustainability in the 1980s (remember Gro Harlem Brundtland), the Progress Party stood out domestically. In 1989 all parties except the Progress Party set concrete targets for stabilizing emissions. The party occupied a maximalist position in both pumping up as much oil as absolutely possible and siphoning even more revenues into the state budget. The term 'petroleum populism' became a mainstay of its politics in the 1990s – two decades later the party had earned the nickname the 'oil party'. The party voted against the first Kyoto Protocol in 2002 when it was ratified in the Norwegian parliament; in 2008 the then centre-left government invited all the opposition parties except the Progress Party for negotiations on Norway's climate policies – which resulted in the Climate Agreement (Sæther, 2019; Ramnefjell, 2017). Chairman Jensen[6] argued in 2008 that not all researchers agree that climate change is caused by humans, and that 'climate scepticism' could be a new vote magnet for the party: 'we might lose a bit in the short term, but in the long run I think the question on climate can be just as important [for us] as immigration' (Jensen, quoted in Nielsen, 2008).[7] Two years later Jensen argued that 'we must not take dramatic measures when it turns out that the basis for the report is not correct', referring to the climate science (quoted in Nrk.no, 2010). In 2012, Per-Willy Amundsen, the party's climate policy spokesman, argued that 'climate scepticism' is inextricably linked to the Progress Party; and that Karl Marx is dead so socialists have found a replacement in 'the CO2-theory' (quoted in Vg.no, 2012).

While such statements sought to undermine the climate science, it soon became clear that the Conservative Party would only let the Progress Party into a government if it accepted this science. Already in 2007 media reported from the national congress that the Progress Party had now got itsself a climate policy. As a first step into new territory for the party, a resolution was approved (with three votes against) that stated there was a difference between 'raising critical questions' and 'rejecting the whole problem' (Vg. no, 2007). When Kyoto-2 (Doha) was being debated in 2013, the Party's parliamentary group first voted unanimously against the bill, but the party then changed course and voted in favour (Falnes, 2013).

The Party's manifesto 2017–2021 (Prinsipp- og handlingsprogram 2017–2021) is a very crude and unpolished version of the Norwegian fossil ideology. While acknowledging that the IPCC's warnings 'provide a basis for caution', the programme also emphasizes how much it respects private property and that the 'earth is always changing and we still know too little about what causes these changes'. The programme presupposes that Norway will conduct reasonable action to cut emissions of climate gases, both nationally and internationally, but is sceptical of 'precautionary principles' and assumes that measures should be results oriented and based on long-term cost–benefit analysis. Further, Norway should not introduce any national rules or tariffs for Norwegian businesses, and a red line for the party would be any climate policies that might 'weaken our international competitiveness and risk putting jobs in danger' (Fremskrittspartiet, 2017: 12, 47).

The real secret behind the Progress Party's climate politics – as so often with climate policies – is found not in the chapter called 'Environment', but rather in the chapter on 'Energy'.[8] Here it is clear that Norwegian oil and gas politics should be stimulated to continue 'wealth creation, profitability and competitiveness in the industry' (Fremskrittspartiet, 2017: 42). The petroleum industry faces challenges because much of its resources are located deeper, in smaller volumes and further from the land – requiring 'niche and tail production'. This must therefore be made profitable to increase the lifetime of the fields and get the highest possible extraction rates (Fremskrittspartiet, 2017: 42). This new climate policy can be exemplified by the party's reaction to the IPCC report 2018. The parliamentary group became 'concerned', and according to Gisle Saudland, MP and environmental policy spokesperson, 'the climate report is a wake-up call'. The logical conclusion, according to Saudland, was therefore to pump up as much gas as possible as soon as possible from the Norwegian continental shelf (Fjellberg, 2018).

The Progress Party and the Norwegian fossil ideology and policy

The government's policy platform from 2013 said that the new government will pursue a 'proactive climate policy' and 'strengthen the climate agreement' (Regjeringen Solberg I, 2013: 4). This is a vocabulary very similar to the 'red-green' government that it preceded. The Progress Party was now part of a government that emphasized the importance of climate change, but also that met that challenge with the Norwegian fossil ideology: solutions should come within market-based systems; dreams of functioning carbon price mechanisms (Trædal, 2018: 220); a continued support for the EU Emissions Trading System; lobbying the EU to export more gas (Sæther, 2019: 74–75); a strong technology-optimism (although the *massive* project under the red-green government on developing cost-effective CO_2 capture and storage technologies was cancelled in 2013), as well as continuing with the plan to electrify the shelf (Regjeringen Solberg I, 2013: 61).

When in government, which positions did the Progress Party aim for? It was neither the Ministry of Culture nor Climate nor Environment. It was the Ministry of Petroleum and Energy: with Tord Lien (2013–2016), Terje Søviknes (2016–2018), Kjell-Børge Freiberg (2018–2019) and Sylvi Listhaug (2019–2020) as ministers. All four were adamant that Norway should *expand* its production of oil several decades into the future. Lien reproduced the fossil ideology when arguing that 'the entire resource base will be exploited, as far as it is socio-economically profitable' (quoted in Trædal, 2018: 191). Søviknes – dubbed the 'lobby minister' for his cosy relations with Norwegian Oil and Gas – called the closing of the oil spigots a 'utopia' (Fremstad, 2017).[9] Freiberg dismissed critics as 'climate romantics' (Thanem, 2018), but it was his successor, Sylvi Listhaug – leader of the party since 2021 – who made most headlines. Listhaug had previously argued that all this talk about CO_2 emissions was 'first and foremost an excuse to introduce more taxes and fees' (Welander, 2020). And as Minister of Agriculture (2013–2015) she combined anti-Muslim and anti-climate politics by demanding *more pork* on the menus in Norwegian prisons (Vojislav Krekling, 2018). When Listhaug was inaugurated as Minister of Petroleum and Energy, Erna Solberg, the then Prime Minister, needed to clarify at a press conference that Listhaug was *not* a climate denier. Only minutes later this became less clear, when Listhaug herself explained to the media that climate change was *also* due to human action, but did not want to answer journalists' questions of how much.

In power, the Progress Party continued the path laid out by, primarily, the Labour Party since the early 1990s. To some degree it even accelerated the pace. The 'red-green' coalition (2005–2013) they succeeded consisted of the Labour Party, the Socialist Left Party and the Centre Party. One of the few victories for the environmental movement (and thus the Socialist Left Party) under this government was that areas outside of Lofoten, Vesteralen and Senja – known together as LoVeSe – should not be opened for exploitation. These areas have remained untouched by extraction activities as they are home to unique ecosystems, being, for example, the spawning grounds for the largest cod stock in the world and one of Europe's largest nesting areas for sea birds, with incredible nature with much tourism. Not even the Progress Party managed to open these areas for extraction under its time in government, and author and politician for the Green Party, Eivind Trædal, noted that the largest victory for the Socialist Left Party was no more significant than the Progress Party could accept when it entered government (Trædal, 2018: 190).[10] Accepting this with one hand, the Progress Party continued with the other to argue for searching for oil outside LoVeSe as well as Møreblokkene, and areas in the far north, such as Jan Mayen and Barents Sea north, considered especially vulnerable. The Progress Party wanted to send in the rigs and the drills 'as soon as possible' (Fremskrittspartiet, 2017: 42; see also Ryggvik & Kristoffersen, 2015). Or, as the leader of the parliamentary group formulated it at the party congress in 2017: 'We will pump up every last remaining drop' (Ramnefjell, 2017).

The number of new licences awarded to new petroleum explorations increased with the Progress Party in government (Bang & Lahn, 2020: 6). In 2019, a record high 88 oil and gas fields were operating (NTB, 2019). Such a record could indeed have happened even without the Progress Party in government, but the party did not miss the opportunity to brag about 'its record'. In 2018 it was pleased to announce in a press release that the 'expansion of exploration areas is the second largest ever and the largest ever in the Barents Sea' (Fremskrittspartiet, 2018b; see also 2018a, 2018c).[11] The main reason why the Progress Party could fairly smoothly shift its position from climate denialism to a 'proactive climate policy' is because the hegemonic fossil ideology already provided enormous possibilities for extracting oil and gas.

Denial that never died

Climate denial is seemingly not needed to legitimize the fossil sector in Norway. Nonetheless, there *is* a lot of it. A survey from 2011 covering 51 countries showed that Norwegians were second-least concerned about climate change – only after Estonians (Nielsen, 2011). One international poll published in 2019 compared denialism in 28 countries, and put Norway at the top, together with Saudi Arabia (Smith, 2019). A recent study shows that more than 36 per cent believe climate change is happening but disagree that human activities are the main cause (Krange et al., 2021: 4).[12] Another survey has shown that no less than 45 per cent of those voting for the Progress Party partly or totally disagree that climate change is caused by humans – to which Carl I. Hagen responded that 'I was hoping it would be many more' (see Cosson-Eide & Hirsti, 2017). Before the election in 2013, 18 of 19 top candidates from the Progress Party believed there were doubts over the UN Climate Panel's claims that climate change is largely due to human activity (Sandvik et al., 2013).

When the former leader Carl I. Hagen launched a comeback in national politics in 2016 it was with climate scepticism as the core issue. He argued, 'the climate hysteria is pure fraud. There is no appreciable correlation between CO_2 emissions and temperatures'; it was also warm in the Viking age when 'nobody drove diesel cars', and that the 'IPCC … holds closed meetings, deceiving world leaders' (quoted in Solvang & Skjelbostad Yset, 2016; see also Ramnefjell, 2016). When the party leadership accepted the fossil ideology in order to remain in control of the Ministry of Petroleum and Energy, Hagen proposed in 2016 the following sentence for the party programme: 'The Progress Party considers climate change to be caused by natural variations, and distances ourselves from the claim that climate change is caused by humans' marginal emission of climate gases'. This did not win a majority, which according to Hagen was because people were 'mobbed into silence' by the 'elite' within the party (Nettavisen, 2016). Hagen also expressed support for Trump for withdrawing from the Paris Agreement and argued that if the truth came out, 'a lot of people [would] lose their income because what they do is totally unnecessary' (quoted in Zachariassen, 2017).

Another high-profile denialist in the party, Christian Tybring-Gjedde, argued at thenational congress in 2019 that the party should focus on two main topics: critiques against environmental science and Islam:

> I am a climate sceptic because I don't think we should relinquish a success. Oil and gas are a success in Norway, and it's a blessing for the world that we have this energy that we can sell. The CO2 hysteria is exaggerated. I just don't believe in it. It's the new idol of the left to believe in this and we should not be a part of it. It's a big lie! We shouldn't speak with a forked tongue! Be clear – be climate sceptics, because that's what the people are! I don't trust the experts! (Quoted in Solås Suvatne & Gilbrant, 2019)

Christian Eikeland, a regional leader, wrote on Facebook that much of what the socialists are doing today reminds him of what Hitler did, and he mentioned 'monopolies, power and propaganda (climate)'. To explain the latter, he argued 'there is a massive propaganda on climate, a climate hysteria' (Skybakmoen, 2019; for more quotes from prominent politicians, see Lia Solberg, 2018).

It should come as no surprise that Greta Thunberg and the Fridays For Future movement are particularly disliked in these circles. 'Sad for children', Hagen commented, 'who are brainwashed to believe that the life-giving gas CO_2 has any negative impacts on the climate!' (Skybakmoen, 2019). When Thunberg decided not to accept the Nordic Council Environment Prize she was awarded in 2019 as a protest against the lack of national climate action – Thunberg mentioned explicitly the high ecological footprint in Nordic countries and that the Norwegian government had given a record number of licences for oil exploration – the denialist far right launched an attack. Gisle Saudland's critique was in a more pragmatic tone: 'The rejection shows how radical and uncompromising parts of the environmental movement have unfortunately become.... I do not think the climate debate benefits from that' (Henden, 2019). Where Saudland wanted to educate Thunberg on how to be an environmental activist, Hagen came with a different tune: 'The 16-year-old girl [Norwegian: *jentungen*] Greta Thunberg is now being listened to as an outstanding climate scientist. Absolutely incredible, and this should make every adult person think' (quoted in Prestegård & Fyen, 2019). Hagen then referred readers to the Breitbart news platform to show that climate research is simply wrong.

The connections that Malm and the Zetkin Collective (2021) identify between racism and climate denialism can be recognized within the Progress Party: the more racist and national-conservative, the more climate denialist. The uncompromising critique of the environmental movement was problematic for those concerned about losing support in cities and especially among young people. Previous State Secretary for the Progress Party, Kai-Morten Terning, responded by saying that while scepticism towards unreasonable climate action is a good thing, Hagen's attack on Thunberg 'was embarrassing to read'. He followed up with a rhetorical question: 'is the person who posted this aware that the Progress Party is in government?' (quoted in Prestegård & Fyen, 2019). The Progress Party left the government in January 2020. The triggering cause was the government's decision to bring home from Syria a woman suspected of affiliation to the Islamic State and her two children – one being seriously ill. One underlying reason – at least according to the national-conservatives within the party – was that popularity decreased because the party had become more 'responsible'. Interestingly, leaving the government had nothing to do with petroleum policy. Sylvi Listhaug replaced Jensen as leader in 2021, which signalled a move towards increased focus on 'anti-environmentalism' and immigration.

Denialists in Norway pick up international discourses, convert them and become part of them – references to Trump and Breitbart show this explicitly. Already from the few quotes included in this chapter we can easily recognize many of the known ingredients from international discourses.

We find conspiracies (e.g. researchers avoid telling the truth as it will cost them their jobs), the 'anti-Marxism'/'anti-left' rhetoric (CO_2 is needed to raise taxes; climate replacing communism), the well-known anti-feminism (e.g. Hagen's *jentungen* ['little girl'] in Norwegian is highly patronizing) and connections to racism (especially from 'hardliners' like Tybring-Gjedde).

Internationally, the history of climate denialism is often associated with large corporations hiding facts or simply lying, with fossil industries being allied with (far-)right movements and conservative think-tanks (see for example Klein, 2014: ch. 1; Oreskes & Conway, 2010: ch. 6). This remains very much the case, even though some companies have shifted more towards greenwashing and capitalist climate governance (cf. Malm & the Zetkin Collective, 2021: ch. 1). Here the Norwegian story is slightly different. The major Norwegian oil company was founded by the state, or, more precisely, Statoil (later Equinor) was founded in 1972, from day one with close ties to the Labour Party.[13] In contrast to fossil ideology, denialism has always been a fringe phenomenon in Norway.

Nevertheless, denialism indeed *is* prominent, and *continues* to be a vital public discourse. The fossil industry can apparently function well without denialists, but did also seem pleased with having them in government. That deniers and delayers so easily can co-exist makes it necessary to further examine relations between them.[14]

Fossil ideology meets climate denial: differences and connections

The fossil ideology and climate denialism constitute two different ideologies which draw legitimacy from *different social relations*. The former is state sanctioned. For everyone who thinks Althusser's (2014) concept of the Ideological State Apparatus is too rigid and deterministic: have a look at how the fossil ideology has been produced in Norway: backed by top economists and the largest Nordic company (Equinor); developed over decades in collaboration among politicians, state managers and the fossil fuel industry; a massive sponsorship of art, culture, sport and research; and a massive PR apparatus (Trædal, 2018: 253; on culture, see for example Jacobsson, 2016).[15] The social forces behind denialism in Norway are very different. These are found more on Facebook groups than in teaching at top universities. It is the delayers, not deniers, that have direct connections to fossil fuel industries.[16]

The two positions differ concerning *knowledge*. Where deniers need to maintain and fabricate lies and fake news, delayers in Norway articulate arguments that are edgy, partly true, always questionable and certainly convenient for their own political-economic interests. Rather than manufacturing lies, this is a selected and cynical use of the truth. In blunt terms, where the deniers seek to alter the truth, delayers seek to hide it.

We can also identify differences between deniers and delayers when it comes to *conflict*. Advocates for the fossil ideology seek to mute and hide conflicts; denialists seek to intensify them. Equinor, for example, wants to discuss openly with the climate movement and climate scientists; a form of communication that indicates that, after all, we are all in the same boat.[17] Conflicts are then mitigated through apparently neutral questions like 'technology' or 'market mechanisms' but always firmly within an eco-modernist framework that seeks to neutralize highly political questions. In sharp contrast, proponents of denialism have a rhetoric that seeks to amplify conflicts: confronting environmental activists, scientists or 'the left', so often in combination with anti-feminism and racism.

As proponents of the fossil ideology argue they are contributing to keeping global warming below 1.5 degrees, we can say they certainly *plan to fail*. Denialism, on the other hand, is an offensive political campaign to crush feminism, cultural Marxists, 'scientists' and others. In this sense they *plan to win*.

Despite said differences – where climate delayers seek status quo and deniers seek war![18] – climate delayers and deniers in Norway live easily together, and can even nourish, legitimize and strengthen each other. We can identify three important connections.

First, the fossil ideology and far-right denialism are – with minor exceptions – based on the same policy for oil and gas extraction: that is, extracting as long as it is profitable. This is why the Progress Party notoriously supported the petroleum policy of the Labour Party and the Conservative Party even before it became 'responsible' enough to join the government.[19] Together, these three parties have formed a solid majority in Parliament over decades.[20] What unites them is 'business friendliness', understood as defending the interests of the fossil industry. It is worth noting that the Progress Party has historically not been included in broad 'climate agreements' (e.g. in 2008) in the Norwegian Parliament, but has always been part of the majority concerning petroleum policy. And to no surprise: petroleum policy trumps environmental policy. Tensions that existed between deniers and delayers both within the government (2013–2020) and within the Progress Party were easily manageable because they had a common petroleum policy.

Secondly, the two discourses both imply that we do not have to change our way of living. Denialism is discursively a reaction to (real or imagined) transformations; a defence against those who – openly or in conspiracy – want to ruin 'our' way of life. The fossil ideology is a heterodox set of ideas, but one common denominator in proposals like trading schemes, carbon markets and the REDD mechanism is that Norway can pay its way out. When the

Norwegian state bought 1 million climate quotas in Bangladesh to subsidize new kitchen ovens for some of the absolute poorest people on the planet, it was clear that it is people in the Global South that must change *their* everyday life in order to save the planet (Martiniussen, 2013). One difference between the two main discourses is that delayers can argue that climate change should be mitigated through consumption-side policies. It is within this framework that we must understand the irony that an oil nation like Norway is world leading in electrifying its car park. These changes are meaningless compared to the transformations that would have to occur if the country shut down its production of oil and gas.

Thirdly, the two approaches share a *nationalist* view on oil and gas in particular, and on climate policy in general. For delayers, *Norwegian* oil and gas is cleaner and better than other nations' fossil fuels. For the deniers, climate science is a direct attack on *Norwegian* interests. Norway is a force for good, but operating in a cruel world where everyone else simply defends their interests.

Deniers and delayers might even *strengthen* each other, not least through providing mutual legitimacy. Deniers legitimize delayers as the Labour Party and the Conservative Party become 'reasonable' and 'accountable' in contrast to the far-right conspiracists. Even those within the Progress Party that for pragmatic reasons 'accept' the science appear sane compared with someone who doesn't believe in it. Proponents of fossil ideology can be shocked and upset over conspiracy theories and denialism from the far right. The Norwegian fossil ideology can then present itself as the reasonable older sibling of denialism.

Delayers also give legitimacy to denialists. Proponents of fossil ideology have over decades contributed to degenerating and obscuring any reasonable debate on oil production and climate in Norway. It is reasonable to believe that the high levels of climate denialism have been nourished by this fact. Equinor, Norwegian Oil and Gas, the Labour Party and the Conservative Party, as well as leading experts and economists, and others, have for decades avoided questions of how severe the climate crisis is, blurred relations between oil and climate change, constantly repeated arguments that are part-truths, hidden information and steered conversations in certain directions. As a consequence, the climate discourse in Norway has been seriously damaged. With unclear arguments,[21] postponing of deadlines[22] and always avoiding the one measure that would mitigate climate change – reducing production – it is no wonder that people think that climate change might not be *that* urgent after all.

Both delayers and deniers will need to acclimatize to a changing setting as the planet gets even warmer. For proponents of the Norwegian fossil ideology, it will indeed be a challenge to come up with new complex, rational and technocratic arguments for why *more* Norwegian oil and gas leads to less emissions globally; especially as temperatures keep rising, heatwaves and wildfires intensify, and flooding and storms progress. One could imagine that denialists will face even greater challenges as the consequences of global warming become all the more visible. After all, they are so wrong! However, that climate denialists are 'wrong' is also the very currency of the position. It will arguably become harder to deny that the world is actually getting warmer, but coming up with 'false' arguments for why this happens, and with what consequences, is not necessarily harder in a warmer world than it is today. Blaming immigrants, feminists or cultural Marxists might surely be absurd, but it is no more or less absurd in an even warmer world. Where delayers must articulate new 'rational' arguments, the deniers can simply intensify their position. In this respect, the future might come with greater challenges for delayers than deniers, as fabricating the truth might be easier than constantly coming up with new and 'plausible' arguments for expanded production of fossil fuels in a burning world.

Notes

1 In this chapter we simply see climate change denial as not believing, dismissing or providing unwarranted doubt that climate change is primarily caused by human activity.

2 Norway is an economy embedded in fossil energy: the oil and gas sector accounted for 14 per cent of GDP and 40 per cent of national export revenue in 2017, and the second-largest export product is commodities and services directly related to the oil industry. Norway is the world's seventh-largest exporter of climate gases. Including oil and gas in climate budgets, a population of around 5 million would be responsible for about 2 per cent of global emissions (Ytterstad, 2012: 4–5; Bang & Lahn, 2020: 1).

3 This is currently the world's largest sovereign wealth fund; it has over US$1.35 trillion in assets and holds 1.4 per cent of all the world's listed companies.

4 Helge Lund, CEO at Statoil (Equinor) said in 2012: 'It is important to take the challenge with climate change seriously, it is one of the most serious issues we face. But at the same time, Norwegian oil and gas production is the most climate-friendly oil production in the world – that is, with least CO2 emissions per barrel – so reducing the Norwegian oil and gas production is a particularly bad climate action [*klimatiltak*], as it will be replaced by less CO2-friendly production abroad' (quoted in Sæther, 2019: 47). Apart from being absurd, this has also historically not been the case, as Saudi Arabia, for example, has had lower CO_2 emissions per barrel, which has certainly nothing to do with any environmental concern (Trædal, 2018: 155).

5 The history of climate denialism in Norway is broader than that of the Progress Party (see for example Ytterstad, 2012), but that falls outside the scope of this

chapter. On denialism in Norway: how it is gendered, see Krange et al. (2019); for a strong ethnographic study, see Norgaard (2011); for how lack of trust in environmental institutions is associated with denial, see Krange et al. (2021); on the methodology of questionnaires about denialism, see Neby & Kolstad (2019); for media analysis, see Ytterstad (2012); and for the Norwegian case discussed in relation to other countries, see Malm & the Zetkin Collective (2021), esp. ch. 4.

6 The anti-feminist party had a *formann* (translating to Chairman or foreman) when Jensen was elected in 2006. This was changed to the gender-neutral 'leader' only in 2009.

7 This coincides with the party suggesting closing all borders to people from Muslim countries and limiting asylum seekers to 100 per year (Rønneberg, 2008).

8 For an interesting historical discussion on relations between the politics of environment and politics of energy in the US context, see Aronczyk and Espinoza (2021), ch. 3.

9 Tommy Hansen, Director of Norwegian Oil and Gas, expressed his gratitude upon Søviknes's resignation, for 'great cooperation' and a 'steady course in petroleum policy' (quoted in Steinsbu Wasberg et al., 2018).

10 Ryggvik (2013) also showed that the red-green government did, for the first time, implement some measures that would limit investments in the oil sector just months before it lost the election in 2013.

11 Aside from petroleum policy, we can add the party's subsidies to road (and tunnel) projects, increased subsidies to airports, the battle against windmills and an agricultural policy favouring meat production. MP and transport policy spokesperson, Morten Stordalen, argued that flying should be considered a part of public transport and improving bus and railway was 'a utopia' – soon we will have electric planess and then 'flying will be one of the cleanest things one can do' (quoted in Jordheim, 2019).

12 The same study shows that only 1.6 per cent believe that climate change does not happen at all.

13 In 2007 Statoil merged with Norsk Hydro's oil and gas operations (a company with historical ties to the Conservative Party).

14 A telling example of this co-existence comes from the MP Oskar Grimstad. Although not himself among the denialists within the party, he nonetheless argued: 'we have climate sceptics among us, and that's the way it should be' (quoted in Falnes, 2013).

15 A more recent phenomenon is that politicians, TV series and employers are hailing Norwegians as subjects of a nation made happy by fossil fuels. Oil and gas fields opened in the 2010s were also named after nineteenth-century national heroes: Ivar Andreas Aasen (founder of the written language nynorsk), Aasta Hansteen (artist and advocate of women's rights) and Johan Svedrup (Prime Minister who introduced parliamentarism).

16 On both formal and informal networks, see Sæther (2019). One important formal network is Konkraft: a collaboration platform between the Norwegian Oil

and Gas Association (an employers' organization), the Norwegian Shipowners' Association, the Confederation of Norwegian Enterprise, and the Norwegian Confederation of Trade Unions (through United Federation of Trade Unions and Industri Energi). An interesting informal group is the so-called 'oil network' within the Labour Party; established by 1981, where key persons within the Labour Party meet representatives from the oil business. It has been hard to examine the network as it has been operating in secret, and we know that even central ministers within the Labour Party (e.g. Thorbjørn Berntsen, former Deputy Leader, MP 1977–1997 and Minister of Environmental 1990–1997) were never informed about the network. The 'secret' network has been exposed, and thus criticized, but Sæther (2019) has recently shown that it still exists (see also Martiniussen, 2013; Ryggvik, 2013).

17 As when Equinor CEO Eldar Sætre spoke at a conference in 2018 hosted by ZERO, a Norwegian environmental organization: 'I want to thank Zero for cooperating with others in challenging us. It has made us better, so continue doing so' (cited in Fannemel, 2018).

18 Thanks to Irma Allen for this formulation.

19 One striking example is when the three parties back in 2000 deposed a centre government – the Bondevik's First Cabinet, consisting of the Centre Party, the Christian Democratic Party and the Liberal Party – on a climate question, as the government did not want to build gas-powered power plants without cleaning technology on Norwegian soil.

20 Recently the Centre Party has also turned very 'pro-oil', further strengthening the fossil ideology. The Centre Party's electorate is highly climate sceptic (35%) second only to the Progress Party, as mentioned on 45 per cent. Next on the list comes the Conservative Party with 20 per cent and the Labour Party with 10 per cent (Cosson-Eide & Hirsti, 2017).

21 One example that certainly points to delaying: where 'everyone' thought the Climate agreement [*Klimaforliket*] from 2008 meant Norway aimed at reducing emissions by 30 per cent by 2020, starting from a 1990 baseline, it became clear after a few years that the government, under Jens Stoltenberg's (Labour Party) leadership, had included a 'track of reference'. This estimated how high the emissions *could* become in 2020 if nothing were done, and then aimed to reduce by 30 per cent from that. The level was suddenly 6 per cent, not 30 per cent (Trædal, 2018: 170).

22 Targets from 1989 that aimed at the year 2000 were cancelled in 1996, and new targets towards 2012 were replaced in 2008 by a new deadline in 2020. In 2016 this target was scrapped, and now everyone talks about 2030 (Trædal, 2018: 217).

References

Althusser, L. (2014). *On the Reproduction of Capitalism: Ideology and Ideological State Apparatuses*. London: Verso.

Anker, P. (2018). A Pioneer Country? A History of Norwegian Climate Politics. *Climatic Change*, 151: 29–41.

Aronczyk, M., & Espinoza, M. I. (2021). *A Strategic Nature: Public Relations and the Politics of American Environmentalism.* New York: Oxford University Press.

Bang, G., & Lahn, B. (2020). From Oil as Welfare to Oil as Risk? Norwegian Petroleum Resource Governance and Climate Policy, *Climate Policy*, 28(8): 997–1009.

Cantor, M. (2019). Could 'climate delayer' become the political epithet of our times? *The Guardian*, 2 March, www.theguardian.com/environment/2019/mar/01/could-climate-delayer-become-the-political-epithet-of-our-times (accessed 28 November 2019).

Cosson-Eide, H. & Hirsti, K. (2017). De har landets mest klimaskeptiske velgere. *Nrk.no*, 1 September, www.nrk.no/norge/de-har-landets-mest-klimaskeptiske-velgere-1.13655920 (accessed 28 November 2019).

Falnes, J. (2013). Frp snur – stemmer for ny klimaavtale. *Dagsavisen*, 5 December, https://e24.no/norsk-oekonomi/i/xPeo0p/frp-snur-stemmer-for-ny-klimaavtale (accessed 5 December 2019).

Fannemel, E. (2018). Olja utfordrer miljøbevegelsen på hjemmebane. *Norsk Olje og Gass*, 8 November, www.norskoljeoggass.no/om-oss/nyheter/2018/11/equinor-pa-zerokonferanse/ (accessed 4 February 2021).

Fjellberg, A. (2018). Frp's klimaløsning: – vi må pumpe opp så mye gass som mulig. *Dagbladet*, 23 October, www.dagbladet.no/nyheter/frps-klimalosning---vi-ma-pumpe-opp-sa-mye-gass-som-mulig/70337563 (accessed 5 December 2019).

Fremskrittspartiet (2017). *Prinsipp- og handlingsprogram 2017–2021.* Oslo: Fremskrittspartiet.

Fremskrittspartiet (2018a). Olje og energy: dette har vi gjort. *Fremskrittspartiet.no*, www.frp.no/frp-i-regjering/olje-og-energi (accessed 5 December 2019).

Fremskrittspartiet (2018b). Petroleumsvirksomhet. *Fremskrittspartiet.no*, www.frp.no/tema/energi/petroleumsvirksomhet [FIX] (accessed 5 December 2019).

Fremskrittspartiet (2018c). Klima og miljø: dette har vi gjort. *Fremskrittspartiet.no*, www.frp.no/frp-i-regjering/klima-og-miljo (accessed 5 December 2019).

Fremstad, M. (2017). Oljeministern: – Ikke realistisk att vi kun skal satsa på nye næringer. *ABC Nyheter*, 5 January, www.abcnyheter.no/nyheter/politikk/2017/01/05/195268271/oljeministeren-ikke-realistisk-vi-kun-skal-satse-pa-nye-naeringer (accessed 5 December 2019).

Fæhn, T., Hagem, C., Lindholt, L., Mæland, S., & Rosendahl, K. E. (2017). Climate Policies in a Fossil Fuel Producing Country: Demand versus Supply Side Policies. *Energy Journal*, 38(1): 77–102.

Henden, R. E. (2019). Fremskrittspartiet refser Greta Thunberg: – hoven og overlegen. *Dagbladet*, 30 October, www.dagbladet.no/nyheter/frp-refser-greta-thunberg—hoven-og-overlegen/71765249 (accessed 5 December 2019).

Holmgren, C. (2019). Norge tar inte klimatansvar för oljan. *Sverigesradio*, 2 November, https://sverigesradio.se/sida/artikel.aspx?programid=83&artikel=7335804 (accessed 26 November 2019).

Ihlen, Ø. (2009). The Oxymoron of 'Sustainable Oil Production': The Case of the Norwegian Oil Industry. *Business Strategy and the Environment*, 18(1): 53–63.

Jacobsson, J. (2016). Maja Solveig Kjelstrup Ratkje vill stoppa oljesponsringen av norskt kulturliv. *Hymn.se*, 13 March, hymn.se/2016/03/13/maja-solveig-kjelstrup-ratkje-vill-stoppa-oljesponsringen-av-norskt-kulturliv. 13.03.2016 (accessed 21 November 2023).

Jordheim, H. (2019). Frp er kritisk til 'flyskam': – Å fly vil bli noe av det reneste vi kan gjøre. *E24*, 28 April, https://e24.no/naeringsliv/i/zGlqO4/frp-er-kritisk-til-flyskam-aa-fly-vil-bli-noe-av-det-reneste-vi-kan-gjoere (accessed 5 December 2019).

Klein, N. (2014). *This Changes Everything: Capitalism vs. the Climate*. London: Allen Lane.

Krange, O., Kaltenborn, B. P., & Hultman, M. (2019). Cool Dudes in Norway: Climate Change Denial among Conservative Norwegian Men. *Environmental Sociology*, 5(1): 1–11.

Krange, O., Kaltenborn, B. P., & Hultman, M. (2021). 'Don't confuse me with facts' – How Right Wing Populism Affects Trust in Agencies Advocating Anthropogenic Climate Change as a Reality. *Humanities and Social Sciences Communications*, 8(1): 1–9.

Lia Solberg, K. (2018). Drammen Frp nekter å tro på klimaforskerne. *Dagsavisen*, 23 July, www.dagsavisen.no/nyheter/innenriks/drammen-frp-nekter-a-tro-pa-klimaforskerne-1.1176627 (accessed 28 November 2019).

Malm, A. & the Zetkin Collective (2021). *White Skin, Black Fuel: On the Danger of Fossil Fascism*. London: Verso.

Martiniussen, E. (2013). *Drivhuseffekten: Klimapolitikken som Forsvant*. Oslo: Manifest.

Neby, S., & Kolstad, E. (2019). BT taler klimafornekternes sak. *Bergens Tidende*, 18 November, www.bt.no/btmeninger/debatt/i/b56lmq/BT-taler-klimafornekternes-sak (accessed 5 December 2019).

Nettavisen (2016). Syv Frp-ere på Stortinget tror ikke på menneskeskapte klimaendringer. *Nettavisen, unsigned*, 16 December, www.nettavisen.no/nyheter/innenriks/syv-frp-ere-pa-stortinget-tror-ikke-pa-menneskeskapte-klimaendringer/3423294007.html (accessed 5 December 2019).

Nielsen, A. (2008). Siv skal ta klima-bløfferne. *VG.no*, 28 March, www.vg.no/nyheter/innenriks/i/ggP70/siv-skal-ta-klima-bloefferne (accessed 31 October 2023).

Nielsen, A. (2011). *Sustainable Efforts & Environmental Concerns Around the World: A Nielsen Report*. August 2011, www.nielsen.com/wp-content/uploads/sites/3/2019/04/nieslen-sustainability-report.pdf (accessed 28 November 2019).

Norgaard, K. M. (2011). *Living in Denial: Climate Change, Emotions, and Everyday Life*. Cambridge: MIT Press.

Nrk.no (2010). Jensen kritisk til FNs klimapanel. *Nrk.no*, 31 January, www.nrk.no/klima/jensen-kritisk-til-fns-klimapanel-1.6971091 (accessed 27 November 2019).

NTB (2019). Rekordmange felt i produksjon på norsk sokkel. *Nettavisen News*, 27 September, www.nettavisen.no/nyheter/innenriks/rekordmange-felt-i-produksjon-pa-norsk-sokkel/3423852716.html (accessed 28 November 2019).

Oreskes, N., & Conway, E. M. (2010). *Merchants of Doubt: How a Handful of Scientists Obscured the Truth on Issues from Tobacco Smoke to Global Warming*. New York: Bloomsbury.

Prestegård, S., & Fyen, S. (2019). Statssekretær Tommy Skjervold ut mot 'klimahysteri'-post fra Oslo Frp. *Dagsavisen*, 23 September, www.dagsavisen.no/oslo/statssekreter-tommy-skjervold-ut-mot-klimahysteri-post-fra-oslo-frp-1.1589246 (accessed 5 December 2019).

Ramnefjell, G. (2016). Klimaskeptikere er en stor velgergruppe: Ikke rart Frp plasserer en av dem i regjering. *Dagbladet*, 20 December, www.dagbladet.no/kultur/klimaskeptikere-er-en-stor-velgergruppe-ikke-rart-frp-plasserer-en-av-dem-i-regjering/66560972 (accessed 21 November 2023).

Ramnefjell, G. (2017). Til siste dråpe. *Dagbladet*, 11 May, www.dagbladet.no/kultur/til-siste-drape/67562054 (accessed 21 November 2023).

Regjeringen Solberg I (2013). Sundvolden-plattformen: Politisk plattform for en regjering utgått av Høyre og Fremskrittspartiet. *Sundvollen*, 7 October, www.regjeringen.no/no/dokumenter/politisk-plattform/id743014/ (accessed 31 October 2023).

Rønneberg, K. (2008). Frp vil stenge grensen. *Aftenposten*, 7 April.

Ryggvik, H. (2010). *Til Siste Dråpe: Om Oljens Politiske Økonomi*. Oslo: Aschehoug.

Ryggvik, H. (2013). *Norsk Olje og Klima: En Skisse til Nedkjøling*. Oslo: Gyldendal.

Ryggvik, H., & Kristoffersen, B. (2015). Heating Up and Cooling Down the Petrostate: The Norwegian Experience. In Thomas Princen, Jack P. Manno & Pamela L. Martin (eds), *Ending the Fossil Fuel Era*. Cambridge: MIT Press, pp. 259–60.

Sandvik, S., Sollund, S., & Randen, A. (2013). FrP-topper tror ikke på klimaforskningen. *Nrk.no*, 24 May, www.nrk.no/valg/2013/fortsatt-stor-klimaskepsis-i-frp-1.11040789 (accessed 5 December 2019).

Skybakmoen, J. (2019). Klimafornekterne i Frp holder stand: – kulldioksid er selve livets gass! *Filter Nyheter*, 17 June, https://filternyheter.no/klimafornekterne-i-frp-holder-stand-kulldioksid-er-selve-livets-gass/ (accessed 5 December 2019).

Smith, M. (2019). International poll: most expect to feel impact of climate change, many think it will make us extinct. *YouGov*, 15 September, https://yougov.co.uk/topics/science/articles-reports/2019/09/15/international-poll-most-expect-feel-impact-climate (accessed 28 November 2019).

Solås Suvatne, S., & Gilbrant, J. (2019). NÅ: Tybring-Gjedde vant Frp-kamp etter advarsel om muslimer. Audio recording of speech. *Dagbladet*, 5 May, www.dagbladet.no/nyheter/na-tybring-gjedde-vant-frp-kamp-etter-advarsel-om-muslimer/71042754 (accessed 21 November 2023).

Solvang, F., & Skjelbostad Yset, S. (2016). FrP-Hagen avviser sammenheng mellom klimaendringer og CO_2-utslipp. *NRK*, 13 December, www.nrk.no/norge/Fremskrittspartiet-hagen-avviser-sammenheng-mellom-klimaendringer-og-co_-utslipp-1.13274228 (accessed 31 October 2023).

Steinsbu Wasberg, E., Sagmoen, I., & Morten Skaug, O. (2018). Norsk olje og gass: – en tydelig talsmann. *E24*, 30 August, https://e24.no/norsk-oekonomi/i/0nBqkM/norsk-olje-og-gass-en-tydelig-talsmann (accessed 21 November 2023).

Sæther, A. K. (2019). *De Beste Intensjoner: Oljelandet i Klimakampen*. Oslo: Cappelen Damm.

Thanem, T. (2018). 'Kjell-Børge Freiberg (Frp) blir ny olje- og energiminister', *Verdens Gang*, 30 August, www.vg.no/nyheter/innenriks/i/dd9owo/kjell-boerge-freiberg-frp-blir-ny-olje-og-energiminister (accessed 21 November 2023).

Trædal, E. (2018). *Det svarte skiftet*. Oslo: Cappelen Damm.

Vg.no (2007). Fremskrittspartiet skaffet seg en klimapolitikk. *Vg.no*, 13 May, www.vg.no/nyheter/innenriks/i/rqvGm/Fremskrittspartiet-skaffet-seg-en-klimapolitikk (accessed 26 June 2018).

Vg.no (2008). Frp størst på ny måling. *Vg.no*, 4 June, www.vg.no/nyheter/utenriks/i/rB2E0/frp-stoerst-paa-ny-maaling (accessed 21 November 2023).

Vg.no (2012). Fremskrittspartiet: CO2 er sosialistenes nye Karl Marx. *Vg.no*, 6 December, www.vg.no/nyheter/innenriks/i/Gkvbq/frp-co2-er-sosialistenes-nye-karl-marx (accessed 21 November 2023).

Vojislav Krekling, D. (2018). Her er 11 Listhaug-utspill som har satt fyr på Norge. *Nrk.no*, 13 March, www.nrk.no/norge/her-er-11-listhaug-utspill-som-har-satt-fyr-pa-norge-1.13958713 (accessed 7 February 2022).

Welander, P. (2020). Kända politiker som är klimathotsskeptiker – del 1. *Klimatupplysningen.se*, 3 January, https://klimatupplysningen.se/kanda-politiker-som-ar-klimathotsskeptiker-del-1/ (accessed 5 February 2021).

Ytterstad, A. (2012). Norwegian Climate Change Policy in the Media: Between Hegemony and Good Sense. Diss., University of Oslo, Faculty of Humanities.

Zachariassen, S. (2017). Jeg gir full støtte till Trump. *ABC*, 2 June, www.abcnyheter.no/nyheter/2017/06/02/195307009/carl-i.-hagen-jeg-gir-full-stotte-til-trump (accessed 26 June 2018).

7

Strategic whiteness: how ethno-nationalism is shaping land reform and food security discourse in South Africa

Lisa Santosa

In this chapter, I will use what Du Toit (2019) calls 'policy-sensemaking' to explain the populist right-wing assumptions that play a large part in determining the public response to land reform debates in South Africa:

> Engaging with the politics of the land question requires a serious confrontation with its symbolic and affective dimensions, an appreciation of its salience and significance, and an understanding of its role in the discursive construction of political frontiers in South Africa. (Du Toit, 2019: 23)

It is important to deconstruct the rhetorical strategies that underlie gatekeeping around resource entitlement and how it is based in a logic of enclosure, where viability is defined by liberal, market-based property regimes that are remnants of the colonial era. I argue that post-apartheid-era liberalism allows for the mainstream rhetorical turn to the right, through strategies of discourse Steyn (2012) labels 'epistemologies of ignorance'. Land holds a symbolic significance in the post-apartheid political landscape, often a scapegoat for unresolved racial tensions combined with the persistent economic inequality yet to be significantly addressed, which is why I focus on discussions around land reform to get a sense of how far-right groups engage with civil society and the state at the rhetorical level. Land equates symbolically to property, which signifies human rights and self-determination for proponents of liberalism. For marginalized groups, land signals the opportunity to take back what was stolen from them through colonial conquest and apartheid.

> To talk about land is to talk about belonging; it is to talk about what President Ramaphosa terms South Africa's 'original sin'; colonial dispossession. It is, in other words, to invoke, without saying it in so many words, the national question – and to challenge the terms upon which the post-colonial democratic order has been shaped. (Du Toit, 2019: 23)

Land restitution policies post-apartheid were pursued through a neoliberal economic framework in alignment with major international trade and development organizations dominated by the hegemonic influence of the industrialized world. The initial post-apartheid strategy for land reform was incorporated into the Reconstruction and Development Plan, which was an attempt to kickstart the post-apartheid economy by way of privatization and drawing in foreign direct investment through trade liberalization. The African National Congress (ANC) government initially adopted a market-based 'willing buyer, willing seller' model that compensated current landowners for their land at market rates, making land reform prohibitively expensive, preventing the timely processing of land claim applications (Aliber & Cousins, 2013). For those who did have their land restituted, the government required participation in cooperative schemas that expanded the production capacity of the land to signal commitment to food security as envisioned by industrialized countries (Cousins & Scoones, 2010; Greenberg, 2015). Due to lack of training and inputs for newly minted farmers to produce at this scale, these schemas largely failed. The failure of these projects has provided justification for current agricultural landowners, white farmers that own farmland due to historical colonial territorialization, to underline their entitlement as contributors to national prosperity and underscore the failures of the ANC's post-apartheid policies. Right-wing organizations in South Africa have reshaped the language of former colonial imaginaries by using transformed identity narratives that prompt nostalgia of nationalist discourses prevalent during apartheid. The controversial amendment to the South African constitution, article 25, proposing expropriation without compensation (Parliament of South Africa, 2019), became a lightning rod for controversy because it challenged the liberal state's role in reinforcing property regimes. The amendment would allow for privately held property to be seized by the state for the purpose of land redistribution without compensating the current owners for its value. Privately owned land is still overwhelmingly held by white landowners who use it for large-scale commercial agricultural operations (Ashton, 2012).

In order for white minority groups to include themselves in the post-apartheid liberal democratic 'rainbow nation', the language of colonial trusteeship and racial segregation has to be couched in terms of democratic participation. Groups that represented liberal whites during apartheid such as the Democratic Alliance (DA) and the South African Institute of Race Relations (IRR) have taken a decidedly skewed political orientation to the right, siding them with AfriForum, a right-wing minority Afrikaner interest group, and the apartheid-era white agricultural unions now conglomerated into Agri SA. The commitment to liberalism and property rights is largely what ties together the special interests and language of the political alliances of far-right groups in South Africa and abroad. Similar to other right-wing groups in the industrialized world, market economies and entrepreneurial individualism are conflated with human rights, democracy and free speech, which is reliant on the erasure of past abuse and dispossession that accumulated the capital necessary for European global dominance. By investigating the rhetorical strategies of the far right around land reform and race, we see that many of the tropes of racialization during apartheid are still used to claim gatekeeping and resource entitlement, as the liberalized post-apartheid economy prioritizes large-scale industrial operations with global supply chain linkages over the subsistence needs of the most marginalized. This signals the limitations of the liberal democratic state as a vehicle for emancipatory projects like land reform, as well as its ability to reverse the state-sanctioned violence and territorialization characteristic of the colonial era. Lastly, the findings emphasize the importance of understanding the symbolic and affective dimensions of policy debate as a necessary facet of policy implementation, which emphasizes the importance of historical background in shaping civic cooperation.

Reactionary narratives of the far right in South Africa

I begin by using the research of Steyn (2012) to explicate the rhetorical strategies adopted by white supremacist and far-right groups in South Africa. Steyn uses a framework called *epistemologies of ignorance* to describe discourses around Afrikaner identity and race in post-apartheid South Africa. She draws from McHugh's (2005) definition of epistemologies of ignorance as an active engagement in choosing what is remembered and what is brought to light, which is useful in explaining historical erasure that is characteristic of post-apartheid Afrikaner and white minority discourse. For settler colonial societies such as South Africa, social reproductions of ignorance are dependent on racial imaginaries that enforce social hierarchies and delimit access to resources. Steyn's analysis is useful for outlining the motivations and assumptions of far-right groups and why they deploy reactionary rhetoric in this way.

The Racial Contract by Charles Mills (1997: 18) provides an explanatory framework for white ignorance, describing it as a cognitive dysfunction that renders whites unable to perceive the world that they themselves created. The Racial Contract is a global commitment to ignorance that upholds structures of white supremacy, denying the lived experiences of the subjugated. White ignorance is a strategic move enabled by creating structures of power through legal mechanisms that make *a priori* claims of egalitarianism in settler colonial societies (Applebaum, 2008). Hoagland (2007) states that in contrast, there is a refusal of relationality that white ignorance cultivates, and the lack of accountability or denial of responsibility white ignorance allows. White South Africans tread a thin line of discourse that justifies their continued occupation of dispossessed land after generations of capital accumulation gained from forced labour.

Steyn and Foster dissect what continues to be a resistant whiteness to the transformation of South Africa as an inclusive democracy. The authors demonstrate this by analysing what they come to call *repertoires for talking white* which are deployed as 'New South Africa Speak' (NSAS) and 'white ululation', which 'allows the ideological function of the discourse to operate efficiently while at the same time rendering the position of the speaker/ writer more difficult to pin down and critique. Moreover, the ambivalence enables positive self-presentation even as hard-nosed self-interest is being pursued' (2008: 27). These rhetorical strategies serve to reproduce apartheid-era dominance for whites, while also incorporating the popularized discourses that developed as a result of instituting inclusive democracy. NSAS carries assumptions of democratic principles such as egalitarianism, reconciliation and freedom; seeking to recover a visage of dignity and reconciliation for white South Africans who seek to participate in democratic processes and consensus. Framing rhetoric under these assumptions allows white South Africans to no longer associate with the violence of former racial regimes and signals goodwill efforts to reconcile the wrongs of the previous government. Despite these impressions, NSAS is implemented strategically, embracing parts of an inclusive democracy that do not threaten their status or enforce restitution through non-racialism (MacDonald, 2006). By stressing the notion of an even playing field, poverty and failure are no longer structural factors but individual choices, which allows whites to deflect any responsibility for societal change while also claiming victim status. Despite appearances of commitment to egalitarianism, there is a selective application of inclusive democratic principles (Steyn & Foster, 2008: 29, 32).

In contrast to NSAS, white ululation engages in an inclusive democracy by way of representation politics (Steyn & Foster, 2008), claiming that whites as a minority group risk being victimized by a non-white majority. This rhetorical strategy actually flips the narrative on its head to now claim that the newly inclusive democratic government is targeting or neglecting minorities (whites) by adopting policies that aim to reverse the inequalities created during apartheid. With bureaucratic seats increasingly filled by black politicians through affirmative action and Black Economic Empowerment (BEE) policies, any complex societal ill that has not been successfully addressed becomes evidence of its failure and is linked to societal decline. Crime in South Africa is often a focus of WU, being considered a visible symptom of a society in decline. By shifting blame to the ANC, whites are able to deflect any calls to change, convinced that the apartheid-era government managed societal needs better than the current one (Steyn & Foster, 2008: 35, 38, 40).

The transition from a colonial state to an inclusive democratic one requires hegemonic groups to retool their approach to how they can justify their continued occupation and extraction. Rhetorical strategies based in historical assumptions of white dominance are a key tool for maintaining a sense of entitlement to the services of the state, which has in the past catered to white interests at a large disadvantage to other groups. The rhetorical strategies of white supremacists obscure the complicity and material benefits that structural inequality allows whites by using the discourse of egalitarianism and liberal democracy. The following sections will demonstrate how these rhetorical strategies are deployed around issues of property and entitlement; in this case the land reform debate is the arena of tension in the South African political landscape.

The case of South Africa: land reform, neoliberalism and territorialization

This section will outline the historical basis for assumptions around race, property and resource entitlement in South Africa. I focus on land restitution as an arena where multiple contestations are meted out; the approach to land reform belies post-apartheid commitment to liberal principles of property enclosure and productive fitness, which thwarts any attempts to redistribute the country's resources. Even with the commitment to land restitution written into the post-apartheid constitution, capital accumulation takes precedence, shoring up inequalities produced through colonial territorialization and apartheid. The hegemonic adherence to liberal principles imported through colonization provides legitimacy to the right-wing campaigns that reify the racial tropes of apartheid. This section will provide background to the contestations, with the rhetoric used by right-wing groups in South Africa in the next section.

Historically in South Africa, a system of coerced black labour was necessary to produce agricultural commodities on the scale of industrial-level efficiency, which necessitated subordination of black sharecropping and tenant labour. Colonial agricultural schemas were often a net negative venture that was highly subsidized by the colonial authority and then the apartheid state (Giliomee, 2003: 347). Landowning was a signal of status to the gentry of the metropole, so the actual productive output of the estate was low and depended highly on black indentured labour as the landowners generally made money outside farming (Keegan, 1986: 637). As European demand for wool heightened in the mid-nineteenth century, non-productive farms suddenly became very lucrative ventures which incentivized the transition to large-scale industrial agriculture to increase production for export to the

British metropole. As the boom precipitated, indebted Boers began to sell land in parcels which made cultivation a logical use of the land and soil instead of animal husbandry of game hunting (Keegan, 1986: 638). Black tenants and sharecroppers were used in place of costly technological inputs for their superior knowledge of the soil.

Foreign colonial investment in the farms served to incentivize using black labour, valuing the skill of black farmers while also rendering them subhuman. Black farm labour performed the tasks and duties that Boer landowners were either too unskilled for or were seen as impure labour for whites. This attitude stems from conceptions of civility that were effectively imported to the African continent with them: 'The landed whites saw themselves as an emergent class, a class in the making; and their corporate self-perception was based fundamentally on a pre-existing sense of racial identity as standard-bearers of European civilization' (Keegan, 1986: 640). The ability of black sharecroppers to cultivate the land successfully became a threat to Boers who were economically precarious and unable to survive under the harsh conditions of the climate.

Capitalist accumulation in rural areas was bolstered by the capital influx from urban centres because of lucrative mining in the region in the early twentieth century. The mineral boom provided the capital to support a state intervention in economic sectors; in this case capital was funnelled into the rural areas where Boers were indebted and struggling. State support helped to incorporate them into the capitalist class. The flexible loans given to Afrikaner farmers allowed for the industrialization of farming practices which entailed a scaling up of productive capacity that we now see as large-scale industrial farming (Keegan, 1986: 642). Suppression of black producers and their subsequent proletarianization was a key element of capital accumulation strategies for imperialist and Afrikaner nationalist entrepreneurs. A litany of legislation such as the Group Areas Act of 1950 targeted black South Africans as a mechanism to violently displace and control their resources and labour. As black South Africans became relegated to the Bantustans, sharecropper labour declined in use due to pass controls and shifts to mining labour.

One of the first major acts passed through Parliament after the post-apartheid elections was the 1994 Restitution of Land Rights Act. The *de facto* system used to determine the value of land to be restituted is the 'willing buyer, willing seller' model, which is essentially a market-based supplyand-demand model. The willing-buyer, willing-seller model comes with a litany of stipulations, such as the land is to be used under certain conditions and generational transference of ownership is limited. The proposed plan is that though the constitution seeks to ensure the rightful restitution of land, individuals must *earn* their share of the land through its productive development (INDABA, 2015). Cousins (2017) notes how this schema will likely only benefit those well placed in the system to capture the benefits in backdoor partnerships.

The continuous support of neoliberal economic policies shapes production and supply chains that are reminiscent of the apartheid era. Cousins and Scoones argue that contemporary agricultural production aligns with the international development nexus, which operates on assumptions of technocratic viability:

> The dominant framing of viability is embodied in technical recommendations around 'minimum farm sizes', 'economic units', and 'carrying capacities'. Methods and measures for appraisal of land reform – in planning, monitoring and evaluation – are defined in terms of marginal returns on investment or farm profitability. (Cousins & Scoones, 2010: 32)

Cousins and Scoones identify the normative assumptions in models of economic development which are based in notions of scarcity which require a technological fix at the macro scale to produce sufficient economies of scale. The technocratic model of agriculture is fundamentally rooted in the ideology of progress through modern frameworks of legibility that centre the needs of white European men (Cousins & Scoones, 2010: 35). Because modern progress situates the white European male at the apex, models of agricultural development were based in temperate zone acclimation and not the indigenous African climate:

> These understandings and techniques, often based on temperate zone agro-ecologies and production systems very different than those that were being developed in practice by farmers in Southern Africa, became the standardised tools-of-the-trade for planning and implementing agricultural development. (Cousins & Scoones, 2010: 34)

Even with the known realities of market-based, export-oriented approaches to land reform and its failures, the technocratic narrative of food security conveniently erases the historical pathways of racial coercion and spatial resource segregation that resulted from the colonial era and state-sanctioned apartheid. Instead, the conversation gets reoriented towards large-scale commercial farming that is predominantly monopolized by white farmers and global agrocorps as a result of the retrenchment of centuries of forced removals.

The next section will detail the rhetoric deployed by influential right-wing groups in South Africa aiming to influence public discourse and policy debates. Liberal values are a common over-riding theme in how right-wing groups engage with the state and the civic arena. Groups that were historically progressive during apartheid have taken a hard turn to the right of the political spectrum; paradoxically, these groups, such as the DA and the IRR, which campaigned to end apartheid and racial segregation, now use rhetorical tactics such as non-racialism to obscure the effects that apartheid continues to have on racial inequality. The politics of representation have become a key tool for right-wing and white supremacist groups to lobby the state for access to resources; in this case land is a significant symbolic and material resource. By supporting the *de facto* 'willing buyer, willing seller' model for land restitution, right-wing lobbying groups are gatekeeping the resources taken from colonial territorialization but obscuring that process through the rhetoric of liberal democratic engagement and productive fitness.

Property, land reform and liberal democracy: an arena for racial tension

South African governmental institutions are no longer solely controlled by a white racial minority, which leaves whites uncertain about their representation in post-apartheid politics. In reality, whites in South Africa continue to control the vast majority of privately owned land and corporate monopolies in the country (Du Toit, 2019). The arena of controversy for racial tensions has consolidated in land reform debates, particularly those surrounding agricultural land, which is primarily held by whites. This section will profile influential right-wing organizations in South Africa, and how they spread misinformation and racial panic with the aim of obscuring the ways that the post-apartheid neoliberal economy continues to reinforce the structure of inequality that is still present in the country. There are some key liberal concepts that align these organizations and how they frame political issues and policy interventions. Private property is foundational to how right-wing organizations interface with the state, being framed as the essential basis for rule of law and protection of human rights. This framing is important for erasing the possible generational advantages given to whites; where the ideology of the liberal democratic state presses the notion that the effects of structural barriers and historic pathways are in fact individual failures. The economic orientation of these right-wing groups is unfettered privatization and market-based incentives originating in property regimes. For instance, the DA states in its Value and Principles that it supports 'the right of all people to private ownership and to participate freely in the market economy' (Democratic Alliance, 2019). For the IRR, the commitments are the same: in the 'What We Stand For' section of its website it states that 'Property rights for all and Real Economic Empowerment' are part of its core principles (South African Institute of Race Relations, 2021a). AfriForum's five core principles are vaguely defined as 'safety', 'cultural identity', 'organisation building', 'self-dependence' and 'justice', which underlie its mission and goals (AfriForum, n. d.). Even the national organization of agricultural unions under Agri SA belie their neoliberal leanings when speaking about the 'land debate', especially concerning the section 25 amendment. Instead of the nationalization of parcels of privately held agricultural land, Agri SA pushes titled land deeds as the alternative form for land restitution that achieves 'economic empowerment' (Agri SA, 2021b). I will focus further on these four organizations and how their right-wing political and economic leanings influence debates on race, inequality and land in South Africa.

To begin with AfriForum, the organization considers itself a civil rights organization giving a voice to minority Afrikaners in the country; its civil rights charter promotes non-racialism as a way of offering legal protections to minorities and mirrors global civil rights charters such as those of the United Nations. The language of the charter assumes Afrikaners are now left out of the post-apartheid democracy and that Afrikaans is a language undergoing erasure. The organization comments on political and cultural events perceived to affect Afrikaners. The strategic aim of the organization is to promote Afrikaner interests in the South African political arena. One controversial topic it has commented on is the banning of the apartheid flag and monuments, using loaded language such as 'concentration camps' for statues of apartheid-era leaders that were removed and put into storage (AfriForum, 2020). Its views on historical land dispossession are informed through denial of the historical violence of the voortrekkers' colonization as they made their way from the Western Cape to the interior of the country, instead claiming that any land acquisitions by the Boers were done fairly under mutual agreements with Natives such as the Zulus (Uys, 2019). There is even debate concerning who can be considered 'native' to South Africa, with the presumption that Bantu speakers migrated from northern Africa not long before the settlement of the Dutch, which allows Afrikaners to claim nativity the same as any Bantu-speaking group (South Africa History Online, n. d.). The organization regularly criticizes the ANC government for perpetuating the same human rights abuses conducted by the apartheid regime while also claiming heritage to apartheid-era symbolism and monuments (Roets, 2019). Farm attacks, the perceived targeting of white farmers on their homesteads, are a large area of concern for the organization, as it tracks incidents to promote awareness of the occurrences which it claims is genocide of Afrikaners (Fairbanks, 2017). The organization also generates its own research and reports in order to push its ideology to the national discourse. In conjunction with other research/lobbyist organizations such as those described below, its ideological stance has been influential in shaping the public discourse around race relations and land.

Established in 1929, the IRR is considered one of the oldest liberal organizations in the country; developed by a group of white civic, educational and religious figures who were opposed to the apartheid government; even offering a bursary to Nelson Mandela to complete his legal studies. They also developed a journal where research from an interdisciplinary array of social scientists on racial inequality was published, providing rigorous annual survey data that was trusted by academics and policymakers. The IRR today can effectively be categorized as a libertarian think-tank, with many of its core values echoing the United States Republican Party and global right-wing advocates. The course that the organization has taken post-apartheid has been to promote the interests of neoliberal policymaking, with affiliations with the International Republican Institute, the Heritage Foundation and the Atlas Network, and, more locally, the DA; reflecting a shift in the ideological stance of the organization to the far right from its more emancipatory roots. A number of social leaders and stakeholders have expressed concern about this shift, with an open letter published in the widely read *News24* in September 2021 (News24, 2021). The shift in the organization began in the 1980s, when it began to cut its ties with civic and local community groups to focus on influencing broader policy mandates that would align with its 'free market, small state' ideology, such as lobbying to leave social and economic rights out of the budding constitutional Bill of Rights in 1995.

The IRR promotes libertarian ideals that flatten racial distinction and its histories. A recent publicity stunt pulled by the organization is billboards reading 'www.racismisnottheproblem.co.za' on the M1 South route in Johannesburg. In response to the multiple complaints about the billboard, IRR issued a statement saying that the billboard does not promote racism but simply conveys that racism is not the foremost issue for the country to tackle (South African Institute of Race Relations, 2021b), citing a self-conducted survey that concluded participants simply did not think racism was the most important issue. The methodology of studies conducted by organizations such as AfriForum, the IRR and the DA is considered questionable according to South African academics, framing questions and choosing participants in a way that furthers their political agenda. This attitude is reflected in a number of their stances on social issues, such as being against affirmative action and BEE initiatives. The IRR's stance on the constitutional amendment to section 25 is strongly opposed to the potential of nationalizing land for purposes of restitution, as reflected in its Stop Land Nationalization campaign. A report published in November 2021 by the IRR equates property rights as a human right, citing the United Nations' Universal Declaration of Human Rights article 17 as a source of legitimacy for this claim; also quoting a number of European Enlightenment thinkers such as St Thomas Aquinas,

John Calvin and John Locke to demonstrate the historical legacy of property rights (Corrigan, 2021: 6), much in alignment with AfriForum.

The Democratic Alliance is a historically centrist political party that has endured since 1959 when it was the Progressive Party. The party has a largely Capetonian white liberal voter base, and its popularity rivals the ANC (Reuters, 2021). During the apartheid era, the DA and the multiple parties it subsumed into itself represented the suburban, English-speaking white liberals who were opposed to the apartheid regime. More recently, in 2009, renowned journalist and former Cape Town mayor Helen Zille took the mantle of DA party leadership. Zille's legacy within the DA is rife with controversy, most notably her tweet defending colonialism, stating, 'For those claiming legacy of colonialism was ONLY negative, think of our independent judiciary, transport infrastructure, piped water etc' (Marvin, 2020). As a former journalist and member of the Democratic Party, a precursor to the DA during apartheid, Zille's legacy is recognized as committed to anti-racism and the fall of apartheid. Zille moved up the party ranks to eventually become mayor of Cape Town once the ANC lost its foothold in the Western Cape in post-apartheid South Africa, but her political leanings began to tilt moderate-right as she eventually became the DA party premier in 2009. Since then, Zille's social media presence and political views have garnered controversy for their colonial and apartheid apologist tone. Her book, *#StayWoke: Go Broke: Why South Africa Won't Survive America's Culture Wars* (Zille, 2021), trumpets alt-right talking points such as free speech, identity politics, cancel culture, the 'woke' mob; even equating cancel culture with apartheid in that race is invoked as a structural critique, though conveniently eschewing the motivations of eugenics in the former versus anti-racism in the latter. Black members of the DA have resigned in response to her racist comments and viewpoints after seeing the lax disciplinary policy of the DA for such behaviour (Mhaka, 2019). Zille's supporters within the party commend her for upholding the liberal values on which the party was formed, as well as defending democratic principles such as the rule of law and meritocracy, which they claim are being eroded under the ANC (Centre for Social Science Research, n. d.). The difference in views for black members versus white or coloured members of the DA reveals a continued divide in how racism and the legacy of colonialism are experienced, exposing the tension that remains as a residual effect of apartheid.

Although agriculture contributes a smaller portion of national GDP in relation to mining or manufacturing, the sector is an important contributor to the land reform debates in South Africa and holds a substantial amount of lobbying power. Agri SA is the largest agricultural union in the country and is a successor of the primarily white regional agricultural unions of the colonial and apartheid era, such as the Transvaal, Natal, Rhodesian and

Orange Free State agricultural unions (Agri SA, 2021a). Agri SA has a close relationship to the South African Department of Rural Development and Land Reform, regularly releasing policy advocacy and participating in important governmental summits and conferences related to economic policy and land issues. Its stance towards land reform and economic development is conservative and it often advocates for the status quo which supports white landowners and market intervention. The Expropriation Without Compensation (EWC) amendment was a major threat to stakeholders of Agri SA, who quickly staged interventions such as policy and press releases, also convening stakeholders and bureaucrats in order to intercede in the policymaking process. In the land affairs section of its website, the Agri SA motto reads, 'Ensuring sustainable land reform and enhancing and protecting property rights' (Agri SA, 2021b). Part of Agri SA's commitment to protecting property rights is its Agri Securitas campaign, which is sponsored by major corporations such as Nissan. The Agri Securitas funding campaign primarily highlights the narrative of farm murders and rural crime and advocates for increased militarization (Agri SA, 2021c). Agri SA, along with AfriForum and the Transvaal Agricultural Union (TAU), have been releasing questionable data concerning farm murders and rural violence.

Because Agri SA is considered a national organization representing farmers in all categories, the alignment with AfriForum and TAU gives it legitimacy and a façade of scientific neutrality. In 2017, the South African Department of Rural Development and Land Reform released a long-anticipated land audit which measured private versus public ownership of land by province as well as the racial makeup of private landownership across the country. It was determined that the minority white population still owned 72 per cent of individual private land holdings, signalling the failures of past land reform legislation (Department of Rural Development and Land Reform, 2017). Agri SA also released its own land audit the following year, 2018 (Agri SA, 2017). According to the report, it emphasized the role of the market in the redistribution of land, particularly the 'willing buyer, willing seller' model as one that could be improved upon as a path to restitution. However, the data in this report and governmental figures shows that this model has made little progress in transferring land ownership from white to black hands.

The underlying assumptions of liberal democracy belie a structure and agreement among hegemonic groups to enforce a hierarchy which they are taught they will always remain at the apex of. The campaign of dispossession and the subjugation of black labour that mars South African history continues to influence the stances of minority white groups in post-apartheid South Africa. The epistemologies of ignorance have stymied any consciousness of the historical pathways and white complicity that continue to influence racial inequality in the country. The symbolic importance of land and liberal property regimes is a relic of the colonial and apartheid eras, with whites drawing many of their implicit assumptions from the racial hierarchies developed during that time. The language of inclusive democracy has transformed the rhetoric of white racial entitlement in key ways that allow it to seamlessly reposition itself from the hegemonic group to a group committed to egalitarianism. The rhetoric is also used to concretize a sense of identity and self when there are shifts in the social landscape such as a democratic transition. The aggressive criticism of the ANC government and the agitation around conspiracy theories such as farm attacks are attempts to delegitimize the current inclusive democratic system and create a nostalgia for the order of the former apartheid regime, while also denying that those past associations are in any way racialized. Through these processes, the white racial minority creates rhetorical strategies that suspend dissonance in an attempt to avoid accountability and continue to enjoy the entitlements created through the systematic discrimination of the colonial and apartheid eras.

Conclusion

> The political significance of the discourse on the theft of the land lies, not in the threat of land seizures by the state, nor in debates around the transformation of South Africa's agricultural sector. Rather it lies in the way in which land makes possible the articulation of an indirect but still powerful critique of non-racialism in the post-apartheid constitutional settlement. (Du Toit, 2019: 32)

To return to Du Toit's idea of 'policy-sensemaking': because public rhetoric has the capability to withhold and mask its true motives, it is necessary to contextualize what the discourse is responding to and what its assumptions say about its implicit biases. The central question that this chapter poses is asking why land reform has been a fundamental failure since 1994 and how its symbolic significance creates a discourse which goes on to interrogate larger issues in the country post-apartheid, its unresolved racial tensions and its deep-seated economic inequality. Though land reform policy was largely ignored as a political issue in post-apartheid South Africa, it has in the last five years been catapulted to the national spotlight and become a major electoral issue. In South Africa and globally, endemic economic inequality has polarized populations and spurred populist movements, putting into question the limitations of the state and democratic processes to effectively govern a fractured populace. Imaginaries around land come to serve a variety of symbolic purposes, but in South Africa, land signals an ability to produce independently, creating an entitlement to the nation-state as an integral group of providers; as we see in the *empty land myth*, the attempt to rewrite historical and genealogical accounts of who occupied the land first, colonial accounts of territorialization create mythologies that frame them as stewards to a virgin soil.

On paper, land reform is a primary constitutional tenet that acts as redress for the racially skewed conditions created by apartheid, so its symbolic significance has long preceded the proposal of the EWC amendment. Unfortunately, liberal democracy as an institution may not be the proper vehicle for such a considerable task; we must remember that during apartheid and the preceding colonial era, the tenets of liberalism were still the guiding fabric for the racially segregated system of separate development. In addition, the language of liberal democracy also creates space for right-wing and fascist groups to claim entitlement to the resources of the state that those same groups systematically altered to benefit themselves historically. Further research into the affective dynamics of right-wing groups in settler colonial states would be useful for determining further the rhetorical tactics and connection to hegemonic structures that continue to persist.

References

AfriForum (n. d.) About us. *AfriForum*, https://afriforum.co.za/en/about-us/ (accessed 6 November 2023).

AfriForum (2020). AfriForum opposes announcement of 'concentration camp for statues'. *AfriForum*, 4 September, https://afriforum.co.za/en/afriforum-opposes-announcement-of-concentration-camp-for-statues/ (accessed 6 November 2023).

Agri SA (2017). *Land Audit: A Transactions Approach*. Johannesburg: Agri SA.

Agri SA (2021a). The story behind Agri SA. *Agri SA*, https://agrisa.co.za/overview (accessed 6 November 2023).

Agri SA (2021b). Land solutions. *Agri SA*, https://agrisa.co.za/land (accessed 6 November 2023).

Agri SA (2021c). Rural safety. *Agri SA*, https://agrisa.co.za/safety (accessed 6 November 2023).

Aliber, M., & Cousins, B. (2013). Livelihoods after Land Reform in South Africa. *Journal of Agrarian Change*, 13: 140–165.

Applebaum, B. (2008). White Privilege/White Complicity: Connecting 'Benefiting From' to 'Contributing To'. *Philosophy of Education Archive*, 292–300.

Ashton, G. (2012). Land reform in South Africa: an unfulfilled obligation. *SACSIS*, 1 November, http://sacsis.org.za/site/article/1475 (accessed 6 November 2023).

Centre for Social Science Research (n. d.). Promoting liberalism in post-apartheid South Africa: how liberal politicians in the Democratic Alliance approach social welfare. *CSSR*, http://www.cssr.uct.ac.za/cssr/pub/wp/438 (accessed 6 February 2022).

Corrigan, T. (2021). A true 'human right': why property rights are indispensable. *South African Institute for Race Relations*, 10 November, https://irr.org.za/reports/

occasional-reports/a-true-human-right-why-property-rights-are-indispensable (accessed 6 November 2023).

Cousins, B. (2017). Land and 'radical economic transformation'. *AIDC | Alternative Information & Development Centre*, 19 May, https://aidc.org.za/land-radical-economic-transformation/ (accessed 6 November 2023).

Cousins, B., & Scoones, I. (2010). Contested paradigms of 'viability' in redistributive land reform: perspectives from southern Africa. *Journal of Peasant Studies*, 37(1): 31–66.

Democratic Alliance (2019). Values and principles. *DA*, www.da.org.za/why-the-da/values-and-principles (accessed 6 November 2023).

Department of Rural Development and Land Reform (2017). *Land Audit Report: Phase II Private Land Ownership by Race, Gender, & Nationality*. Pretoria: Republic of South Africa.

Du Toit, A. (2019). Whose land question? Policy deliberation and populist reason in the South African land debate. *Plaas*, 13 November, www.plaas.org.za/andries-du-toit-2019-whose-land-question-policy-deliberation-and-populist-reason-in-the-south-african-land-debate/ (accessed 6 November 2023).

Fairbanks, E. (2017). The Last White Africans. *Foreign Policy*, 16 January, https://foreignpolicy.com/2017/01/16/the-last-white-africans/ (accessed 14 February 2024).

Giliomee, H. B. (2003). *The Afrikaners: Biography of a People*. London: C. Hurst & Co. Publishers.

Greenberg, S. (2015). Agrarian Reform and South Africa's Agro-food System. *Journal of Peasant Studies*, 42(5): 957–979.

Hoagland, S. L. (2007). Denying Relationality: Epistemology and Ethics of Ignorance. In Shannon Sullivan & Nancy Tuana (eds), *Race and Epistemologies of Ignorance*. New York: Suny Press, pp. 95–118.

INDABA (2015). Framework for the Rural Economic Transformation Model – Department of Rural Development and Land. *DRDLR*, https://old.dalrrd.gov.za/Resource-Centre/Portals/0/Conferences/Land Reform Indaba 2015/Framework for the Rural Economic Transformation Model.pdf.

Keegan, T. (1986). The Dynamics of Rural Accumulation in South Africa: Comparative and Historical Perspectives. *Comparative Studies in Society and History*, 28(4): 628–650.

MacDonald, M. (2006). *Why Race Matters in South Africa*. Cambridge: Harvard University Press.

Marvin, C. (2020). DA comes under fire for 'protecting white privilege' in Western Cape. IOL, www.iol.co.za/capeargus/news/da-comes-under-fire-for-protecting-white-privilege-in-western-cape-831f5ae4–0365–4cf1-acf9-eecf01bcdabc (accessed 3 September 2020).

McHugh, N. (2005). Telling Her Own Truth: June Jordan, Standard English and the Epistemology of Ignorance. In V. Kinloch & M. Grebowicz (eds), *Still Seeking an Attitude: Critical Reflections on the Work of June Jordan*. Lanham: Lexington Books.

Mhaka, T. (2019). Helen Zille's return is a bad omen for South Africa. *Aljazeera*, 27 October, www.aljazeera.com/opinions/2019/10/27/helen-zilles-return-is-a-bad-omen-for-south-africa (accessed 5 February 2022).

Mills, C. W. (1997). *The Racial Contract*. Ithaca: Cornell University Press.

News24 (2021). Open letter: We are concerned about the direction the IRR is taking. *News24*, 20 September www.news24.com/news24/opinions/letters/open-letter-we-are-concerned-about-the-direction-the-irr-is-taking-20210919 (accessed 6 November 2023).

Parliament of South Africa (2019). Constitution Eighteenth Amendment Bill: Amendment of Section 25 of the Constitution. Pretoria, Government of South Africa.

Reuters (2021). In blow to ANC, opposition DA mayors elected in major S. African cities. *Reuters*, 23 November, www.reuters.com/markets/rates-bonds/blow-anc-opposition-da-mayors-elected-major-safrican-cities-2021–11–23/ (accessed 28 February 2022).

Roets, E. (2019). 'Old flag' banned: what it's all about. *Afriforum*, 26 August, https://afriforum.co.za/en/old-flag-banned-what-its-all-about/ (accessed 6 November 2023).

South African History Online (n. d.). The empty land myth. *SAHO*, www.sahistory.org.za/article/empty-land-myth (accessed 27 April 2023).

South African Institute of Race Relations (2021a). What we stand for. *IRR*, https://irr.org.za/what-we-stand-for (accessed 2021).

South African Institute of Race Relations (2021b). Complaints laid about Racism Is Not the Problem billboard. *IRR*, 1 July, https://irr.org.za/media/complaints-laid-about-racism-is-not-the-problem-billboard (accessed 6 November 2023).

Steyn, M. (2012). The Ignorance Contract: Recollections of Apartheid Childhoods and the Construction of Epistemologies of Ignorance. *Identities*, 19(1): 8–25.

Steyn, M., & Foster, D. (2008). Repertoires for Talking White: Resistant Whiteness in Post-apartheid South Africa. *Ethnic and Racial Studies*, 31(1): 25–51.

Uys, B. (2019). The Zulus and the Voortrekkers – in search of more truth. *Afriforum*, 19 December, https://afriforum.co.za/en/the-zulus-and-the-voortrekkers-in-search-of-more-truth/ (accessed 6 November 2023).

Zille, H. (2021) *#StayWoke: Go Broke: Why South Africa Won't Survive America's Culture Wars (and What You Can Do about It)*. Independently Published.

8

Fossil fuel authoritarianism: oil, climate change and the Christian right in the United States

Robert B. Horwitz

'Trump Digs Coal' proclaimed the placard brandished by candidate Donald Trump on the campaign trail in 2016. Upon election victory, he followed through on his campaign rhetoric. Pronouncing climate change a hoax, Trump doubled down on an expansive fossil fuel agenda. His administration rolled back or weakened every major federal policy intended to combat dangerous emissions (Baker et al., 2020).

Trump's pro-fossil fuel, anti-climate change stance was not new. It reflected what has become a standard talking point of the US Republican Party in recent years, one that casts doubt not only on climate science but on expertise *per se*. The logic of the position was perhaps best articulated by former Pennsylvania Senator and two-time Republican presidential hopeful Rick Santorum in an interview on the Rush Limbaugh radio show in 2011. 'Man-made climate change', Santorum declared, is 'patently absurd … junk science … a beautifully concocted scheme … by the left … just an excuse for more government control of your life.' The underlying political stance reflects both a deep hostility towards the regulatory functions of government and a fixation on what is understood as the baleful influence on Western contemporary thought by the political left. In some quarters of the right, this malevolent influence is attributed to the evil of 'cultural Marxism' (The Rick Santorum Interview, 2011; Jay, 2011).[1]

My aim in this chapter is to illuminate how American conservatives arrived at this position on climate change, a position that serves to underscore that the Republican Party has become virtually indistinguishable from the far right. The stance entails an outlook that regards fossil fuels – coal, oil and natural gas – as the fundamental pillars of the American energy mix. It sees the private companies that engage in mining, drilling and fracking as entities to be rewarded – even venerated – for their risk taking (and contribution to nationbuilding), and thus deserving of solicitude by government. Energy sources have entered the culture wars in the United States and are imbued with symbolic, in addition to material economic, significance.

Fossil fuel extraction and use are patriotic: the mining of coal and the drilling of oil and gas not only drive the nation's industrial might, but they also secure independence from possible foreign malefactors (Tabuchi & Friedman, 2021).[2] Mining and drilling are coded as masculine: fossil fuels are the product of the physical labour of men joined in the gruelling effort to liberate God's mysterious gifts from the bowels of the (feminine) earth (Daggett, 2018).

Renewable forms of energy, by contrast, are a limited and troublesome addition to the energy mix because their output is intermittent and dependent on forces beyond human control. Moreover, conservatives complain, renewables benefit from unfair subsidies (Johnson, 2011).[3] Environmentalism is typecast as a feminine creed that both exudes weakness *and* animates a massive regulatory apparatus, the result of which is to rob people of their natural freedoms. It should not be surprising that the regulatory system is often denigrated by the right as the 'nanny state' (another belittling gendered construction) (McCright & Dunlap, 2011; Hunt, 2020). Climate science is nothing but politicized claptrap, its claims to expertise bunk. Policies designed to address climate change are nothing but power grabs by the left. At the most abstract edge of this complaint, the environmental regulatory juggernaut is claimed to violate natural law.[4] The overall stance is one that we might call 'fossil fuel authoritarianism'.

The identity of the Republican Party with fossil fuel authoritarianism was not always thus. Protection of the environment was once a bipartisan affair in the United States.[5] Indeed, Republicans were early champions of conservation. The setting aside of public lands to preserve areas of natural or historic interest was championed by President Theodore Roosevelt in the first decade of the twentieth century. Not long thereafter, President Woodrow Wilson, a Democrat, presided over the creation of the National Park Service to conserve the scenery, natural and historic objects, and wildlife within the national parks (Organic Act, 1916). In more recent decades, the National Environmental Protection Act (NEPA), sometimes called the Magna Carta of US environmental law, passed the House of Representatives by an overwhelming 372–15 margin. The Senate vote for the bill was unanimous. Although he did not do much to shape the NEPA bill, President Richard Nixon saw political advantage in embracing and signing it. Nixon created the Environmental Protection Agency in 1970, the same year that the Senate unanimously passed the tough Clean Air Act. When Nixon reversed course and vetoed the Clean Water Act in 1972, a bipartisan Congress over-rode his veto (National Environmental Policy Act, 1970). As late as 1990, a bipartisan majority passed strong amendments to the Clean Air Act, legislation that substantially increased the authority and responsibility of the federal government to control acid rain and issue power station operating permits

(Clean Air Amendments Act, 1990). But by 1992, political polarization on issues of environmental concern had begun to emerge, driven by anti-environmentalism among conservative elites (McCright, Xiao & Dunlap, 2014).

What explains the shift of American conservatives, and the Republican Party specifically, from a general support of environmentalism to fossil fuel authoritarianism? The answer lies in the evolution of the Republican Party from a mainstream conservative political party into one whose policies are increasingly indistinguishable from those of the far right. The reasons for this evolution are complex and multi-faceted, and have been pondered by many scholars (see Perlstein, 2001, 2014; Rogers, 2011; Horwitz, 2013). One important factor – and the factor I think helps best explain the party's particular stance on climate – is the rise to dominance of white, right-wing Protestant evangelicalism within the Republican electoral coalition.

The religious transformation of the Republican Party began with the 1980 election of Ronald Reagan and has accelerated virtually unabated since (Smidt & Kellstedt, 1992; Igielnik et al., 2021).[6] Protestant evangelicalism embodies a set of doctrinal beliefs that our corrupt world is moving towards its 'end times'. Human attempts to halt climate change (or any broad social problem for that matter) are just short of blasphemy; only God can intervene in the world. Historical change takes place not via human actions but through divine intervention, the details of which are revealed in Scripture. From its beginnings, Protestantism exuded a common-sense anti-elitism in opposition to the hierarchical nature of the Catholic Church. That inheritance has been transformed in current American evangelicalism into a strong tendency towards anti-science dogmatism. Religious dogmatism is character-ized by an unchangeable certainty in a set of beliefs and practices, ostensibly rooted in the Bible, without consideration of evidence or contrary opinion. What has happened over the last decades of US political history is that evangelical religion has become politicized and Republican politics has become religious. Dogmatism in the religious domain has become dogmatism in the political domain. In the area of climate, this has manifested in fossil fuel authoritarianism.

The transformation of the Republican Party: an overview

From its creation in the 1850s, the Republican Party (also known as the Grand Old Party, or GOP) was the party of the pro-business, anti-slavery northern modernist Protestant establishment. African Americans supported the GOP after the Civil War because of the emancipation legacy of President

Abraham Lincoln. The Democratic Party, in turn, historically constituted a contradictory political alliance consisting of northern urban working-class ethnic groups (such as Italian and Irish Americans), Catholics, organized labour and the pro-slavery white South. The New Deal, the name for the long presidential administration of Democrat Franklin Roosevelt, permanently transformed US domestic politics through a centre-left embrace of government intervention into the economy and the establishment of a regulatory state in the 1930s and 1940s. The power of the white South in the New Deal coalition, however, meant that little progress was made in the area of race relations/civil rights.

In the immediate aftermath of World War II, President Dwight Eisenhower led the Republican Party's dominant, establishment wing. The party, having vigorously opposed the New Deal in the 1930s and 1940s, made a reluctant peace with it and the institutions of the modest welfare state the New Deal had established. The GOP also signed on to the postwar Democrats' anti-communist agenda, both domestically and in the international arena in the policy of the containment of international communism. The Republican Party was thus part of what scholars have labelled the postwar liberal consensus (Hodgson, 1976).

A minority, *anti*-establishment faction of the Republican Party, instead advocated militant rollback: of international communism and the New Deal (considered communism's domestic version), both. The standard bearer of the anti-establishment conservative faction in the 1950s was Senator Joseph McCarthy. McCarthy denounced social institutions such as labour unions, universities and Hollywood, as well as some government bureaus, as having been taken over by communists. Myriad right-wing organizations and non-mainstream media outlets championed McCarthy and his cause. In the 1960s, the leader of anti-establishment conservatism was Senator Barry Goldwater. Goldwater's 1964 presidential campaign denounced the New Deal state as an attack on private property and liberty. He and his supporters also charged that the mere containment of the Soviet Union was inadequate; the United States must confront international communism militarily, with the nuclear arsenal if need be (Goldwater, 1960).

For all the damage that McCarthyism wreaked on the country, the Senator was censured and the movement he led disparaged. Goldwater, having brought the anti-establishment faction of the GOP to momentary domination, was trounced in the 1964 presidential election by Democrat Lyndon Johnson. The 1960s and 1970s essentially belonged (with many caveats that cannot be discussed here because of space constraints) to liberals.

One way to characterize the success of liberalism in this period is to note the general expansion of individual rights and the concomitant broadening of pluralism and secularism in many domains of American society. Under the pressure and moral gravity of the African American civil rights movement, Congress finally passed the Civil Rights and Voting Rights acts, facilitating the right of racial minorities to belong, in principle, to the US social contract. Pressed by the anti-war, counterculture and feminist movements in the 1960s, the country (often with the help of the courts) moved beyond the protection of minority rights towards pluralistic positions in areas of public life that had historically embedded traditional religious values in such matters as school prayer, contraception, abortion and general individual deportment. In short, government began to secularize the life-world in response to the pluralistic cultural dynamism of the 1960s and the force of logic of judicial decisions involving the Fourteenth Amendment to the US constitution's equal protection and due process clauses (on secularization see Casanova, 1994: 11–39, 135–157).[7]

Growth in the role and size of government, especially the federal government, accompanied these changes. Conservatives bristled. They felt the changes marked not only a ruinous expansion in the size and function of government, but also represented an abdication of moral responsibility and a judicial taking of sides. They saw the cultural enfranchisement of women and racial minorities and the liberalization of sexual mores as moral hazards. The anti-establishment faction of the Republican Party that had been pushed out of party halls of power after the defeat of Barry Goldwater emerged afresh. It recruited religious conservatives who felt that their institutions had come under threat by an intrusive federal government. By the mid-1970s, evangelicals perceived themselves to be losing the moral struggle with liberalism for the soul of America. They saw the principle of the separation between church and state being weaponized to undermine their religious institutions. They saw the liberalization of the life-world as the triumph of 'secular humanism' (which sometimes served as code for cultural Marxism, discussed previously, though the use of the latter concept was limited in that period of time). The Reverend Jerry Falwell mobilized these grievances in a powerful way in the founding of the Moral Majority in 1980 – the year that evangelicals turned out for Ronald Reagan (Falwell, 1980).

The anti-establishment conservative faction of the Republican Party became the Republican Party. Its electoral base was increasingly dominated by white evangelicals whose dogmatic, end-times doctrines began to suffuse generally through the party, including, as years went by, its anti-science stance on climate change. Here the long, complicated nexus between religion and oil in the United States is salient. That nexus is key to the understanding of current day Republican energy and climate politics. We explore the origins of those doctrines through the schismatic history of American Protestantism.

Postmillennialist Protestantism: fossil fuel extraction and rational, godly development

John D. Rockefeller's Standard Oil was the early and long-time leader of the oil industry in the United States. Standard was the first great American business trust, controlling, in 1904, 91 per cent of oil refinement and 85 per cent of final sales in the United States. The company long practised cut-throat pricing to undermine competitors, leading to antitrust litigation and its break-up in 1911 (Yergin, 1991; Desjardins, 2017). Rockefeller, who controlled Standard Oil as Chairman and major shareholder, was a pious northern Baptist Protestant who believed in economic and technological development as the way to build the Kingdom of God on earth in advance of Christ's second coming (Dochuk, 2019). Why Rockefeller's religious orientation is of importance requires examination that situates the centrality of Protestantism and its internal dynamics to American socio-economic life.

The American colonies were founded by religiously devout Christian dissenters. Persecution by state religions in Europe led these dissenters to embrace a conception of political liberty as non-domination or independence from arbitrary power. Independence of religious belief from political authority was embedded in the principle of the doctrine of the separation between church and state.

For most of the nineteenth century, the American Protestant worldview married a deep religiosity to republican political ideology (whose paramount value is political liberty) and moral reasoning based on Scottish common-sense philosophy (rather than the acute rationalism of the continental Enlightenment). Its epistemology held that there is a world outside us, which we can know via the use of induction from facts obvious to the senses. Resting on the implicit assumption that humans are by nature good, and educable, individuals were understood as free agents, naturally capable of understanding Scripture without priestly expertise. The capacity of individuals to read and understand the Bible meant in turn that ordinary free persons were in principle both capable of independent moral judgement and of self-government (Heclo, 2009).

The Protestant approach to knowledge and government was democratic, and hostile to the elite authority of the Catholic priestly hierarchy. Nineteenth-century Protestantism saw science, which it understood as the precise observation of the world, as the complement to the literal reading of the Bible. Science confirmed Scripture. There could be no contradiction between the deist God of the Newtonian universe and the God of the Bible, between natural and revealed religion (May, 1976).[8] But Protestantism's common-sense anti-elitism also revealed a populism that, as we shall see later, would be mobilized to challenge expertise *per se*.

In the nineteenth-century American Protestant worldview, work in the world improved the world. Hence the dominance of what is known as *postmillennialism*, the theological doctrine that understands spiritual and cultural progress as paving the way for the thousand years of God's kingdom, after which Christ will come to earth a second time. Nineteenth-century American Protestants believed that the Holy Spirit, working through Christians, would so Christianize the culture that Christ could return to provide the capstone to a thousand-year reign of perfect peace. In this view, although human history reflects the ongoing struggle between the cosmic forces of God and Satan, each represented by earthly powers, the victory of righteousness is essentially assured. Ethical human effort embodies God's goodness and speeds the advent of a blessed new world (Marsden, 1980).[9]

The Social Gospel, the late nineteenth-, early twentieth-century religious movement focused on the importance of good works and the mobilization of citizens to help the poor and do good politically, embodied the central motifs of the postmillennialist Protestant worldview (White Jr, 1990). In this optimistic, progressive view of history, the fit between the Christian God and republican liberty was natural, even divinely ordained. Postmillennialist Protestants saw the United States as a special nation, a chosen nation, whose self-development and encounters in the world were regarded as speeding the establishment of the Kingdom of God on earth. This tradition is a primary source of the idea of American exceptionalism.

The rational, disciplined engagement with the world to improve it is perhaps the central tenet of postmillennialist Protestant doctrine. Postmillennialism for the most part pervaded American culture writ large, even after religion *per se* receded as the central shaper of public discourse (Bellah, 1967; Marsden, 1980; Dorrien, 2008). Rockefeller, a staunch postmillennialist and equally steadfast Republican, was the epitome of what we call the mainline Protestant establishment, the power bloc that dominated American economic, political and cultural life from the beginning of the republic until late in the twentieth century (Mills, 1956). Rockefeller was convinced that Standard Oil's petroleum quests and his philanthropic missions were one and the same. Building the Kingdom of God on earth entailed making money from oil and giving back generously to various causes and institutions, including foreign religious missions and institutions of higher learning such as the University of Chicago and the historically Black Spellman College. Rockefeller had been a stalwart abolitionist (Chernow, 1998).

The historian Darren Dochuk offers a neat phrase for Rockefeller's doctrine of uplift through oil: 'the civil religion of crude'. Work hard; bring forth oil from the earth; make money; use it in ways that improve the world – in short, the tenets of postmillennialist Protestantism. The civil religion of crude applied not just domestically, it was also linked to foreign policy and

American exceptionalism. Standard Oil pressed onto foreign shores, especially what would become Saudi Arabia, eager to save global humanity with a redemptive message of benevolent faith, capitalism and oil (Dochuk, 2019: 10–13, 405–446).

As industry leader, Standard Oil embodied ordered, disciplined, managerial capitalism. Rockefeller detested the uncontrolled boom and bust that typified the oil industry outside of Standard's orbit; he was repulsed by the social mayhem characteristic of petroleum strikes and manic oil boomtowns. Of course, Standard Oil's ordered managerial capitalism meant establishing an integrated monopoly of refineries and pipelines in order to manipulate a scarcity of supply. Standard first manipulated supply domestically, then pursued the practice in the international market (Mitchell, 2011).

Premillennialist Protestantism: the rush to drill before the end times

Opposing Rockefeller and Standard with both economic and religious fervour were the western independent oilmen, also known as wildcatters. These were the struggling oilmen largely frozen out by Standard's dominance. They tended to be Protestants of a very different orientation and doctrinal worldview from the Protestant mainline. These were the dispensational premillennialists – religious men who believed that the end of the world was imminent because of moral decay. In their view, the entire edifice of postmillennialism and its Social Gospel was blasphemous, an attempt to improve the world when the world was in God's hands alone (Marsden, 1980).

Premillennialism grew out of schisms as Protestant theology intersected with material and ideological conflicts. American Protestantism fractured not just along denominational lines (e.g. Methodists, Lutherans, Baptists, etc.), but also within denominations over slavery, the basic view of God's word and, later, Darwinism. Individual congregations of the same denomination on different sides of the Mason–Dixon line (the line demarcating the North from the South) found that they did not share the same values on the crucial issue of slavery, and in part because of the slavery question, no longer interpreted the Bible in the same way.

In the decades before the Civil War, northern congregations eventually denounced slavery, finding biblical warrant in opposing the evil of what was called euphemistically 'the peculiar institution'. Their southern counterparts likewise recited biblical passages in the effort to legitimize a slavery-based moral order. The application of Enlightenment rationality to the Bible precipitated another fault-line. The Higher Criticism was a scholarly movement coming from German academies under the broad influence of Kant and Hegel. It applied critical methods derived from other scholarly disciplines to Scripture and opened a process of exposing the Bible to close textual reading and hermeneutic analysis. Practitioners applied rational textual analysis to the Bible and in so doing cast doubt on scriptural verities such as the virgin birth and the miracles performed by Jesus. As these views filtered through scholarly and ministerial circles, many Protestants came to doubt the inerrancy of the Bible.

Darwinism posed another challenge as the nineteenth century moved into the twentieth. Recall that nineteenth-century American Protestantism revered science and believed there was no contradiction between science and Scripture. But faced with growing scientific evidence that the earth had a very long geological history and that numerous biological species had appeared and disappeared during the eons, many Protestants came to believe that the Genesis story of creation could not be sustained. The Protestant modernists began to downplay the supernatural and to view theology as no longer a fixed, God-given body of eternally valid truths. They continued to identify the Kingdom of God with the progress of civilization, but they increasingly came to view the essence of religion as morality, not blind faith, and, over time, they embraced the pluralism of values. To be sure, this liberal shift in the mainline churches was gradual and took place over several decades (Ahlstrom, 1972).

Those holding onto the old understandings denounced the modernists. The Bible, the traditionalists declared, was God's very word, inerrant and perfect. They viewed slavery as biblically sanctioned. They viewed Darwinian theory as undercutting the central biblical tenet of humanity's special creation. Their rejection of the Higher Criticism embodied Protestantism's original and integral anti-elitist dismissal of priestly expertise and professional knowledge. Indeed, for traditionalists, modernist teachings were themselves evidence of the decline of civilization. Contrary to postmillennialism's optimism, late nineteenth-century traditionalists pronounced that the world was becoming increasingly corrupt. In contrast to postmillennialism's progressive story, history was, rather, the story of eras of regression, owing to the fact that human beings are by nature sinful. History, in the view of the premillennialists, is the sad story of the stages of human degeneration from its Edenic beginning.

According to this theory, history is the story of divine intervention, revealed in Scripture. History doesn't just reflect the Bible; the Bible *is* history. The present age, marked by apostasy in the churches and the moral collapse of Christian civilization, is *prior* to Christ's kingdom. The millennium lies wholly in the future, *after* Christ returns to a very troubled world. Linking verses from the biblical books of Revelation, Daniel and Ezekiel, premillennialists described Christ's second coming as at the end of an apocalyptic period called the tribulation – a period of war, famine and social chaos during the seven-year rule of the Antichrist. As the end times commence, true Christian believers and innocents will be transported by God from earth to heaven in an event called the Rapture. Those left behind will be subject to violence, suffering and strife in the battle between the forces of God and the forces of Satan. Terrible suffering will ensue, but the forces of God will emerge victorious. Following Armageddon, Christ will return to establish a kingdom in Jerusalem, where he will reign for a thousand years (Clark, 2007: 27–144).

Because they understood the secular world as effectively under Satan's rule, traditionalists scorned efforts to make the world better through social activism, charity and politics. Traditionalists viewed the Social Gospel's emphasis on good works and serving the poor as undercutting the basic doctrinal concern for repentance from sin and dependence on God's grace. What mattered before the end times was to accept Christ as one's personal saviour and proselytize others to do so (see Marsden, 1987; Riesebrodt, 1993).[10]

The wildcatters: drill, baby, drill

Premillennialism became increasingly popular within conservative circles during the years between the world wars, conspicuously in the oil patches. It was the primary religious orientation of the wildcatters. Texas wildcatters underwrote the rise of J. Frank Norris and John R. Rice, the two most prominent fundamentalist ministers in mid-century America (Dochuk, 2019: 246–249). Premillennialist belief informed the wildcatter worldview: oil was God's gift to men; it was God's will for humans to harvest the earth. But a driller had to take risks, work hard and be devout to be rewarded in the release of God's mysterious endowment. Against John D. Rockefeller's managerial capitalism, the wildcatters held to an intense libertarian individualism that must not be suppressed by bigger businesses or the state.

Like other conservative Protestants, the wildcatters displayed a kind of populist defiance towards the establishment, whether religious or business. To wildcatters, the fact that the world would soon come to an end meant they must extract oil deposits swiftly *and* save souls before God's final decree. There was little time to waste as the end times neared, and no reason to safeguard the fossil resource or forestall the despoilment of the land from whence it came. Besides, as we know from the Book of Revelation, those who will be left behind in the wake of the Rapture will be the sinners and the unbelievers. Why leave any of God's gift for *them*?

In their swashbuckling libertarian zeal, wildcatters built not only oil rigs across Texas, Oklahoma and California, but they also built fundamentalist and conservative evangelical churches in the settlements around the wells. The wildcatters were promoters of the peculiarly American mixture of radical market freedom and religious moral traditionalism. It is not coincidence that it was Lyman Stewart, founder of the independent Union Oil, who bankrolled *The Fundamentals*, the foundational texts of Protestant fundamentalism, published between 1910 and 1915. It is also not coincidence that it was Sun Oil owner, J. Howard Pew, who financed Fuller Seminary, evangelicalism's key institution of theology. Pew also was the money behind evangelicalism's house media organ, the magazine *Christianity Today*. And Pew acted as bundler of western oil money for Barry Goldwater's presidential campaign in 1964 (Perlstein, 2001).

Conclusion

The story of the evolution of the Republican Party is the story of the transfer of the dogmatism embedded in its key evangelical constituency to the party as a whole. Metaphorically, evangelicalism is a religion of the heart. What matters is that one personally accepts Jesus and his love. It is not a religion of the head. By the time of the George W. Bush presidency, one could argue that the GOP had become essentially a religious party. That transformation began to have an impact on the character of public discourse and the reasoning offered to justify public policies writ large. President Bush came to legitimate the Iraq war in both secular and religious registers. Alongside the realist foreign policy official National Security Policy of the United States document were Bush's references to 'a Third Great Awakening' of religious devotion in the United States that had coincided with the nation's struggle with evil international terrorists (National Security Strategy, 2002; Baker, 2006). The Christian right, which strongly backed Bush and the war, saw Saddam Hussein as the anti-Christ and the Iraq war as the hoped-for beginning of the end times (Boyer, 2003).

The story of the Republican Party in the energy–climate domain is in part the story of the ascendance of the libertarian premillennialist wildcatter ethos embodied in the evangelical religious doctrine of the end times. As the Republican Party has become a party dominated by its evangelical base, it has rejected climate science, and expertise generally, as inherently political. *Everything* is politics, including facts and science. This radical scepticism can be traced, in part, to the old populist, anti-elitist character of the Protestant theory of knowledge, seen earlier in the traditionalist rejection of the Higher Criticism. That attitude, which also informed the battle against Darwinism, is now applied to climate science and expertise generally (Zimmerman, 2011). The latter is understood as just the latest in a long effort by liberal elites to expand the state and undermine freedom, private property and traditional cultural norms. The rejection of climate science and expertise is joined to the older and broader culture war of polarized politics against liberals and Democrats.

The contemporary Republican Party adopted the premillennialist wildcatter view of dominion over the earth. The looming of the end times made it unnecessary to conserve, or steward or act to avert climate change. Together with the old traditional Protestant distrust of experts and expertise, the old wildcatter ethos to exploit the earth fortifies the party's commitment to fossil fuel authoritarianism.

Now, here's the wrinkle. While we understand the doctrinal *religious* underpinnings of the GOP's denial of climate change and climate science, the public position is primarily a *political* one. A study of survey data on attitudes towards climate science shows that there is no particular difference between the Christian right's scepticism about human-made climate change and that of Republican voters generally. The survey data on the rejection of climate science does not show a lot of end times talk; the data show political talk (Evans & Feng, 2013). How should we understand this?

Religion may have shaped the contemporary Republican Party as a pro-extraction, anti-climate science party. The premillennialist Protestant embrace of resource extraction, fully consonant with the historical oil wildcatter ethos, has now been institutionalized in the Republican Party writ large. Its overtly religious origins no longer matter. Republicans without a religious bone in their body (such as Trump himself) adopt the drill, baby, drill perspective for purely partisan reasons (Antonio & Brulle, 2011). It remains strategic in a pluralistic polity (and even to sway Republicans not drawn to evangelicalism) to continue to couch religious reasons in more secular argument.

The sociological element here is that as political affiliation becomes less of an ideology and more of an identity, as it has in the last couple of decades, it is risky to the self to break from the positions of one's political community. Those evangelicals who break ranks with evangelical dogma (whether theological or political) have been drummed out of leadership positions and sometimes even out of their churches (O'Connor, 2017).[11] Republican officeholders who may believe in climate science generally keep quiet.[12]

The interpenetration of religion and politics has taken a fairly astonishing turn. White conservative Americans of non-Protestant faiths – or even no faith – are identifying as evangelicals because of the perception of identity between evangelicalism and the Republican Party under Trump's dominance. To be a conservative or right-wing white Republican is to be an evangelical Christian, even if one is Catholic, Hindu, Muslim or an unbeliever (Smith, 2021). This bodes ill for American politics. As the Republican Party has become more religious, it has become more dogmatic. Dogmatism is the enemy of politics; indeed, dogmatism undermines the political, because it substitutes emotion and preconceived opinion/judgement for reason. No one should gainsay how important religion has been and continues to be as a source of inspiration and fount of moral judgement influencing politics. Religious belief has animated any number of consequential political stances in American history, from the abolition of slavery, to Prohibition, to civil rights, to efforts to reduce poverty.

But religious argument is not political argument. That is, religious argument ultimately is based on some form of revelation or revealed truth, and thus is not argument *per se*. Rather, it is a foundationalist, pre-rational appeal not amenable to counterclaims outside of its faith-based framework. A democratic political public sphere is in principle the space for reasoned communicative exchange, wherein people exchange reasons in public in order to assess validity claims that have become problematic or subject to conflict. Religious claims are not of this character, because they are true not through argument; they are true through revelation or faith and thus not accessible to those outside the revelatory framework. The problem with religion in politics is that some religions are absolutist. There's little compromise or negotiation (the heart of democratic politics) with faith-based systems.

But politics is a domain that cannot be governed by dogmatism, or it ceases to be the domain where people talk and act in common (Habermas, 2006). As a political system and a culture, democracy is messy, frustrating, often unsatisfying. Although animated by ultimate values, in principle democracy requires a process of continuous negotiation and argument based on reason and evidence (Weber, 1946). A dogmatic or religious approach to politics, one in which belief overwhelms evidence or responsibility, is an authoritarian politics. It is the deep nihilism of the Republican far-right authoritarian project that confounds the United States politically and foils the effort to avert climate disaster.

Notes

1 The obsession with cultural Marxism has coursed through right-wing circles in the United States since the 1990s, and is a core meme of the global far right. The gist is that virtually all the ills of current Western culture, from feminism, affirmative action, sexual liberation, gay rights and environmentalism to the decay of traditional education, are ultimately attributable to the insidious influence of the (mostly Jewish) members of the Frankfurt Institute for Social Research (including Max Horkheimer, Theodore W. Adorno and Herbert Marcuse, among others), who fled Nazi Germany for the United States in the 1930s and influenced generations of American scholars and students thereafter.

2 'God bless Chevron', exclaimed Congressman Jim Jordan (R–Ohio), exasperated with the interrogation of oil executives at a congressional hearing about their industry's role in disseminating climate disinformation.

3 While it is true that there are now various governmental incentives and subsidies for renewables, the conservative complaint about them overlooks the many decades of lucrative subsidies to fossil fuel companies embedded in tax policies. Moreover, hidden subsidies abound. The ability of energy companies to dump on public lands without charge is a massive hidden subsidy. The fact that the cost of cleaning up of soil and water pollution emanating from mines and oil and gas fields has often been borne by government constitutes a hidden subsidy. The public health externalities of pollution generated by the burning of fossil fuels is another massive hidden subsidy.

4 Natural law theory posits that law is bestowed by God and is authoritative over all human beings. Human liberty arises from the natural law. Positive or human-made law cannot supersede natural law. In the United States, natural law theory has tended to skew to the conservative side of the political spectrum (see Kirk, 1954). Kirk, considered the father of modern American conservatism, posited that private property is the functional basis of liberty. Government regulations that inhibit the use of private property violate liberty. The Federalist Society, the influential conservative legal organization (that recommends nominees for the judiciary to Republican presidents), expounds on the connections among natural law, the American founding documents and originalism (the notion that constitutional text should be interpreted by judges according to the original public meaning that it would have had at the time that it became law) – and their effective abandonment since Franklin Roosevelt's presidency, known as the 'New Deal' (The Federalist Society, n. d.).

5 This is, of course, a qualified appraisal that brackets the history of the racial dimensions pertaining to concern over the environment, as well as the historic exclusion of Native Americans from their lands.

6 Prior to 1980, evangelicals tended to be significantly less engaged in American political life. But they turned out for Reagan, who received approximately two-thirds of the evangelical vote in 1980, and significantly higher in 1984. The permanent realignment of white evangelicals was seen in the 1988 George H. W. Bush presidential election totals. George W. Bush received 68 per cent of the white evangelical vote in 2000 and 78 per cent in 2004, the same percentage that Mitt Romney received in 2012. Seventy-seven per cent of white evangelicals voted for Trump in 2016, increasing to 84 per cent in 2020. White evangelicals accounted for 19 per cent of all voters in 2020, but a much higher share of Trump's voters (34 per cent) (Smidt & Kellstedt, 1992; Igielnik et al., 2021).

7 The Fourteenth Amendment, passed in 1876 in the aftermath of the Civil War, reads: 'No State shall make or enforce any law which shall abridge the privileges or immunities of citizens of the United States; nor shall any State deprive any person of life, liberty, or property, without due process of law; nor deny to any person within its jurisdiction the equal protection of the laws.'

8 Deism posits belief in the existence of God based solely on rational thought and revealed through nature, without any reliance on revealed religions or religious authority.

9 In contrast, as we shall see shortly, was *premillennialism*, an emergent, competing Protestant doctrine that viewed the world in moral decline and would end violently in the Apocalypse.

10 Readers should note that terminology regarding these matters is often confusing. Nineteenth-century Protestantism in general is described as *evangelical*, that is, resting on the individual emotional experience of the spiritual and of personal conversion. But, after the acceptance of modernism, the mainline churches could no longer be considered evangelical. Traditional, anti-modernist Protestants, whom we now call fundamentalists, sought to maintain the old evangelical beliefs and theology, including the inerrancy of Scripture and authenticity of biblical miracles. Fundamentalism can be understood as an extreme form of evangelicalism; it is tradition made self-aware and consequently defensive. It counselled its adherents to minimize their contact with, even withdraw from, the secular world. The New Evangelicalism movement of the post-World War II era constitutes what we usually now call, generically, *evangelicalism*. What is the difference between evangelicalism and fundamentalism? Both believe, to various degrees, in biblical authority and the inerrancy of the Bible, the authenticity of biblical miracles, and the centrality of a personal, devotional relationship with God, that is, being born again. But, unlike the fundamentalist withdrawal from the secular world, the New Evangelicals counselled joining the world in order to spread the gospel. Evangelicals were optimistic. In their political manifestation, fundamentalists and evangelicals are often grouped under the label 'Christian right'.

11 The story of Richard Cizek is a case in point. Cizek had served as the Vice-President for Governmental Affairs of the National Association of Evangelicals (NAE) and was described as one of the most prominent evangelical lobbyists in the United States. He had pushed for the NAE to endorse a cap-and-trade bill and move the organization towards a stewardship model of humans and the earth. Cizek's efforts were derailed by hard-right Christians who often received significant material support from the fossil fuel industry. And, after he voiced support for same-sex civil unions on National Public Radio's Fresh Air in December 2008, Cizek was forced to resign his position with the NAE.

12 There is some suggestion that younger evangelicals have rejected GOP political dogmatism and have come to believe, among other things, that climate change is real and must be addressed. There was even speculation that these younger evangelicals might desert the GOP in the 2016 and 2020 election. Indication is that they did not.

References

Ahlstrom, S. E. (1972). *A Religious History of the American People*. New Haven: Yale University Press.

Antonio, R. J., & Brulle, R. J. (2011). The Unbearable Lightness of Politics: Climate Change Denial and Political Polarization. *Sociological Quarterly*, 52(2): 195–202.

Baker, P. (2006). Bush tells group he sees a 'Third Awakening'. *Washington Post*, 13 September, www.washingtonpost.com/archive/politics/2006/09/13/bush-tells-grou p-he-sees-a-third-awakening/03bf58a0-5160-45f4-83b2-e4d532a45f99/?itid=sr_1 (accessed 2 November 2021).

Baker, P., Friedman, L., & Kaplan, T. (2020). As Trump again rejects science, Biden calls him a 'climate arsonist'. *New York Times*, 14 September, www.nytimes. com/2020/09/14/us/politics/trump-biden-climate-change-fires.html (accessed 2 November 2021).

Bellah, R. N. (1967). Civil religion in America. *Daedalus*, 96(1): 1–21.

Boyer, P. (2003). When U.S. foreign policy meets biblical prophecy. *AlterNet*, 20 February, www.alternet.org/2003/02/when_us_foreign_policy_meets_biblical_prophecy (accessed 2 November 2021).

Casanova, J. (1994). *Public Religions in the Modern World*. Chicago: University of Chicago Press.

Chernow, R. (1998). *Titan: The Life of John D. Rockefeller, Sr*. New York: Random House.

Clark, V. (2007). *Allies for Armageddon: The Rise of Christian Zionism*. New Haven: Yale University Press.

Clean Air Amendments Act (1990). S.1630 — 101st Congress (1989–1990), www. congress.gov/bill/101st-congress/senate-bill/163 (accessed 2 November 2021).

Daggett, C. (2018). Petro-masculinity: Fossil Fuels and Authoritarian Desire. *Millennium: Journal of International Studies*, 47(1): 25–44.

Desjardins, J. (2017). Chart: the evolution of Standard Oil. *Visual Capitalist*, 24 November, www.visualcapitalist.com/chart-evolution-standard-oil/ (accessed 2 November 2021).

Dochuk, D. (2019). *Anointed with Oil: How Christianity and Crude Made Modern America*. New York: Basic Books.

Dorrien, G. (2008). *Social Ethics in the Making: Interpreting an American Tradition*. Malden: Wiley-Blackwell.

Environmental Protection Agency (2021). EPA history. *EPA*, www.epa.gov/history/origins-epa (accessed 2 November 2021).

Evans, J. H., & Feng, J. (2013). Conservative Protestantism and Skepticism of Scientists Studying Climate Change. *Climatic Change*, 121: 595–608.

Falwell, J. (1980). *Listen, America!* Garden City: Doubleday.

Goldwater, B. M. (1960). *The Conscience of a Conservative*. Shepherdsville: Victor Publishing Co.

Habermas, J. (2006). Religion in the Public Sphere. *European Journal of Philosophy*, 14(1): 1–25.

Heclo, H. (2009). *Christianity and American Democracy*. Cambridge: Harvard University Press.

Hodgson, G. (1976). *America in Our Time*. Garden City: Doubleday.

Horwitz, R. B. (2013). *America's Right: Anti-establishment Conservatism from Goldwater to the Tea Party*. Cambridge: Polity Press.

Hunt, E. (2020). The eco gender gap: why is saving the planet seen as women's work? *The Guardian*, 6 February, www.theguardian.com/environment/2020/feb/06/eco-gender-gap-why-saving-planet-seen-womens-work (accessed 2 November 2021).

Igielnik, R., Keeter, S., & Hartig, H. (2021). Behind Biden's 2020 victory. *Pew Research Center*, 30 June, www.pewresearch.org/politics/2021/06/30/behind-bidens-2020-victory/ (accessed 2 November 2021).

Jay, M. (2011). Dialectic of counter-Enlightenment: the Frankfurt School as scapegoat of the lunatic fringe. *Salmagundi*, 22 December, http://canisa.org/blog/dialectic-of-counter-enlightenment-the-frankfurt-school-as-scapegoat-of-the-lunatic-fringe (accessed 2 November 2021).

Johnson, J. (2011). Long history of U.S. energy subsidies. *Chemical and Engineering News*, 19 December, https://cen.acs.org/articles/89/i51/Long-History-US-Energy-Subsidies.html (accessed 2 November 2021).

Kirk, R. (1954). *The Conservative Mind: From Burke to Eliot*. London: Faber & Faber.

Marsden, G. M. (1980). *Fundamentalism and American Culture: The Shaping of Twentieth-Century Evangelicalism, 1870–1925*. New York: Oxford University Press.

Marsden, G. (1987). *Reforming Fundamentalism: Fuller Seminary and the New Evangelicalism*. Grand Rapids: Eerdmans.

May, H. F. (1976). *The Enlightenment in America*. New York: Oxford University Press.

McCright, A. M., & Dunlap, R. E. (2011). Cool Dudes: The Denial of Climate Change among Conservative White Males in the United States. *Global Environmental Change*, 21(4): 1163–1172, www.sciencedirect.com/science/article/abs/pii/S095937801100104X (accessed 2 November 2021).

McCright, A. M., Xiao, C., & Dunlap, R. E. (2014). Political Polarization on Support for Government Spending on Environmental Protection in the USA, 1974–2012. *Social Science Research*, 48: 251–260.

Mills, C. Wright (1956). *The Power Elite*. New York: Oxford University Press.

Mitchell, T. (2011). *Carbon Democracy: Political Power in the Age of Oil*. London: Verso.

National Environmental Policy Act (1970). Public Law 91–190, https://uscode.house.gov/statutes/pl/91/190.pdf (accessed 2 November 2021).

National Security Strategy (2002). https://georgewbush-whitehouse.archives.gov/nsc/nss/2002/ (accessed 2 November 2021).

O'Connor, B. (2017). How fossil fuel money made climate denial the word of God. *Splinter*, 8 August, https://splinternews.com/how-fossil-fuel-money-made-climate-denial-the-word-of-g-1797466298 (accessed 2 November 2021).

Organic Act (1916). Act to Establish a National Park Service U.S.C., title 16, www.nps.gov/grba/learn/management/organic-act-of-1916.htm (accessed 2 November 2021).

Perlstein, R. (2001). *Before the Storm: Barry Goldwater and the Unmaking of the American Consensus*. New York: Hill & Wang.

Perlstein, R. (2014). *The Invisible Bridge: The Fall of Nixon and the Rise of Reagan*. Riverside: Simon & Schuster.

Riesebrodt, M. (1993). *Pious Passion: The Emergence of Modern Fundamentalism in the United States and Iran.* Don Reneau, trans. Berkeley: University of California Press.

Rogers, D. T. (2011). *Age of Fracture.* Cambridge: Harvard University Press.

Smidt, C., & Kellstedt, P. (1992). Evangelicals in the Post-Reagan Era: An Analysis of Evangelical Voters in the 1988 Presidential Election. *Journal for the Scientific Study of Religion,* 31(3): 330–338.

Smith, G. A. (2021). More white Americans adopted than shed evangelical label during Trump presidency, especially his supporters. *Pew Research Center,* 15 September, www.pewresearch.org/fact-tank/2021/09/15/more-white-americans-adopted-than-shed-evangelical-label-during-trump-presidency-especially-his-supporters/ (accessed 2 November 2021).

Tabuchi, H., & Friedman, L. (2021). Oil industry executives grilled over industry's role in climate disinformation. *New York Times,* 28 October, www.nytimes.com/2021/10/28/climate/oil-executives-house-disinformation-testimony.html (accessed 2 November 2021).

The Federalist Society (n. d.). 'Natural Law' https://fedsoc.org/search?term=%22natural+law%22 (accessed 2 November 2021).

The Rick Santorum Interview (2011). *The Rush Limbaugh Show,* 8 June, www.rushlimbaugh.com/daily/2011/06/08/the_rick_santorum_interview/ (accessed 2 November 2021).

Weber, M. (1946). Politics as a Vocation. In H. H. Gerth & C. Wright Mills (eds), *From Max Weber: Essays in Sociology.* New York: Oxford University Press.

White, Jr, Ronald C. (1990). *Liberty and Justice for All: Racial Reform and the Social Gospel, 1877–1925.* San Francisco, Harper & Row.

Yergin, Daniel (1991). *The Prize: The Epic Quest for Oil, Money, and Power.* New York: Free Press.

Zimmerman, M. (2011). From creationism to anti-environmentalism: the religious right's attack on science expands. *Huffington Post,* 25 May, www.huffpost.com/entry/from-creationism-to-antie_b_801783 (accessed 2 November 2021).

9

Conspiracy theories and anti-environmentalism in Bolsonaro's Brazil

Rodrigo D. E. Campos, Sérgio B. Barcelos and Ricardo G. Severo

Far-right politics has become an explosive phenomenon in Brazil since the presidential election of Jair M. Bolsonaro in 2018. In his reactionary political platform – based, among other things, on a neoliberal political economy set to destroy social security and an educational policy which aims to legalize persecution of teachers deemed 'leftists' – lies a promise to deregulate environmental norms that currently constrain deforestation and guarantees natives the right to land demarcation. In this chapter, we analyse how conspiracy theories about environmentalism in Brazil have found space in the far-right government and impacted the country's current environmental policy.

Conspiracy theories have played a central role in Bolsonaro's strategy of 'organized chaos' which, much like Trump's communication strategy, 'feeds on, and fosters, a climate of confrontation and uncertainty that helps him secure the loyalty of his base' (Nunes et al. 2020).[1] As a result, fascist groups such as the '300 do Brasil' and the green-shirts 'Integralistas' have directly threatened Parliament and the Supreme Federal Court with outright support from Bolsonaro and top government officials, echoing a long and much-alive tradition of coup plotting that involves large sectors of the military, intellectuals and businessmen.[2]

The tragedy of Brazil's post-transitional period – which after 21 years of military rule chose to reconcile with its past instead of seeking both justice for the crimes of the dictatorship and ways to curb military influence over politics – is that it has allowed a proliferation of conspiracy theories, similar to those that created the breeding ground for the 1964 military coup (dos Santos, 1994), to spread and find political representation in mass democracy. Thus, there is a move away from enclosed conspiracy circles such as the 'Clube Militar' – a reactionary association of retired military men – and the 'Philosophy Seminar' of Olavo de Carvalho – the 'intellectual Guru' of Bolsonarism – to organized political parties, security forces, religious institutions and even armed militias in urban as well as in rural areas

(Pinheiro-Machado and de Freixo, 2019; Webber, 2020). In this context, neoliberal subjectivity has found resonance in far-right ideology where market fundamentalism, anti-statism and radical Christian family moralism have spurred bizarre and well-articulated conspiracies of a globalist communist strategy involving billionaire elites and the Chinese government attempting to impose 'cultural Marxism' in schools and universities. These alleged conspiracies would ultimately destroy the traditional patriarchal family, promote generalized abortion, stimulate the transmission of transgender ideas to children, and give away lands with valuable natural resources to non-governmental organizations (NGOs) that hide behind the façade of promoting Indigenous people's rights (Gallego, 2018; de Almeida, 2019; Alves Cepêda, 2018).

While far-right conspiracy theories in Brazil have been analysed in relation to their impact on the 2018 elections (Recuero, 2020), educational policies (Severo et al., 2019), gender debates (Messenberg, 2019; Miguel, 2021) and scientific denialism (Oliveira, 2020), there is still a considerable gap of knowledge in how the conspiracy theories of cultural Marxism are affecting the current environmental situation in Brazil. In order to explore this issue, we first provide some contextual background to the inquiry by highlighting the main threads of Bolsonaro's environmental policy. Secondly, we offer a theoretical account of far-right conspiracy theories and introduce the main conspiracy animating the Brazilian far right: cultural Marxism. Thirdly, we provide an overview of the Brazilian far right under Bolsonaro and explore the main conspiracy thinkers and their theories related to the environment and show how this has been instrumentalized in the government to advance deregulation of environmental policies. We conclude by reflecting on the impact of the far-right government in environmental activism and struggle for land and recognition in rural Brazil.

The state of depletion

Since colonial times, the agricultural exports sector has been the dominant thrust of capital accumulation and exploitation in Brazil (Marini, 2000). In today's international division of labour, Brazil sits as one of the major exporters of primary resources such as wood, cereals, oil and minerals. A broad, structural dynamic is currently at play in the territoriality of Brazilian capitalism. First, the increased concentration of control over natural resources by fewer actors, which demands ever-larger scales of production and intensified integration into new social spaces. Secondly, the privatization of public spaces that are rich in natural resources, in particular water and minerals, combined with the intensification of labour productivity in the environment

(Acselrad, 2004, 2010). This context points to the re-primarization of the Brazilian economy, which can be understood as a combination of deindustrialization with the outgrowth of commodity exports *vis-à-vis* manufactured or semi-manufactured exports since 2010 (Lamoso, 2020).

Historically, the large landowning elites or *ruralistas* have been linked to reactionary forces in the country, and were one of the main backers of the military dictatorship that spanned from 1964 to 1985 (Dreifus, 1989). The structural power of *ruralistas* can be seen both in terms of their capacity to mobilize financial resources and in constructing majority coalitions in representative institutions and regulatory agencies within the state (Bruno, 2016). *Ruralistas* constitute the most powerful elite supporting Bolsonaro's government, alongside the arms industry and Evangelicals (Firmiano, 2020).[3] Far-right ideology in Brazil can be said to have one of its most important roots in a ruralist worldview, blending a nostalgia for settler colonial expansion and monocultural plantations with anti-Indigenous activism. Below we explore the main threads of Bolsonaro's environmental policy.

Bolsonaro's agribusiness agenda arrived even before he was sworn into office, when the powerful Brazilian Rural Society and the Ruralist Caucus in Congress declared support for his campaign. In the run-up to the 2018 election, he had already announced his intentions to shut down the Ministry of the Environment and merge it with the Ministry of Agriculture, Livestock and Supply. Once in office, strong domestic and international criticism, coming even from international markets, forced Bolsonaro to abandon the project, although changes were still programmed inside the ministry to benefit sectors that defended a more intensive exploitation of natural resources. Ricardo Salles, the appointed Minister in charge of this dismantling project, had been previously condemned by a Justice Court in São Paulo on grounds of contractual fraud when he was State Secretary of the Environment in the state of São Paulo.

The first expression of this process of change was the ministerial restructuring defined by Decree no. 9672 of January 2019, which extinguished the Environmental Education Directorate. The effect was to limit all environmental education initiatives to the Secretary of Ecotourism. The National Agency of Waters was also moved to the Ministry of Regional Development, and the Brazilian Forestry Service to the Ministry of Agriculture, to be under the command of well-known ruralist politicians and lobbyists.

In May, Minister Salles announced the revision of all Conservation Units in the country, from the Itatiaia National Park (created in 1934) to the Refúgio da Vida Silvestre Ararinha Azul (created in 2018), on the grounds that they had been created without meeting technical criteria. In the same month, the ministry disregarded a technical report from the Brazilian Institute of the Environment and Renewable Natural Resources (IBAMA) which pledged to veto oil exploitation near the Abrolhos National Park. The Executive Secretary of the ministry, Ana Pellini, rejected the report alleging 'strategic relevance of the subject matter', and then authorized a public auction offering seven oil blocs to be exploited in the region (Metrópoles, 2019).

Another similar reversal was the change of categorization of the Lagoa do Peixe Park, in the state of Rio Grande do Sul, to an Environmental Protection Area, which will allow varied sorts of private exploitation in the region. The Park hosts around 270 animal species throughout all seasons of the year, including species threatened by extinction and migratory birds coming from different parts of the world such as Canada, the US, Chile and Argentina. But perhaps the most astounding U-turn of the dismantling of the protective apparatus has been a legislative bill (191/2020) sent by the government to the Chamber of Deputies, which aims to liberalize intensive mining and other environmentally damaging activities within Indigenous lands of the country.

A process of militarization of environmental policies followed the first year of Bolsonaro's presidency. In the Amazon Council, all representatives from IBAMA, the Chico Mendes Institute for Biodiversity Conservation (ICMBio) and the National Indian Foundation (FUNAI) were sacked and substituted by 19 army representatives and 4 sheriffs from the Federal Police. In ICMBio, its President, Adalberto Eberhard, a well-known conservationist, was sacked alongside other directors, opening the way for the appointment of a colonel, a tenant and a major of the Military Police to the Board of Directors. Further, Bolsonaro published Decree 10342/2020, which authorized the deployment of the Armed Forces for missions under the Guarantee of Law and Order (GLO)[4] statute in border regions, Indigenous lands, environmental conservation units and other federal areas comprising the states of the so-called Legal Amazon. The same decree subordinates all environmental agencies to the Ministry of Defence.

In line with the new policy, the Ministry of Agriculture, Livestock and Supply liberated 290 new pesticides in the first 205 days of government. Of these, 41 per cent are classified as either highly or extremely toxic, while at least 4 products have been banned in other countries (DW, 2019). In 2020 alone, 405 new pesticides had been registered, and another 241 new requests will likely follow the same path. In all, the speed of pesticide permission is record breaking if compared with the rate of the previous ten years.

Environmental surveillance mandates have also suffered drastic setbacks under Bolsonaro. Up to May 2020, there had been a decrease of 34 per cent in the number of environmental fines related to illegal deforestation applied by IBAMA – the lowest rate in 11 years. The peak of this was when Minister Salles publicly reproached environmental inspectors who had destroyed equipment used for illegal deforestation in a Conservation Unit in the state of Pará, although their action had been sanctioned by force of a federal decree. Towards the end of August, Minister Salles announced the halt of all surveillance and deforestation-fighting operations. As a result, catastrophic fires occurred in the Pantanal natural region – in the states of Mato Grosso and Mato Grosso do Sul – affecting a staggering 30 per cent of the biome, its biodiversity and local communities. There was also a delay in the appointment of fire brigades, as well as frequent interruptions in the fire-fighting activities. The number of fires from 1 January to 22 October 2020 reached 89,604 (Fante, 2020).

According to the National Institute for Spatial Research (INPE), the number of deforestation and environmental degradation alerts increased 88 per cent in comparison to the same month in the previous year. In the first semester, alerts of deforestation in Indigenous lands increased 38 per cent, and by a staggering 85 per cent inside Federal Conservation Units (INPE, 2021). In response, Bolsonaro claimed that the data from INPE had been manipulated, and accused its Director, Ricardo Galvão, who was later sacked from the institute, of working 'at the service of NGOs'. 'We understand the importance of the Amazon for the world, but the Amazon is ours. We will not accept the type of politics that used to be done in the past', Bolsonaro further added (Brasil de Fato, 2019).

In August 2019, farmers and land grabbers who supported Bolsonaro organized 'fire day' – a coordinated incineration of pasture. One of the organizers declared that 'we need to show the president that we want to work, and the only way to do so is by knocking it down. And to form and clean our pasture, we need fire.' As a result, on 19 August, the skies of São Paulo became dark at 3pm with the black smoke that had travelled all the way from the Amazon. Minister Salles associated the fire with 'fake news', and on 21 August Bolsonaro suggested that NGOs could have orchestrated the Amazon fires as a form of retaliation for cuts in federal funding (Brasil de Fato, 2019).

In September, INPE had already registered an increase of 64 per cent of fire occurrences in the country compared with 2018 (DW, 2020a). Deforestation alerts had also risen by 321 per cent in August. In that month, Bolsonaro delivered a speech at the UN, attacking political opponents such as the Indigenous leader Roni Metyktire and the President of France, Emmanuel Macron, who had severely criticized the Brazilian government's mismanagement of the Amazon crisis. At the end of November 2019, Bolsonaro pledged that money donated to NGOs should be halted and went so far as to accuse Hollywood actor Leonardo DiCaprio of paying organizations to spread fires in the Amazon.

On 26 November, massive oil slicks of unknown origin had reached 779 areas in the Brazilian coastline since the end of August. The substance was raw petrol, which can affect the lives of maritime animals and coastal cities. Minister Salles ignored the Contingency Plan for Incidents of Oil Pollution in Waters under National Jurisdiction and insinuated that Greenpeace could have orchestrated the spills. Four and a half thousand tons of oil mixed with sand had been collected in the north-eastern coast by November 2019. According to a survey carried out by *Piauí* magazine, this amount is enough to fill 27,000 barrels (Mazza et al., 2019).

With this brief outline of the current state of decay of environmental public policies in Brazil, we turn to how the far right was able to ideologically justify such transformations and streamline a more aggressive anti-environmental agenda.

Living in sin with cultural Marxism

Broadly speaking, conspiracy theories are 'an explanation, either speculative or evidence-based, which attributes the causes of an event to a conspiracy or a plot' (Byford, 2011: 21). Conspiracy theories can however become politically charged when they are seen to threaten a group's identity and existence, leading it to create narratives that strengthen boundaries of difference with the outside world, whereby the out-group may provide justification for collective fear. When this happens, conspiracy theories can elevate social anxieties to a point of permanent obsession, channelling all frustrated experiences with modern life – economic self-realization, social recognition, cultural authenticity and so on – to marginalized scapegoats who become the bearers of 'evil'. The victimized 'we' identity is incapable of realizing its true moral nature (i.e. gifted by the mythical past of tradition) because the world has become profane, and all the violence, war and greed that exists is reductive to one, or a cluster, of social groups, such as Jews, Palestinians, Feminists, Gays, Blacks, Arabs, Communists, Natives.

The bizarre theories often brought forth about them are *conspiratorial* because they point to networked actions of corruption, moral degradation, plots of overtaking power and ideas that can lead down the road to violence and criminality. And such conspiracies are *theoretical* because they cannot ever be proved, or yet, any loose evidence can automatically prove the theory right and cannot be rationally debated without new, sub-theories arising to support them.[5] Whichever their contours, conspiracy theories are always about the creation and personalization of the public enemy (Kurz, 2017) through a 'single overarching plot that supposedly explains everything' (Byford, 2011: 33).

The far right has historically been the group most prone to embracing conspiracy theories and of articulating 'politics as conspiracy' (Saull et al.,

2015: 5). Radicalizing the conservative's commitment to *preserve*, it turns instead to a quest for *transformation* of society given the emergency to protect, or to further develop, its idealized self-notions of racial supremacy, masculine warrior *ethos*, religion, patriarchy and domination over nature (Davidson and Saull, 2017). What unites most of the far right today is a shared perception of enmity geared towards a global, pervasive conspiracy branded as 'cultural Marxism'. Once part of the propaganda repertoire of the German Nazi party in the 1930s to combat 'cultural Bolshevism', the obsession with the supposed erosion of traditional values operating swiftly through leftist intellectuals and artists became rebranded as cultural Marxism after the end of the Cold War. This conspiracy asserts that, with the collapse of really-existing-socialism and the failure of socialist revolutions to spread worldwide, the left devised new strategies of cultural domination – inspired by Gramsci and authors of the Frankfurt School – which would in the long term destroy capitalism from its superstructures of representation. As Olavo de Carvalho – Bolsonaro's 'intellectual Guru', whom the far-right strategist Steve Bannon believes to be one of the most brilliant minds alive (Teitelbaum, 2020) – suggests in his outlandish caricature:

> Gramsci discovered the 'cultural revolution', which would reform the 'common sense' of humanity, leading it to see the martyrdom of the Catholic saints as a sordid capitalist publicity campaign, and would transform the intellectuals, instead of the proletariat, as the elected revolutionary class. The Frankfurt men, especially Horkheimer, Adorno and Marcuse, had the idea to mix Freud with Marx, thereby concluding that Western culture was a disease, that anyone educated in it suffered from the 'authoritarian personality', that Western peoples should be reduced to the condition of a hospice patient and submitted to a 'collective psychotherapy'. (De Carvalho, 2019: 125–126)

Themes such as human rights, feminism and reproduction rights, homosexual marriage, and quotas for minorities and historically oppressed populations are, in this depiction, all 'Gramscist' strategies aiming to erode the family and traditional hierarchies which are the founding stone of capitalism. This explains the obsession of the far right with a 'culture war' or 'metapolitics' at all levels, as the communist public enemy is seen to be omnipresent in public education, mainstream media, the entertainment industry and in environmental regulatory institutions (Carapanã, 2019; Teitelbaum, 2020).

The most striking example of 'metapolitical activism' against cultural Marxism comes not from an angry intellectual, but from Brazil's former Minister of Foreign Affairs, the diplomat Ernesto de Araújo, who hosts an online blog named *Metapolics 17: Against Globalism.*[6] In a meeting among diplomats held in August 2019, where a report on climate change was presented, Araújo intervened to defend his view: 'I do not believe in Climate

Change. You see, I was in Rome in May and it was very cold. This shows how the theory is wrong. ... This the media chooses to ignore.' (see IG, 2019) This was not a side comment or a silly joke. Araújo was the man personally appointed by Olavo de Carvalho to shape Brazil's foreign policy. However nerve-wracking it may sound, his statement is in fact interwoven into a system of belief to which the Chancellor subscribes and around which similar conspiracies abound, such as that Nazism was a left-wing movement, that the left has an anti-natalist project to keep people from being born, and that 'globalist cultural Marxism' began with the French Revolution (see Esquerda Diário, 2018).

Such iterations are not casual or incidental. They are consistently outlined and articulated in philosophical writings linked to a broad tradition of thought. Take, for instance, Araújo's two articles published in Brazil's leading diplomatic journal, *Cadernos de Política Exterior*. In 'Trump and the West' (Araújo, 2017), he hails the victory of Trump as the saviour of Western civilization. In 'Globalism: A View Based on Nietzche's Thinking' (Araújo, 2019), he describes how Marxism occupied what he calls the desert of nihilist values and created its own form of religion, 'Globalism', a merging of the cultural revolution from the 1960s with Frankfurt School theories and Gramsci's ideas to pave the terrain for a new cultural hegemony of the left.

In these writings we can derive essential topics such as the decay of Western civilization – threatened both by a foreign enemy, Radical Islamic Terrorism, and a domestic one, people's very own loss of self-identity. According to Araújo, 'Pan-nationalism' is what defines the spirit of the West, the sense of a 'birth-culture'[7] as the overarching edifice of world politics which rests on the mutual existence of nations with no claims of sovereignty below or beyond them (Araújo, 2017: 332). By looking at history, he reminds us of the great deeds of Western civilization in fencing off enemies to preserve its self-image, such as when the Greeks defeated the Persians in 480 BC, when the Europeans deterred the Ottomans from invading Vienna in 1683, or when the counterrevolutionaries suppressed the proletariat in the upheavals of 1848 onwards.

By insisting on such 'Great Restorations', Araújo believes he is engaged in a moral crusade to restore Christian values. Not by chance, Araújo has been characterized by people both on the left and right in Brazil as a 'Knight Templar' in a moral crusade against cultural Marxism. Roberto Freire, a former right-wing Minister, Tweeted prior to Araújo's appointment as Chancellor in November 2018 that 'unfortunately, Brazil will not have a minister of foreign affairs, but a Templar Knight preaching on Gods, the Devil, and prophets of a new age'.[8] This depiction becomes less a caricature when confronting Araújo's claim that what Trump's platform offered to the West was a Jungian geo-psychic, civilizational therapy 'whose key is to recover the contact with an abandoned collective unconsciousness that has been suffocated by the blows of technocratic liberalism and political correctness' (Araújo, 2017: 331). In fact, there have been some public displays of Knights Templar symbology by Araújo and other far-right figures in Brazil, which suggests stronger links with its international counterparts like the alt-right (Pachá, 2019; Chade, 2021). This type of civilizational imagery has been termed 'conspiratorial medievalism', a form of discourse 'centred on the existence of a transhistorical, White Christianity that is permanently threatened by a variety of agents' (Millar and Lopez, 2021: 5).

The moral crusade against the 'green mafia'

Cultural Marxism played a fundamental role in the election of Jair Bolsonaro in October 2018 and in the ensuing environmental policies of the far-right government. The large-scale dissemination of fake news during the presidential campaign against the candidate of the Worker's Party, Fernando Haddad, provided Bolsonaro with a quasi-religious aura against fears that the left wanted to 'teach sex in schools' with the platform of 'gender ideology', and that generalized, state-led corruption was to become legalized.[9] Winning over the majority of the votes of the Evangelicals – the most morally conservative group in the electorate that voted as a bloc – allowed Bolsonaro to secure a wide margin over his opponent in the second round of the elections.[10]

Running on an internally fragmented far-right platform with declining popular support, Bolsonaro's strength lies in the contingent support he receives from certain state factions such as cultural authoritarians, militarists and neoliberal technocrats – all sharing with him the basic tenets of the conspiracy theories alluded to in the last section (Webber, 2020). The environmental dimension of this could already be felt in his inauguration speech, where he claimed that the agricultural sector – that is, monocultural farming, cattle ranching, extractivism – would have a decisive role in Brazil's development strategy, 'in perfect harmony with environmental preservation' (see Veja, 2019) This he said after having spent the campaign complaining that environmental policies and rights of Indigenous people block economic development (see Bragança, 2018). Let us turn to how this 'harmony' is understood and interwoven with the tenets of the Brazilian brand of cultural Marxism.

The former Chancellor Ernesto de Araújo is perhaps the most authoritative and articulate voice among conspiracists. In a speech at the Heritage Foundation, he claimed that globalism, that is, 'economic globalization highjacked by cultural Marxism', operates through three main threads: the ideology of climate change (or 'climatism'), gender ideology and 'oikophobia' – the opposite of xenophobia, that is, hatred towards one's own nation (FUNAG, 2019). He focuses on climatism as the main pressing issue of the day, pointing to supposedly faulty evidence in the 2018 IPCC report on climate change to conclude that 'it doesn't seem like a climate catastrophe to me' (FUNAG, 2019). Climatism, in this view, seeks to end political debate in order to impose exceptional measures that limit countries' sovereignty and attempt to steal away freedom of speech. Further, climatism is a tactic that seeks to destroy the 'symbolic order' of things: whereas classical Marxism reduced men to an economic animal, the 'new Marxism' introduces the *'reductio ad climaticum'*, and hence any utterance of a 'climate crisis' becomes the rationale for a communist plot to overthrow democratic countries in the West (FUNAG, 2019). Elsewhere, Araújo (2018) specified that

> This dogma has served to justify the increase of states' regulating power over the economy and the power of international institutions over nation states and their people, as well as to suffocate economic growth in democratic capitalist countries and to favour China. ... Climatism is basically a globalist tactic of instilling fear in order to obtain more power. Climatism says: 'hey you, you will destroy the planet. Your only choice is to hand everything over to me, your way of life and your thinking, your freedom and individual liberties'.

Here, climate change denialism becomes a position of conscious resistance against an alleged communist objective to steal away the fundamental liberties of a market economy.

Araújo is not alone in this crusade. A very influential work among the Latin American moralist crusaders is the *Dark Book of the New Left* (Marquez and Laje, 2018). According to its authors, with the collapse of the Soviet Union, many leftist groups in Latin America united to create, in 1990, the 'São Paulo Forum', having as its main leaders Fidel Castro, Lula from the Worker's Party and the Revolutionary Armed Forces of Colombia. They claim the Forum gave the opportunity for the left to reinvent its Leninist orientation and invest in a new hegemonic strategy inspired by Gramsci, Laclau and Mouffe. Indigenous and environmental movements would play a central role in this new phase, especially from 1992 onwards, 'when a number of strange, innovative and seemingly disconnected movements began appearing in many different parts of the world and in Latin America in particular' (Marquez and Laje, 2018: 16). The Rio de Janeiro Earth Summit (Eco-92) and the Indigenous March in Bolivia under the leadership of Evo Morales in the same year, were symbolic of this new era:

> With the absence of Soviet support and the consequent need to remedy this void, all leftist structures had to fabricate NGOs and different sorts of organizations to accommodate not only its primer, but also its activism, its flags, its clients and its sources of funding. (Marquez and Laje, 2018: 17)

Another source of inspiration is an older conspiracy that can be referred to as 'far-right decolonialism', which leaves aside the obsession with leftist regimes and focuses instead on a diffuse elite project from the Northern hemisphere that supposedly manipulates progressive social movements in the South. Rejecting any form of social identity based on gender, race and class, it derives the substance of the nation mainly from adherence to Christian values, in particular the principle of man's creation in the image of God, which would justify full domination over nature. To reject this truth is to fall into the traps of 'green neo-colonialism', according to the Ibero-American Solidarity Movement, a transnational conservative think-tank that disseminates this conspiracy. Reportedly, this conspiracy has significant resonance among militarists and ruralists in Brazil and has become a guide for Bolsonaro's environmental policy (see BrasilAgro, 2019). Its main ideas come from the book *Green Mafia: Environmentalism in Service to the World Government* (Carrasco et al., 2017), published in 2001 and currently in its twelfth edition. The authors claim that the 'green mafia' is a:

> Complex network of powerful supranational interests that created, funded and manipulated the international environmental-indigenous movement as a political weapon to divide and hinder the sovereign development of countries like Brazil, endowed with important natural resources, in order to exert control over its use, according to the exclusivist criteria of its hegemonic agenda. (Carrasco et al., 2017: 45–49)

As a consequence, the elites behind this project would be capable of controlling the population and natural resources of those countries, establishing a neo-colonial agenda through a cultural strategy deployed by the 'environmental apparatus'. The world government elite, or 'Anglo-American oligarchy', would be guided by values that make environmentalism a successor to Malthusianism, economic liberalism and the vision of an intrinsic Anglo-Saxon superiority as its model of world domination (Carrasco et al., 2017: 158–164).

In this setting, environmentalism is seen by the conspiracy theorists as a form of 'hybrid war' waged for 'social engineering', seeking to discredit national identity, the family unit and Christian values. The counterculture of the 'new left' became a strategy of this Anglo-American oligarchy, which from the end of the 1960s began investing in cultural tactics at universities with the spread of post-modern theories, the LGBT movement, 'gender ideology' and the 'environmental-indigenous' apparatus – which operates with the infiltration of scientists and environmental activists in national governments.

In Brazil, the authors claim this was first disseminated with Liberation Theology, a popular theological strand in the 1960s and 1970s that opposed military rule. In the 1980s, it then turned to NGOs promoting ideas such as global warming and ozone depletion. Further, 'human zoos' were implemented with the creation of Indigenous reserves, hindering exploration of God-gifted natural resources. For instance, this agenda resulted in the land demarcation of the 'gigantic and absurd Yanomami indigenous reserve, an area comprising 90.000km ^{2} located at the border with Venezuela and inhabited by a few thousand wandering foresters that have yet to overcome the civilizational phase of the Neolithic' (Carrasco et al., 2017: 613).

In sum, NGOs, infiltrated institutions – such as the INPE and IBAMA – and social movements – such as the Landless Workers' Movement and its branches – have allegedly created barriers to sovereign economic development: on the one hand, by denying the use of natural resources according to the 'national interest' (which in Brazil is intimately linked to notions of 'national security' in the military's mindset) and, on the other, producing a preservationist ideology that discredits national identity and prepares room for the exploitation of the Amazon by the 'neo-colonialist international consortium' (Carrasco et al., 2017: 84–90).

Taken together, these conspiracies form a consistent backbone of the ideology of Bolsonaro's government, although here we are only able to present a brief sketch of a much broader and transnationalized conspiracy theory. The main problem is that such views are not just limited to the elected government but have a long spill-over trajectory within the Armed Forces and relate to their ongoing politicization. The military has been a key actor in the process of de-democratization that Brazil has gone through in recent years (Ortega and Marín, 2020), with recurrent blackmail and tutelage on the part of the military against the judiciary. An example was in April 2018, when former Commander of the Army, General Villas-Bôas, threatened on Twitter to intervene in the event of a favourable decision on the Habeas Corpus by the Supreme Court to prevent former President Luiz Inácio Lula da Silva (2003–2010) of the Workers' Party from being arrested after being sentenced to 12 years in jail on dubious charges of passive corruption and money laundering (see Betim, 2018). In his recently published memoir, Vilas Bôas admits that the Tweet had been not a personal decision but meticulously articulated within the High Command of the army (see DW, 2021). As a result of their ideological affinity, Bolsonaro's government has been completely militarized. He chose four-star General Hamilton Mourão as his Vice-President, appointed (as of February 2021) 11 military officials as ministers (out of 23 ministries), and around 2,900 military personnel have been allocated to other echelons in the public administration (see Monteiro and Fernandes 2020).

According to Leirner (2020: 12), the Brazilian military has been actively engaged, at least since 2007 in 'full spectrum psychological', warfare against what the higher chains of command perceived as the new asymmetric threats arising from the post-Cold War era. These threats are pretty much the same as those identified by the far-right conspiracy theories outlined above,[11] the 'environmental-Indigenous apparatus' and the greed over the Amazonian forest, of which the left, under the Workers' Party, had been an international agent. With the demarcation of the Indigenous land 'Raposa Serra do Sol' under Lula's presidency in 2008, a widespread rebellion took shape in the army, with Vilas Bôas and General Augusto Heleno – currently a Minister in the far-right government – at the head of the insurgency that ultimately paved the way to Bolsonaro's election. With over 1,700,000 acres of land in the state of Roraima, at the border with Venezuela and Guyana, the Raposa Serra do Sol reserve has been the centre stage of many rural conflicts between Indigenous communities and non-Indigenous rice planters, who were forced to leave the land following the demarcation. With the judicialization of those conflicts, General Heleno claimed that the reserve was on its way to becoming an 'autonomous state' with the activities of NGOs and Indigenous movements (Fernandes, 2018). But, as already mentioned, the threats to the Amazon are perceived exclusively from the diffuse activism of environmentalists, and not from the greed of the transnational agricultural and mining sector, for which Bolsonaro lobbied during his campaign. In a video posted on social media, he said he would work to allow exploitation of natural resources in the Raposa Serra do Sol reserve: 'I dream, who knows one day, that we also have the Niobium Valley' in that region (Fernandes, 2018).

Perhaps no other event in the Bolsonaro presidency illustrates more the correlation between beliefs in conspiracy theories and its functionality in the interests of *ruralistas* than the infamous ministerial meeting held in April 2020 that was released to the public by a Supreme Court order. This meeting, which was recorded on video, gives a rare insight into the mentality of far-right politicians in their daily exchanges, and how conspiracy theories are nourished both in a vulgar and a more structured, ideological fashion. For instance, amid an escalating hate speech against the 'omnipresent' communist enemy and the glorification of the military dictatorship, the former Minister of Education, Abraham Weintraub, intervened to suggest the forced arrest of all Supreme Court ministers and the radicalization of the government in their 'struggle for freedom', to then conclude that 'I hate the term "indigenous population", I hate it. … There is only one people in this country. If you like it, you like it. If you don't like it, leave it on reverse gear.'. The Minister for Women, Family and Human Rights, Damares Alves, claimed she had information that the left had a plot to spread coronavirus against Indigenous populations in the Amazon, with the sole aim to 'blame it on the government'. Bolsonaro himself could not hold his excitement. Echoing Chancellor Araújo's well-articulated conspiracy that state intervention is a communist tactic to steal away one's freedom, the

President burst out in fury to say that the imposition of isolation measures during the pandemic – which he always minimized – was equivalent to imposing a dictatorship: 'what those sons of horses want ... is our freedom. Look how easy it is to implement a dictatorship in Brazil. ... People are at home. This is why I want ... people to be armed!' (see G1, 2020).

The above remarks highlight the extent to which there is a conspiracist mindset within the far-right government that is conducive to anti-democratic politics. But the 'horror show', as the meeting has been called, also reveals the level of sheer pragmatism of the neoliberal agenda in the environmental sector, with conspiracy theories being self-consciously used as a smoke screen for advancing the interests of the rural elite. The then-Minister of the Environment, Ricardo Salles, perfectly outlined the guide for action, suggesting that 'in this current moment where media attention is almost exclusively turned to Covid', it was the perfect time to 'pass infra-legal reforms to de-regulate, simplify' the legal structure of environmental protection in Brazil; or, in his words, to 'let the cattle pass through to change the whole rule' (see G1, 2020).

To Salles, to 'let the cattle pass through' means to facilitate the unimpeded exploitation of natural resources. Meanwhile, all scientific evidence pointing to increases in forest fires, deforestation, irregular cattle ranching, violence against rural communities and the like, is considered an 'international campaign against Brazil' – as Bolsonaro claimed in his speech at the UN Biodiversity Summit in September 2020 (DW, 2020b). Thus, cultural Marxism and related environmental conspiracies, as has been shown in this section, sit in perfect harmony with the economic interests of the backward power structure of *ruralistas* and have therefore facilitated the anti-environmental policies undertaken by Bolsonaro's presidency. The coup plotter General Vilas Bôas could not have made this clearer in his memoir when he stated that Minister Salles, suffering a 'massacre of accusations' from foreign audiences, 'dares to denounce what lies behind international indigenism and environmentalism' (de Castro, 2021: 221–222).

The intensification of land struggle

In this chapter, we have argued that the ongoing environmental catastrophe in Brazil has been widely facilitated by the use of conspiracy theories by the far right in their moral crusade against so-called cultural Marxism. We claim that the conspiracy theory of cultural Marxism played a fundamental role in agitating not only the more radical base of Bolsonaro's supporters, but more significantly in informing environmental policies that perfectly harmonize with the interests of *ruralistas*. By way of conclusion, we briefly look at how this situation is currently affecting the state of class struggle in rural Brazil, in particular the unprecedented increase in environmental conflicts in the country.

According to a survey carried out by Project Latentes (2018), there are currently 4,536 areas in Brazil where settlements, *quilombos*, Indigenous reserves or preservation sites neighbour, or intersect with, active regions of mineral exploitation, which more often than not precipitates land conflict. This reality reflects the escalation of rural violence and land struggle in contemporary Brazil, stretching to disputed territories comprising waters, land and the subsoil (Gonçalves, 2016). According to the Conflict Map Involving Environmental Injustice and Health in Brazil, as of March 2021 around 611 socio-environmental conflicts had been reported by local communities or academics in the country.[12] Another mapping platform, Ejatlas, shows that, from the 2,840 environmental conflicts that have been registered worldwide by social movements and NGOs, 133 were self-reported in Brazil, making it the country with the third-highest number of environmental conflicts in the world.[13] Further, in 2019, about 860,000 people were involved in land conflict, according to the latest Land Conflict Map, which is annually published by the Land Pastoral Commission. Mining companies are responsible for 38.8 per cent of those conflicts in rural Brazil (Land Pastoral Commission, 2019).

Aside from fulfilling his promise of not demarcating any centimetre of Indigenous land, the Bolsonaro government returned 27 demarcation lawsuits to be reviewed by FUNAI in the first session of 2019 alone. This implies larger obstacles, as well as impediments, to the fulfilling of the constitutional rights of the Indigenous population who claim their ancestral territory. In 2019, 113 homicides of Indigenous natives were registered by the Special Secretary of Indigenous Health, a little fewer than in 2018, with 135 homicides. The states of Mato Grosso do Sul and Roraima registered the highest rates, at 40 and 26, respectively. There have been even reports of torture against children in the state of Mato Grosso do Sul (CIMI, 2020). In parallel to this context, the Bolsonaro government is currently pushing to criminalize progressive rural social movements through a punitive turn in the legal apparatus that regulates land occupation, as well as relaxing legislation concerning the right to carry firearms on rural properties (Firmiano, 2020).

In Brazil, there are many movements reacting against and resisting the environmental policies of the far-right government, such as the Landless Workers' Movement and the Via Campesina. Peasants, local communities, landless populations and social movements are at the forefront of the land struggle, spanning nationwide demonstrations against mining projects from the south to the north of the country, questioning large, multinational fishing industries and standing up to environmental racism, among other pressing issues. Meanwhile, Bolsonaro's base of supporters has shrunk after a disastrous mishandling of the economy and the COVID-19 pandemic, although what remains of it has radicalized even further. Threats to the division of powers and coup plotting against democracy – fuelled by ever-emerging conspiracy theories – also continue under the far-right government as Bolsonaro's chances of winning the 2022 elections for a second term seem all the more distant, as shown by polls throughout the country. Possibly for the first time in Brazil, the environmental issue will become highly politicized during the elections, given the scale of the anti-environmentalist catastrophe represented by Bolsonaro's office.

Notes

1 In 771 days as President, Bolsonaro has made 2,411 false or distorted declarations, 20 of which are related to environmental issues (Aosfatos, 2022).

2 The global COVID-19 pandemic has only strengthened the conspiratorial nature of Bolsonaro's government and its supporters. For instance, Bolsonaro has repeatedly claimed COVID-19 was nothing more than 'a little flu' and a 'hysteria' and mobilized the state machinery to campaign for the use of hydroxychloroquine as a treatment for the virus, despite widespread alerts from the scientific community that it was ineffective and could lead to dangerous side effects.

3 This triad of support constitutes a relatively cohesive legislative bloc in Congress named *Bancada do Boi, da Bala e da Bíblia* (Beef, Bullet and Bible caucus, or BBB).

4 GLO operations are a constitutional provision that can be summoned by executive powers in the cases of depletion of security forces, severe disturbances of order, or security of events. The GLO has been one of the main instruments of militarization in democratic Brazil since the end of the military dictatorship.

5 Rosenblum and Muihead (2020) claim that while classic conspiracism involved some degree of detective work to amass data for generating a comprehensive narrative, the new conspiracism practised by figures such as Trump and Bolsonaro lets go completely the burden of explanation – they are conspiracies *without* theories – in order to delegitimize democratic institutions.

6 Araújo was in office from January 2019 to the end of March 2021. He was sacked after strong political pressure from Congressmen and diplomats, who considered his accusations against China – widely publicized in his Twitter account and blog posts, reproducing tropes such as 'comunavirus' or 'communist-virus' – had impacted the delivery of raw materials from Chinese ports for the production of vaccines against coronavirus.

7 The concept of the birth-culture draws on contemporary French far-right thinking and is tied to the idea that culture is an immutable element defining individuals from birth (de Orellana and Michelsen, 2019).

8 See Roberto Freire's X account, 27 December 2018: https://bit.ly/3rjApDT (accessed 25 February 2021).

9　In 2020, Alexandre de Morais, a Minister of the Supreme Court, opened an investigation called *Hate Cabinet*, which sought to identify the funded network of coordinated disinformation against political opponents (see Correio Braziliense, 2020).

10　Bolsonaro was elected with 55.13 per cent of the vote (57.7 million votes), whereas Haddad, from the Worker's Party, received 44.87 per cent (47 million). Representing only one-third of the electorate, the Evangelicals gave 11 million votes to Bolsonaro, which is more than the difference that separated him from Haddad (Webber, 2020: 8).

11　The main book inspiring this type of reasoning within the Armed Forces is entitled *Orvil* (see Brandão and Leite, 2012). It was produced by army officials under the order of former Minister of Defence, Leônidas Gonçalves, during the presidency of José Sarney, just after the military regime ended. It was devised as a response to the book *Brazil: Never Again* (Archdiocese of São Paulo, 1985).

12　More information available at: http://mapadeconflitos.ensp.fiocruz.br/ (accessed 1 March 2021).

13　More information available at: https://ejatlas.org/ (accessed 1 March 2021).

References

Acselrad, H. (ed.) (2004). *Conflitos Ambientais no Brasil*. Rio de Janeiro: Relume Dumará.

Acselrad, H. (2010). Ambientalização das Lutas Sociais – O Caso do Movimento por Justiça Ambiental. *Estudos Avançados*, 24(68): 103–119.

Alves Cepêda, V. (2018). A Nova Direita no Brasil: Contexto e Matrizes Conceituais. *Mediações: Revista de Ciências Sociais*, 23(2): 40–75.

Aos Fatos (2022). Em 1.459 dias como presidente, Bolsonaro deu 6.685 declarações falsas ou distorcidas. *Aosfatos.org*, 30 December, www.aosfatos.org/todas-as-declarações-de-bolsonaro/ (accessed 28 February 2021).

Araújo, E. (2019). Globalismo: Uma Visão a Partir do Pensamento de Nietzsche. *Cadernos de Política Exterior*, 5(8): 5–15.

Araújo, E. (2018). Sequestrar e perverter. *Metapolítica 17. Contra o Globalismo*, www.metapoliticabrasil.com/blog/sequestrar-e-perverter (accessed 12 February 2020).

Araújo, E. H. F. (2017). Trump e o Ocidente. *Cadernos de Política Exterior*, 3(6): 323–357.

Archdiocese of São Paulo (1985). *Brasil: Nunca Mais*. Petrópolis: Vozes.

Betim, F. (2018). Pressão política de militares no HC de Lula revela como Exército ganha espaço com Temer. *El País*, 11 April, https://bit.ly/3r5Um0M (accessed 27 February 2021).

Bragança, D. (2018). Bolsonaro defende o fim do Ministério do Meio Ambiente. *(O)eco*, 1 October, https://bit.ly/2NRUa6H (accessed 26 February 2021).

Brandão, P., and Leite, I. (2012). Nunca Foram Heróis! A Disputa pela Imposição de Significados em Torno do Emprego da Violência na Ditadura Brasileira, por Meio de Uma Leitura do Projeto ORVIL. *Anos 90*, 19(35): 299–327.

BrasilAgro (2019). Autor da bíblia de ruralistas critica ONGs estrangeiras na Amazônia. *BrasilAgro*, 14 October, https://bit.ly/3q7QURZ (accessed 26 February 2021).

Brasil de Fato (2019). Estimulados por Bolsonaro, fazendeiros promovem 'dia do fogo' na Amazônia. *Brasil de Fato*, 15 August, www.brasildefato.com.br/2019/08/15/estimulados-por-bolsonaro-fazendeiros-promovem-dia-do-fogo-na-amazonia/ (accessed 3 March 2020).

Bruno, R. (2016). Desigualdade, Agronegócio, Agricultura Familiar no Brasil. *Estudos Sociedade e Agricultura*, 24(1): 142–160.

Byford, J. (2011). *Conspiracy Theories: A Critical Introduction*. New York: Palgrave Macmillan.

Carapanã (2019). A Nova Direita e a Normalização Do Nazismo e Do Fascismo. In Esther Solano Gallego (ed.), *O Ódio Como Política: A Reinvenção Das Direitas No Brasil*. São Paulo: Boitempo Editorial, pp. 33–39.

Carrasco, L., Palacios, S. e Lino, and Luís, G. (2017 [2001]). *Máfia Verde: O Ambientalismo a Serviço do Governo Federal*, 12th ed. Rio de Janeiro: Capax Dei.

Castro, C. (ed.) (2021). *General Villas Bôas: Conversa com o Comandante*. Rio de Janeiro: FGV.

Chade, J. (2021). Símbolos monárquicos e religiosos geram críticas contra Araújo no Itamaraty. *UOL*, 27 February, https://noticias.uol.com.br/colunas/jamil-chade/2021/02/27/bandeiras-alimentam-criticas-contra-araujo-no-itamaraty.htm (accessed 28 April 2023).

CIMI (2020). Relatório. Violência contra os povos indígenas no Brasil. Conselho Indigenista Missionário (Missionary Indigenist Council (CIMI), https://cimi.org.br/wp-content/uploads/2021/11/relatorio-violencia-povos-indigenas-2020-cimi.pdf (accessed 22 April 2022).

Correio Braziliense (2020). STF fecha o cerco contra o 'Gabinete do Ódio'; confira quem são os alvos. *Correio Braziliense*, 28 May, https://bit.ly/2OdeYpj (accessed on 1 March 2021).

Davidson, N., and Saull, R. (2017). Neoliberalism and the Far-Right: A Contradictory Embrace. *Critical Sociology*, 43(4–5): 707–724.

De Almeida, R. (2019). Bolsonaro Presidente: Conservadorismo, Evangelismo e a Crise Brasileira. *Novos Estudos Cebrap*, 38(1): 185–213.

De Carvalho, O. (2019). *A Nova Era e a Revolução Cultural: Fritjof Capra & Antonio Gramsci*. 4th ed. Campinas: Vide Editorial.

De Orellana, P., and Michelsen, N. (2019). Reactionary Internationalism: The Philosophy of the New Right. *Review of International Studies*, 45(5): 748–767.

Dos Santos, T. (1994). *Evolução Histórica do Brasil: Da Colônia à Crise da 'Nova República'*. Petrópolis, RJ: Vozes.

Dreifuss, R. (1989). *O Jogo Da Direita Na Nova República*. Petrópolis: Vozes.

DW (2019). Ministério da Agricultura libera novos agrotóxicos. *DW*, 22 May, https://bit.ly/3uLPtMi (accessed 28 February 2021).

DW (2020a). Brasil: deforestación en la Amazonía sube un 64 por ciento. *Deutesche Welle*, 8 May, www.dw.com/es/brasil-deforestaci%C3%B3n-en-la-amazon%C3%ADa-sube-casi-un-64-por-ciento/a-53375405 (accessed 15 November 2023).

DW (2020b). Na ONU, Bolsonaro ataca ONGs e critica cobiça estrangeira. *DW*, 1 October, https://bit.ly/3kC82hi (accessed 28 February 2021).

DW (2021). Projeto Bolsonaro presidente foi construção de generais. *DW*, 18 Frebruary, https://bit.ly/3kBMYYE (accessed 27 February 2021).

Esquerda Diário (2018). Conheça o que pensa o reacionário Ernesto Araújo, chefe do Itamaraty de Bolsonaro. *Esquerda Diário*, 15 November, https://bit.ly/3b71158 (accessed 25 February 2021).

Fante, E. (2020). Causas e efeitos da mudança do clima nos biomas Amazônia e Pampa. *Fundação Rosa Luxemburgo*, 17 December, https://rosalux.org.br/causas-e-efeitos-da-mudanca-do-clima-nos-biomas-amazonia-e-pampa/ (accessed 20 January 2021).

Fernandes, L. (2018). Raposa Serra do Sol | A questão de honra do general Augusto Heleno. *BrasildeFato*, https://bit.ly/3bNZ64F (accessed 27 February 2021).

Firmiano, F. D. (2020). 'Quem lamenta os estragos – se os frutos são prazeres?' O Bloco de Poder Agro do Governo Bolsonaro. *Estudos Sociedade e Agricultura*, 28(2): 364–387.

FUNAG (2019). Speech by the Minister of Foreign Affairs, Ambassador Ernesto Araújo, at the Heritage Foundation. *FUNAG*, 11 September, https://bit.ly/3sF4vSw (accessed 26 February 2021).

G1 (2020). Leia a transcrição do vídeo da reunião que Moro diz provar a interferência de Bolsonaro na PF. *G1*, 22 May, https://glo.bo/3bPnTp5 (accessed 28 February 2021).

Gallego, E. S. (2018). *O Ódio Como Política: A Reinvenção das Direitas no Brasil*. São Paulo: Boitempo.

Gonçalves, R. J. A. F. (2016). No horizonte, a exaustão: disputas pelo subsolo e efeitos socioespaciais dos grandes projetos de mineração em Goiás. 504f. Tese (Doutorado em Geografia). Universidade Federal de Goiás, Programa de Pós-graduação em Geografia.

IG (2019). 'Não acredito em aquecimento global. Estive em Roma e estava frio', diz ministro. *IG*, 3 August, https://bit.ly/3dWNA9E (accessed 25 February 2021).

INPE (2021). A taxa consolidada de desmatamento por corte raso para os nove estados da Amazônia Legal em 2020 foi de 10.851 km2. 2021. *INPE*, www.inpe.br/noticias/noticia.php?Cod_Noticia=5811 (accessed 25 September 2021).

Kurz, R. (2017). Hysterical populism. *Libcom.org*, 12 June, https://libcom.org/article/hysterical-populism-robert-kurz (accessed 9 November 2023).

Lamoso, L. (2020). Reprimarização no Território Brasileiro. *Espaço e Economia: Revista Brasileira de Geografia Econômica*, IX(19): 1–31. doi: 10.4000/espacoeconomia.15957.

Land Pastoral Commission (2019). *Comissão Pastoral da Terra. Conflitos no Campo Brasil 2018*. Goiânia: Land Pastoral Commission.

Leirner, P. C. (2020). Hybrid Warfare in Brazil: The Highest Stage of the Military Insurgency. *HAU: Journal of Ethnographic Theory*, 10(1): 41–49.

Marini, R. M. (2000). *Dialética da Dependência: Uma Antologia da Obra de Ruy Mauro Marini*. São Paulo: Editora Vozes.

Marquez, N., and Laje, A. (2018). *O livro Negro da Nova Esquerda*. Curitiba: Danúbio.

Mazza, L., Rossi, A., and Buono, R. (2019). Sobre o óleo derramado. *Revista Piauí*, 4 November, https://piaui.folha.uol.com.br/sobre-o-oleo-derramado/ (accessed 15 November 2023).

Messenberg, D. (2019). A Cosmovisão da 'Nova' Direita Brasileira. In Rosana Pinheiro-Machado and Adriano de Freixo (eds), *Brasil em Transe: Bolsonarismo, Nova Direita e Desdemocratização*. Rio de Janeiro: Oficina Raquel.

Metrópoles (2019). Bolsonaro nomeia acusada de improbidade para 2° posto do Meio Ambiente. *Metrópoles*, 18 January, www.metropoles.com/brasil/politica-brasil/bolsonaro-nomeia-acusada-de-improbidade-para-2o-posto-do-meio-ambiente (accessed 30 March 2020).

Miguel, L. F. (2021). O Mito da 'Ideologia de Gênero' no Discurso da Extrema Direita Brasileira. *Cadernos Pagu*, (61): 1–14. e216216.

Millar, K. M., and Lopez, J. C. (2021). Conspiratorial Medievalism: History and Hyperagency in the Far-Right Knights Templar Security Imaginary. *Politics*, 0(0): 1–17. doi.org/10.1177/02633957211010983.

Monteiro, T., and Fernandes, A. (2020). Com 2.019 cargos, Forças Armadas temem desgaste. Estadão, 31 May, https://bit.ly/3raBnlB (accessed 27 February 2021).

Nunes, J., Ventura, D., and Lotta, G. (2020). Brazil: Jair Bolsonaro's strategy of chaos hinders coronavirus response. *The Conversation*, 23 April, https://theconversation.com/brazil-jair-bolsonaros-strategy-of-chaos-hinders-coronavirus-response-136590 (accessed 9 November 2023).

Oliveira, T. (2020). Desinformação Científica em Tempos de Crise Epistêmica: Circulação de Teorias da Conspiração nas Plataformas de Mídias Sociais. *Revista Fronteiras – estudos midiáticos*, 22(1): 21–35.

Ortega, A., and Marín, P. O. (2020). Coronavírus e a propaganda anti-China. *Revista Opera*, 24 March, https://operamundi.uol.com.br/coronavirus/63726/o-coronavirus-e-a-propaganda-anti-china (accessed 23 November 2023).

Pachá, P. (2019). Why the Brazilian far right loves the European Middle Ages. *Pacific Standard*, 12 March, https://psmag.com/ideas/why-the-brazilian-far-right-is-obsessed-with-the-crusades (accessed 9 November 2023).

Pinheiro-Machado, R., and Adriano de Freixo (eds) (2019), *Brasil em Transe: Bolsonarismo, Nova Direita e Desdemocratização*. Rio de Janeiro: Oficina Raquel.

Project Latentes (2018). Brasil tem 4.536 conflitos socioambientais latentes. *Livre. jor*, https://livre.jor.br/brasil-tem-4-536-conflitos-socioambientais-latentes/ (accessed 1 March 2021).

Recuero, R. (2020). #FraudenasUrnas: Estratégias Discursivas de Desinformação no Twitter nas Eleições 2018. *Revista Brasileira de Linguistica Aplicada*, 20(3): 383–406.

Rosenblum, N.L., and Muirhead, R. (2020). *A Lot of People Are Saying: The New Conspiracism and the Assault on Democracy*. Princeton: Princeton University Press.

Saull, R., Anievas, A., Davidson, N., and Fabry, A. (eds) (2015). *The Longue Durée of the Far-Right: An International Historical Sociology*. Oxon: Routledge.

Severo, R. G., Gonçalves, S. da R. V., and Duque Estrada, R. (2019). A Rede de Difusão do Movimento Escola Sem Partido no Facebook e Instagram: Conservadorismo e Reacionarismo na Conjuntura Brasileira. *Educação & Realidade*, 44(3): 1–28.

Teitelbaum, B. (2020). *War for Eternity: The Return of Traditionalism and the Rise of the Populist Right*. London: Penguin Books.

Veja (2019). Leia a íntegra dos dois primeiros discursos do presidente Jair Bolsonaro. *Veja*, 1 January, https://bit.ly/37ZqJ9M (accessed 26 February 2021).

Webber, J. R. (2020). A Great Little Man: The Shadow of Jair Bolsonaro. *Historical Materialism*, 28(1): 3–49.

10

Necromancers and rebirth: bodily ideals of masculinity among far-right traditionalists in London

Amir Massoumian

Nature is a fascist and nature is the greatest teacher. If you want to climb a mountain, but you're not prepared, nature's going to teach you a lesson. If you want to hunt, but you're not prepared, nature's going to teach you. That's what being one with nature is about, it's not extinction rebellion, or some degenerate hippie shit, it's being what nature chooses. If these cucks were left to fend for themselves for 2 days nature would eat them alive. But that's what a traditionalist system is for. It's the best way that nature has taught us that ethnic groups should organize and live. All people belong in their rightful places on the globe in harmony. Anytime someone tries to mess around with that, you see the results.

Thomas explains to me: 'What we're involved in is necromancy. It's about raising our own consciousness to match what nature requires of us, and by doing that, we're saving Britain from the filth it's in.'

Necromancy, according to its dictionary definition, is 'a method of divination through alleged communication with the dead; black art magic in general, especially that practiced by a witch or sorcerer; sorcery; witchcraft; conjuration'.[1] In this context, however, Thomas speaks of necromancy as a rejuvenation of the ideology of 'traditionalism' which will harmonize human beings within their 'rightful places'. The appropriation of medieval entanglements by ethno-nationalist groups means that the 'logics of the past' are seen to be bastions of white ethnic history where a homogeneous existence once reigned within a conflict-free nation (Rambaran-Olm et al., 2020: 356). As Kao (2020) argues, the use of racialized medievalism and paganism by eco-fascists is rooted in an identitarian ecology that is always alert to the potential threat of pollution. It is this very attempt to resurface and re-embody these logics of a past tradition and prevent 'pollution' in both the environmental and physical sense that the word 'necromancy' was used by Thomas. Well versed in both English history and forms of paganism, we spend the afternoon drinking and smoking in an overpriced bar in Clapham. With nervous energy and a rapid pace of speech, Thomas informed me of the differences between Wicca, Odinism and Druidry, while my minuscule knowledge of British occultism managed to keep the conversation somewhat reciprocal. Though we spoke for a couple of hours, this was one of the few interviews I was unable to record. The very presence of my recording device would conjure an apprehensive and uneasy body language. I asked if he was okay, seeing how his enthusiasm and tone had dimmed. 'Being recorded really brings out my anxiety, I just freeze and can't think', he told me, and after two brief attempts, and many apologies on his behalf, I decided it best not to record the conversation, seeing the embarrassment it seemed to bring about.

'It's tripped me up so many times', he continued. 'How come?' I ask. 'You know, just … life, when you need to be ready.' He explained while looking at the table, 'I used to be on Diazepam to treat it, then I tried Xanax for a while, but I've purged myself of that stuff since. Had to detox for ages … those things rot much more than they heal.'

The words 'purge', 'rot' and 'heal' make an appearance time and time again throughout this chapter, pertaining not only to the body but also to the 'health' of the nation-state. In this particular context, Diazepam, a medicine used to treat anxiety prescribed by Thomas's General Practitioner (GP), and Xanax (which I later learnt was purchased off the internet), not only failed in their healing effect, but apparently caused a form of corrosion which required a 'detox' of fasting, prayer and constant hydration. Thomas detailed to me that part of the detox was his strict abstinence from any medication prescribed by his GP to avoid this 'rot'. Far from being perceived as a medical side effect such as depersonalization or muscular numbness, I soon learn that this is perceived to be due to modern pharmaceutical corporations' intent to keep his body and country in a state of false consciousness resulting in climate change, physical decay and the destruction of the environment.

The data presented in this chapter is situated within a two-year ethnographic project in London that was conducted as part of my master's and present doctoral research. Reflecting the fragmented and multilayered nature of the contemporary far right, my fieldwork led me to research a variety of groups and individuals that often embodied disparate and contradictory beliefs and practices. In the context of this chapter, I became acquainted with Thomas (28 y/o) in the summer of 2018, who later introduced me to the other two interlocuters: David (26 y/o) and Jay (21 y/o). My first interaction with Thomas was at a private talk given by a famous right-wing historian where we did not speak. The following summer, however, we met once again during the Free Tommy Robinson protests in Trafalgar Square and instantly recognized one another, connecting on the fact that we had both come alone and found it bizarre that a naked bike tour of London was passing through at the same time as the protest was happening. Though we exchanged numbers after the protest and engaged in a long discussion on Heidegger, Thomas was completely reluctant to be interviewed or become my interlocuter. After a few months of sporadic meetings, however, I received his trust and he finally agreed under the condition of full anonymity. He later introduced me to Jay and David whom he had met the previous year through mutual friends loosely affiliated with the now dissolved Generation Identity UK. The data presented in this chapter is sourced from interviews and participant observation in the field where we would either meet together or individually throughout the year that followed.

The common thread between them seemed to reflect comradery as well as a common desire in the purification of both their bodies and the environment in which they lived. When asked how they would identify themselves, the word 'traditionalists' was used, which embodied the view that notions of progress and individualism were opposed to a transcendental order of natural hierarchy as espoused by figures such as Julius Evola.[2] A state of political decadence, racial mixing, all perpetuated by a loss of masculinity in the West, were believed to be the core reason why Europe was heading towards ecological – and cultural – degeneracy and collapse. A strict eco-praxis, including vegan diets, avoidance of any form of vehicle transport, and the growth of fruit and vegetables in their respective households, were seen as solutions.

My encounter with my interlocuters presented a stark contrast to the assumptions I had been building before my aforementioned interactions. Indeed, from a gendered perspective, it is often assumed that ecological concerns are considered to be 'stereotypically feminine' by the far right (Bloodheart & Swim, 2010), while anti-environmentalist sentiments and meat consumption are seen to reflect masculinity and industriousness (Gelfer, 2013; Anshelm & Hultman, 2014).

This group of traditionalists, however, dispelled this assumption that I had been building with the data, echoing Lubarda's (2020) claim that the label 'far right' inhabits a wide, complex variety of beliefs regarding the environment. While beliefs concerning leftist infiltration and cultural Marxism were strongly held, an esoteric view, similar to the myriad of 'neo-Romantic anti-industrialist' thought among early twentieth-century nationalists, was evident; man and nature are not only far from separate, but there is also a strong and eternal link between the environment in which people live and the resulting character of said peoples (Dietz, 2008: 809; Turner-Graham, 2019: 58). Thomas's feelings of anxiety were not simply in his mind and body but were seen as intimately connected with the nation-state and its nature. Healing in the 'real' sense, I was told, for this group, comes from a combination of environmental activism, a vegan diet, strenuous physical exercise including yoga, waking early to see the sun rise and, most importantly, abstinence from any form of 'degenerate' behaviour. This chapter thus wishes to highlight how it is that conspiratorial thinking regarding climate change (in this case Jewish conspiracies of cultural Marxism) can embed itself within eco-fascistic thinking and the consequences this has in terms of the body.

The importance of bodies

The ruthless emphasis of far-right ideologies on the subordination of the individual to a 'pure' ethnic community is well documented (Heineman, 1999; Sinke, 1989; Proctor, 1997; Koonz, 2003; Nolan, 2005). This obsession with health and purity was itself one outcome of the long modern European turn from the ancient preoccupation with the soul as an intimation of cosmic order, to the body as the location not only of pleasure, pain, demand and desire but also of 'personal identity' (Cocks, 2007: 96). Striving towards purity, in this context, is a discursive judgement made regarding the future in relation to a supposed past ideal (rural, non-cosmopolitan, white, cis gendered, heteronormative, able bodied, etc.), free from heterogeneous or inferior (i.e. non-white, non-heteronormative, etc.) elements. Adherents, then, purport to defend the white race against the threats of 'impurity', by working towards the redemption and rejuvenation of the nation; this is summarily known as the 'rebirth myth' or 'palingenetic ultranationalism', which is then intertwined with personal sensations of religious revival and personal rebirth (Coupland, 2016: 120; Griffin, 1995: 13).

While such notions of racial hygiene seem like a haunting memory of Europe's past, they are proving to have an increasingly coercive influence on the present. Considering increasing electoral success from populist radical right parties, commentators point to traces of the rebirth rhetoric in the Brexit campaign's slogan 'Take Back Control' (Green et al., 2016). Manifestations of this rhetoric reared their ugly head on 16 June 2016, when far-right terrorist, Thomas Mair repeatedly shot and stabbed Labour MP, Jo Cox in an attack during the EU referendum campaign. Police discovered Mair's house to be sparse and obsessively orderly, with tinned food carefully arranged in precise rows, with each label pointing in exactly the same direction. According to members of his family, he had been treated for obsessive-compulsive disorder, with such a great deal of anxiety about cleanliness that he had been known to scrub himself with pan scourers (Cobain, 2016).

The reason I bring this to the reader's attention is that while the historical, social and political aspects of the far right are of great importance to its studies, it is, as Mosse (1999: 10) argues, 'only ... when we have grasped fascism from the inside out, [that we can] truly judge its appeal and its power'. The study of bodies matters (Connell, 1995: 51), for they are the site of symbolic interpretation, where personal and social identities coalesce (Mangan, 2000: 32). This chapter argues that, for my interlocuters, both the nation and the body are seen as having been corrupted and require redemption and purification through a return to pure tradition reflecting ideologies of purity and their physical embodiments as a desire for 'order and stability, for clear (symbolic) boundaries' (Forchtner, 2019: 296).

Rising from the ashes

As a teenager from Iran, I remember receiving the odd British National Party (BNP) leaflet in the post. I would throw it in the bin as soon as I caught sight of the logo on the corner, as if the paper would come to life if I wasn't fast enough. Being left with the chilling thought that the BNP had been in front of our door, I often wondered whether they had any success in converting people through paper.

Though the British far right has been represented by several parties, from the British Union of Fascists (BUF) in the 1930s, League of Empire Loyalists in the 1950s, to the present-day BNP, none of my interlocutors detailed in this chapter claimed to have membership of any official political party. Radicalization was not done through leaflets, nor from being stopped by party members next to stalls of right-wing literature and migration statistics, but rather from behind their computer screens at home. David tells me how he would hear about the increase in 'halal restaurants', 'rising immigration, grooming gangs, and Islamism in Europe' but doesn't recall taking it seriously or having much interest in politics generally. 'I remember thinking ... who are these nutters?' he tells me while smoking a cigarette on Hampstead Heath – a large park in north London. 'Saying that, I do come from a very liberal family so I'd always been brought up to live as though nothing's wrong ... like sheep waiting to get the cut', he says while throwing his cigarette on the floor and stomping it out. As we walk away, he turns back, picks up the cigarette butt and puts it in the small pocket on his t-shirt. 'Old habits die hard', he says smiling, which I later realize, is not in reference to smoking – but to his former anti-ecological carelessness.

According to my interlocutors, a mixture of researching online theories on various forums, along with the rise of what they call 'leftist politics' in their everyday life, culminated in a 'wake-up call' which radically changed them. This 'wake-up call' is also referred to as being 'red pilled', a metaphor taken from the movie *The Matrix* which has been central to fascist rhetoric within anti-feminist masculinist political subcultures (Nagle, 2017: 144). The other side of 'waking up' is a constant awareness of 'race realism'. The corruption of the white race by a Jewish Zionist elite. David elaborates on how he started noticing the semblance of what he was reading online to his lived experience: 'I remember reading this thing … how everyone gets to be proud, right? Black pride, gay pride, this pride, that pride, everything except for being white and being male … that you're supposed to be ashamed of.' He goes on to say: 'I saw book shops push critical race theory to the forefront, movies and news reports had clear leftist messaging, adverts always had white women with a Black or Asian man … and I was like hang on … something's not right here.'

Hermansson et al. (2020: 114) write that by cloaking Nazi propaganda in movie references such as *The Matrix*, the viewer is provided with a new framework through which genocidal notions can be interpreted in an appealing manner. While the question may arise as to how anyone can seriously adhere to the same ideology which was responsible for the Holocaust through the lens of Hollywood movie references, Ernst Bloch reminds us that, when studying fascism, one's focus should not exclusively rest on the 'seriousness' of its rhetoric, but rather its 'energy', 'the fanatic-religious impact' which does not simply come from 'despair and ignorance', but rather from 'the uniquely stirring power of belief' (Rabinbach, 1977: 13–14). The term 'necromancy' coincides with this imagery of 'energy' and 'rejuvenation'; a form of shock which wakes what is dormant.

Indeed, during a meeting with David and Thomas, I ask about the BUF badges which they wore on the lapels of their bomber jackets. David simply replies, 'The symbol spoke to me', while Thomas, the more esoterically minded of the two, informs me that 'it's a symbol of energy and electricity, waking Britain up. … I feel dangerous when I wear it', he smirks. The symbol itself is that of a lightning bolt, similar to those one would usually see on a warning sign for high voltage. This 'awakening', however, is not seen to be sufficient, as Thomas elaborates: 'people think being red pilled is enough, like "okay, I clocked onto the subversion, I'm red pilled about the Jews", but now what? You're still lost.' He starts tapping his finger on the table: 'it doesn't mean anything unless you're actually connected to something'. Among the interlocutors outlined in this chapter (Thomas, David and Jay) there is a shared experience regarding life before traditionalism which is characterized as a 'lost' state. A state without this 'connection' Thomas speaks of. Most stories revolve around 'decadent' behavioural patterns such as taking drugs, eating meat, playing video games and rarely engaging in physical activity. 'How I used to live was disgusting', enunciated David. 'You don't even want to know the shit I used to get up to … I was rotting away. You know the worst bit? I had no shame about it. No shame at all.' This 'disgusting' past was seen as a byproduct of the decadent times they situate themselves in, from being educated in schools where they were taught to value diversity and egalitarianism, to indoctrination through films and advertising that they were exposed to. There seems to be a corrupt past life which they tirelessly try to move away from. As Ahmed (2014: 104) points out, shame involves a 'different orientation from disgust towards the subject and others' where the subject may be 'filled up' with something bad, but this 'badness gets expelled and sticks to the body of others'.

The figure of the Zionist Jew who seems to be pulling the strings behind every problem they as individuals, and Britain as a whole, seem to face, is a theme that is in almost every single one of our conversations. Seen to be plotting against the white race on two fronts: a) the mental (film, music, entertainment, media) and b) the biological (pharmaceutical drugs, fluoride in tap water, hormones in meat products, fast food), Jews are seen to be attempting to emasculate the white male by reducing his sperm count and testosterone levels, and ideologically 'subverting' him into emasculation. Racial mixing (specifically white women having relations with non-white men), the perceived loosening of national borders and ecological pollution are said to be a consequence of this emasculation; a giving up of territory to the foreign entities.

Indeed, there is a long history of 'whiteness' being conceived in part as a sort of physical hygiene, representing 'the lack of a mark of pollution' (Berthold, 2010: 2). I initially interpreted such beliefs as also relating to the 'whiteness as innocence' discourse, where whiteness is seen as not being able to 'do wrong', due to being inherently on the moral and ethical high ground, while also a guiding 'light' to other peoples and nations (Jonsson, 2021; Wekker, 2016). Hence when one lives in an apparently corrupt state, any personal failures can always be put down to an external 'Other' – as is elaborated in Sartre's anti-Semite and Jew, where he writes that 'the existence of the Jew merely permits the anti-Semite to stifle his anxieties at their inception by persuading himself that his place in the world has been marked out in advance, that it awaits him, and that tradition gives him the right to occupy it' (1948: 38).

However, Thomas assures me that 'Jews can't help but do what they do because they're genetically primed to do it – it's a survival strategy'. 'So, is everything everyone does a survival strategy?' I ask. 'More or less', he shrugs. 'I don't blame Blacks or Muslims for wanting to live in the greatest civilization humanity's ever come up with. Who would blame them? The blame is with us. White men who allowed this to happen by going back on our ancestral responsibilities.'

The only actor who has been endowed with intellect and rational thought is the white man, who makes it his responsibility: 'The blame is with us.' Those not part of this in-group of white men – Jews, Black people, Muslims – are reduced to beings without agency, a type of Othering which, when taken to the extreme, is the backbone to genocides and death camps (Dehzani, 2008).

What strikes me is how similar this is to the rhetoric espoused by far-right terrorist Brenton Tarrant, who in 2019 took the lives of 51 Muslims when attacking a mosque in Christchurch, New Zealand (see chapter 1 by Thomas in this volume). In his Great Replacement manifesto he writes that

> the people who are to blame most are ourselves, European men. Strong men do not get ethnically replaced, strong men do not allow their culture to degrade, strong men do not allow their people to die. Weak men have created this situation and strong men are needed to fix it.

Contrary to my expectations, David and Thomas's response to the attack was wholly negative: 'What do these retarded acts of nihilism accomplish?' Thomas says in anger:

> It's hard to do what we do. It's hard to change your diet. To be militant about your spirit while living in this shit hole. You know what's easy? To just say 'fuck it' and blow some shit up or even worse, to kill yourself. So no, I don't ascribe to any of that lone wolf nonsense, it just rakes in more money for Jewish agendas, same old story.

The feeling seems to be mutual among my interlocutors, along with the idea that their own 'consciousness raising' has an impact on the land and its people. It is within this discourse that two distinctions arise that highlight the stark difference between left-wing eco-activism, and the variant of eco-fascism espoused by my interlocutors. The first pertains to the fascist hermeneutics surrounding the term 'consciousness raising'. While it is often associated on the left with figures such as Lukács, pertaining to a practice of collective awareness of the inequalities under which people live (Lukács & Livingston, 1971), the interlocutors in this chapter take a non-materialist approach to the matter. The agent of the struggle shifts from proletariat under capitalist rule, its systems of exploitation which seek profit in spite of its ecological ramifications, to white men under the rule of the Jewish elite whose systems of subversion and plotting have caused an imbalance in the 'natural' ecosystem: environmentally, racially and against their bodies. This also shifts the terrain on which struggle against 'Jews' is conducted – that is, not the economy – where Jews are the capitalists – but now the terrain of culture and the inner landscape – the body, the self, where Jews are now perceived as targeting. The second difference exemplified is the concept of 'struggle'. They thus saw it as their responsibility as white men to purge themselves from this decadence through highly specific routines in physical exercises, rituals which I am told are variants of sun worship, and an inner expulsion of any sort of 'Jewish media'.

The combination of these two distinctions (the first being the term 'consciousness raising' and the second being the concept of struggle) leads to the most significant difference – namely, that their view on climate change is rooted in mysticism. As Zimmerman (1990: 213) argues, 'National Socialists promoted a perverted "religion of nature"', as opposed to ecologists, who gave a more nuanced, demystified and rational perspective on the matter (Garrard, 2010: 261). This reflects clearly on Peter Staudenmaier's (2011) essay *Fascist Ecology*, where he points to the refusal of Nazi ideology to locate the sources of environmental destruction in social structures, instead laying the blame on Jews through conspiracies. The struggle against climate change is thus not purely on a material basis, but reflects a mysticism associated with blood and soil ideologies (Klemperer, 2013), which is then embodied in the struggle to maintain their bodies and the environment in the face of decadence. This view reflects Smith's (2009: 50) suggestion that for nationalists, people and their homeland become increasingly 'symbiotic' in 'ethno-scapes' where environmental destruction is a symptom of alienation from the homeland and the community's culture.

Both the nation and the body are seen as having been corrupted which simultaneously require redemption and purification. This respect for one's body is seen to go hand in hand with respect and adoration for the environment, relating to what David calls a bad 'habit' when he threw his cigarette butt on the grounds of Hampstead Heath. A strict vegan diet, avoidance of any form of vehicle transport (for which I was gravely admonished), and the growth of fruit and vegetables in their respective households was a cornerstone of their practices. The importance of physical exercise, and the cultivation of a 'sports-friendly image' which contrasts 'powerful bodies' with 'physical degeneration' in the service of an ideal of 'racial quality' has been well documented in fascist thought (Mangan, 2000; Reichel, 1999; Schmitz & Kazyak, 2016).

I previously alluded to Griffin's (1995: 26) argument that fascism is a genus of political ideology whose mythic core orbits the rejuvenation of the nation following a period of perceived decline. Mann (2004: 12), in his critique of Griffin's idealism, argues that 'surely, fascists must have *offered* something more useful than the mythical rebirth of the nation' (my emphasis). In the framework of Mann's argument, 'usefulness' is translated as 'power organizations', 'economic programs' and 'political strategies' (2004: 12). I wish to point out that what seems to be 'offered' in this state of 'knowing' or being 'red pilled' is what marks a fundamental break for my interlocutors. Both David and Thomas assure me that they feel fitter, happier and 'more at one with nature' since 'taking on this responsibility'.

Such modes of being and acting are seen to be dictated by nature itself. In line with Thomas's quote at the start of this chapter, the term 'necromancy' entails not the raising of the 'dead', but a dormant consciousness or potential of a mystical harmony and order. Ecological disasters, while caused by material factors, are here believed to be primarily manifestations of this 'meddling' with this mystical 'harmony'. A harmony which relates to ethno-pluralism – where the preservation of mutually respecting (but separate) bordered regions based on ethnicity is seen to be the most 'correct' way to exist (Spektorowski, 2003).

More important, however, is Thomas's assertion that these are not 'his' truths since traditionalism is the way in which nature 'teaches' humans how to be. This is highlighted in Thomas's elaboration on 'being what nature chooses' along with his belief that white men are the only ones with agency. Ecological collapse is seen to be in my participants' hands. The correct way to *be* is not determined by them, it is an outside imposition. This signifies how their ideas on climate change activism are simultaneously situated in neoliberal discourses of individual responsibility (Featherstone, 2013). Furthermore, the view of nature being able to 'teach' echoes a view of nature posited by Ernst Haeckel, who 'contributed to that special variety of German thought which served as the seed bed for National Socialism' as he argued that there are laws put forth by nature for civilizations to thrive (Gasman, 1971: xvii–34).

Other than the evident Social Darwinism in their thought, ideas surrounding necromancy, consciousness raising and mysticism emanate, at least partly, from figures such as Julius Evola, a twentieth-century occultist who advocated for a form of radical traditionalism, while necessitating male domination over women, strict gender roles, elitism and rigid hierarchical structures (Furlong, 2011: 163–164).[3] Through following Evola's guidelines, my interlocutors reclaim their bodies from corruption through techniques such as abstention from any form of sexual pleasure. Thomas later shows me a passage from Evola's book *Introduction to Magic*, where Evola posits that sexual desire 'paralyses' and weakens, 'especially in people with nervous temperaments', going on to advise that 'the fluidic body is energised by a vegetarian diet, fasting, and even magical aromas' (Evola, 1927: 73).

In this section of the chapter, I have attempted to elaborate on how my interlocutors conceive of their decadent pasts and how the 'health' of the nation is juxtaposed with their own conceptions of their 'improved' health, embodying Griffin's notion of a rebirth and rejuvenation in thought – and surely how by focusing on their own improved health they are also improving the health of the nation – they are becoming the strong men that the nation needs in order to rescue it from degeneracy; the enactment of their symbolic necromancy. Before moving on to the next section, I wish to briefly point to David's conception of shame. Specifically, the two sources of shame that he alluded to: 1) the liberal system which he believes is trying to shame him for being a white male, and 2) the shame he feels about his own 'disgusting' past. In reference to the former, this shame is rejected on the basis that it is essentially an attack on his identity from an enemy which aims to strip white men of certain rights to the benefit of (weaker) women and minority groups in general. This is widely noted as being a key rhetorical technique in the far right's pattern of targeting young white men for radicalization – that they are the real victims – and that by joining them, there is a potential for reclaiming those very privileges that have been taken away from them (Davey & Ebner, 2017; Gartenstein-Ross & Grossman, 2009; Kimmel, 2003, 2017; Kimmel & Ferber, 2000). As Marks (2020: 109) puts it: 'fascism aligns with misogyny of necessity, as the armourisation of the male self'.

According to David, the latter form of shame, namely the one in reference to his past life, was not believed to be 'the worst bit'. It was not his actions, but rather the lack of 'shame' that he had towards those actions. In this case, shame is deemed to have a positive influence, as it is an outcome of the 'awakening' which led him to a better life. Shame becomes 'crucial to the process of reconciliation or the healing of past wounds' where 'one's body seems to burn up with the negation that is negation that is perceived' (Ahmed, 2014: 101–103). The next section will elaborate on my observations of how this shame is not only always present but harshens with every transgression of the patriarchal norms which have been set as an ideal.

Eternal fall

He starts to set up his speakers while I look at his bookshelf. Expecting to find texts from prominent fascist writers like Evola, Faye and Dugin, I instead find a list of what can only be described as self-help books: *The Power of Now*; *The 7 Habits of Highly Effective People*; *Thinking, Fast and Slow*; *Rich Dad Poor Dad*. While there was only one row of books, my skim of the titles didn't find anything that could merit the explicit label 'nationalist literature'. When finished setting up, he shows me a very old book containing black and white pictures of muscular men flexing in a variety of positions. Each chapter illustrated the ways in which a particular exercise should be executed correctly to achieve the optimal body. Jay is 21, incredibly hyperactive, and has come to London from Coventry to study history at university.

Initially, I found him to be the most difficult person of the three to speak to. Mainly because he was incredibly suspicious of my presence and not the least shy in voicing his mistrust and dislike. The feeling was very much mutual. I found him incredibly irritating as he had a remarkable talent of speaking incessantly with a combination of arrogance and pessimism. After a few months of interaction, and the realization of a mutual love for the band Death Grips, tensions gradually subsided, and he became one of my most vital interlocutors. While the group was vocal on virtually every aspect of society they felt had a defect, it was Jay who first opened up to me about his feelings towards his own. While slim in stature, he would speak endlessly about the importance of a muscular physique. 'I don't care who you are, if you've got a body like a tank then nobody can say anything to you', he would tell me while showing me his arms and pointing out every flaw he could find: 'look at this shit, man ... I look like a fucking swami!'

From their first interviews which were rampant with passionate rhetoric about country and the preservation of the white race, the intensive training routines they had set up and the vitality that they assured me their ideology had brought them, all this, I later found, was glued together with patterns of deep nihilism, anger, self-defeatism – and shame. An obsessive concern with specific body parts like the forearms and neck was consistently contrasted to an ideal of masculinity – referred to in the ideal as being 'alpha'.

Thomas, who is of similar physique to Jay, informed me of the research he'd done into testosterone injections. 'It's different from steroids', he told me: 'it's like the supplements we take to supply with whatever we're missing from a vegan diet, but just a lot more expensive.' To afford the treatment, he'd been working double shifts at his job as a security officer at an entertainment centre. The decision was applauded by both Jay and David, who also have similar intentions of acquiring the treatment, but don't have a stable income, and are therefore unable to save up for it. While desires to be more muscular are generally common among young men (Pope et al., 2005), Thomas, while dealing with the experience of being diagnosed with anxiety in his assessment by mental health workers, alluded to being diagnosed with body dysmorphia too. While I did not press on this point when it was brought up, I questioned him regarding the diagnosis during a meet-up at a bar after he seemed frustrated about the lack of progress on his physique. 'Look, there's nothing wrong with me', he tells me. 'They probably say that shit to anyone who's not in line with their Jew science', he asserts after shrugging off my questions and showing a mounting irritation. Jay chipped in with his take on psychotherapy being an inherently Jewish practice, and that 'they'll do anything to stop white dudes from improving'. The subject then changes to how therapy as a whole is part of an elaborate Jewish scheme. While one would think that notions of self-improvement linked with psychotherapy would be resonant to the overall mission of the participants, the discipline or any kind of therapeutic practice in line with an institution was itself was seen as highly suspicious, aligning with anti-Semitic notions of a 'Jewish science' as 'corrupting' and 'directed at poisoning the health of the Aryan nations' (Frosh, 2015: 9).

While a combination of cold cynicism and passionate idealism was embedded in most of their conversations, they were compassionate and empathetic towards each other's failures. Stories of bingeing on fast food, drug relapses, skipping exercises and rituals, waking up late became more and more common as the months went by. The reaction to these stories was one of encouragement and motivation to do better next time. However, the goal was very much fixed – the past of the nation needed to be resurrected just as they believed their own greatness and sense of masculinity needed to be too. They were stuck in a cyclical pattern where mental health issues formed bonds of intimacy and friendship, with an ideology that exasperated and encouraged the worst of the symptoms resulting in hyper vigilance towards their minds and bodies, with little room for questioning of the ideal.

The term 'body fascism' normally refers to someone with extreme views about how somebody should look.[4] Kimmel (2014) writes that while many think the word 'fascism' is a bit extreme, he points to the vital similarity in the way in which fascism views political violence and war as a means to achieve national rejuvenation towards an ideal, and violence towards our own bodies in the way that we assert that stronger, healthier-looking bodies have the right to displace (and replace) weaker, less perfect-looking bodies. This ideal has its historic legacy within fascist thought. Mirzoeff (1995: 277) highlights the profound relevance to the body as political icon, the image of a cosmic human body – 'image of the vast contained in a little'. Through masculinist stereotypes, fascism works not only with abstract symbols of strength and resilience, but with living human symbols as well (Mosse, 1996: 247). The true fascist man must

> through his looks, body, and comportment, project the ideal of male beauty … men of flesh and blood were given a symbolic dimension, a fact which added to the fascist appeal. Here was an aesthetic which was not confined to the public realm, but one which penetrated daily life. (Mirzoeff (1975: 277)

As Klemperer (2013: 15) explains: 'Nazism permeated the flesh and blood of the people through single words, idioms and sentence structures which were imposed on them in a million repetitions and taken on board mechanically and unconsciously'. At the heart of these efforts to establish ideals of masculinity through increasingly sophisticated measurement schemes was the pervasive anxiety at the turn of the 20th century to link problems in society with the weaknesses of individuals – and in turn to identify the weaknesses of individuals with their somatic makeup (Vertinsky, 2002: 144).

Equally important, however, is how this aesthetic sharpened and refined the image in contrast to a 'decadent Other'. While in Nazi Germany, images of Jewish physiology were made to contrast a pure Aryan race, today this same contrast can be found in the far right's rejection of body acceptance movements, which they deem to be a result of the propagation of cultural Marxist thought. Here it is important to note that, for my interlocutors, their own superiority was not a given. Just because they were able-bodied white men did not automatically render them to be in line with their own ideal, only the potential. Equally as important to note is the paradoxical notion of how the ideal past was always present. Thus, the temporality of a great past and the 'potential' for a great future was always in their hands, and by purifying their body they realize not only their own potential, but that of a nation free from ecological disasters. As obvious as it may seem, I think it is vital to note that the golden past that is imagined does not have the industrial, technological or material factors which could have ever brought about such ecological disasters. Thus, in a sense, the potential is always already an impossibility. Due to their perception of the nation and their bodies' temporalities, any perceived issue is instantly put down to their own individual failings. The more I got to know my interlocutors, the more this unreached potential and ideal seemed to be a source of torment.

Conclusion

In this chapter I have outlined the importance in recognizing the body's significance in the study of eco-fascism and to understanding the far right in general. Specifically, how far-right rhetoric surrounding the idea of 'control' has the potential to produce idealizations of a reasserted sense of masculinity and the rejuvenation of British ecology. Practices which aim at 'necromancy' attempt to reassert the values of a pure past when order, hierarchy and strict gender relations resulted in a supposed harmonious society. Attempts at this rejuvenation are, however, laced with failure and consequently result in feelings of shame and self-negation. Indeed, while progressive movements, arts and sciences have attempted to exorcise the present from oppressive and corrupting spectres of the past, the interlocutors in this chapter seek to conjure these spectres to the fore of British life in order to purify it; a form of necromancy. While vegan diets and environmentalism are often associated with leftist politics, such cases remind us of the importance of not essentializing lifestyles with ideological outlooks and not to make assumptions about inevitable causal and ideological links. It is a necessary reminder that environmentalism can conjure white supremacist feelings of a connection to 'roots' and racist understanding of ancestry too.

During my time with Thomas, David and Jay, while they would espouse the most extreme rhetoric, I could see that they were very much suffering with serious mental health issues which were exacerbated by the ideas they strongly upheld. The increase of ecological disasters was consistently aligned with their own worsening state of being. This chapter thus wishes to contribute to the further understanding of eco-fascism, not purely through the rhetoric used and the consistency within its ideological outlook, but also the symptoms of mental health issues evident within its praxis and the consequences of eco-fascistic outlook, specifically concerning the body.

Notes

1 www.dictionary.com/browse/necromancy, *Dictionary.com* (accessed 10 November 2023).
2 Julius Evola was an Italian 'traditionalist' philosopher who has been cited as a leading figure in fascist circles advocating for male domination over women as part of a purely patriarchal society where women stay in complete subordination to male authority.
3 Incidentally, he was also the philosopher cited by Donald Trump's chief strategist Steve Bannon during his speech at the Vatican (Horowitz, 2017).
4 www.oxfordlearnersdictionaries.com/definition/english/body-fascism?q=body+fascism (accessed 28 November 2023).

References

Ahmed, S. (2014). *The Cultural Politics of Emotion*. Edinburgh: Edinburgh University Press.
Anshelm, J., & Hultman, M. (2014). A Green Fatwā? Climate Change as a Threat to the Masculinity of Industrial Modernity. *NORMA*, 9(2): 84–96.
Berthold, D. (2010). Tidy Whiteness: A Genealogy of Race, Purity, and Hygiene. *Ethics and the Environment*, 15(1): 1–26.
Bloodheart, B., & Swim, J. (2010). Equality, Harmony, and the Environment: An Ecofeminist Approach to Understanding the Role of Cultural Values on the Treatment of Women and Nature. *Ecopsychology*, 2: 187–194.
Cobain, I. (2016). The slow-burning hatred that led Thomas Mair to murder Jo Cox. *The Guardian*, 23 November, www.theguardian.com/uk-news/2016/nov/23/thomas-mair-slow-burning-hatred-led-to-jo-cox-murder (accessed 23 November 2023).
Cocks, G. (2007). Sick Heil: Self and Illness in Nazi Germany. *Osiris*, 22(1): 93–115.
Connell, R. W. (1995). *Masculinities*. Berkeley: University of California Press.
Coupland, S. R. (2016). *The Cripps Mission*. London: Normanby Press.
Davey, J., & Ebner, J. (2017). *The Fringe Insurgency: Connectivity, Convergence, and Mainstreaming of the Extreme Right*. London: ISD.
Dehzani, J. (2008). *Nihilism and Technologies of Othering: The Kurds in Iran, Iraq and Turkey*. Ottawa: Carleton University.

Dietz, B. (2008). Countryside-versus-City in European Thought: German and British Anti-Urbanism between the Wars. *European Legacy*, 13(7): 801–814.

Evola, J. (1927). *Introduction to Magic: Rituals and Practical Techniques for the Magus*. Rochester: Inner Traditions.

Featherstone, D. (2013). The Contested Politics of Climate Change and the Crisis of Neo-liberalism. *ACME: An International Journal for Critical Geographies*, 12(1): 44–64.

Forchtner, B. (2019). Nation, Nature, Purity: Extreme-Right Biodiversity in Germany. *Patterns of Prejudice*, 53(3): 285–301.

Frosh, S. (2015). *Hate and the 'Jewish Science': Anti-Semitism, Nazism and Psychoanalysis*. London: Palgrave Macmillan UK.

Furlong, P. (2011). Riding the Tiger: Crisis and Political Strategy in the Thought of Julius Evola. *The Italianist*, 31(1): 25–40.

Garrard, G. (2010). Heidegger Nazism Ecocriticism. *Interdisciplinary Studies in Literature and Environment*, 17(2): 251–271.

Gartenstein-Ross, D., & Grossman, L. (2009). *Homegrown Terrorists in the US and UK: An Empirical Examination of the Radicalization Process*. Washington, D. C.: FDD Center for Terrorism Research.

Gasman, D. (1971). *The Scientific Origins of National Socialism: Social Darwinism in Ernst Haeckel and the German Monist League*. London: Macdonald & Co.; New York: American Elsevier.

Gelfer, J. (2013). Meat and Masculinity in Men's Ministries. *Journal of Men's Studies*, 21(1): 78–91.

Green, S., Gregory, C., Reeves, M., et al. (2016). Brexit Referendum: First Reactions from Anthropology. *Social Anthropology*, 24: 478–502.

Griffin, R. (1995). *Fascism*. Oxford: Oxford University Press.

Heineman, E. (1999). Nazi Family Policy 1933–1945. By Lisa Pine. Oxford and New York: Berg Publishers. [Book Review]. *Central European History*, 32(4): 503–504.

Hermansson, P., Lawrence, D., Mulhall, J., & Murdoch, S. (2020). *The International Alt-Right: Fascism for the 21st Century?* 1st ed. Abingdon: Routledge.

Horowitz, J. (2017). Steve Bannon cited Italian thinker who inspired fascists. *New York Times*, 10 February, www.nytimes.com/2017/02/10/world/europe/bannon-vatican-julius-evola-fascism.html (accessed 23 November 2023).

Jonsson, T. (2021). *Innocent Subjects: Feminism and Whiteness*. London: Pluto Press.

Kao, W. C. (2020). Identitarian Politics, Precarious Sovereignty. *Postmedieval*, 11, 371–383.

Kimmel, M. (2003). Globalization and its Mal(e)contents: The Gendered Moral and Political Economy of Terrorism. *International Sociology*, 18(3): 603–620.

Kimmel, M. (2014). *Life Beyond Therapy: The Rise of Body Fascism*. New York: EGN.

Kimmel, M. (2017). White Men as Victims: The Men's Rights Movement. In *Angry White Men: American Masculinity at the End of an Era*. New York: Nation Books, pp. 99– 134.

Kimmel, M., & Ferber, A. L. (2000). White Men Are This Nation: Right-Wing Militias and the Restoration of Rural American Masculinity. *Rural Sociology*, 65(4): 582–604.

Klemperer, V. (2013). *The Language of the Third Reich: LTI – Lingua Tertii Imperii: A Philologist's Notebook*. London: Bloomsbury Academic.

Koonz, C. (2003). *The Nazi Conscience*. Cambridge: Harvard University Press.

Lubarda, B. (2020). Beyond Ecofascism? Far-Right Ecologism (FRE) as a Framework for Future Inquiries. *Environmental Values*, 29(6): 713–732.

Lukács, G., & Livingstone, R. (1971). *History and Class Consciousness: Studies in Marxist Dialectics*. Cambridge: MIT Press.

Mangan, J. A. (2000). *Superman Supreme: Fascist Body as Political Icon: Global Fascism*. London: Frank Cass.

Mann, M. (2004). *Fascists*. Cambridge: Cambridge University Press.

Marks, L. U. (2020). *Which Came First, Fascism or Misogyny? Reading Klaus Theweleit's Male Fantasies*. London: Pluto Press.

Mirzoeff, N. (1995). *Bodyscape – Art, Modernity and the Ideal Figure*. London and New York: Routledge.

Mosse, G. L. (1996). *The Image of Man: The Creation of Modern Masculinity*. New York: Oxford University Press.

Mosse, G. (1999). *The Fascist Revolution*. New York: Howard Fertig.

Nagle, A. (2017). *Kill All Normies: Online Culture Wars from 4chan and Tumblr to Trump and the Alt-Right*. Alresford: Zero Books.

Nolan, M. (2005). Germans as Victims during the Second World War: Air Wars, Memory Wars. *Central European History*, 38(1): 7–40.

Pope, C. G., Pope, H. G., Menard, W., et al. (2005). Clinical Features of Muscle Dysmorphia among Males with Body Dysmorphic Disorder. *Body Image*, 2: 395–400.

Proctor, R. N. (1997). The Nazi War on Tobacco: Ideology, Evidence, and Possible Cancer Consequences. *Bulletin of the History of Medicine*, 71: 435–488.

Rabinbach, A. (1977). Unclaimed Heritage: Ernst Bloch's Heritage of Our Times and the Theory of Fascism. *New German Critique*, 11: 5–21.

Rambaran-Olm, M., Breann Leake, M., & Goodrich, M. J. (2020). Medieval Studies: The Stakes of the Field. *Postmedieval*, 11: 356–370.

Reichel, P. (1999). Festival and Cult: Masculine and Militaristic Mechanisms of National Socialism. *International Journal of the History of Sport*, 16(2): 153–168.

Sartre, J.-P. (1948). *Anti-Semite and Jew*. Paris: Schocken Books.

Schmitz, R. M., & Kazyak, E. (2016). Masculinities in Cyberspace: An Analysis of Portrayals of Manhood in Men's Rights Activist Websites. *Social Sciences*, 5(2): 18–22.

Sinke, S. (1989). Mothers in the Fatherland: Women, the Family and Nazi Politics. *Oral History Review*, 17(1): 177–178.

Smith, A. (2009). *Ethno-symbolism and Nationalism*. Abingdon: Routledge.

Spektorowski, A. (2003). The New Right: Ethno-regionalism, Ethnopluralism and the Emergence of a Neo-fascist 'Third Way'. *Journal of Political Ideologies*, 8(1): 111–130.

Staudenmaier, P. (2011). *Ecofascism Revisited: Lessons from the German Experience*, 2nd ed. Porsgrunn: New Compass Press.

Turner-Graham, E. (2019). 'Protecting Our Green and Pleasant Land': UKIP, the BNP and a History of Green Ideology on Britain's Far Right. In B. Forchtner (ed.), *The Far Right and the Environment*. London: Routledge, pp. 57–71.

Vertinsky, P. (2002). Embodying Normalcy: Anthropometry and the Long Arm of William H. Sheldon's Somatotyping Project. *Journal of Sport History*, 29(1): 95–133.

Wekker, G. (2016). *White Innocence: Paradoxes of Colonialism and Race*. Durham and London: Duke University Press.

Zimmerman, M. (1990). *Heidegger's Confrontation with Modernity*. Indianapolis: Indiana University Press.

11

Climate science vs denial machines: how AI could manufacture scientific authority for far-right disinformation

David Eliot and Rod Bantjes

We originally wrote this text for the Political Economies of the Far Right Conference in 2019. At the time, the most advanced publicly known text generating AI was GPT-2. Our social theories were originally developed in reference to our technical understanding of GPT-2. After being selected for this publication, OpenAI announced and demoed GPT-3. In response we updated the technical exploration to include the initial advancements made in the technology. As is highlighted in the text, at the time of initial authorship GPT-3 was not publicly available; however, in early 2023 OpenAI launched Chat-GPT, a web application that provided public access to GPT-3 (OpenAI, 2023). In March of 2023 OpenAI released GPT-4, and provided public access to the system via Chat-GPT (Weitzman, 2023). Unfortunately, due to publication time constraints and concerns regarding appropriate rigour, we were unable to update our technical analysis and explore the repercussions of these recent developments. However, we believe that recent advances demonstrate the viability of the predictive technical claims made in this text. In March 2023 *The Guardian* reported that peer reviewers for an education journal unknowingly approved the publication of a paper written completely by Chat-GPT, providing concrete support for our claims that the peer-review system will soon be under threat from the machines (Fazackerley, 2023).

Introduction

Dunlap and McCright (2012) have used the metaphor of a machine – the 'denial machine' – to characterize the institutional complex that produces and distributes artificial, knowingly fictional counterclaims against the incontrovertible evidence of catastrophic risk from climate change. 'Machine' is a good metaphor for an institutional system that follows a determinate logic (i.e. the logic of profit for fossil capital). In this chapter we analyse the increasing automation of this machine – a theme that has so far been overlooked in the literature. We extrapolate from automation processes already underway to argue that near-future developments will involve artificial intelligence (AI) able to write persuasive denialist arguments at unprecedented speed and volume. Our argument relies in part on an analysis of new technological affordances that are not well understood outside the tech community – for example, OpenAI's GPT3. However, we place our discussion of AI, climate denial and its uptake by the far right within the context of structural and historical trends that have developed since the start of the neoliberal revolution in the 1970s.

The denial machine and the Intergovernmental Panel on Climate Change (IPCC) are institutional mediations of our knowledge of the climate and its historical dynamics. When denialists believe that they are challenging climate science based on 'their own research' they are rather trusting the denial machine, accessed through the mediation of the internet, right-wing talk radio and the like. Theirs is not, as many have represented it, a problem of distrust in institutions, it is a problem of trusting the wrong institutions. Oreskes and Conway (2010: 154, 269) argue that one of the best reasons for non-scientists to trust the knowledge produced by the IPCC is that it is extensively vetted through peer review. Peer review, a feature of institutional design, is our best available guarantee of the empirical and theoretical adequacy of knowledge (our closest approximation of 'truth'). Not surprisingly, attempts to undermine the authority of peer review have already been part of the denialist project (Dunlap & McCright, 2012: 5). Our aim in this chapter is to assess near-future risk, much in the same way that the IPCC does. The risk that we focus on, both for its probability and for the seriousness of its implications, is that text-generating AI will soon develop to the point where it could deceive peer reviewers and thereby breach the barrier of peer review. The result would be an epistemological crisis in which all institutionally mediated knowledge could genuinely be placed in doubt.

Until now, the institutions of climate change denial – corporate funders, think-tanks, front groups, ersatz experts, lobbyists – have attempted to manipulate what we call 'downstream mediation' – formal and informal news media, internet chat and policy discussion. AI-generated peer-reviewed denial would distort upstream mediation – where reliable scientific knowledge is produced and can currently be accessed to discount downstream disinformation. Hard denial – that the climate is not changing or that that change is not caused by human institutions – still circulates with impunity downstream in what Benkler (2021: 44) calls the right-wing media ecology 'anchored by Fox News and Breitbart'. We expect that upstream denial would attack softer targets – minimizing the severity of climate change risks and supporting overblown claims for technological solutions, what McLaren and Markusson (2020) call 'technological prevarication'.

The neoliberal project and ideological misdirection

Dunlap and McCright (2012), along with Oreskes and Conway (2010), have made clear the neoliberal logic of denial. Neoliberal market solutions cannot solve the climate crisis (Klein, 2014). To acknowledge climate change was to invite regulatory solutions to it – a prospect that the neoliberal faithful were unwilling to face. The radical anti-state position of neoliberal theorists like Hayek had an epistemological basis. According to Hayek (1945), individual minds are incapable of encompassing system complexities at the scale of a society (and, presumably, of interrelated global climate systems). All collective planning efforts – their main target here was socialist planned economies – are therefore doomed to failure. Individuals know only how to pursue local self-interest and must allow market systems to 'automatically' calculate and coordinate system-level complexities. They were advocating total subordination to the most abstract, disembedded, global institution of modernity – the market – and to do so in a way that was sure to benefit elite interests. (Note also the theme of automation here – to link any human endeavour to market logic is to place it under a supposedly automatic control system.)

This was a radical, fringe idea with few adherents when it was floated in the 1940s, a period when popular mobilization was firmly behind the expansion of the welfare state. Neoliberalism shifted from a set of ideas to a societal project when it was taken up by what David Harvey (2005) characterizes as a social movement of the corporate elite in the United States. The aim of the neoliberal movement was always primarily structural – to change laws and policies in ways that would expand market dominance (privatization, global free trade, etc.) and also to change the structure of civil society in order to create publics willing to accede to deeply unpopular policies. The assault, beginning in the 1970s, was directed against the new social movements (notably, for our purposes, the environmental movement) and the labour unions, but also, importantly and frequently overlooked, the farm unions and the protections from market forces that had created security for the rural petty bourgeoisie. The latter was to become a core constituency for the 'New Right' that has morphed into the twenty-first-century far right.

The rise of right-wing populism and the authoritarian far right is one of the fruits, perhaps an unintended consequence, of neoliberal efforts to engineer civil society (hardly a precise science). What was intentional was the fusion of incompatible ideologies and interests – neoliberal libertarianism with religious, patriarchal and racial authoritarianism – evident in the American 'New Right' as early as the 1980s (Himmelstein, 1983). Fusing – Ernesto Laclau (1977) would say 'articulating' – ideas that serve the interests of the corporate elite to worldviews of the working class and petty bourgeoisie creates ideological monsters and a good deal of ideological misdirection. Populist rage against the abstract projects of 'globalist' elites (e.g. the UN Framework Convention on Climate Change (UNFCCC)) is paradoxically fused to the uncritical support of the abstract projects of 'globalist' elites (neoliberal market dominance). Populist rage against false 'experts' creating fake climate science for financial gain (purportedly the IPCC) is paradoxically fused to the uncritical support of false 'experts' creating fake climate science for financial gain (the denial machine).

The denial machine is one element of a larger neoliberal project. Understanding how the two work in tandem, originating in the United States but increasingly exported worldwide (Kaiser, 2020), is key to understanding the ideological perplexities of the far right. The European far right, for instance, raises the alarm about putative global threats to the local – such as global migration and immigration, global free trade and global spread of invasive species. Despite an environmentalism that links the preservation of ethno-nationalist identities to the preservation of local nature, they are wilfully and perversely blind to the global climate threats to all local nature (Forchtner, 2020: 7). This contradiction is a product of Laclauian articulation. It is no surprise that in Sweden, for example, far-right climate denial was mobilized 'from above' by a think-tank, the Stockholm Initiative, that closely followed a climate-denialist playbook developed and tested in the US (Hultman et al., 2020: 122–123).

Mediated knowledge, trust and risk

Ulrich Beck's seminal analysis of the politics of risk perception in 'risk society' hinges on an epistemological conundrum. He laments that amid the claims and counterclaims about the safety of trace chemicals in drinking water, radiation from nuclear accidents or genetically modified foods, citizens can no longer rely on direct, sensory evidence to assess the truth – they no longer have 'cognitive sovereignty' (1992: 27, 53–54). To sense nuclear radiation, they must rely on technological mediation – a Geiger counter. To make sense of their exposure to that radiation they must further rely on scientific experts who have built the device and can interpret its readings and assess associated health risks in relation to long-term epidemiological studies. Beck, like many on the left at the time, was acutely aware of the role that scientific experts, institutionally bound to corporate and state interests, played in minimizing many of the risks of the risk society. How could environmental activists critique scientific perceptions of risk when they were equally dependent on the 'sensory organs of science' to detect risk (Beck, 1992: 27)?

Individuals have perhaps never had privileged, unmediated access to the truth, whether by sense perception or Cartesian pure reason (Bantjes, 2019). However, this personally empowering idea has been a core myth of liberal democracies. Epistemological individualism still makes it difficult to see the complex institutional mediations through which we come to know our world. Beck's solution to his conundrum is not less, but more politicization of knowledge – an opening up of science to the voices of the public and organized social movements. An exemplar of this would be the anti-toxics movement of the 1980s. In the case of Love Canal, Lois Gibbs (2011) and her Love Canal Homeowners Association did 'citizen science', going door to door to collect data on the incidence of diseases such as cancer. In no instance here were the patients or the door-to-door canvassers 'observing' cases of different types of cancer. The sufferers sense pain, but identifying pancreatic cancer requires diagnostic technology, tests and interpretative expertise – an institutional complex whose rationality is validated in peer-reviewed medical literature. Similarly, to establish the causal connection between rates of illness and the witch's brew of chemicals seeping into people's basements, they contacted a scientist who was a relative of one of their members and he put them in touch with the relevant peer-reviewed literature.

They were mobilizing experts against experts. And to make sense of the contradictory claims of competing experts they learned to do a kind of lay sociology of knowledge. Gibbs was warned, for example, that test samples of urine could not be entrusted to the New York State Health Department because of its contractual relations with the polluter, Hooker Chemical, and that university labs feared appearing to be in conflict with the Department or the State (Gibbs, 2011: 112–113). What we are calling lay sociology of knowledge, Frank Fischer treats somewhat pejoratively as 'social cognition', which he characterizes in the following terms:

> Citizens want to know how and why decisions were reached, whose interests are at stake, if the process reflects a hidden agenda, who is responsible, what protection they have if something goes wrong and so on. If, for example, citizens have experiences that suggest they should be distrustful of particular government officials, such information will tend to override the data itself. (2019: 140)

Fischer seems not to understand that these are questions we all must attempt to answer, citizens and experts alike, when faced with scientific claims outside our expertise. We cannot appeal to our individual sense data (as he seems to imply with his invocation of Popperian falsification); we need to assess the reliability of the institutional complexes that produce the knowledge in question.

The Love Canal Homeowners' Association was doing relatively good sociology of knowledge, placing trust where there were institutional guarantees of science quality (peer review). Peer review is an instance of a general set of mechanisms of transparency and accountability designed to minimize corruption and incompetence in all of the 'expert systems' (Giddens, 1990) worthy of our trust. The Homeowners' Association was also doing a power analysis of the conflicts of interest that might distort science mediation – focusing in particular on the sources of experts' research funding. The climate change deniers whose 'social cognition' Fischer (2019: 148) gives ambivalent support for, are, by contrast, doing bad sociology of knowledge. They are taking at face value tendentious claims that false 'experts' are creating fake climate science for financial gain in the case of the IPCC, and wilfully ignoring strong evidence that false 'experts' are creating fake climate science for financial gain in the case of the denial machine.

The epistemological thrust of strategies to mobilize the far right has been to amplify distrust of institutional mediation. The idea is that elite 'experts' have robbed us, the people, of cognitive sovereignty and we need to take it back. Online forums and 'news' platforms that promote far-right conspiracy theories, such as OANN news, RSBN, Parler, 8Chan and Reddit, adopt a tone that implies that the reader is too smart to be deceived by the media, censored Google searches, '"official" scientific authorities' or 'globalist' experts (Work, 2019). Don't trust the groupthink 'experts': you must do your own research to find the truth about a 'hoax' such as climate change, readers are cautioned (The Rush Limbaugh Show, 2020). What is on display here is not so much the 'irrationality' that some think is definitive of the far right, but rather the delusions of liberal reason. When it is up to you, personally, to get to the bottom of the Pizzagate conspiracy, it makes sense to show up in person at the Comet Ping Pong restaurant and demand, by force if necessary, to be shown the basement where Hillary Clinton is running a child-sex-trafficking operation (Fisher et al., 2016). The purpose of this invocation of cognitive sovereignty is ideological misdirection whose aim is to make the institutional structure of the disinformation machine disappear from view.

Appeals to local knowledge resonated with rural constituencies – farmers, ranchers, woodworkers – who were the recruiting grounds both for the anti-environmental 'wise use' movement (Helvarg, 1994; Bantjes, 2007: 264–272) and the far-right militias of the 1980s and 1990s (Freilich & Pridemore, 2005). Even where the interests of these groups coincided with those of environmentalists, the right was successful in amplifying divisions based on class and epistemology (Dunk, 1994). Anti-environmentalism worked on a binary opposition between authentic/inauthentic, trustworthy/ suspect, freedom/tyranny. On the trustworthy side: hands-on practical knowledge through direct experience with nature. On the suspect side: over-educated government experts peering at data models on their computer screens (Dunk, 1994). On the one hand individual freedom, self-sufficiency and property rights; on the other government overreach and intrusive regulation. These ideological threads of locally conceived freedoms and authority were effectively articulated, at least in the US, to the deregulation interests of a (global) corporate class. We want to stress that there was nothing inevitable about this articulation. As Dunk's study of woodworkers and the literature on the environmental justice movement makes clear, there was tremendous potential to mobilize working-class and petty-bourgeois environmentalism that was explicitly anti-corporate. Indeed, it was precisely this 'threat' that fuelled the corporate counter-attack, carried out by proxy through a network of think-tanks, front groups, PR firms and the like (Bantjes, 2007: 258–275).

The myth of cognitive sovereignty dovetails with the liberal faith in 'counter-speech' and the 'marketplace of ideas' as means of challenging and correcting misinformation. Denialists have championed this supposed open democracy of ideas, setting it in contrast to peer review and scientific consensus as though these were forms of irrational 'groupthink' (Dunlap & McCright, 2012: 5). The implication is that the peer-reviewed scientist, as an individual knower, has no more authority than you or I. The true test of her beliefs is how well she stands up to reasoned debate within the free marketplace of ideas. The appeal here is again to an implicit localism, as though we all debated together in the same coffee house, or as though we were all part of the same small reading circle, a 'republic of letters', and could hear and adequately assess the arguments of every one of our Enlightenment colleagues (Habermas, 1989).

Napoli (2018) makes a strong case for the growing irrelevance of these liberal assumptions in the age of AI-driven disinformation. The first problem, according to Napoli, is that increasingly effective targeted marketing ensures that we inhabit separate ideological market spaces. Our 'filter bubbles' filter out the counter-speech that is supposed to help us challenge and critically reassess bad information. The second problem has to do with the increased volume and speed of circulation of disinformation. Lies (which rely only on invention) are easier to produce than truths (which rely on research). Automation tools such as text-generating AI and online bots can accelerate the production and distribution of lies, making it all the more easy for far-right strategists like Steve Bannon to 'flood the zone with shit' (Stengel,

2020). Regardless of how easy it might be to rebut each new piece of disinformation, the overwhelming flood will mean that there is never enough time to do so. Counter-speech in this way becomes ineffective and free-speech ideology is invoked by the far right to protect the flood of lies.

Artificial intelligence, text-generating AI and the economic forces driving it

The right has long been quick to capitalize on new technological affordances to promote the circulation of ideology and disinformation – such as computer databases to perfect direct-mail mobilization in the 1980s (Beder, 2002: 32–34), unregulated talk-radio in the 1990s (Benkler, 2021; Benkler et al., 2017) and the deployment of online 'bot armies' in the early twenty-first century (Bessi & Ferrara, 2016; Marlow et al., 2021). The publics that have been cultivated in this way are increasingly disembedded from face-to-face personal networks and are largely animated from above by those who design and sponsor the mediation. The bot army is pure automation, pure astroturfing, in which actual humans have been replaced by machines.

The recent dramatic shift towards digital mediation of personal interaction, political mobilization, state governance, and consumer and corporate activity has led to two quick-succession revolutions in capital accumulation: surveillance capitalism (Zuboff, 2018) and an as-yet-unnamed revolution based in AI (Eliot & Murakami Wood, 2021). The growing digital technosphere simultaneously mediates and records human behaviour. The tech-based companies best positioned to harvest this unimaginable new data stream – Apple, Amazon and, pre-eminently, Google – developed powerful software tools to analyse it, modelling human behaviour in detail with the aim of prediction and control. The first strategy to monetize big data analytics was to sell its capabilities to advertisers, in other words, to manipulate consumer behaviour. The next wave of capital accumulation, that the big tech firms are already jockeying to dominate (Eliot & Murakami Wood, 2021), will be to model all forms of work that can be digitally mediated with the aim of replicating it so that expensive human workers can be replaced by digital machines. The new wave of automation will rely on big data and artificial intelligence.

Despite the varied connotations that we attach to the term 'intelligence', AI experts such as Stuart Russell give the term a quite restricted meaning. An intelligent actor is an entity that 'does what is likely to achieve what it wants, given what it has perceived' (Russell, 2019: 14). This is a kind of instrumental rationality where the 'agent' does not necessarily determine its own goals, nor does it necessarily have intentionality and certainly not consciousness. Something as simple as an E-coli bacterium is 'intelligent' by this definition because it pursues a goal (consuming glucose); it 'perceives' its environment (the intestinal tract); and, importantly, it adapts its behaviour to changes in that environment – moving always towards more glucose-rich regions. There have been efforts to make intelligent machines using genetic engineering (e.g. Craig Venter's artificial bacteria) and mechanical hardware, but all of the recent advances have been with computer programs or algorithms operating in digital media.

The key innovation has been the shift from machine programming to machine learning. In the former, the rules of action are exhaustively defined by a human engineer; in the latter, the machine itself develops its own rules under controlled 'training' conditions. Training, for example, the categories of perception that enable the machine to distinguish between a dog and a cat follows a logic similar to the learning of a human child. Through exposure to dogs and cats in differing contexts, the child makes labelling attempts and is corrected. It tries out rules – large four-legged creatures versus small four-legged creatures – and abandons or modifies them as new data emerges – for example a small Pug. The AI develops complex rules quickly because of the scale of data – potentially every dog and cat image on the internet – and the speed of its exposure and processing – fractions of a second. An important feature of current AI is that the internal logic of its 'neural networks' is 'black boxed' so that we cannot reverse engineer its decision-making architecture.

Machine learning is a kind of automation of automation. But it still requires a training engineer. 'Competitive self-play' is a technique that reduces further the amount of time the software engineer needs to spend in training. In this model the AI is trained by competing with itself. An illustrative example is Google's AlphaZero chess-playing AI. Within only four hours it was able to learn not just the rules of chess, but the secrets of chess strategy sufficient to defeat the previous chess-playing AI champion, Stockfish 8, which had in turn beaten every human chess master in 2016 (Harari, 2018). The core learning algorithms of these AIs are marvels of engineering but are often relatively simple. It is the training data, amassed by a few key tech firms at incomprehensible scale, that makes them powerful.

The competition among tech giants to lead in AI is currently focused on producing the best AI personal assistant (Eliot & Murakami Wood, 2022). For this application what needs to be automated is intelligent speech recognition (to perfectly understand our commands) and speech generation (to speak to booking agents on our behalf and troubleshoot travel arrangements, for example). In the tech world this is called natural language processing (NLP). The personal assistant will work in highly abstract areas of competency – doing research for us, writing up summaries, making arrangements with clients, friends, colleagues, perhaps making arguments for us. Once designed, it can be easily replicated and offered to millions, such that its access to data, experience and training snowballs exponentially. We should point out that devices such as this will likely use the recently developed strategy of 'federated learning', where the learning algorithm drops into your local device and learns from your personal data but does not extract it from the device. The algorithm keeps the slightly fine-tuned rules (black boxed), but not the data that it used to do the fine tuning (Eliot & Murakami Wood, 2021). Federated learning was developed to allay privacy concerns and facilitate the widespread acceptance of this and similar data-gathering devices. In what follows, we will indicate how far NLP has so far gotten towards the possibility of writing peer-reviewed academic articles, but we want to emphasize that, given the logic of machine learning and the economic interests at stake in developing NLP, near-future developments are likely to accelerate.

Natural language processing advancements are already being applied to the writing of increasingly complex texts – an application that IT specialists call text-generating AI (TGAI). TGAI term papers are already being marketed to students through Essaybot. Provided only with a simple prompt (e.g. 'the risks of TGAI'), Essaybot advertises that they will completely generate your term paper – complete with citations – with a zero percent chance of being caught for plagiarism (Winkie, 2019). Readers may also be surprised to learn that a significant amount of the news they consume is now also generated by TGAIs. In fact, Bloomberg News, an industry leader in AI-assisted news reporting, in 2019 used some form of the tech on roughly a third of its articles (Peiser, 2019). Bloomberg is not alone in this practice, as TGAIs are currently used by reputable publications like the *Washington Post*, *Associated Press*, *Forbes* and *The Guardian*. The software accesses relevant information and compiles a rough draft that human writers work into finished pieces. The TGAI speeds production and cuts costs (Peiser, 2019). TGAIs currently in use still produce crude results that need significant human revision; however, new developments, such as OpenAI's GPT project, show promise for more autonomous high-quality text generation.

The GPT model that was available when we first presented our research in 2019 was GPT-2. GPT-2 was trained on a dataset of Reddit articles (Hern, 2019; Martin, 2019; Radford et al., 2019). OpenAI was already concerned about potential malicious use in areas such as 'fake news' generation. While they typically release their innovations as open-source code, they initially held back GPT-2, before eventually releasing it, first, as a watered-down demo, then in full form (Hern, 2019; Martin, 2019). Unlike previous TGAIs, GPT-2 demonstrated its ability to produce convincing text from human prompts, and had little problem replicating human syntax (Hern, 2019). GPT-2 could gauge the tone of its prompts and produce writing that matched the implied genre (e.g. dystopian fiction, newspaper, academic text) (Hern, 2019). Tests of the system revealed that a watered-down version of GPT-2 released to the public could produce articles almost as convincing as real articles by the *New York Times* 72 per cent of the time (Jack et al., 2019). To the researchers' surprise, GPT-2's machine-learning system had acquired abilities that it had not been designed for: excelling at such tasks as question answering, reading comprehension, summarization and translation (Radford et al., 2019). Building on GPT-2's reading comprehension abilities, OpenAI has now issued an even more advanced GPT-3.

GPT-3 was trained using a diverse mix of professionally curated data sets, and other text samples, including books and Wikipedia pages (Brown et al., 2020: 8). Millions of academic texts are now available online through Google's digitization efforts and in proprietary academic databases. The new GPT-3 could be trained on this data, and its academic style prompted by one (one-shot) or multiple (few-shot) tailored sample texts (Brown et al., 2020: 5). Others are now beginning to recognize the risks that we warned of in 2019 (Eliot, 2019). The text produced by GPT-3 is still not strong enough, in our opinion, to threaten academia; however, it is another step towards a TGAI with that capability. GPT-3's creators themselves are aware of the risk. Brown et al. (2020: 35) write:

> Any socially harmful activity that relies on generating text could be augmented by powerful language models. Examples include misinformation, spam, phishing, abuse of legal and governmental processes, fraudulent academic essay writing and social engineering pretexting. Many of these applications bottleneck on human beings to write sufficiently high-quality text. Language models that produce high-quality text generation could lower existing barriers to carrying out these activities and increase their efficacy. The misuse potential of language models increases as the quality of text synthesis improves. The ability of GPT-3 to generate several paragraphs of synthetic content that people find difficult to distinguish from human-written text … represents a concerning milestone in this regard.

OpenAI has sought to minimize the risk by refusing to release GPT-3's source code and instead offering GPT-3 only as an application programming interface. Those interested in using GPT-3 must apply to OpenAI, and OpenAI retains the right to cut off access if an actor is misusing the program (OpenAI, 2020). However, there is currently strong economic motivation and intense competition to produce ever-more sophisticated natural language processing AI. OpenAI's proof of concept will certainly be replicated and there is no guarantee that others will not put similar TGAIs to malicious purposes.

Why the far right is likely to lead the trend towards automated disinformation

Since the 1970s, disinformation, particularly on the scale and audacity of climate change denial, has been almost exclusively a product of the right, initiated and financed by neoliberal interests. The neoliberal project of social and environmental deregulation was bound to produce what Beck (1992) calls 'negative side-effects' – widespread economic precarity and worsening environmental degradation. From the start, that project was advanced and 'popularized' under cover of deception (McLaren & Markusson, 2020) and ideological misdirection. Neoliberal precarity had real effects on that segment of the public that has since been mobilizing under the banner of the far right. To the injury of increasing economic failure, liberal ideology added the insult of personal responsibility and blame (Peacock et al., 2014). The powerful sense of injury and abandonment that fuels far-right rage is real (Hochschild, 2016). The neoliberal right has had unmatched success in deflecting that rage away from themselves (i.e. the corporate elite) and redirecting it towards governmental and scientific elites, as well as furnishing emotionally potent identity-compensations for those that they have injured, compensations that take the form of racial and gender supremacy or (particularly in the US) religious righteousness (Benkler, 2021: 62) (see chapter 8 in this volume by Robert Horwitz).

An extensive empirical analysis has recently confirmed that systematic disinformation is primarily a right-wing phenomenon in the US (Benkler, 2021). Disinformation is produced and amplified within a right-wing media ecology that includes television news (Fox), talk radio (e.g. Rush Limbaugh) and online outlets (e.g. Breitbart, Drudge Report). Outside that echo chamber (left and liberal) disinformation is produced, but its spread is still contained by competitive criticism and fact checking between news sources. Benkler's work is a corrective to the idea that political polarization is driven by algorithms that create 'filter bubbles' across the ideological spectrum. A bubble exists, one that excludes fact checking and counter-speech, but its boundaries are maintained by competitive ideological policing among far-right news outlets and exclusive loyalty from far-right publics. Far-right outrage is now demand driven and has fanatically loyal 'consumers', but that is a somewhat perverse and misdirected demand that has been carefully cultivated over a long sweep of history.

We argue further that there is a social constructivist neoliberal tendency, an arrogance that power can simply make truth. Oreskes and Conway (2010) have shown that the corporate politics of risk, pioneered by the tobacco industry, has from the outset involved the denial of accepted science and the promotion of what firms and their PR consultants knew to be disinformation.

Exxon's own scientists were aware of the risks of climate change in the early 1980s (Franta, 2021). Firms get seduced by their own marketing culture that values the simulacrum above the thing in itself (Klein, 2000). Ideas and meanings become products like any other, and if you succeed in selling them, then they are effectively 'true'. 'Truth' is merely what works, what has effects in the world. A cavalier attitude towards the truth is also a mark of those who believe that they have the power to remake the world. 'When we act', a senior Bush official famously proclaimed in 2004, 'we create our own reality.' The power-fuelled arrogance of the neoliberal right seemed to justify contempt for facts, and for those in the 'reality-based community' who respect them (Suskind, 2004).

The corporate sector has an interest in conflating the kind of free speech that serves the public interest in a democracy and advertising or paid speech that serves private, commercial interests often at the expense of the public (Bantjes, 2019). The corporate elite command financial resources that make it possible to flood downstream media with paid speech. Acquiring the big data and software engineering needed to produce powerful AI also takes money, or else, for the emerging players in surveillance capitalism, the data resources that they are already accumulating. The paid speech model will generally favour the neoliberal ideals of elites articulated, as they have been since the 1980s, with the authoritarianism of the far right.

However, it may be that the costs of producing AI will drop sufficiently that climate science 'truth bots' and left-wing counter-speech bots might become potential tools for less powerful actors to wield in the battle over disinformation. We suggest that genuine democrats should be reluctant to take this route. The risk is that AI-versus-AI debate will function like competitive self-play, rapidly 'training up' powerful automated speech on both sides, and crowding out human speech. A democracy of robots would be difficult to distinguish from authoritarianism.

The future of peer-reviewed disinformation extrapolated from existing trends

The automation of human capacities has historically followed two steps, the first of which is to make actual human activity machine like before fully replacing the human component with machine systems (Bakardjieva, 2015). We take the private, for-profit 'contract research organization' (CRO), as analysed by Mirowski and van Horn (2005), to be a good example of the first step towards a fully automated AI 'researcher'. The CRO gives important hints as to what the final automation will look like in terms of the type of disinformation it will produce. CROs are mainly contracted to conduct drug trials, and their clients are pharmaceutical firms seeking regulatory approval. Within the CRO, research leading up to publication is subject to the division of labour in detail and deskilling of the component tasks. The model is 'efficient' in terms of speed and the lowered costs of deskilled labour. It also reduces the autonomy of these 'assembly line' researchers to pursue intellectual aims, such as free inquiry, careful replication of results or critique, that are at odds with those of their employer. The CRO's aim, Mirowski and van Horn put it quite bluntly, is to deliver 'positive' results to its pharmaceutical clients. In other words, like the Denial Machine, their purpose is to minimize evidence of risk. To that end they produce tendentious arguments, cherry pick evidence, and suppress counterevidence or lines of inquiry likely to uncover it (Mirowski and van Horn, 2005; Bantjes, 2019).

These are the techniques that we expect AI to be trained to follow in order to breach genuine peer review. They will not invent fake evidence (the 'unicorn' style of falsification) in ways that human peer reviewers should be able to catch. Steering clear of pure fantasy would give what we call the 'Sokal bot' (after the famous breach of peer review by Alan Sokal (Hilgartner, 1997)) the greatest likelihood of passing peer review. The Sokal bot will rather 'massage' evidence tendentiously but persuasively. We also think it unlikely, at this point, that AI could – even by following the 'credible doubt' strategy – produce convincing 'hard denial', that is, denial that climate change is occurring or is caused by the fossil economy. The target is more likely to be risk response and policy. McLaren and Markusson (2020) have shown that policy at the level of the UNFCCC has been steered away from effective regulatory measures by what they call 'technological prevarication'. By this they mean overstated promises of technological fixes such as carbon capture and storage that have little to no hope of being scaled up without regulatory intervention. AI publication could plausibly add peer-reviewed authority to technological prevarication.

We need to remember, however, that the power of AI will not simply be in persuasiveness, but also in the speed and volume with which it will be capable of producing disinformation. So, a possible effect could be to erode peer-review standards by overwhelming the peer-review process. Changes in for-profit academic publishing are setting the stage for a pre-emptive weakening of peer review. Peer review is time consuming and increasingly onerous for faculty who are expected to provide it for free in productivity-oriented neoliberal universities. Private, often predatory, enterprise has responded to this situation in which peer review is in short supply and the papers seeking publication are in oversupply. Most academics are now bombarded with offers of quick-turnaround peer-reviewed publication for a fee. Some of these publishers may be defraying the costs of genuine peer review. Most are in the business of turning peer-reviewed publication into paid speech. In the growing pay-to-publish world, unicorn-style AI falsification could easily 'flood the zone' of ersatz peer-reviewed publication. While academics might have the resources to distinguish genuine from fake peer review within their own specialty, non-specialists, including academics in other fields, journalists and the general public, will not.

Conclusion

In this chapter we have assessed rapidly evolving capabilities of existing text-generating AI, and extrapolated a near-future scenario where AI will be able to produce work that can pass the test of peer review. We have also documented the long-term structural trends driving a disinformation campaign (with climate change denial as its flagship achievement) on the far right. We offer a risk assessment, and the grave risk that we think merits serious attention is an epistemological one. The lodging of disinformation 'upstream' in our systems of knowledge production could result in a systemic failure to discriminate between scientific truth and the fictions that flatter the interests of power. At the very least, public discourse would be robbed of any moorings in reliable research, with fatal consequences for already weakened democratic decision making and informed public opposition.

We argue that climate change denial is the exemplar of malicious disin-formation in risk societies. It is a special case of a much broader project of the denial of the environmental and social risks that attend the kind of unregulated economic activity that neoliberalism promotes. Those who benefit from such disinformation have a long track record of promoting it and of harnessing far-right authoritarianism to mobilize broad popular support for it.

Our main intent has been to demonstrate the seriousness of the risk. However, our discussion here is not sufficient to ground policy recommenda-tions. We invite others to begin that discussion. OpenAI is aware that its software poses the kinds of risks we outline here. So far, their approach to minimizing those risks has been careful licensing of the release of the software. We expect that now that proof of concept is in place, equally powerful software is likely to be independently developed and widely distributed. So, much more far-reaching measures need to be taken.

Our analysis suggests that the AI threat is part of a larger set of institutional developments that are transforming knowledge production generally. It is to those larger developments in addition to the particular technology that we need to address our attention. Long-held liberal assumptions about cognitive sovereignty, free speech and the marketplace of ideas that direct our attention towards the individual knower need to be questioned and more attention directed towards the institutional design of our systems of knowledge production. The trend towards privatization and marketization of universities, research and academic publication needs to be rethought. A simple first step towards reform could be the regulation of for-profit peer review and increased public support of independent academic peer review.

References

Bakardjieva, M. (2015). Rationalizing Sociality: An Unfinished Script for Socialbots. *Information Society*, 31(3): 244–256.

Bantjes, R. (2007). *Social Movements in a Global Context: Canadian Perspectives*. Toronto: Canadian Scholars' Press.

Bantjes, R. (2019). The epistemic crisis of liberalism and the rise of the far right. (Conference paper) Political Ecologies of the Far Right, Lund University, Lund, Sweden, 16 November, www.academia.edu/41081072/The_Epistemic_Crisis_of_Liberalism_and_the_Rise_of_the_Far_Right (accessed 13 November 2023).

Beck, U. (1992). *Risk Society: Towards a New Modernity*. Newbury Park: Sage Publications.

Beder, S. (2002). *Global Spin: The Corporate Assault on Environmentalism*. Totnes: Chelsea Green Publishing.

Benkler, Y. (2021). A Political Economy of the Origins of Asymmetric Propaganda in American Media. In W. L. Bennett & S. Livingston (eds), *The Disinformation Age: Politics, Technology, and Disruptive Communication in the United States*. New York: Cambridge University Press.

Benkler, Y., Faris, R., Roberts, H., & Zuckerman, E. (2017). Study: Breitbart-Led Right-Wing Media Ecosystem Altered Broader Media Agenda. *Columbia Journalism Review*, 3 March, www.cjr.org/analysis/breitbart-media-trump-harvard-study.phpm (accessed 13 January 2020).

Bessi, A., & Ferrara, E. (2016). Social bots distort the 2016 US presidential election online discussion. *First Monday*, 21(11), http://firstmonday.org/ojs/index.php/fm/article/view/7090/5653 (accessed 13 November 2023).

Brown, T. B., Mann, B., Ryder, N., et al. (2020). Language Models Are Few-Shot Learners. *arXiv Preprint*, arXiv:2005.14165 (accessed 13 November 2023).

Dunk, T. (1994). Talking about Trees: Environment and Society in Forest Workers' Culture. *Canadian Review of Sociology and Anthropology*, 31(1): 14–34.

Dunlap, R. E., & McCright, A. M. (2012). Organized Climate Change Denial. In John S. Dryzek, Richard B. Norgaard & David Schlosberg (eds), *The Oxford Handbook of Climate Change and Society*. Oxford: Oxford University Press, pp. 144–160.

Eliot, D. (2019). Climate science vs. the machines: how the radical right can use AI tech to undermine climate science. (Conference paper) Political Ecologies of the Far Right, Lund University, Lund, Sweden, 16 November.

Eliot, D., & Murakami Wood, D. (2021). Minding the flocs: Google's marketing moves, AI, privacy and the data commons. *Centre for International Governance*

Innovation, 20 May, www.cigionline.org/articles/minding-flocs-googles-marketing-moves-ai-privacy-and-data-commons/ (accessed 30 August 2021).

Eliot, D., & Murakami Wood, D. (2022). Culling the FLoC: Market Forces, Regulatory Regimes and Google's (Mis)steps on the Path away from Targeted Advertising. *Information Polity*, 1–16. doi.org/10.3233/IP-211535.

Fazackerley, A. (2023). AI makes plagiarism harder to detect, argue academics – in paper written by chatbot. *The Guardian*, 19 March, www.theguardian.com/technology/2023/mar/19/ai-makes-plagiarism-harder-to-detect-argue-academics-in-paper-written-by-chatbot (accessed 28 March 2023).

Fischer, F. (2019). Knowledge Politics and Post-Truth in Climate Denial: On the Social Construction of Alternative Facts. *Critical Policy Studies*, 13(2): 133–152.

Fisher, M., Cox, J. W., & Hermann, P. (2016). Pizzagate: from rumor, to hashtag, to gunfire in D.C. *Washington Post*, 6 December, www.washingtonpost.com/local/pizzagate-from-rumor-to-hashtag-to-gunfire-in-dc/2016/12/06/4c7def50-bbd4-11e6-94ac-3d324840106c_story.html (accessed 22 November 2023).

Forchtner, B. (2020). Far Right Articulations of the Natural Environent. In B. Forchtner (ed.), *The Far Right and the Environment: Politics, Discourse and Communication*. New York: Routledge.

Franta, B. (2021). Early Oil Industry Disinformation on Global Warming. *Environmental Politics*, 30(4): 1–6.

Freilich, J. D., & Pridemore, W. A. (2005). A Reassessment of State-Level Covariates of Militia Groups. *Behavioral Sciences & the Law*, 23(4): 527–546.

Gibbs, L. M. (2011). *Love Canal: And the Birth of the Environmental Health Movement*. Washington: Island Press.

Giddens, A. (1990). *The Consequences of Modernity*. Stanford: Stanford University Press.

Habermas, J. (1989). *The Structural Transformation of the Public Sphere: An Inquiry into a Category of Bourgeois Society*. Cambridge: MIT Press.

Harari, Y. N. (2018). Why technology favors tyranny. *The Atlantic*, October, www.theatlantic.com/magazine/archive/2018/10/yuval-noah-harari-technology-tyranny/568330/ (accessed 27 August, 2020).

Harvey, D. (2005). *A Brief History of Neoliberalism*. Oxford: Oxford University Press.

Hayek, F. A. (1945). The Use of Knowledge in Society. *American Economic Review*, 35(4): 519–530.

Helvarg, D. (1994). *The War Against the Greens: The Wise-Use Movement, the New Right and Anti-environmental Violence*. San Francisco: Sierra Club Books.

Hern, A. (2019). New AI fake text generator may be too dangerous to release, say creators. *The Guardian*, www.theguardian.com/technology/2019/feb/14/elon-musk-backed-ai-writes-convincing-news-fiction (accessed 29 May 2022).

Hilgartner, S. (1997). The Sokal Affair in Context. *Science, Technology, & Human Values*, 22(4): 506–522.

Himmelstein, J. (1983). The New Right. In R. C. Liebman & R. Wuthnow (eds), *The New Christian Right: Mobilization and Legitimation*. New York: Aldine.

Hochschild, A. R. (2016). The Great Paradox. In *Strangers in Their Own Land: Anger and Mourning on the American Right*. New York: New Press.

Hultman, M., Bjork, A., & Viinikka, T. (2020). The Far Right and Climate Change Denial: Denouncing Environmental Challenges Via Anti-establishment Rhetoric, Marketing Doubts, Industrial/Breadwinner Masculinities, Enactments and Ethno-Nationalism. In B. Forchtner (ed.), *The Far Right and the Environment: Politics, Discourse and Communication*. New York: Routledge.

Jack, C., Brundage., M & Solaiman, I. (2019). GPT-2: 6-month follow-up. *OpenAI*, https://openai.com/blog/gpt-2–6-month-follow-up (accessed 29 May 2022).

Kaiser, J. (2020). In the Heartland of Climate Scepticism: A Hyperlink Network Analysis of German Climate Sceptics and the US Right Wing. In B. Forchtner (ed.), *The Far Right and the Environment: Politics, Discourse and Communication*. New York: Routledge.

Klein, N. (2000). *No Logo: Taking Aim at the Brand Bullies*. Toronto: Random House.

Klein, N. (2014). *This Changes Everything: Capitalism Vs. The Climate*. New York: Simon & Schuster.

Laclau, E. (1977). Toward a Theory of Populism. In *Post-Marxism, Populism and Critique*. London: NLB, ch. 6.

Marlow, T., Miller, S., & Roberts, J. T. (2021). Bots and Online Climate Discourses: Twitter Discourse on President Trump's Announcement of US Withdrawal from the Paris Agreement. *Climate Policy*, 21(6): 765– 777.

Martin, N. (2019). New AI development so advanced it's too dangerous to release, says scientist. *Forbes*, 19 February, www.forbes.com/sites/nicolemartin1/2019/02/19/new-ai-development-so-advanced-its-too-dangerous-to-release-says-scientists/?sh=2a2488d4a801 (accessed 29 May 2022).

McCright, A. M., & Dunlap, R. E. (2010). Anti-reflexivity: The American Conservative Movement's Success in Undermining Climate Science and Policy. *Theory, Culture & Society*, 27(2–3): 100–133.

McLaren, D., & Markusson, N. (2020). The Co-evolution of Technological Promises, Modelling, Policies and Climate Change Targets. *Nature Climate Change*, 10(5): 392–397. doi: 10.1038/s41558-020-0740-1.

Mirowski, P., & van Horn, R. (2005). The Contract Research Organization and the Commercialization of Scientific Research. *Social Studies of Science*, 35(4): 503–548.doi: 10.1177/0306312705052103.

N. C. (2019). Conspiracy theories are dangerous – here's how to crush them. *The Economist*, 12 August, www.economist.com/open-future/2019/08/12/conspiracy-theories-are-dangerous-heres-how-to-crush-them (accessed 13 November 2023).

Napoli, P. M. (2018). What If More Speech is no Longer the Solution? First Amendment Theory Meets Fake News and the Filter Bubble. *Federal Communications Law Journal*, 70(1): 55–87.

OpenAI (2020). 'OpenAI API.' *OpenAI*, https://openai.com/blog/openai-api/ (accessed 18 January 2020).

OpenAI (2023). Introducing ChatGPT. *OpenAI*, https://openai.com/blog/chatgpt (accessed 28 March 2023).

Oreskes, N., & Conway E. M. (2010). *Merchants of Doubt: How a Handful of Scientists Obscured the Truth on Issues from Tobacco Smoke to Global Warming*. New York: Bloomsbury Press.

Peacock, M., Bissell, P., & Owen, J. (2014). Shaming Encounters: Reflections on Contemporary Understandings of Social Inequality and Health. *Sociology*, 48(2): 387–402. doi: 10.1177/0038038513490353.

Peiser, J. (2019). The rise of the robot reporter. *New York Times*, 5 February, www.nytimes.com/2019/02/05/business/media/artificial-intelligence-journalism-robots.html (accessed 23 November 2023).

Radford, A., Jeffrey, W., Amodei, D., et al. (2019). Better language models and their implications). *OpenAI*, https://openai.com/blog/better-language-models/ (accessed 29 May 2022).

The Rush Limbaugh Show (2020). 15-Year-Old credits your host for making her a critical thinker. *The Rush Limbaugh Show*, 3 April, www.rushlimbaugh.com/daily/2020/04/03/15-year-old-credits-your-host-for-making-her-a-critical-thinker-2/ (accessed 29 August 2021).

Russell, S. J. (2019). *Human Compatible: Artificial Intelligence and the Problem of Control*. New York: Viking.

Stengel, R. (2020). Domestic disinformation is a greater menace than foreign disinformation. *Time*, 26 June, https://time.com/5860215/domestic-disinformation-growing-menace-america/ accessed 22 November 2023).

Suskind, R. (2004). Faith, certainty and the presidency of George W. Bush. *New York Times Magazine*, 17 October, www.nytimes.com/2004/10/17/magazine/faith-certainty-and-the-presidency-of-george-w-bush.html (accessed 23 November 2023).

Weitzman, T. (2023). Council post: GPT-4 released: what it means for the future of your business. *Forbes*, 28 March, www.forbes.com/sites/forbesbusinesscouncil/2023/03/28/gpt-4-released-what-it-means-for-the-future-of-your-business/?sh=762e4bf62dc6 (accessed 28 March 2023).

Winkie, L. (2019). Essaybot will do your homework. But it won't get you an A. *Vox*, www.vox.com/the-goods/2019/4/15/18311367/essaybot-ai-homework-passing (accessed 20 September 2020).

Work, D. (2019). Climate alarmists blissfully ignorant of globalist agenda. *Cowichan Valley Citizen*, 17 December, www.cowichanvalleycitizen.com/opinion/climate-alarmists-blissfully-ignorant-of-globalist-agenda/ (accessed 29 August 2021).

Zuboff, S. (2018). *The Age of Surveillance Capitalism: The Fight for a Human Future at the New Frontier of Power*. New York: PublicAffairs.

The 'fake' virus and the 'not necessarily fake' climate change: ambiguities of extreme-right anti-intellectualism

Balsa Lubarda

Arguably similar to previous years, 2022, in which this chapter was written, will be remembered as a year marked by wars, pandemic, climate change and, as a consequence, constant fears for the lives of our loved ones. Some of these crises have also revealed a striking distrust of science, followed by continuous doubt mongering in relation to some of the established scientific findings. The pandemic has, together with climate change, amplified this contestation of science and the rejection of scientific authority in the name of personal freedoms. Although they might have originated elsewhere on the ideological spectrum (including the more 'moderate' right), these protests are commonly associated with the far right. This is not surprising given the link between this ideological spectrum and anti-intellectualism informing their conspiracism (Bergmann, 2018), arising from the antagonism towards the political order of liberal democracy (Pirro & Taggart, 2023; Uscinski et al., 2021).

Indeed, the anti-lockdown, anti-vaccine and other protests against measures taken in the cause of public health amid the pandemic have been spurred around the world, reiterating the connection between the far right and anti-intellectualism (Bieber, 2022). In Eastern Europe, where far-right parties have assumed power in several countries (e.g. in the Visegrad Four region), managing the pandemic was particularly challenging, with Hungary, Czechia and Slovakia all being in the top 10 of the world's COVID-19 death per capita list. This in part had to do with the politicization of expertise and the contestation of legitimacy, which led to disarrayed and virtually unenforceable policies (Buštíková & Baboš, 2020). Unsurprisingly, this caused a notable backlash and open resistance towards the measures proposed by the governing bodies. The reasons for this backlash were numerous: from sheer denialism of the threat, the existence of the virus or the effectiveness of the vaccine, to more nuanced (and more founded) ones related to personal data management and the implementation of specific measures. Either way, the far right,[1] and in particular its (more) extreme portion, has either bandwagoned or openly contributed to the anti-lockdown and, subsequently, anti-vaccine or COVID-pass protests. Accusations of dystopian realities and 'Orwellian regimes' generated in the name of the 'mild flu' have been commonly voiced by, among others, the far right and other sceptics, even though research has shown that the far right's response to the pandemic is far from monolithic (van Dongen & Leidig, 2021). On the one hand, the majority of far-right organizations around the world exploited the pandemic-related restrictions (such as lockdowns) to assert their indexical orders and Manichean, binary outlooks on the world in order to broaden their appeal. On the other hand, there are (rare) cases of the far right acknowledging the scientific positions and governmental policies related to the pandemic, or at least being ambivalent about the existing regulations (van Dongen & Leidig, 2021).

As explained above, the spectrum of responses to a crisis, from openly contesting the (emerging) science to endorsing and embracing the measures in order to mitigate harmful consequences, including everything in between, has already been noticed with the far-right responses to anthropogenic climate change. Until the last couple of years, there has almost been a scientific consensus concerning the far right's role in spreading climate scepticism or even straightforward denialism (Rahmstorf, 2004). Notwithstanding the rare cases of climate acceptance, the far right has long been perceived as a hindrance to the vote for progressive climate policies (Lockwood, 2018) and this has been mirrored by the individual attitudes of the voters and supporters of the far right (Huber et al., 2021; Krange et al., 2021) and even conservative parties (McCright & Dunlap, 2011). Even in those cases where the far, and especially the extreme, right offers an elaborate ecological agenda, building on the profound ideological link with origins in the nineteenth century (see, among others, Staudenmaier & Biehl, 1995; Olsen, 1999), this 'green nationalism' is, more often than not, considered a concomitant of climate scepticism (Malm & the Zetkin Collective, 2021). Only recently has the scholarship attempted to answer what the argumentation of radical- and extreme-right climate acceptance looks like (see Lubarda & Forchtner, 2023). However, such a task with respect to the morphology of COVID-related scepticism coming from the extreme right has not yet been performed.

With this missing part of the puzzle, and taking into account the relationship of the far right to anti-intellectualism that informs these policy positions, this chapter aims to reconstruct the ideological rendition of science by the far right, in relation to climate change and the pandemic. Of course, these two challenges do not exist in a vacuum. In other words, reasons for acceptance, scepticism or denialism are conditioned by the political context, ideological trajectories and strategic positioning. However, attitudes towards the pandemic and climate change are mutually informing due to their immense contemporary salience and the common ideological grounds from which positioning on these issues is derived. To respond to the central aim of canvassing the spectrum of COVID-19 scepticism and its relationship with the similar claims associated with climate change, as well as understanding what this (in)congruence may mean for the extreme right's relationship with science, this chapter will commit to the following tasks. First, it will explore the role of anti-intellectualism in the ideological space of the extreme right. Secondly, it will present the data and method operationalized in this chapter, providing also a background of three extreme-right organizations from the V4 region used in this study: Czech Republic's Národní demokracie (National Democracy), Mi Hazánk Mozgalom (Hungarian Our Homeland Movement), and Slovak Kotlebovci – Ľudová strana naše Slovensko (Kotlebists – People's Party: Our Slovakia) and its breakaway party, Republika (Republic). Thirdly, building on the analysis of the social media posts and 12 qualitative interviews conducted with the representatives of these parties, the chapter will outline the spectrum of sceptical arguments related to COVID-19 and its overlaps with the scepticism related to anthropogenic climate change. Fourthly, and finally, the chapter will use these results to revisit the far right's attitude towards science, intellectualism and authority in light of the contemporary crises.

Anti-intellectualism and authority of the far right

It may seem surprising that the terms 'anti-intellectualism', referring to the mistrust of intellectuals and scientists, is a concept virtually confined to the analysis of US politics (Hofstadter, 1963). In the US, anti-intellectualism was 'the heart of McCarthyism' in the 1950s, leading to a populist crusade on the wings of religious fundamentalism and fervid anti-communist sentiment (Peters, 2019). The core features of this American anti-intellectualism are its individualistic bent, venerating 'self-made men', strong religious background and utilitarian logic (Hofstadter, 1963). Rigney (1991) added 'populist anti-elitism' and 'anti-rationalism' to this conceptualization, all to indicate the right-wing garb of this conceptualization (for the left and centrist variants of anti-intellectualism, see Featherstone et al., 2004). Even though its mainstreaming was particularly evident in the era of Donald Trump, anti-intellectualism and its consequence, conspiratorial framing, has been a permanent shadow of right-wing populism and, consequently, the far right (Gauchat, 2012), which is what makes it relevant for international politics beyond the US context.

What made anti-intellectualism particularly suitable for its conjunction with fascism and the extreme right is the logic of scapegoating, commensurate with the Manichean distinction between the absolute moral categories of good and evil, core values of fascist, far right and populist ideological morphologies (see Kallis, 2003; Mudde, 2007), paired with a sense of victimhood and 'ambivalence towards representative politics' (Pirro & Taggart, 2023: 7). In fact, anti-intellectualism and the downplaying of art, philosophy, literature, and overall education and scientific expertise were pronounced in the works of Giovanni Gentile, the main theorist of Italian fascism. Gentile was not straightforwardly opposed to science and education, but claimed that the role of anti-intellectualism is to bring together 'thought and action' and re-establish concern for the 'practical world' (Gentile, 1928: 300). Hence, fascist suspicion of science is based on science devoid of interest to the 'laypeople', fuelling the agenda of both the populist radical and the extreme right. This may also lead to a spill-over effect, where the negative popular attitude towards some experts or expertise brings about broader and more general distrust towards matters where scientific consensus has already been established. The alternative reading is the 'mitigation thesis', which indicates the possibility of reducing anti-intellectualism through 'verbal intelligence' (for an overview, see Motta, 2018).

Irrespective of the scholarly focus on the US, anti-intellectualism is a common feature of the contemporary extreme right worldwide. Juxtaposing it with 'traditional wisdoms', science and education in this reading are framed as obstacles and constraints imposed by the epistemic elite that acts as a 'gatekeeper' on the individual's pathway to the truth (see Tebaldi, 2021). In Europe, and in particular its eastern part, such conclusions may be less popular on the grounds of their contextual detachment (e.g. the relatively weak tradition of libertarianism). In the internet and 'meme' era, these political and ideological traditions bear much less relevance, as messages traverse these geographical boundaries and challenge the established standards or 'truths' in a polity (Reyes, 2020). There is already ample evidence on the links between anti-intellectual sentiments and climate scepticism or denialism (Merkeley, 2020) and vaccination (Stecula et al., 2020). At the same time, research has indicated the importance of offering a closer look at the important outliers and caveats, such as the one that anti-intellectuals do not tend to avoid exposure to expertise or COVID-related news (Merkley and Loewen, 2021: 711).

The conspiracism and anti-intellectualism of today are heavily reliant on the conceptualization of authority. In the ideological morphology of the extreme right, including psychological research, authority figures are an indispensable component, possibly even superseding ethno-nationalism. However, authority as a concept and a feature of politics is not only associated with right-wing ideologies (see Manson, 2020 on how left-wing authoritarianism impacts the responses to the pandemic). Authority in its ecological reading has long been considered one of the central features of 'right-wing ecology' as well (Olsen, 1999), although its position has been deemed peripheral to the ideology over the last couple of years (see Lubarda, 2019). In other words, far-right ecologists of today, including the most extreme eco-fascists, are placing authoritarian leadership in developing an ecological polity.

The extreme-right reading of authority departs from several basic premises. First, authority is legitimized by a fundamental conviction that human beings are unequal, from which the call for a social and political hierarchy is derived. Secondly, authority is a resolutely anti-liberal concept, which is why, for example, authoritarian, far-right populism has been perceived as an antidote to liberal democracy (Müller, 2016: 31). Thirdly, authority in the extreme-right ideology rests on the conceptualization of order: be it through the authority of experience or through harking back to a nostalgic polity and family (see Lubarda, 2019), authority requires a 'punitive state'. These principles, however, do not imply that the extreme right's rendition of authority is homogenic, but it is, more often than not, central to their ideological appeal and policy positions. Studies linking far- (thus, not only extreme-) right authoritarianism and the pandemic or other infectious diseases have indicated that viewing the pandemic as an existential threat moderates authoritarian predispositions (Hartman et al., 2021). While the rejection of anthropogenic climate change may seem to go hand in hand with the scepticism related to the origins of, and the measurements taken to mitigate, the pandemic, it is not entirely clear what the idiosyncrasies, for example the acceptance of anthropogenic climate change paired with the anti-lockdown stance, may imply for the notion of authority in the extreme right.

Data and method

As noted in the introduction, this chapter focuses on the attitudes of four extreme-right parties towards anthropogenic climate change and the COVID-19 pandemic. The parties were selected on two main grounds. First, their extreme-right ideological position differs from that of the radical-right parties in their explicit rejection of liberal democracy – examples include Freedom and Direct Democracy in Czech Republic, Fidesz and Jobbik in Hungary, and the Slovak National Party. Secondly, the parties included in the analysis share broader regional, political and ultimately far-right contexts, belonging to the Visegrad 4 region, representing post-socialist and Eastern European countries. Finally, the case parties were also selected on the grounds of their exceptional engagement with environmental issues and politics in comparison to other extreme-right organizations in the region.

Národní demokracie (full name 'No to Brussels – National Democracy') was founded in 2005, even though its official webpage claims that the party is 'continuing a 170-year long tradition of preserving and developing the nation' (Národní demokracie, 2017). The two pillars of the party ideology are 'defence' and 'revival', signalling the palingenetic component (Griffin, 1991) epitomized in departure from the EU and NATO and the prevention of immigration (Národní demokracie, 2017). Moreover, the party defines itself as a 'conservative' and 'patriotic' party with an aim to 'cultivate a healthy mental state of the nation, love of country, knowledge of one's own identity and history' (Národní demokracie, 2017). It is interesting that even in the declaration of ideological principles, Národní demokracie outlines the importance of environmental protection through the conservative responsibility towards future generations and protecting the resources of the national wealth (see Scruton, 2012). The party had little success in the elections, peaking at only 0.79 per cent at the 2019 European Parliamentary elections and winning no seats in the national Parliament. The leader of the party is Adam Bartoš.

Unlike Národní demokracie, as of 2022 Mi Hazánk has two seats in Parliament. Founded in 2018, the party attempted to occupy the ideological space of Hungarian extreme-right nationalism vacated by Jobbik, the then-leading opposition party. Based on the principles of 'camaraderie, patriotism, credibility, and anti-compromise', the party advocates for the 'salvation of the Homeland' and of all Hungarians who live in the Carpathian basin (which overlaps with the borders of the Greater Hungary that existed before the Treaty of Trianon, signed in 1921). The leader of the party is László Toroczkai, a well-established figure in the Hungarian far right, being one of the founders of the extreme-right HVIM and one of the highly prominent leaders of Jobbik for more than a decade. The party also has its ecological cabinet, Zöld Hazánk (Green Homeland), led by Krisztina Csereklye.

Kotlebovci – Ľudová strana naše Slovensko was founded in 2010 as one of the many offshoots of the extreme-right Slovenská pospolitosť (Slovak Togetherness). Both organizations were founded by Marián Kotleba, arguably the most emblematic figure on the Slovak far right and a candidate for the 2019 Slovak presidential elections in which he finished fourth (out of 15 candidates). In the 2020 national elections, the party won a total of 17 seats, 3 seats better than in the previous elections in 2016, when the party won about 8 per cent of the popular vote. Kotlebovci has always been an unambiguous extreme-right party, with pronounced ties with historical revisionism and anti-Semitism and its militia unit (Mareš, 2018). In October 2020, Kotleba was sentenced to 4 years and 4 months in prison, after being found guilty of 'supporting organizations oppressing fundamental human rights' (Spectator, 2020). His sentencing led to turmoil within the party, when a group led by Milan Uhrík, Member of the European Parliament, decided to form a faction called 'The Republic', building on the existing and then-inactive centre-right political party formed in 2002. However, the party has, for the most part, preserved the ideological positioning of Kotlebovci, although somewhat assuaging its position by emulating the principles of the American national conservatives. For instance, the party is less stern on its positioning on the European Union (calling for 'a fundamental reform' instead of immediate departure), simultaneously calling for the protection of 'human rights' and 'conservative values' (Republika, 2021).

The data used in the analysis comprises the official party documents containing policy or ideological positions (electoral and ideological manifestos) and Facebook posts related to the environment and/or (not necessarily COVID-19) vaccination, as well as 12 qualitative interviews (2 with representatives of Národní demokracie, 5 with Mi Hazánk and 5 with Kotlebovci/ Republika). The interviews were conducted as part of a larger (doctoral) project on far-right ecologism in Eastern Europe, mostly conducted before the beginning of the pandemic. Because of that, I specifically focused on the answers of my respondents to two questions posed during the interview: 'What is your opinion on anthropogenic climate change?' and 'How do you envisage the role of scientists in your ideal, ecologically prosperous polity?' Since I did not have the chance to ask the questions about the pandemic (even though I managed to follow up with two of my respondents from Kotlebovci and Mi Hazánk in January 2022), I focused on social media posts on the official webpages about the pandemic and science.

The analytical framework used in the coding of the data was van Rensburg's (2015: 7) typology of evidence, process and response scepticism. Whereas evidence scepticism constitutes the 'core' scepticism or straightforward denialism of climate science, with respect to the trend, causes or impact (see also Rahmstorf, 2004), process and response scepticism represents 'concomitant' scepticism or scepticism-related claims.[2] Process scepticism refers to scientific knowledge generation or decision-making processes, while response scepticism is related to particular policies (van Rensburg distinguishes between policy instruments and policy styles). While this threefold typology was useful in pinpointing climate change scepticisms (van Rensburg, 2015: 7), it was not particularly helpful in drawing boundaries between COVID-19 sceptic claims. For this reason, the primary focus was in identifying as many individual claims as possible. The following section presents the overview of the most commonly voiced claims associated with both climate and COVID-19 scepticisms, before turning to the conclusions related to the position of anti-intellectualism and scientific authority within extreme-right ideology.

Reconstructing the positioning: locating climate and COVID-19 scepticisms on the spectrum

Evidence scepticism about climate change has long been entrenched in far-right climate denialism. A lot has changed over the last decade: the increased evidence on the anthropogenic causes of climate change, but also the emphasis on energy security following the war in Ukraine – these push and pull factors, however, still seem to be going in the direction of response scepticism or even acceptance (see Lubarda, 2023). Although these categories are not watertight and frequent shifts in claims, from evidence to response scepticism and vice versa is possible, Národní demokracie is the only case party in this analysis that has combined all three of the subcategories (trend, cause, impact) within the 'evidence' label. In an interview we conducted a few months before the beginning of the pandemic, Jan Sedláček, the leader of the youth section (Národní mládež) and the main spokesperson of the party on climate- and pandemic-related matters, combined evidence scepticism with derogatory claims about climate science being alarmist:

> I know the climate is changing, and this happens every time – with or without human population. It has changed in history … I think the climate change brings us both positive and negative consequences. The positive, for example, is when people say that 50 or 60 years ago the winter in Czech Republic lasted from September to April. I think that this would be very bad because, if it continued this way until today's times, it would have been very uncomfortable to live under those winters. (Jan Sedláček, Národní demokracie, 11 December 2019)

Even though he also emphasized the negative effects of climate change, such as the increased temperatures of the urban zones (for which he suggests allocating resources to plant more trees instead of mitigating the issue globally), Sedláček's remarks fit perfectly the 'significant positive impacts' claim within van Rensburg's typology. Perhaps contrary to ideological expectations, Sedláček and Národní demokracie (or any other extreme-right organization in this analysis) did not espouse any of the suggested forms of 'carbon vitalism', in which carbon is perceived as constitutive of the natural order (Pasek, 2021). However, authoring a book, *Climate Ideology vs. Nature Conservation*, Sedláček has been vocal about the 'alarmism' of climate science, arguing that climate science is ultimately detrimental to the natural environment. Evidence scepticism of climate change was occasionally voiced also by some of my respondents from Kotlebovci, who linked this scepticism with a (rather flamboyant) criticism of Greta Thunberg.

> You know that green parties are very leftist. I think that the meaning of this topic is different in their understanding as compared to what we have to say. I am following the situation with Greta, this little girl from Sweden who is

telling everyone how to live and not to travel by airplanes, but ... I am not
saying it [anthropogenic climate change] is true, but I am not saying it is fake
either, because I am not an expert. It is possible, it is warm today, in these
years, but it could be some phases of our planet, there has been a little ice
age in the medieval, the weather has always been changing. But it is true that
the plastic in our seas, forests, and rivers make the situation fucked up. (Kuba,
Kotlebovci, 25 June 2019)

That dissatisfaction with the figure of Greta Thunberg and her climate
activism may lead to an entrenching of denialism was clear in the cases of
my other respondents from the same party. To this day, Kotlebovci or
Republika have not publicly expressed their lack of trust in climate science,
although they have advocated for keeping the Slovak coal mines open, on
the grounds of the economic arguments and workers' rights. The 'inconclusive'
'yes-but' claims acknowledging the harmful effect of human beings on the
environment but not fully accepting climate science is the most commonly
announced form of climate change scepticism among the Kotlebists and
Republika members:

There are too many facts about it that denying it is so insane. The question
is how big an impact people have on it. There is also problem with people,
some of them don't have inhibitions and want make money from everything,
I personally think there is a possibility that some of them want to make money
from this problem and some facts can be garbled. People are sceptical about
the statements of our elites and they don't know to identify a lie. (Ana,
Kotlebovci, 17 March 2019)

The archetypal populist fears of the corrupted elites who use climate
change to deceive the people (van Rensburg's 'Climate decision-making
process') provides an example of how the logic of scepticism flows in a way
that binds together evidence denialism and a more subtle (and warranted)
scepticism towards the policy responses greasing a neoliberal capitalist
machine. In other words, evidence scepticism conditions both process and
response variants, accentuating the importance of 'spectral' understanding
of this phenomenon, where the positions may easily shift from one imagined
analytical container to another.

In the three cases, process and response scepticism were particularly visible
in the extensive critique of the Green New Deal, being linked to 'climate
mafia' (Národní mládež, Facebook, 10 January 2022). One of the recently
raised claims is linked to the looming 'energy collapse' amid increasing prices
and the demand for electricity during COVID crisis and the war in Ukraine,
which cannot be met solely from renewable resources. This argumentative
constellation allows both the Národní demokracie and Kotlebovci/Republika
to re-establish themselves as defenders of 'the little guy' (Forchtner, 2019)

and his/her interests against the discursively constructed 'climate elites'. The actual response scepticism referring to the policy instruments or the policy style is present mostly concerning the economic arguments, that is, the costs of an energy transition (see Capstick & Pidgeon, 2014). This can be explained on three major grounds. First, the relatively weak position of the extreme-right parties in the political systems of the three countries (with the partial exception of Hungary). Secondly, the lack of party expertise in the specific domains of energy and environmental politics evidenced also in the interviews I conducted with the representatives of the three parties. Thirdly, the disinterested electorate (Jylhä et al., 2020). Although all four parties included in this analysis offered a form of far-right ecologism in their official party documents, the ideological content was situated around the idea of a 'rational' or 'conditional' ecologism (see Caiani & Lubarda, 2023), or ecologism that does not stand in the way of capitalist development.

What is particularly interesting about these forms of climate scepticism is that they are disturbingly similar to the claims related to the existence and responses to COVID-19. After two years and almost 100,000 lives lost due to COVID-19 in Czechia, Slovakia and Hungary, scepticism related to the virus is still in full bloom. However, given the length of the pandemic and its outcome thus far, it may seem as if evidence scepticism, that is, scepticism related to the very existence of the virus and its harmful effects, is intellectually obsolete. Indeed, the claims commonly voiced in the first month of the pandemic, such as 'COVID-19 being nothing but a flu' or the more eschatological ones, such as the disease being 'God's punishment for immoral behavior' have virtually evaporated even from the extreme-right discourse. Yet, this is not to claim that these were absent. Even though most of these arguments are converging around 'personal freedoms', these scepticisms are ultimately about contesting the scientific evidence. Claiming that 'everyone should have the right to choose', Dóra Dúró, member of the Hungarian Parliament and former spokesperson of Mi Hazánk, called for an 'open discussion about the real consequences of the vaccinations' (Dóra Dúró, Facebook, 24 January 2022). The official Facebook page of Mi Hazánk also cites Andrew G. Bostom's claim that 'COVID-19 vaccination is three times as dangerous as the virus itself' (Mi Hazánk, Facebook, 2022). The most recent, omicron variant also served the case of Mi Hazánk to reiterate the mild nature of the disease, making the restrictions and 'stigma' fundamentally unnecessary (Mi Hazánk, Facebook, 7 January 2022). Likewise, Milan Uhrík, MEP from Republika (formerly 'Kotlebovci') exquisitely argued that 'the virus is no longer here', alluding to the inappropriate response of the government to the pandemic and 'the measures that lack basic logic':

Most of the measures are no longer about fighting the pandemic (the measures lack basic logic), but about moving wealth from the middle class into the hands of the richest, those whose assets grew to billions during the coronavirus crisis. The second goal is to teach people to be constantly controlled. Teach them to sit at home. Politicians in governments do this because coronavirus will overshadow all other cases ... if we replaced the politicians, the epidemic would weaken in a moment ... when politicians and the media employ other issues, the epidemic suddenly disappears.

Thus, it becomes immediately clear that Uhrík and Republika's populist intervention belongs to concomitant, process and response claims of scepticism, rather than the core objects of scepticism (evidence). The spectrum of claims related to response scepticism to COVID-19 is conspicuously similar to the original, van Rensburg's typology of climate change scepticism. Process scepticism mostly refers to the manipulation of scientific evidence, such as when Uhrík argued in the European Parliament that COVID is 'a mere scam from the pharmaceutical corporations' (Uhrík, Facebook, 12 November 2021). Found at the intersection of the negative attitudes towards the scientific process and the industry that is abusing the science to call for ever-more restrictions or mandatory vaccinations, process scepticism queries both the logic of scientific discovery and the process through which these findings are communicated to the decision-making entities: political coordination bodies assembled amid the pandemic. This unfolds the extreme-right anti-intellectualism by linking these bodies and the scientists who are, among others, composing them, to leftist or elitist politics. Be it through the 'communist mentality of the West', or the 'covid hysteria' (Uhrík, Facebook, 12 March 2021), these bodies are held responsible for the measures that are leading to wealth redistribution and a lucrative pharmaceutical industry, responsible for imposing vaccinations. Indeed, the response to the pandemic, that is, the thrust behind the vaccinations, is the main object of COVID-related scepticism coming from the extreme right: while Národní demokracie and Kotlebists immediately rejected the very existence of the virus, Mi Hazánk became involved in the COVID-sceptic movement only after the first wave of lockdowns, March – May/June 2020, and particularly after the first vaccines were tested.

Vaccinations were thus perceived as a 'money-making scheme' for the profit of well-established discursive villains, such as Bill Gates (according to Toroczkai from Mi Hazánk, see 24.hu, 2021). Similar to climate scepticism and in line with the 'rational' 'cost–benefit' logic, the bulwark of response scepticism claims is situated around the economic domain: the costs of the pandemic-related restrictions and the infringements upon the businesses and incomes of ordinary people. What is also interesting is that these calls for ever more 'openness' in the name of the people were also funded by denialist networks, such as the Koch family. Within such a logic, COVID-19 (climate)-related regulations are nothing but another invention of the detached elites obstructing the lives of those who are struggling to make ends meet (Forchtner & Özvatan, 2019). As an example, Národní demokracie protested against the government decision to ban the Christmas markets, accusing the government of being influenced by the elites and big businesses against 'Czech self-employed sellers' (Facebook, 12 July 2021). While this is present across the four cases and possibly beyond, the reference to incompetent elites noted in, for example, research on climate and COVID-19 scepticism in Germany, is virtually missing from the Eastern European realms (Forchtner & Özvatan, 2022).

With these restrictions in mind, Mi Hazánk in Hungary also advocated for the 'epidemic solidarity tax' which would entail a 'taxation of casinos, pharmaceutical companies, vitamin manufacturers, and retail chains', all with an intention to support 'the working Hungarians' (Telex, 15 March 2021). Similar claims from the spectrum of 'response' scepticisms include statements such as 'no problem – no response needed' (Lubarda and Forchtner, 2023), implying that the COVID-19 virus is not fundamentally different from other types of viruses. However, this may also point to the deficiency of van Rensburg's typology, as this comment refers more to the evidence scepticism querying the very existence of the virus and the extent to which it is a problem, but also the importance of spectral understanding of such typologies, where the individual arguments may easily permeate the established containers of analytical frameworks.

Another commonly voiced claim belonging to response scepticism and shared by all four parties in the analysis is the one on COVID-19 being an instrument of the totalitarian 'New World Order'. The principal idea of this 'New World Order', in accordance with the well-established conspiracy fable, is in defining 'first'- and 'second'-class citizens based on the mandatory vaccinations (see Kalil et al., 2021 for similar discussion in the Brazilian case). Milan Mazurek, a member of the Slovak Parliament from Republika (formerly Kotlebovci), made frequent parallels between the COVID-19 regulations and Nazi-era laws. He warned that Slovakia is becoming a 'concentration camp' under the 'fascist Slovak government' and imposing 'reserved lanes for the vaccinated and paid mandatory tests for the unvac-cinated is the same as banning Jews from walking on sidewalks in German-occupied zones during the war, or paying a special tax to unbelievers in states conquered by Islamic troops' (Milan Mazurek website, 10 July 2021). Similar references were also made by other politicians from Republika, as well as Národní demokracie:

> How else can you comment on the madness demonstrated by idiots who call themselves government experts? Please tell me which expert signed under the order that overcoming the disease is enough for you for just 90 days? No normal person can do that, let alone a doctor.

It is generally known that natural immunity is incomparably better and lasts longer. However, the idiots in the government, parliament and all those 'organisms' don't care, because science and medicine go aside. The interest is to vaccinate, vaccinate until you go crazy. Healthy, sick, young, old … everyone must eventually vaccinate, no matter the consequences. (Milan Mazurek, website, 12 January 2022)

Overall, the congruence between climate and COVID-19 scepticist claims is striking. With notable differences related to evidence scepticism (see Table 12.1), conditioned by the different nature of the problems at hand but also the speed with which the pandemic has swept the world, individual claims associated with process and response scepticism show extensive overlap. In the case of COVID-19, most of these two scepticisms are derived from anti-vax and, ultimately, anti-science sentiments. While I encountered interesting outlooks on authority, politics and education, nothing in my interviews conducted with the representatives of Kotlebovci and Mi Hazánk in 2018 and 2019 indicated a belonging to the anti-vax movement. This change in positioning may well be attributed to political opportunism, as the extreme right in Eastern Europe capitalized on the emerging discontent with the way the COVID-19 pandemic was managed. Through frame bridging, or 'linkage of two or more ideologically congruent but structurally unconnected frames regarding a particular issue or problem' (Snow et al., 1986: 467), the opposition to vaccine mandates on the grounds of, first, the unknown long-term effects of the vaccines, and, secondly, economic freedoms has gradually turned into the (at the moment, still implicit) opposition to mandatory vaccination in general. This became most visible in the opposition to the vaccination of children, for example when the post on Mi Hazánk's Facebook page reiterated the old populist blueprint, indicating that 'child poverty increased by 20% during the epidemic, and giant companies increased their income and profit to a level never seen before' (Mi Hazánk Facebook, 26 December 2021).

In lieu of a conclusion: levelling the grounds between authority and anti-intellectualism

The similarity of claims voiced by COVID-19 and climate sceptics may seem unsurprising – however, what happens when those on the far right who accept the basic tenets of climate science are also among the COVID sceptics? Unlike the obvious case of Národní demokracie, which has extensively engaged with all three types of scepticism, and Republika/Kotlebovci, whose members were less clear about the scientific evidence related to the anthropogenic background of climate change but objected to the policy

Table 12.1 Overview of climate change and COVID-19 sceptic claims in accordance with van Rensburg's typology

Evidence	Process	Process	Response	Response
COVID-19 is God's punishment for immoral behaviour	Peer review by 'buddies'/not all views are heard	World government agendas	Goes against our natural habits (save the children)	Economy and jobs should not be harmed
We don't talk about the consequences of vaccinations	Climate change/COVID-19 is a hoax	Irrationalism (alarmist, hysteria)	A money-making scheme	Vaccines are not working
COVID-19 is a flu	Scientists manipulate/hide the evidence	Wealth redistribution	No problem – no response needed	A pragmatic and measured response is best
Holocaust repeats itself	A lucrative COVID industry now exists	Socialists and Greens drive the climate/COVID-19 agenda	The costs of mitigation outweigh the benefits	
		Media sensationalism distorts public opinion	No problem – no response needed	Do not forget our poor!
			Manufacturers are not responsible	COVID-19 is a pretext to define second-class citizens

Key: Black font – claims shared by COVID-19 and climate sceptics (according to van Rensburg's typology); grey font – claims made by COVID-19 sceptics only.

responses, Mi Hazánk is one of the prominent cases of the extreme right in Eastern Europe which has acknowledged the findings of climate science.

> The main reason is that people don't have enough education and knowledge about it [climate change]. The average people don't know how to save the environment and protect everything around them, so you cannot be surprised that they don't care about the climate … but honestly, until Asian countries and the US make a move, we can't expect Europe to solve the problem. (Krisztina Csereklye, Mi Hazánk, 6 June 2019)

Csereklye, who is also chairing Zöld Hazánk, the party's green cabinet, is not the only party official who has acknowledged the existence of anthropogenic climate change. In his interview, Toroczkai also confirmed that he believes in anthropogenic climate change because its consequences have been made clear (Lubarda, 2023). Toroczkai went on to accentuate the importance of engaging with other nationalists on this issue, in an effort to combat climate change which is now evidently affecting 'the people on the ground – the farmers' (Lubarda, 2020). What Mi Hazánk self-admittedly offers to climate change mitigation are 'locally flavoured' responses, dependent on contextual circumstances and realms (János Árgyelán, 30 October 2018). Irrespective of the particular claims associated with response scepticism, Mi Hazánk, much like the other far-right organizations in Hungary (Jobbik, HVIM), acknowledges the existence of anthropogenic climate change. Such a position on climate change (and the broader stances on the environment) has mostly been justified on the grounds of the scientific authority that would, in an ideal world, contain the (overly) emotionally loaded environmentalism of the left.

> So LMP [Hungarian green party] made a programme, but I talked to my party members, they never had any scientific publications related to this. They never had scientific conferences on the subject – because they can't do real scientific work and present the results. I have the feeling, and in West Europe, the result is the same, that these parties don't have real knowledge. They make a campaign, but they can't develop a valuable programme because they don't have knowledge for this. (Krisztina Csereklye, Mi Hazánk, 6 June 2019)

The clear epistemic hierarchy with science and scientists at the helm of decision-making processes, calling for an 'expertocracy' may seem to fit the authoritarian principle in the extreme-right ideology. Yet, when the scientific findings conflict with that same ideology or strategic positioning, the trust in scientific authority seems to lose priority to the populist principle of protecting 'the people' and their freedoms. The extreme right is well aware of this contention and its potentially damaging impact on its ideological core. Even when this contention is resolved through scepticism, all four parties included in this analysis justify their stances through their 'own' science and scientists. In the case of Národní demokracie, these 'proper' scientists are to be found in their ranks, often equating scientific reasoning with common sense deduction (see Oreskes & Conway, 2011). For Republika, earlier the Kotlebists, and to some extent Mi Hazánk, the scientists are 'borrowed', articulating climate and COVID-19 scepticism at guest lectures and panel discussions organized by the parties. Mi Hazánk even set up the Coronavirus Research Centre, a shadow of the equivalent governmental body, gathering 'professionals' with an aim to focus on 'the facts, tips, and useful advice' related to the pandemic (Mi Hazánk, Facebook, 11 April 2021).

Thus, in spite of the harmful effects of misinformation related to both COVID-19 and climate change, the extreme right, or at least its representatives in Eastern Europe, is not necessarily downplaying the role of science in its ideal polity. In the case of climate change denialism, it is the integrity of the scientific method that is fundamentally contested, as scientists are presented as insincere or distrustful (Philo & Happer, 2013: 14). But science is never about the imagined purity of 'facts', as uncertainties are a constitutive part of science. However, this is not to argue that everything is unresolved (Conway & Oreskes, 2010: 34). With COVID-19, the problem is not so much with the scientists but with the communication of these uncertainties, that is, response scepticism, and the effect governments and corporations have on science communication. Still, these are only speculations: similar to Hoffman's (2012) finding, the public debate about climate change, and, I add, COVID-19, is not about science as much as it is about values and ideology.

Notes

1 In line with the scholarship, I consider 'far right' to occupy a part of the ideological spectrum comprising the 'radical right' and the 'extreme right', where the latter is openly disputing liberal democracy and seeking to overthrow it through violent means. With the mainstreaming of the far right (see Mudde, 2019), the line between the radical and the extreme right becomes ever more blurred, as both have undermined, more or less timidly, liberal democratic procedures. However, this (sub)ideological differentiation remains well established in the scholarship, which is why it will also be used in this chapter.
2 While van Rensburg uses 'arguments' and 'claims' interchangeably, I specifically decided upon the latter.

References

24.hu (2021). Néhány száz ember tüntetett a Mi Hazánkkal a lezárások ellen [A few hundred people protested with Mi Hazánk against the lockdowns]. *24.*

hu, 15 March, https://24.hu/belfold/2021/03/15/nehany-szaz-ember-tuntet-a-mi-hazankkal-a-lezarasok-ellen/ (accessed 21 January 2022).

Bergmann, E. (2018). *Conspiracy and Populism: The Politics of Misinformation*. Cham: Springer International Publishing.

Bieber, F. (2022). Global Nationalism in Times of the COVID-19 Pandemic. *Nationalities Papers*, 50(1): 13–25.

Biehl, J., & Staudenmaier, P. (1995). *Ecofascism: Lessons from the German Experience*. Edinburgh: AK Press.

Buštíková, L., & Baboš, P. (2020). Best in Covid: Populists in the Time of Pandemic. *Politics and Governance*, 8(4): 496–508.

Capstick, S. B., & Pidgeon, N. F. (2014). What is Climate Change Scepticism? Examination of the Concept using a Mixed Methods Study of the UK Public. *Global Environmental Change*, 24: 389–401.

Caiani, M., & Lubarda, B. (2023). Conditional Environmentalism of Right-Wing Populism in Power: Ideology and/or Opportunities? *Environmental Politics*, 1–21. doi: 10.1080/09644016.2023.2242749.

Featherstone, L., Henwood, D., & Parenti, C. (2004). 'Action will be taken': left anti-intellectualism and its discontents. *LiP Magazine*, 11.

Forchtner, B. (2019). *Far Right and the Environment: Discourse, Politics, Communications*. London: Routledge.

Forchtner, B., & Özvatan, Ö. (2019). Beyond the 'German Forest': Environmental Communication by the Far Right in Germany. In B. Forchtner (ed.), *The Far Right and the Environment*. London: Routledge, pp. 216–236.

Forchtner, B., & Özvatan, Ö. (2022). De/legitimizing Europe through the Performance of Crises: The Far-Right Alternative for Germany on 'Climate Hysteria' and 'Corona Hysteria'. *Journal of Language and Politics*, 21(2): 208–232.

Gauchat, G. W. (2012). Politicization of Science in the Public Sphere: A Study of Public Trust in the United States, 1974 to 2010. *American Sociological Review*, 77: 167–187.

Gentile, G. (1928). The Philosophic Basis of Fascism. *Foreign Affairs*, 6(2): 290–304.

Griffin, R. (1991). *The Nature of Fascism*. London: Pinter Publishers Limited.

Hartman, T. K., Stocks, T. V. A., McKay, R., et al. (2021). The Authoritarian Dynamic During the COVID-19 Pandemic: Effects on Nationalism and Anti-immigrant Sentiment. *Social Psychological and Personality Science*, 12(7): 1274–1285.

Hoffman, A. J. (2012). Climate Science as Culture War. *Stanford Social Innovation Review*, 10(4): 30–37.

Hofstadter, R. (1963). *Anti-intellectualism in American Life*. New York: Knopf.

Huber, R., Greussing, E., & Eberl, J.-M. (2021). From Populism to Climate Scepticism: The Role of Institutional Trust and Attitudes towards Science. *Environmental Politics*, 31(7): 1115–1138.

Jylhä, K. M., Strimling, P., & Rydgren, J. (2020). Climate Change Denial among Radical Right-Wing Supporters. *Sustainability*, 12(23): 1–15.

Kalil, I., Silveira, S.-C., Pinheiro, W., et al. (2021). Politics of Fear in Brazil: Far-Right Conspiracy Theories on COVID-19. *Global Discourse*, 11(3): 409–425.

Kallis, A. A. (2003). 'Fascism', 'Para-fascism' and 'Fascistization': On the Similarities of Three Conceptual Categories. *European History Quarterly*, 33(2): 219–249.

Krange, O., Kaltenborn, B. P., & Hultman, M. (2021). 'Don't confuse me with facts' – How Right-Wing Populism Affects Trust in Agencies Advocating Anthropogenic Climate Change as a Reality. *Humanities & Social Sciences Communications*, 8: 255.

Lockwood, M. (2018). Right-Wing Populism and the Climate Change Agenda: Exploring the Linkages. *Environmental Politics*, 27(4): 712–732.

Lubarda, B. (2019). Far-Right Agricultural Alternatives to Right-Wing Populism in Hungary: The 'Real' Caretakers of the Blood and Soil. *Culture della Sostenibilità*, 24: 1–17.

Lubarda, B. (2020). 'Homeland Farming' or 'Rural Emancipation'? The Discursive Overlap between Populist and Green Parties in Hungary. *Sociologia Ruralis*, 60(4): 810–832.

Lubarda, B. (2023). *Far-Right Ecologism: Environmental Politics and the Far Right in Hungary and Poland*. London: Routledge.

Lubarda, B., & Forchtner, B. (2023). Far-Right Narratives of Climate Change Acceptance and their Role in Addressing Climate Skepticism. *Journal of Environmental Education*, 54(6): 1–11.

Malm, A., & the Zetkin Collective (2021). *White Skin, Black Fuel: On the Danger of Fossil Fascism*. Verso Books.

Manson, J. H. (2020). Right-Wing Authoritarianism, Left-Wing Authoritarianism, and Pandemic-Mitigation Authoritarianism. *Personality and Individual Differences*, 167: 1–14.

Mareš, M. (2018). How Does Militant Democracy Function in Combating Right-Wing Extremism? A Case Study of Slovakian Militant Democracy and the Rise of *Kotleba – People's Party Our Slovakia*. In A. Ellian & B. Rijpkema (eds), *Militant Democracy: Political Science, Law and Philosophy*. Berlin: Springer, pp. 61–76.

McCright, A. M., & Dunlap, R. E. (2011). Cool Dudes: The Denial of Climate Change among Conservative White Males in the United States. *Global Environmental Change*, 21(4): 1163–1172.

Merkley, E. (2020). Anti-intellectualism, Populism, and Motivated Resistance to Expert Consensus. *Public Opinion Quarterly*, 84: 24–48.

Merkley, E., & Loewen, P. J. (2021). Anti-intellectualism and the Mass Public's Response to the COVID-19 Pandemic. *Nature Human Behavior*, 5: 706–715.

Motta, M. (2018). The Dynamics and Political Implications of Anti-intellectualism in the United States. *American Politics Research*, 46(3): 465–498.

Mudde, C. (2007). *Populist Radical Right Parties in Europe*. Cambridge: Cambridge University Press.

Mudde, C. (2019). *The Far Right Today*. Cambridge: Polity.

Müller, J.-W. (2016). *What is Populism?* Philadelphia: University of Pennsylvania Press.

Národní demokracie (2017). O nás [About us]. *Národní demokracie*, https://narodnidemokracie.cz/strana/proc-jdeme-do-toho/ (accessed 1 May 2022).

Olsen, J. (1999). *Nature and Nationalism: Right Wing Ecology and the Politics of Identity in Contemporary Germany*. New York: St Martin's Press.

Oreskes, N., & Conway, E. M. (2011). *Merchants of Doubt: How a Handful of Scientists Obscured the Truth on Issues from Tobacco Smoke to Global Warming*. London: Bloomsbury.

Pasek, A. (2021). Carbon Vitalism: Life and the Body in Climate Denial. *Environmental Humanities*, 13(1): 1–20.

Peters, M. (2019). Anti-intellectualism is a Virus. *Educational Philosophy and Theory*, 51(4): 357–363.

Philo, G., & Happer, C. (2013). *Communicating Climate Change and Energy Security: New Methods in Understanding Audiences*. London: Routledge.

Pirro, A. L., & Taggart, P. (2023). Populists in Power and Conspiracy Theories. *Party Politics*, 29(3): 413–423.

Rahmstorf, S. (2004). *The Climate Sceptics*. Potsdam: Potsdam Institute for Climate Impact Research.

Republika (2021). Programme. *Republika*, www.hnutie-republika.sk/program/ (accessed 1 August 2022).

Reyes, D. (2020). I, Trump: The Cult of Personality, Anti-intellectualism and the Post-Truth Era. *Journal of Language and Politics*, 19(6): 869–893.

Rigney, D. (1991). Three Kinds of Anti-intellectualism: Rethinking Hofstadter. *Sociological Inquiry*, 61(4): 434–451.

Scruton, R. (2012). *Green Philosophy: How to Think Seriously About the Planet*. London: Atlantic Books.

Snow, D. A., Rochford, E. B., Worden, S. K., & Benford, R. D. (1986). Frame Alignment Processes, Micromobilization, and Movement Participation. *American Sociological Review*, 51(4): 464–481.

Spectator (2020). Judge explained to Kotleba why he is an extremist. *Slovak Spectator*, 14 October, https://spectator.sme.sk/c/22509979/judge-explained-to-kotleba-why-he-is-an-extremist.html (accessed 16 November 2023).

Stecula, D. A., Kuru, O., & Jamieson, K. H. (2020). How trust in experts and media use affect acceptance of common anti-vaccination claims. *The Harvard Kennedy School Misinformation Review*, 1(1): 1–9.

Tebaldi, C. (2021). Speaking Post-truth to Power. *Review of Education, Pedagogy, and Cultural Studies*, 43(3): 205–225.

Uscinski, J. E., Enders, A. M., Seelig, M. I., et al. (2021). American Politics in Two Dimensions: Partisan and Ideological Identities versus Anti-establishment Orientations. *American Journal of Political Science*, 65(4): 877–895.

Van Dongen, T., & Leidig, E. (2021). Whose side are they on? The diversity of far-right responses to COVID-19. *ICCT Hague*, https://icct.nl/publication/whose-side-are-they-on-the-diversity-of-far-right-responses-to-COVID-19/ (accessed 26 December 2021).

Van Rensburg, W. (2015). Climate Change Skepticism: A Conceptual Re-evaluation. *SAGE Open*, 5(2): 1–13.

Afterword: extinguishing the flames: a call for future research and action on far-right ecologies

The Zetkin Collective (contributing authors, in alphabetical order: William Callison, George Edwards, Ståle Holgersen, Alexandra McFadden, Jacob McLean and Tatjana Söding)

As the world burns, the far right worships at the flaming altar of fossil capital. Whether through denial, deflection or delay, their goal is not to alleviate but to accelerate the climate and biodiversity crisis. Our goal – the goal of all who refuse this collective death drive and who fight for a habitable planet – is to understand and extinguish these flames before it is too late.

When the Zetkin Collective published *White Skin, Black Fuel* back in 2021, the political ecologies of the far right still comprised a field of research in the making. A few years later, with this volume and an increasing number of scholarly publications, it is clearly becoming a well-established field. While our book mainly focused on the Global North, *Political Ecologies of the Far Right* has shown that the phenomenon is (unfortunately) not only alive but thriving far beyond countries in the capitalist core. The volume has surveyed the thematic and geographical diversity of far-right political ecology: from agricultural ethno-nationalism in South Africa to reactionary militants benefiting from global warming conspiracies in Nigeria; from eco-fascism in Aotearoa New Zealand to anti-environmentalism in Brazil; from Christian nationalism and idealized masculinity to new far-right communication strategies in Europe and North America; and the unclear lines between denialists and climate delayers around the globe.

Broadening the geographical scale of the political ecologies of the far right – as *Political Ecologies of the Far Right* does – is a crucial step forward. But more chapters, cases and volumes must be written. Many such studies would need to account for the geopolitical reconfiguration that has occurred since February 2022, when the ultra-nationalist Vladimir Putin ordered the military invasion of Ukraine. Having long built the pipelines ensuring international dependency on Russian fossil fuels and the communication infrastructure connecting the international far right, the invasion kicked the politics of fossil fascism into a higher gear.

This new phase of far-right organization was not primarily the product of some Putinist master strategy, however. It was also the consequence of a fossil-hungry European establishment committed to business-as-usual with an increasingly authoritarian and murderous regime. 'A cautious u-turn with regards to Russia', as Oleksiy Radynski (2022) observed, 'was only made by these elites when it became clear, in the early days of the invasion, that Ukrainian resistance had halted the Russian blitzkrieg.' Meanwhile, the neo-colonial invasion was justified by appropriating the left's rhetoric of 'anti-fascism' and fabricating narratives about a 'Nazi' government in Kyiv (Bilous, 2023). Inside and outside Russia, the far right has violently mobilized against feminist, queer and trans politics in both word and deed. While some parts of the international right have pivoted away from supporting the Russian government, other parts have filled the vacuum, thereby ensuring that Russia's lines of finance, communication and influence continue to expand. The invasion is not just transforming the trajectory of international trade and energy policy. It is providing fuel for the fire of xenophobic, anti-environmental and anti-LGBTQ politics for decades to come.

As sanctions and sabotage made it harder to sell Russian oil and gas to Europe, exports flowed in other directions. From less than 1 per cent before February 2022, India imported about 35 per cent of its oil from Russia only a year later (Outlook India, 2023). Modi's ruling Bharatiya Janata Party (BJP) emerged out of and remains intimate with the world's longest-running fascist group, the Rashtriya Swayamsevak Sangh (RSS), an all-male paramilitary organization which has been in operation for nearly a century. One fixation of the Hindu nationalist ideology is the restoration of an 'unbroken India', an imagined land of 'cultural unity' spreading from Afghanistan in the west to Myanmar in the east. Speaking of the advance of this Hindu nation, the chief of the RSS warned that a 'vehicle is on the move which has an accelerator but no brakes … those who want to stop it will be either removed or finished, but India will not stop' (Express News Service, 2023). Much of the fuel for the Indian engine flows through the Adani Group's many pipes. The industrial empire, formed of coal, oil, gas, airports, cement and shipping, stretches far beyond the Indian subcontinent, with one recent acquisition being Israel's largest port. But when an American hedge-fund shorted the company amid allegations of widespread fraud, the RSS came to Adani's defence. The principal magazine of the fascist organization recognized these to be attacks on the nation – analogous to those perpetrated by environmental activists, George Soros and the producers of a BBC documentary that defamed Modi – intended to slow down the country's economic rise (Mehta and Singh, 2023). The moving vehicle that is the Indian nation is defended by an aura of conspiratorial thinking.

Adani has also reached across the Indian Ocean to plug into another fossil empire – Australia. Adani's Carmichael mine, supported heavily by the Australian government and fossil industry, sits in the Galilee Basin in Queensland, an untouched region at the edge of the Great Barrier Reef. The colossal mine violates Indigenous ancestral land rights and is set to add 4.6 billion tonnes of carbon to the atmosphere. Uncoincidentally, the state of Queensland houses some of the country's most prominent public climate deniers and fossil fuel advocates. This includes Frazer Anning, former Queensland Senator who blamed the Christchurch mosque attack on immigration and mocks any meek attempts by Australian politicians to address environmental crises. Another figure is Pauline Hanson, leader of the right-wing One Nation party, who infamously wore a burqa to Parliament to protest Muslim immigration, and regularly engages in anti-Aboriginal rhetoric and climate change conspiracies. After visiting the Great Barrier Reef following a heavy bleaching period in 2016, Hanson earned ridicule from marine conservationists when she put her head under the water and promptly declared that 'it' – a living structure larger than the United Kingdom – was in 'pristine condition'.

Beneath this circus of climate apathy and white nationalism that belies Australia's fossil engine lies the ideology of civilizationism. This entails the belief that the superiority of white Europeans is embedded in 'civilized' technological capacities and the 'civilized' treatment and management of the environment, as 'evidenced' by historical feats over 'uncivilized' lands and peoples. 'Civilizationism' helps to draw together our understanding of the ethnic, racial and cultural boundaries of far-right ideology and ground them in specific historical-contemporary relations with technology and the environment. The most overt and vicious defenders of Australian civilization-ism are far-right activist groups and online media platforms. Groups like Antipodean Resistance and the Lads Society have attempted to infiltrate mainstream political parties, while online platforms XYZ and The Unshackled campaigned semi-officially for Anning's 2019 federal election run. These fringe groups are a symptom and an echo of the fossil hegemony and white Eurocentrism that define Australian politics. The settler colonial project that founded Australia was a civilizationist project, and far-right actors are driven to protect and project these sentiments of white technological and ecological dominance (McFadden, 2023). Fossil extractivism is seen as a natural consequence of superior white technology, which entitles White Australia to an unchecked supply of ecological resources. The lands and cultures stamped down on this path are dismissed as vestiges of 'uncivilized' technologies and ways of managing lands and resources. Notably, far-right civilizationism aims to maintain Australia's fossil industry free from non-white foreign investment and control, including that of Adani, which is ironic given the anti-Muslim and civilizationist ideals the Australian far right shares with the BJP. In contrast, the mainstream liberal and labour parties prioritize filling their coffers as long as the national character and population base remain 'white' and 'civilized'.

Major tectonic shifts are also occurring in the Middle East, with China taking a mediating role in a longstanding conflict between Saudi Arabia and Iran in March 2023, thereby ensuring pipelines will allow oil to flow in its direction. Through OPEC+, these oil-producing countries still wield outsized and often disruptive influence over global prices in a period of high inflation, as seen in Saudi Arabia's decision to slash oil production for the rest of the year (Singh, 2023).

All the while Iran has been shaken by progressive political resistance from within its own borders. In the wake of the murder of 22-year-old Iranian Kurd Masha Jina Amini in September 2022, thousands of women took to the streets, setting their head scarfs aflame in tyre-rim pit fires or burning them on poles resembling firing flare guns. Though women are leading the protests and their struggle for 'life and freedom' is at the forefront of the movement, it has become a nation-wide, cross-class uprising supported by men and ethnic and political minorities alike. Shouting 'Zan, Zendegi, Azadai', a broad fraction of Iranian society is taking to the streets, risking their life over the struggle for the political, religious and personal freedom of the many. But the movement also has a climate dimension, as becomes evident in its anthem, 'Baraye' (For the Sake of), whose 28 lyrical lines dwell on the fights for the sake of which the Iranian population is rising. 'For this polluted air; for the worn-out plane trees on Vali 'Asr Street; for the cheetah and its possible extinction; for the innocent banned stray dogs' are four lines indicating that the struggle against authoritarianism, poverty and repression is also a fight against environmental deterioration (Afary & Anderson, 2022). As much as the movement is building upon grievances and structures from previous feminist uprisings, it is likewise continuing the legacy of the protests against water shortages and food scarcity that shook the country in 2021 and 2022. With predictions of a 2.6°C rise in mean temperatures and a 35 per cent decline in precipitation in the next decades (Mansouri Daneshvar et al., 2019), Iran refuses to ratify the Paris Agreement despite being the eighth-biggest emitter in the world and acutely vulnerable to climate change.

One implication of the work collected in *Political Ecologies of the Far Right* is that the environmental struggle is linked with the anti-fascist struggle. And yet this link needs to be made more visible, both on the ground and in writing. Further research on far-right ecologies must specifically connect the fascist spectre with the growing literature on the socio-ecological transition. Current models for this transition – be they individualist or collectivist, techno-optimist or based on war-time mobilization – should be evaluated as to how they may serve or avert far-right crisis narratives. One crucial element of such an evaluation is questioning how political subjects are interpellated by the fossil capitalist system and which subject positions are offered by different narratives of a socio-ecologically just future. As the devastation wrought by climate change mounts and alternative ecological visions proliferate, how to conceptualize the forms of subjectivity that drive far-right political formations, without falling back on the rigid interpretations of fascism that have often characterized socialist theories? How can a materialist analysis simultaneously advance the imperative to transform economic production and illuminate the politics of identity, subjectivity and affect that are intertwined with this world-historic task? And how can anti-fascist, environmental, feminist, anti-racist and abolitionist struggles be connected on an international level? These questions may not be novel but, precisely because they remain open, engaged scholarship must put considerable effort into formulating new theories and tools.

Concretely, though, what does this mean for praxis? If the far right is 'fanning the flames' of climate change, then the challenge of extinguishing them is (at least) twofold: not only to obstruct primitive fossil capital itself, but to destroy the bellows that is the far right. Despite the growth in research on the political ecology of the far right, a remaining lacuna concerns the anti-fascist response to explicitly pro-fossil fuel far-right movements. If on a theoretical level we can say that fossil fuel expansion today materially produces the conditions for a fascistic politics and even climate genocide, then, on the level of praxis, does this lead us to the conclusion that anti-fossil fuel protest is also inherently anti-fascist? If so, then anti-hate and anti-fascist advocacy groups would need to elevate climate denialism and obstructionism to a key vector worth monitoring in their respective national contexts, akin to other 'classic' far-right issues like anti-immigration and racism.

One problem with doing so, however, has to do with collapsing the boundaries of the mainstream and the far right. If fossil fuel expansionism in a time of climate crisis is inherently far right in that it produces futures where far-right politics becomes more palatable and even 'reasonable' sounding to masses of people struggling with insecurity of various kinds, then we must conclude that much of the political spectrum, insofar as they remain committed to fossil fuels, is pushing towards this far-right horizon. In doing so, however, we run the risk of repeating the mistake of some German communists who viewed the Social Democratic Party as 'social fascists' – the mistake, in short, of conflating our opponents. Take recent developments in the US, for example. On 23 February 2023, Joe Biden announced a change to US immigration policy that critics argue 'effectively resurrects Donald Trump's asylum ban' (Goodfriend, 2023). Then, three weeks later, Biden approved the Willow Project in Alaska, which, in terms of emissions, is the 'equivalent of adding two new coal-fired power plants to the U.S. electricity system every year' (Lefebvre & Colman, 2023). While such decisions undoubtedly move us closer to a world governed by the logic of the 'armed lifeboat', it would be a mistake to argue that Biden is fascist, let alone far right. If fossil fascism is the purest form of the reactionary political bloc, then what about these hybrids like Biden, who simultaneously deploy market incentives for energy transition while approving fossil mega-projects, and who simultaneously offer relief from the worst excesses of far-right immigration policy, only to implement marginally less severe versions of the same thing? Theoretically, how should we understand the relationship between the political ecologies of centrist liberalism and the far right? And tactically, how should socialists relate to centrist liberalism to make concrete policy gains?

When more radical alternatives are lacking, it is hard to categorically reject the idea that socialists could be forced to lend strategic support to centre-left governments, as a form of electoral self-defence. But this must always be coupled with social movements muscular enough to force their hands. At the same time, however, the pandemic seems to have set us back on this front. With the exception of Black Lives Matter in 2021, the left largely stayed at home at the height of the pandemic, forfeiting the streets to the far-right, anti-lockdown, anti-vaccine movement. The climate left is a long way off from its 2019 peak, and we must urgently rebuild momentum. We must recognize the limitations of the old tactics, and develop new ones. The global climate strike model, for example, should be expanded with the goal of bringing in trade unions and moving towards multi-day strikes of both students and workers. The one-day strikes are far too non-disruptive to shake anybody in power; if Justin Trudeau is willing to participate in such actions, as he did in Montréal at the height of the global climate strike wave in September 2019, then we should probably rethink our approach.

Glimmers of hope, however, come from France. Attempts to articulate the ecological alongside the social followed in the wake of the pension age hike pushed through by Macron in the spring of 2023. The struggle against raising the retirement age carries an environmental dimension, since working less slows ecologically destructive economic growth. Additionally, as hundreds of thousands protested and mobilized against the policy in cities and towns throughout the country, climate activists carried some of this fury to Saint-Soline, a rural town in the west. Marching beneath the banner of Les Soulèvements de la Terre – the Earth's Uprising – thousands of demonstrators (30,000 by some estimates, 6,000 according to the police) gathered to oppose the construction of a giant reservoir, built to secure water supply for the large agri-businesses while diverting water away from smaller farms in the region. This part of the country was scorched in the summer of 2022 as France experienced its most severe drought in history. The demonstration was met by the full force of the state: the police hailed down stun grenades and tear-gas, all the while blocking medical support reaching those in need. Les Soulèvements de la Terre was the first resistance action specifically targeting a policy of 'climate adaptation', or rather maladaptation (Budgen, 2023).

If the climate movement is now resisting the form which adaptation takes, the far right is seeking to profit from the backlash against what is cast as mitigation. The Dutch tractor protests against ecological agriculture reforms, for example, cleared the way for the Farmer-Citizen Movement's landslide in the March 2023 provincial elections. Italy and Poland joined Germany to force the handbrake on the original EU plans to phase out the internal combustion engine, while the Christian Democratic Union won the Berlin elections on a racialized and pro-car ticket. The technologies of the transition are in the headlights too, especially with regards to the electrification of private mobility. From electricity transformers overloaded with charging cars to child labour lifting rare battery minerals from the earth, the lines to attack what gets brandished as environmentalism are multiple. Presenting themselves as 'climate realists', the far right attempt to exploit some of these contradictions, waging common sense against the 'climate alarmists', said to be in thrall to the World Economic Forum and the Chinese Communist Party. The British far right have been rehearsing a version of this script in opposition to urban planning schemes designed to reduce car usage in towns and cities. In practice amounting to little more than bus lanes and bollards, these innocuous designs are portrayed as a sinister ploy to curtail freedom of movement, which left unchecked they claim will be worse than any gulag or ghetto. These demonstrations draw crowds beyond the usual far right: peace campaigners march alongside street-fighting hooligans, disgruntled local residents join up with savvy online influencers. The danger here is of the far right steering a broader anti-environmental coalition converging in defence of fossil fuel freedoms. The left must remain vigilant to these emerging alliances, anticipating the conditions where such movements may flourish.

At the same time, as we rebuild our own movements, we must connect the project of scaling down the fossil economy with the aim of improving the material conditions and strengthening the democratic freedoms of workers across the globe. We need to reckon with the affective popularity of fossil fuels and their technologies, especially in places where they continue to provide uniquely high-paying working-class jobs. There are worrying signs that such communities are becoming a part of the far right's political base. In such contexts, building buy-in for a just transition will require a diversity of tactics, and the toolkit of the left ought to be expanded beyond protest, climate strike and blockade. Fossil capital and authoritarian far-right actors are organizing internationally, making an even stronger case that any left response to the climate crisis must take on a global character. Just as capital's reach is global, so must our understanding of the global working class encompass care labourers and communities on the fringes of the world economic system on whose labour the Global North is materially dependent. In this, we can take inspiration from our namesake, Clara Zetkin, who in 1923 saw a growing fraction of the international working class falling under the sway of fascism and, in response, called for her comrades to 'initiate the most energetic campaign' to gain their allegiance (Zetkin, 1983: 110). Indeed, the anti-fascist campaign today must be 'energetic' in two senses: urgent, of course, but also aimed squarely at energy transition. The choice today, it seems, is as stark as it was then: eco-socialism or climate barbarism.

References

Afary, J., & Anderson, K. (2022). Woman, life, freedom: the origins of the uprising in Iran. *Dissident Magazine*, 2 December, www.dissentmagazine.org/online_articles/women-life-freedom-iran-uprising-origins (accessed 15 November 2023).

Bilous, T. (2023). The far right in Ukraine. *Commons*, 16 February, https://commons.com.ua/en/far-right-ukraine/ (accessed 15 November 2023).

Budgen, S. (2023). 'France's social explosion w/ Sebastian Budgen'. Interview by Alex Doherty. *Politics Theory Other Podcast*, 1 April, www.patreon.com/poltheoryother (accessed 2 May 2023).

Express News Service (2023). https://indianexpress.com/agency/express-news-service/ (accessed 2 May 2023).

Goodfriend, H. (2023). Joe Biden is bringing back Donald Trump's asylum ban at the border. *Jacobin*, 7 March, https://jacobin.com/2023/03/joe-biden-immigration-migrants-asylum-seekers-neoliberalism-capital (accessed 15 November 2023).

Lefebvre, B., & Colman, Z. (2023). Biden expected to OK Alaska oil project – a blow to his green base. *Politico*, 11 March, www.politico.com/news/2023/03/11/joe-biden-climate-alaska-willow-oil-00086659 (accessed 15 November 2023).

Malm, A., & the Zetkin Collective (2021). *White Skin, Black Fuel: On the Danger of Fossil Fascism*. London: Verso.

Mansouri Daneshvar, M. R., Ebrahimi, M., & Nejadsoleymani, H. (2019). An Overview of Climate Change in Iran: Facts and Statistics. *Environmental Systems Research*, 8(7): 1–10.

McFadden, A. (2023). Wardens of Civilisation: The Political Ecology of Australian Far-Right Civilisationism. *Antipode*, 55(2): 548–573.

Mehta, S., & Kumar Singh, B. (2023). Hindenburg–Adani controversy: attack on Adani is continuation of assaults on Indian economy. *Organiser*, 5 February, https://organiser.org/2023/02/05/107224/bharat/attack-on-adani-is-continuation-of-assaults-on-indian-economy/ (accessed 15 November 2023).

Outlook India (2023). Indian oil imports from russia touch all-time high in February, amount to 35% of all imports. *Outlook*, 5 March, www.outlookindia.com/national/

indian-oil-imports-from-russia-touch-all-time-high-in-february-amount-to-35-per-cent-of-all-imports-news-267372 (accessed 2 May 2023).

Radynski, O. (2022). Russian fossil fascism is Europe's fault. *Soniakh Digest*, 4 October, https://soniakh.com/index.php/2022/10/04/russian-fossil-fascism-is-europes-fault/ (accessed 15 November 2023).

Singh, N. (2023). Oil prices surge as Saudi and other OPEC nations slash production in shock move. *Independent*, 3 April, www.independent.co.uk/news/business/saudi-arabia-oil-price-usd-b2312913.html (accessed 15 November 2023).

Zetkin, C. (1983). The Struggle Against Fascism. In D. Beetham (ed.), *Marxists in Face of Fascism: Writings by Marxists on Fascism from the Inter-war Period*. Manchester: Manchester University Press, pp. 102–113.

Index

EU authorised representative for GPSR:
Easy Access System Europe, Mustamäe tee 50,
10621 Tallinn, Estonia
gpsr.requests@easproject.com